Humour in Asian Cultures

This innovative book traces the impact of tradition on modern humour across several Asian countries and their cultures. Using examples from Japan, Korea, Indonesia and from Chinese cultures in Mainland China, Hong Kong and Taiwan, the contributors explore the different cultural rules for creating and sharing humour.

Humour can be a powerful lubricant when correctly interpreted; misinterpreted, it may cause considerable setbacks. Over time, it has emerged and submerged in different forms in all these countries but even today, conventions about what is appropriate in creating and using humour still reflect many traditional attitudes and assumptions. Using close examination, Milner Davis and her colleagues show how forms and conventions that differ from those in the west can nevertheless be seen to possess some elements in common. Examples include Mencian and other classical texts, Balinese traditional verbal humour, Korean and Taiwanese workplace humour, Japanese laughter ceremonies, performances and cartoons, as well as contemporary Chinese-language films and videos, as they engage with a wide range of forms and traditions.

This fascinating collection of studies will be of interest not only to students and scholars of many Asian cultures but also to those with a broader interest in humour. It highlights the increasing importance of understanding a wider range of cultural values in the present era of globalised communication as well as the importance of reliable studies of how cultures that may be geographically related differ in their traditional uses of and assumptions about humour.

Jessica Milner Davis PhD FRSN is an honorary research associate at both the University of Sydney, Australia, and Brunel University London's Centre for Comedy Studies Research. She is a member of Clare Hall, Cambridge, and a Fellow and Councillor of the Royal Society of New South Wales. She has twice served as president of the International Society for Humor Studies (ISHS) and founded and coordinates the Australasian Humour Studies Network (AHSN: https://ahsn.org.au/). An editorial board member for leading humour research journals and book series, her most recent books are:

Satire and Politics: The Interplay of Heritage and Practice (Palgrave Macmillan, 2017) and *Judges, Judging and Humour* (with Sharyn Roach Anleu, Palgrave/Springer, 2018). With Jocelyn Chey, she has co-edited two volumes on *Humour in Chinese Life and Culture* (Hong Kong University Press, 2011 and 2013). Her 2006 book, *Understanding Humor in Japan* (Wayne State University Press), won the 2008 AATH book prize for humour research. In 2018, the International Society for Humor Studies presented her with its Lifetime Achievement Award for her interdisciplinary research in humour studies.

Routledge Studies on Asia in the World

Routledge Studies on Asia in the World will be an authoritative source of knowledge on Asia studying a variety of cultural, economic, environmental, legal, political, religious, security and social questions, addressed from an Asian perspective. We aim to foster a deeper understanding of the domestic and regional complexities which accompany the dynamic shifts in the global economic, political and security landscape towards Asia and their repercussions for the world at large. We're looking for scholars and practitioners – Asian and Western alike – from various social science disciplines and fields to engage in testing existing models which explain such dramatic transformation and to formulate new theories that can accommodate the specific political, cultural and developmental context of Asia's diverse societies. We welcome both monographs and collective volumes which explore the new roles, rights and responsibilities of Asian nations in shaping today's interconnected and globalized world in their own right.

The Series is advised and edited by Matthias Vanhullebusch and Ji Weidong of Shanghai Jiao Tong University.

Eldercare Issues in China and India
Edited by Longtao He and Jagriti Gangopadhyay

The Shanghai Cooperation Organization
Exploring New Horizons
Edited by Sergey Marochkin and Yury Bezborodov

Humour in Asian Cultures
Tradition and Context
Edited by Jessica Milner Davis

City, Environment, and Transnationalism in the Philippines
Reconceptualizing "the Social" from the Global South
Koki Seki

Find the full list of books in the series here: https://www.routledge.com/Routledge-Studies-on-Asia-in-the-World/book-series/RSOAW

Humour in Asian Cultures
Tradition and Context

**Edited by
Jessica Milner Davis**

LONDON AND NEW YORK

First published 2022
by Routledge
4 Park Square, Milton Park, Abingdon, Oxon OX14 4RN

and by Routledge
605 Third Avenue, New York, NY 10158

Routledge is an imprint of the Taylor & Francis Group, an Informa business

© 2022 selection and editorial matter, Jessica Milner Davis; individual chapters, the contributors

The right of Jessica Milner Davis to be identified as the author of the editorial material, and of the authors for their individual chapters, has been asserted in accordance with sections 77 and 78 of the Copyright, Designs and Patents Act 1988.

All rights reserved. No part of this book may be reprinted or reproduced or utilised in any form or by any electronic, mechanical, or other means, now known or hereafter invented, including photocopying and recording, or in any information storage or retrieval system, without permission in writing from the publishers.

Trademark notice: Product or corporate names may be trademarks or registered trademarks and are used only for identification and explanation without intent to infringe.

British Library Cataloguing-in-Publication Data
A catalogue record for this book is available from the British Library

Library of Congress Cataloguing-in-Publication Data
A catalog record has been requested for this book

ISBN: 978-1-032-00916-2 (hbk)
ISBN: 978-1-032-00918-6 (pbk)
ISBN: 978-1-003-17637-4 (ebk)

DOI: 10.4324/9781003176374

This book is dedicated to Cecil Robert Burnett
Quentin (1917–1979) who first introduced me to
the rich cultural histories of Asia

Contents

List of Figures	xi
List of Tables	xiii
List of Contributors	xiv
Preface	xviii

1 **Humour and cultural context: Tradition and practice in six Asian cultures**   1
JESSICA MILNER DAVIS

2 **Humour as rhetorical discourse in ancient Chinese philosophy: *The Works of Mencius***   19
SHIRLEY CHAN

3 **Humour in the *huaben* novellas of the Ming Dynasty: The *Guzhang Juechen* 鼓掌絕塵 in context**   40
ANTONIO LEGGIERI

4 **Linguistic devices in traditional forms of Balinese humour**   62
NENGAH ARNAWA

5 **Pluri-modal poetic performance of banter: The *Angama* ritual on Ishigaki Island in Japan**   88
MAKIKO TAKEKURO

6 **Themes, cultural context and verbal exchanges in the cartoons of Machiko Hasegawa**   117
SACHIKO KITAZUME

7 **The *makura* of *rakugo*, tradition and modernity**   136
M.W. SHORES

8 To joke or not to joke?: Politeness, power and the
   impact of tradition in Korean workplace humour 170
   HEESUN KIM AND BARBARA PLESTER

9 Chinese conversational humour over time: Contemporary
   practice and tradition in Taiwanese cultures 188
   WEI-LIN MELODY CHANG AND MICHAEL HAUGH

10 *We Are Real Friends*: Women constructing friendship
   via teasing in a Chinese reality TV show 211
   YING CAO

11 *My Unfair Lady*: Gender, *sajiao* and humour in a
   Hong Kong TV series 238
   MARJORIE K. M. CHAN

   Index 268

List of Figures

2.1	Mencius (anonymous artist, 1922).	22
2.2	A *shi* gentleman, by Gengle Jushi Yunong 耕樂居士雨農 (Han Yong 韓勇).	23
3.1	Illustration from *Guzhang Juechen* 鼓掌絕塵, 1631.	44
3.2	Illustration from *Guzhang Juechen* 鼓掌絕塵, 1631.	45
3.3	Illustration from *Guzhang Juechen* 鼓掌絕塵, 1631.	57
4.1	Still of *wayang kulit* performance by Cenk Blonk, Jembrana District Government News, Bali, 2011.	64
4.2	Photograph of *wayang kulit* puppets (Nengah Arnawa, 2019).	72
4.3	Photograph of Cenk Blonk *wayang kulit* puppets (Nengah Arnawa, 2019).	73
4.4	Photograph of Cenk Blonk *wayang kulit* puppets (Nengah Arnawa, 2019).	79
5.1	Map of Ishigaki, Japan, by Motoki Saito, 2018.	89
5.2	Photograph of *angama* performance, Ishigaki (Makiko Takekuro, 2017).	93
5.3	Photograph of *angama* performance, Ishigaki, Makiko Takekuro, 2017.	95
5.4	Photograph of *angama* performance, Ishigaki, Makiko Takekuro, 2017.	104
6.1	*The Wonderful world of Sazae-san* (Vol. 12, p. 68; *Sazae-san*, Vol. 43, p. 98), by Machiko Hasagawa, 2004.	123
6.2	*The Wonderful world of Sazae-san* (Vol. 6, p. 100; *Sazae-san*, Vol. 21, p. 71), by Machiko Hasagawa, 2003.	125
6.3	*The Wonderful world of Sazae-san* (Vol. 11, p. 111, *Sazae-san*, Vol. 40, p. 126), by Machiko Hasagawa, 2004.	127
6.4	*Granny Mischief*, p. 29 (*Ijiwaru Baasan*, Vol. 1, p. 30), by Machiko Hasegawa, 2001.	129
6.5	*Granny Mischief*, p. 37 (*Ijiwaru Baasan*, Vol. 1, p. 41), by Machiko Hasegawa, 2001.	130
6.6	*Granny Mischief*, p. 96 (*Ijiwaru Baasan*, Vol. 1, p. 113), by Machiko Hasegawa, 2001.	132

xii *List of Figures*

7.1	Photograph of Tenma Tenjin Hanjōtei in Osaka (Kamigata Rakugo Kyōkai 上方落語協会).	141
7.2	Photograph of Katsura Ayame III performing (Katsura Ayame III 三代目桂あやめ).	153
7.3	Photograph of Katsura Bunza V performing (Katsura Bunza V 五代目桂文三).	155
7.4	Photograph of Shōfukutei Tama performing (Shōfukutei Tama 笑福亭たま).	160
8.1	Photograph of office-workers, Seoul, Korea, by HeeSun Kim, 2021.	176
9.1	Photograph of office-worker, Yilan, Taiwan, by Wei-Lin Melody Chang, 2010.	197
9.2	Photograph of office-worker, Yilan, Taiwan, by Wei-Lin Melody Chang, 2010.	197
9.3	Photograph of office-worker, Yilan, Taiwan, by Wei-Lin Melody Chang, 2010.	198
10.1	Still from *Wo Men Shi Zhenzheng De Pengyou* 我们是真正的朋友 (*We Are Real Friends*), 2019.	218
10.2	Still from *Wo Men Shi Zhenzheng De Pengyou* 我们是真正的朋友 (*We Are Real Friends*), 2019.	218
10.3	Still from *Wo Men Shi Zhenzheng De Pengyou* 我们是真正的朋友 (*We Are Real Friends*), 2019.	223
11.1	Still from *Budong Sajiao De Nüren* 不懂撒嬌的女人 (*My Unfair Lady*), 2017.	251
11.2	Still from *Budong Sajiao De Nüren* 不懂撒嬌的女人 (*My Unfair Lady*), 2017.	257

List of Tables

4.1	Sangut and Délem discuss the kidnapping of Rama	71
4.2	Key to *bladbadan* in Table 4.1	72
4.3	Key to *bladbadan* in Example 5	74
4.4	Key to *bladbadan* in Example 6	74
4.5	Rhyming in *Wewangsalan* 1 and 2	76
4.6	Rhyme and interpretation in *Wewangsalan* 3 and 4	77
4.7	Sonority in *Wewangsalan* 5	78
4.8	Sonority in *Wewangsalan* 6	78
4.9	Tualén and Merdah discuss the cost of education	79
7.1	Selected *makura* elements	139
9.1	Overview of studies of conversational humour in Chinese	191
10.1	Transcription conventions	234
11.1	Group text messages	242
11.2	Molly warns Cherry about men	243
11.3	Gordon to Molly: "Your boyfriend?"	254
11.4	Cracking Hanson's Facebook code	258
11.5	Rhyming pun, Example 1	259
11.6	Rhyming pun, Example 2	259
11.7	Molly to Gordon, "You betrayed me!"	260

Contributors

Nengah Arnawa is a Lecturer at the Mahadewa University of Indonesia with research interests in semantics and pragmatics. He is a member of the Indonesian Linguistic Society (MLI) and the Local Language Researchers Association (APBL). Dr Arnawa has made a deep study of linguistic constructions in Balinese, such as *bladbadan* and *cecimpedan* which are often used as a medium for humour in traditional theatre, and has written and published articles in both Balinese and English on humorous Balinese discourse.

Ying Cao holds her PhD from the School of Humanities and Communication Arts at Western Sydney University, Australia, and lectures in the School of Foreign Languages at Wuhan Polytechnic University, PRC. Her research interests focus on humour, gender, (im)politeness and identity construction in the discourse of TV fictional dialogues, Chinese conceptions of humour, and linguistic studies of humour in translation and interpreting. A multiple graduate scholarship winner with the Australasian Humour Studies Network (https://ahsnhumourstudies.org/), Dr Cao has published with colleagues a study of aggressive humour in Chinese sitcom discourse in *The European Journal of Humour Research* (Vol. 9/4, 2021).

Marjorie K. M. Chan is an Associate Professor in the Department of East Asian Languages and Literatures at the Ohio State University. She received her BA and MA in Linguistics from the University of British Columbia, PhD in Linguistics from the University of Washington, and was a post-doctoral fellow at UCLA's Phonetics Lab. Her teaching and research focus on Chinese Linguistics: phonetics and phonology; dialectology; historical linguistics, especially historical phonology; the Chinese writing system, including dialect-writing; socio-pragmatic issues pertaining to language and gender as well as to humour and topics dealing with Chinese operatic traditions, especially Cantonese regional opera.

Shirley Chan is an Associate Professor and Head of Chinese Studies in the Department of Media, Communications, Creative Arts, Language and Literature at Macquarie University, Sydney. She is a member of the Macquarie University (MQ) Research Centre for Cultural Heritage and Environment. Dr Chan served as President of the Chinese Studies Association of Australia (2015–2017), and as Editor-in-chief for the "Journal of the Oriental Society of Australia" (2018–2021). She teaches Chinese language, literature and culture, Chinese history and Chinese philosophy and has published in her broad research interest areas of Chinese culture, Chinese philosophy and textual studies, including humour.

Wei-Lin Melody Chang is a Lecturer in Chinese at the School of Languages and Cultures, University of Queensland. Her research focuses on pragmatics, intercultural communication and business negotiation, especially studying face, (im)politeness and humour. She is the author of *Face and Face Practices in Chinese Talk-in-Interactions: An Empirical Analysis of Business Interactions in Taiwan* (Equinox, 2016), as well as a number of papers in edited volumes and journals, including the *Journal of Pragmatics, Intercultural Pragmatics, International Review of Applied Linguistics in Language Teaching, Journal of Politeness Research, Pragmatics, Multilingua, Lingua* and *East Asian Pragmatics*.

Michael Haugh FAHA is Professor of Linguistics and Applied Linguistics in the School of Languages and Cultures at the University of Queensland. His research interests include pragmatics, conversation analysis, intercultural communication and humour studies, with a particular focus on the role of language in social interaction. His more than 100 papers and books include the *Cambridge Handbook of Sociopragmatics* (CUP, 2021, with Dániel Z. Kádár and Marina Terkourafi), *Doing Pragmatics Interculturally* (Mouton de Gruyter, 2017, with Rachel Giora), *Im/Politeness Implicatures* (Mouton de Gruyter, 2015) and *Pragmatics and the English Language* (Palgrave Macmillan, 2014, with Jonathan Culpeper). He is the founding Co-Editor of *Cambridge Elements in Pragmatics* (Cambridge University Press) and was Co-Editor-in-Chief of the *Journal of Pragmatics* (Elsevier) from 2015 to 2020.

HeeSun Kim is an Assistant Professor in the Department of Business Administration at Yonsei University, Mirae Campus. Her research interests include organisational humour, work-life balance and East-Asian cultural perspectives on organisational behaviour. Dr Kim's teaching spans across undergraduate, postgraduate and professional level courses, including subjects in international management, organisational behaviour, research methods, business strategy, career development and design management. She is engaged in diverse interdisciplinary research and teaching groups, and her work aims to help bridge the gap between different academic areas and boundaries.

Sachiko Kitazume has authored many papers on English linguistics including "Middles in English" (*WORD: Journal of the International Linguistic Association*, 47 (2), 1996) and "A linguistic study of 'Show the Flag'" (in *The Deep/True Phase of Language*, Eihosha, 2004). For the last decade, her research has focused on humour, resulting in *How to Do Things with Humor* (Eihosha, 2010) as well as "Do the Japanese have a sense of humor?" (*Society*, 47 (1), 2010). An Emeritus Professor at Kindai University, she served as Mayor of an English immersive facility established in 2006 called "e-cube", a Japanese pioneering project in communicative English education, reflected in her contribution to *Eigomura of Kindai University* (Eihosha, 2010). An expert committee member, in 2017 she contributed to the establishment of Tokyo Global Gateway, a large-scale education project initiated by the Tokyo Metropolitan Board of Education. Since 2010, she has been an executive board member of the Kindai Educational Cooperation.

Antonio Leggieri holds a PhD in comparative literature from Beijing Language and Culture University and is currently completing a second Doctorate from the Universities of Salento and Vienna jointly. His main research interest is in late-imperial Chinese literature, especially humour in jestbooks and narratives, but he is also interested in the theory and practice of literary translation between Mandarin Chinese and Italian. He has published on the connections between Western and traditional Chinese concepts of humour and is a member of the Humours of the Past research group (https://humoursofthepast.wordpress.com/). He currently resides in Taipei.

Jessica Milner Davis FRSN is an honorary research associate at the University of Sydney, Australia, and at Brunel University London's Centre for Comedy Studies Research, a member of Clare Hall, Cambridge, and a Fellow of the Royal Society of New South Wales. Twice president of the International Society for Humor Studies (ISHS), she coordinates the Australasian Humour Studies Network (AHSN: https://ahsn.org.au/). Her most recent books are *Satire and Politics: The Interplay of Heritage and Practice* (Palgrave Macmillan, 2017) and *Judges, Judging and Humour* (with Sharyn Roach Anleu, Palgrave/Springer, 2018). She co-edited (with Jocelyn Chey) two volumes on humour in Chinese life and culture (Hong Kong University Press, 2011 and 2013) and *Understanding Humor in Japan* (Wayne State University Press, 2006) won the 2008 AATH book prize for humour research. In 2018, the International Society for Humor Studies recognised her interdisciplinary research in humour studies with its Lifetime Achievement Award.

Barbara Plester is a Senior Lecturer in the Department of Management and International Business at the University of Auckland, Aotearoa/ New Zealand. Although this is a serious job, she laughs a lot because her research explores workplace humour, fun, play, organisational culture, food rituals and critical perspectives of organisational life. Part of the Organisation Studies group, Barbara teaches Organisational Behaviour, Organisational Theory and HRM infused with humour stories, at both undergraduate and postgraduate levels. Her current research investigates fun and well-being in the social spaces of work. Prior to her academic career, Barbara worked in Publishing and Information Technology companies and has practical experience in Sales, Marketing and Human Resource Management, where she once was accused of laughing too much at work!

M.W. Shores is a Lecturer in Japanese at the University of Sydney, Australia. He is a scholar of Japanese literary arts and entertainment, with a focus on modern comic storytelling (*rakugo*) and its early-modern precursors, literary and otherwise. His most recent book is *The Comic Storytelling of Western Japan: Satire and Social Mobility in Kamigata Rakugo* (Cambridge University Press, 2021). After receiving a PhD in Japanese literature from University of Hawai'i at Mānoa, Shores was Director of East Asian Studies and a Governing Body Fellow at Peterhouse, Cambridge's oldest constituent college. He spent over a decade in postgraduate study in Japan at Tezukayama University as well as undertaking research at Ritsumeikan University's Art Research Center and Waseda University's Tsubouchi Memorial Theatre Museum. He has also undergone two informal *rakugo* apprenticeships.

Makiko Takekuro is Professor in the School of Law at Waseda University, Japan, where she teaches English and linguistic anthropology. Her research interests include poetics and performance, honorifics and discordance in social relations. Her work and many resultant publications in both English and Japanese explore how cultural practices are brought into being through social interaction, including humour. She has also published a chapter comparing conversational jokes in Japanese and English in *Understanding Humor in Japan* (ed. J. Milner Davis, Wayne State University Press, 2006).

Preface

This book is the product of a delightful collaboration between people I regard as old friends and also some very new ones. It was born of my desire to expand beyond the work I had already done on humour and laughter in Japanese and Chinese contexts (working with Marguerite Wells and with Jocelyn Chey, respectively). The Asian region is so rich in cultural variation and history as to be inexhaustible, and I wanted to explore its humour further. While the result is necessarily only a limited further contribution to the subject, I hope the selection of topics and themes in this book proves as interesting to other readers as it does to me.

The fascinating book of Asia was first opened for me as an undergraduate student by the foundation Professor of Drama in what was then the very new Faculty of Arts at the University of New South Wales in Sydney. The year was 1961 and Robert Quentin, a quiet but scholarly former Naval Intelligence officer and manager for the London and Bristol Old Vic Companies (before he then joined J. C. Williamson's company in Australia[1]), was teaching his inaugural class on the history of world theatre. Unlike some of the Faculty's Schools, his Department of Drama actually meant "world" when it said "world" in its syllabi. As he shared with us, a handful of students, Quentin was himself inclined to Buddhism and he wanted us to know not just about the Western tradition in drama dating back to Classical Greece, but also about Japanese *noh* and *kabuki*, about Chinese classical opera (then known as Peking Opera), Sanskrit drama and Javanese *wayang kulit* shadow puppet plays. We listened to scratchy old LP recordings and watched 33-mm films of these novel media; we read and discussed plays in translation, and later, in Honours class, we were set the challenge of re-writing *Hamlet* from a Buddhist perspective to make a *noh* revenge drama. The world was our very rich oyster.

As a student, I was lucky enough to travel to the Philippines and India (unbeknownst to me, this was funded by the CIA—but that is another story for another time and place). However, I had to wait to experience Japan, Indonesia and China. Nevertheless, in 1971 and thus well before the 1980s when it began to be fashionable for Japanese couples to honeymoon in Australia, my husband, Jeremy Davis, and I were privileged to spend our honeymoon in Japan and to see *kabuki* at first hand. In 2000, when Kansai University in Osaka hosted the 12th Conference of the International Society of Humor Studies (of which I had earlier served as President), the two of us managed to have a second such honeymoon. Since Ōsaka is known as the laughter capital of Japan, the conference was an excellent preamble to a memorable trip up the Hida Valley with its historic towns.

I was lucky enough to be introduced to the People's Republic of China (PRC) in 1987 by my sister, Dr Jocelyn Chey AM, who was then resident in Beijing as Trade Commissioner for Australia, and also later in Hong Kong as Australia's Consul-General before the handover of the Territory by the United Kingdom to the PRC in 1997. Although I have learned much from family, friends and colleagues in all these and other countries, I know very well that I have only managed to scratch the surface of true knowledge. I am not a specialist on Asia and, sadly, I speak no Asian languages. Nevertheless in this book, by contributing my expertise in studying humour around the world, and by combining that with the expertise of others in their own cultures, I believe that my colleagues and I have together arrived at some valuable insights. Certainly, there is much to attract the general reader as well as the specialist and each author has striven to provide all the necessary background information to render their writing accessible.

The different chapters in this book reflect very different disciplinary approaches. Several focus on pragmatic and linguistic exchanges, others have a more discursive literary approach and still others reflect the insights derived from anthropology, sociology, personal interview and observation and even regional politics. Some chapters focus on long-standing cultural traditions and practices in humour: these can then illuminate the contemporary forms and uses of humour that are examined in the others. All the chapters are informed by a consciousness of cultural tradition and social convention, which is what gives the book its unifying theme: the interplay in humour between continuity and change. Many forms of humour are capable of surviving effectively unchanged from times past, while others transform themselves to a greater or less extent in order to adapt to modern circumstances, especially to new media—and new ones are being created all the time. Nevertheless, whatever shape humour takes now and has taken in the past, whatever it has been called (and its terminology varies greatly from one place and time to another), it has always been present in these cultures of Asia, and also in others not within the purview of the present book. Its forms and modes have ranged from verbal to visual and performative, and also combinations of these. Humour may be written, spoken, enacted or exchanged interpersonally, in writing or online. As the following chapters demonstrate, humour is thus indigenous and familiar as well as being novel and modernising in Asia as elsewhere.

I think that my old professor, Robert Quentin, would be pleased by the publication of this book and so have taken the liberty of dedicating it to him. I happily acknowledge that it is to his prompting that I owe my life-long interest in comedy and humour. When he and I were considering a topic for my doctoral thesis in 1965, I suggested tragedy: he replied, "Oh Jessica, don't study tragedy, study comedy; you'll never be bored". He was right and I am still fascinated by it. Humour in all its forms and manifestations is an amazingly rich and varied subject and studying it has led me around the world and back home to Australia many times, always in the company of colleagues for whose lasting friendship and collaboration I am eternally grateful.

It now remains for me to thank most sincerely all those who have contributed to the making of this book: the authors themselves, first and foremost; likewise the cartoonists and their curators in Australia and Japan who have so generously given permission for their work to be reproduced; my sister Jocelyn Chey, who very kindly reviewed several of the chapters concerning Chinese culture; Lucien Leon for expert assistance with images, the editorial staff at Taylor and Francis/Routledge, and in particular, Simon Bates of that publisher's Singapore office, who patiently waited until I could say to him, yes, I think I do have a book for you. Finally, and above all, I thank my family, whose forbearance about yet another book on humour is deeply appreciated.

Jessica Milner Davis PhD FRSN
Sydney November 2021

Note

1 A brief biographical note is available at: https://adb.anu.edu.au/biography/quentin-cecil-robert-11470. It fails to do justice to this remarkable pioneer of theatre in Australia and sadly neither the University of which he became an Emeritus Professor nor the National Institute of Dramatic Art of which he was the Founding Director have any memorial to him. He lives on however in the memories of those who were touched by his life and work.

1 Humour and cultural context

Tradition and practice in six Asian cultures

Jessica Milner Davis

The serious process of bringing a modern scholarly lens to bear on humour and laughter has been in train now since 1978, if not earlier. It was in that year that the first inter-disciplinary conference on humour and laughter was convened by the Welsh Branch of the British Psychological Society in Cardiff (I was lucky enough to attend this ground-breaking event). While literature and philosophy have long treated the comic with the same seriousness as the tragic and the romantic, following the conference, psychologists and linguists have also adopted humour and laughter as topics for serious study. From a range of different perspectives, then, scholars have tried to decode the complexities of creating and experiencing humour as a form of human behaviour. Although much still remains mysterious, a great deal is now known about these topics, including the importance of distinguishing between the two, since laughter is only one potential response to humour and can also result from non-amusing causes such as anxiety, embarrassment and malice. The issue of whether "getting" humour is purely a cognitive process (as maintained by many linguists over the years) or also involves the emotions has been resolved by cognitive studies using functional magnetic resonance imaging (fMRI). This kind of research has confirmed what seems obvious after the event: that humour must first be perceived as intended to be humorous before it can be processed at all (Goel and Dolan 2001; Moran et al. 2004), and also that affective neural nets are just as deeply implicated in sensing and responding to humour as are cognitive ones. Enjoying funny cartoons triggers subcortical reward pathways in the brain and the funnier they are perceived to be, the stronger the reward response (Mobbs et al. 2003). These findings underlie the increasing use of humour in carefully designed therapeutic uses such as clown doctors in hospitals and other settings (see Warren 2007; Dore 2021) and as an educational tool (see Rucynski and Prichard 2020 for its use in ESL; and Tunnisa et al. 2019 for school-teaching in Indonesia). In psychology, the range of personal styles in using and responding to humour has also been explored in some depth, as is further discussed below.

DOI: 10.4324/9781003176374-1

Humour and cultural exchange

Many issues concerning cultural differences in habit, taste and tradition of humour-use nevertheless remain to be examined, despite their importance for understanding, appreciating and sharing humour. This is particularly true when the gaps to be bridged are those between West and East. Until quite recently, linguistic barriers as well as the persistent myth of the mysterious and enigmatic Orient have resulted in a scarcity of English-language scholarly works on humour in many Asian cultures. This book is conceived as a contribution to those few that have appeared.[1] It focusses on the importance of cultural context and tradition in interpreting humour in four very different Asian cultures: those of Japan, China (interpreted broadly to embrace but also insist on the cultural and linguistic distinctiveness of present-day Taiwan and Hong Kong as well as the People's Republic of China [PRC]),[2] Indonesia and South Korea. Studies dealing with humour in any of these cultures are still rather limited, usually tucked away in somewhat obscure specialist journals[3] and they often deal more with laughter than humour itself since the former is much easier to identify than humour. Humour notoriously takes an infinite number of shapes, comes in a variety of styles from gently amusing to bitterly sarcastic and scornful and can be used for all kinds of different purposes. It is also difficult sometimes to spot, particularly when irony is at hand or when it lurks within the confines of a revered and ancient text such as the *Works of Mencius*, as discussed by Shirley Chan in this volume.

Despite such challenges, the topic is highly relevant to the modern age as readers and travellers increasingly traverse temporal and geographic separations. Cultural exchange and business and diplomatic relations must be pursued.[4] East and Southeast Asia are important destinations, despite the travel disruptions of the 2020–2021 COVID-19 pandemic. If tourism is currently down, then the spotlight is on print and electronic resources for businesspeople, international students and the intelligent public as they seek to locate knowledge about cultural differences. It is as important as ever to understand how to bridge the gap between one's own mindset and that of someone from another culture without giving or taking offence if personal relations are to be successfully maintained (Mullan and Béal 2021). Studies in both business and tourism demonstrate that humour can be a powerful lubricant for interpersonal exchange when used and interpreted correctly but that when it is misinterpreted, relationships are at risk of setback (Schnurr and Chan 2009, 2011; Chen, G-H. et al. 2013; Murata 2014; Pearce and Pabel 2015; Jiang et al. 2019; Plester and Kim 2021).

One illustrative disaster story comes from Australia, where in 2017, the National Meat and Livestock Board decided to develop a humorous advertising campaign promoting the consumption of lamb—a choice Australian export. Invoking diversity in both present Australia and the potential markets of neighbouring Asia, the ad designers dreamed up the concept of a light-hearted "feast of the gods" that would show parodies of various divine incarnations and prophetic figures joining in a cheerful toast to lamb as a shared delicacy. What could go wrong? The short video clip depicted figures modelled on the Norse pantheon, a Roman god and goddess, Christ, the Laughing Buddha, a Star Wars guru and, as hostess, a nice but agnostic young Australian–Asian woman. Lord Ganesha is the life of the party, proposing they all should meet more often and make the galaxy a friendlier and better place. But—associating Ganesha with meat (even if he does not appear to be eating it) when he is well-known to be a vegetarian? Complaints flooded in from Australia's Hindu community and also from overseas. One local press headline read: "GODS. Prophets. Messiahs. All may come to the table under this Australian meat industry ad. But some of their followers are seeing red—and are fuming" (Seidel 2017). The ad was dropped.[5] Cultural sensitivity is vital to humour and particularly awareness of how cultures that are distinct but related in important ways like geography and trade differ in their conventions about the use of humour. Hence the vital contribution of reliable studies such as this book seeks to offer.

Humour in Asian cultural contexts

Although the cultures under consideration in this book are only a selection of those that deserve study across Asia more widely, they all demonstrate that in European culture historically, humour has taken different shapes and been called by different names long before the word itself came into use in the languages concerned. The present term thus reveals a modernising tendency wherever it came into effect. Even in English, before the late nineteenth century, humour had a different and specific meaning as the particular form of kindly and self-deprecating humour adopted by a well-bred and good-natured person (Wickberg 1998). This harked back to the ancient theory of bodily humours in which all elements should be present in harmonious balance to ensure health and happiness (Arika 2007).[6] By the first decades of the twentieth century, the general umbrella sense of humour had developed in which it is now used around the world—including in Asian non-English contexts—to refer to any and all forms of what is amusing. In French, however, *l'humour* still carries the connotations of a benign English humour as opposed to the witty and acerbic French *l'esprit* (Noonan 2011). At Harvard University in the 1930s, the idea of a good sense of (general) humour was first included by Gordon Allport as a sign of maturity and self-actualisation in his pioneering instruments for psychological assessment (Allport 1937; Wickberg 1998: 222).

Around the same time, the word arrived in China to overtake but also coexist with older indigenous terms for the laughable, the comic, satire, witticism and many other form-specific terms (Liao 1998; Wells 2006). In Chinese cultures, for example, the presently prevailing linguistic usage dates from the 1930s when the writer Lin Yutang, acclaimed as the Master of

Humour (*youmo dashi* 幽默大師), published a seminal essay, *Lun youmo* 論幽默 (*On humour*, 1934).[7] He and his group used the term *youmo* to advocate for a new sensibility in Chinese society. Interestingly, as with the English word humour as opposed to terms like wit and satire, *youmo* implies more gentleness than older indigenous terms like *huaji* 滑稽 and *xiao* 笑 (laughter and the laughable; see Liao 2003; Chey 2011: 19; also Shirley Chan this volume, Note 4). It is thus both a loanword in its form and a neologism in the sense in which Lin introduced it.

In Japan, the situation is rather similar. First adopted during the period of the opening to the West by literary writers and critics as early as the 1890s (Wells 1997: 69), the loanword *yūmoa* ユーモア now coexists with older terms such as *fūshi* 諷刺 (satire, see Wells 2006) and other borrowed terms such as *uitto* ウィット (wit, see Condren 2020). In Indonesian and Balinese, the word is simply *humor*, but the novelty of the concept is evident from the naming of the Indonesian Modern Humor Institute (IHIK), founded in 2016.[8] In the various Balinese languages, a plethora of terms still identify different formats of humorous material, which can all be summed up as *bebanyolan* or Balinese humour (Nengah Arnawa this volume). The coexistence of older terms for various types of humour and laughter with the modern loanword holds true for the other cultures represented in this book. Accordingly, when the term humour is used in English or in a neological form by the present authors, it is intended in the modern umbrella sense, while other specific terms identify particular forms or modes of humour.

Whatever humour has been called, it has always been present in these cultures, in forms and modes that range from verbal to visual and performative, and also in combinations of those. Humour everywhere may be written, spoken, enacted or exchanged interpersonally or online. As the following chapters demonstrate, many forms survive effectively unchanged from times past, while others have transformed themselves to a greater or less extent in order to adapt to modern circumstances, especially to new media. Humour is thus indigenous and familiar as well as being novel and modernising. The theme of this book is the interplay between these kinds of continuities and changes.

Humour and its cultural conventions

Over time, it seems that cultures develop not only special forms of humour but also sets of conventions about when, where and how to use humour, and that these reflect national differences. While these could be and often are described as national senses of humour, the implications of that terminology are not always helpful. Most cultures laugh at or are amused by the same things, although some of the recognised forms that humour takes differ. More importantly, different countries have internalised over time different cultural conventions about the use of humour and the times and places where it is considered appropriate—and not. Hence, it is preferable to talk about humour *in* a certain nation or culture, rather than "Chinese humour" or "Japanese humour".

These rules about humour reflect in part the different natures and values of the societies, and they continue to exert influence even as cultures modernise and transform with international exchange and natural evolution (Milner Davis 2013; Cai et al. 2019). As a review of studies by Jiang et al. (2019) has shown, the chief impact of these conventions is on attitudes to and the use of humour in daily life, particularly as a coping strategy. Speaking of behaviour by students, the authors sum up the differences: "Westerners and Easterners do differ in the relationship between humor and psychological well-being, not qualitatively but quantitatively ... Chinese students tend to appreciate and use humor less than Western students do, Chinese are more likely to embrace adaptive humor styles, which have the greatest influence on their mental health, while maladaptive humor styles are less influential" (2019: 5). Adaptive humour styles are those considered to build affiliation and enhance self, while maladaptive ones are using humour aggressively and in self-deprecation.

For psychological studies such as these, there are some legitimate questions about how well Western assessment instruments translate into Asian languages: for example, Chinese people may well regard self-deprecating humour as self-enhancing, given politeness norms (Jiang et al. 2019). There is no doubt, however, that the reported findings are consistent with other observations about cultural differences. Researchers since Geert Hofstede (1980, 2011) have sought to develop ways of measuring differences in cultural values between nations which must relate to humour along with many other things.[9] Differences in the social value accorded to hierarchy, autonomy and individualism, harmony and considerations of face, must all inevitably impact on attitudes to humour (Liao 1998; Chen, G-H. et al. 2013; Chen, H-C. et al. 2013). The continuing influence across Chinese societies of the Confucian traditions of respect and politeness undoubtedly affects humour and joking—indeed, this is attested to by several chapters in this book, as well as by other studies (Xu 2011; Yue 2011, 2018). And similarly, both Japanese and Balinese rules about politeness privilege some forms and uses of humour over others. In Japan, for example, the preference is for interpersonal exchange of word-play rather than canned jokes (Nagashima 2006; Takekuro 2006). In Balinese culture, this is matched by an amazing richness of punning which is ubiquitous in both entertainment and personal conversation (Sherzer 1993; Arnawa this volume). These two cultures both privilege the more subtle and depersonalised forms of humour involved in verbal play over jokes, which tend to be aimed at a particular target, are sometimes personal and often controversial. In any society, then, current views about using humour will reflect the continuing influence of traditional values and practices.

Regardless of such shared cultural values, individuals in any country will differ greatly in their tastes for and ways of using humour in daily life.[10]

Personal aesthetic preferences differ, as do temperaments. Their relevance to humour is confirmed by a large body of sociological and psychological studies (e.g., Martin et al. 2003; Ruch 2007; Heintz and Ruch 2019). Within almost every culture, there are identifiable groups of people who shrink from the sound and use of laughter as well as those who actively seek it out. There will be some who enjoy laughing at others and some who enjoy being laughed at (Ruch and Proyer 2009). Some people love joke-telling sessions and some prefer more high-brow forms of humorous entertainment (Kuipers 2015). Such personal differences additionally complicate any effort to talk about a typical or national sense of humour. Every country possesses a huge range of individual variations within its shared cultural boundaries. Even the national identity is a construct that evolves slowly over time, is affected by history and political events and continues to be impacted by the modernising effects of international culture, particularly American popular culture in the age of the internet. Hence the culture wars that in many places are so hotly debated these days: the clash between different political groupings over what is truly national.

Continuity and change in humour

As in other things, countries sometimes deliberately set out to adopt a particular overseas humour practice or form. It was in this sense that Lin Yutang recommended to his countrymen the refined comic style of the English novelist and man of letters, George Meredith (1828–1909), over what he saw as the less humane native traditions of *huaji* (Sample 2011; see also Shirley Chan this volume, Note 3). In Japan, today's talented performers of *manzai* 漫才 (formerly written 萬歳, a stand-up comedy duo)[11] can be traced back to the age-old Lunar New Year village performances by a pair of strolling funny men (Katayama 2008). But these rustic comic dialogues were transformed, first to something more suited to the popular stage and then, under the growing influence of Western culture and its commercial imperatives in the 1920s, to Western models adapted for radio and finally the age of television. Today, young *manzaishi* wear casual Western clothing and perform like rock stars (*aidoru* アイドル) rather than adopting the conventional garb and demeanour of the more traditional artists who recite *rakugo* 落語 or sit-down comedy. Nevertheless, retaining tradition does not mean irrelevance to today's world: elsewhere in this book, M.W. Shores outlines the inventive means that these highly trained *rakugoka* 落語家 adopt in order to relate to and entertain their audiences with their age-old art. Similarly, in Bali, as Nengah Arnawa shows (this volume), today's village *wayang kulit* performances (shadow puppet plays) adapt themselves seamlessly to contemporary worries such as bureaucratic bungling and government-run schools, as well as using the new media to reach much wider audiences via the equivalent of YouTube and mobile phone apps.

Arguments persist about the continuity of some native traditions in humour. In China, for example, the pattern of humour as truth-telling was established by the witty and urbane *huaji*-ists 滑稽師 who served in the Imperial courts of the Spring and Autumn and Warring States periods (722–221 BCE) and the Qin Dynasty (221–206 BCE). Their use of humour as a technique of political advice and teaching was certainly advocated by sages such as Mencius (Mengzi 孟軻, see Shirley Chan this volume). Does this tradition lie behind contemporary manifestations such as *xiangsheng* 相聲 (cross-talk, see Cai and Dunn 2020) and internet *e'gao* 惡搞 (spoofing, see Rea 2013), both of which have been viewed at times as disruptive and disrespectful by internet censors? Or are these contemporary styles of irreverent humour altogether remote from ancestral predecessors? Equally importantly, do they fit either the traditional Confucian or the PRC's neo-Confucian concept of appropriate humour? In the final result, continuity and change in humour probably depend not only on state initiatives like the Japanese deliberate adoption of Western (German and American) models but also on generational social change. Research in South Korea by Kim and Plester (this volume) and in Taiwan by Chang and Haugh (this volume) shows that younger people in both those Confucian-influenced cultures feel able to adopt styles of humour in their daily repertoire that are more aggressive than those used by older people.

Tradition and continuity

Taken as a whole, the studies collected in this book demonstrate that ancient themes in humour are indeed still playing out centuries later and that today's media facilitate modern humourists reinterpreting familiar forms and topics. As Marjorie Chan points out (this volume), the Chinese ancient taboo on imperial names established a tradition of nicknaming and witticism involving other people's names that exploits the rich homophony of Chinese languages. This kind of word-play lies at the core of the very funny Hong Kong TV series that her chapter examines. Illustrating the continuity of this traditional practice, earlier examples occur in the Ming dynasty (1368–1644) novella *Guzhang Juechen* 鼓掌絕塵 (*Clap your hands and rid yourself of dust*) examined by Antonio Leggieri in his chapter. And from Japan, another series of amusing examples of the technique comes from the pen of the remarkable woman cartoonist Machiko Hasegawa 長谷川町子 (1920–1992). As explained by Sachiko Kitazume (this volume), in one popular Hasegawa cartoon strip, a whole family of characters rejoice in fish-related names, signalling their bond as a tight-knit group but also their endistancing from reality as stereotypical characters. Comic naming is both traditional in its technique and modern in its cheekiness.

In the examples of humour presented here from the six cultures of Japan, PRC, Hong Kong, South Korea, Taiwan and Bali, other recurring themes concern trickery and deception, official corruption and bureaucratic red tape, the battle of the sexes and the use of humour for persuasion and instruction. It takes very little reflection to perceive that these differ not at all from but rather are held in common with Western humour. From medieval farce to the films of Charlie Chaplin, from Molière to American sitcoms, the same kinds of butts for humour can be found. Casual inspection of humorous memes on the internet or of the jokes and quips exchanged on social media will reveal plenty of lampoons directed at bureaucratic bungling and the opposite gender, as well as the sharing of humorous advertising. Many of these topics and targets of humour appear to be universal. Further, while cultural rules certainly differ between European cultures and the Sinosphere about the use of humour, as Shirley Chan points out (this volume), the recommendations for its proper practice promulgated by Confucius and his disciples bear a remarkable resemblance to Aristotle's influential teachings on *eutrapelia*.[12] Other parallels include the fact that, while Japan is well known for its reticence in expressing public criticism even under the cloak of humour (Wells 2006), its traditional *kyōgen* comic playlets share many plot structures with European farce (Wells and Milner Davis 2006). Similarly, in Makiko Takekuro's chapter describing a surviving traditional laughter ritual on one of the outlying Japanese islands, the humorists' jibes at modern celebrity culture and materialism read suspiciously like the playwright Ben Jonson inveighing against modish nonsense in Elizabethan London. Elsewhere, the longstanding tradition of political satire expressed in Korean masked dance-drama has much in common with the Carnival celebrations of Europe which in medieval times especially enjoyed temporary licence to celebrate social topsy-turvydom (Bakhtin 1968; Van Leest 1991).

Humour and cultural tradition

Given such similarities and shared tropes in humour, the first chapters in this book focus on relevant cultural traditions and practices in humour. These then illuminate the contemporary forms and uses of humour that are examined in other chapters. The book commences with two studies of humour found in classical sources which resonate down the ages to influence more contemporary examples. The first is Shirley Chan's exploration of how Mencius (according to his disciples) cleverly used irony and rhetorical humour in parables that taught the Confucian way. Hidden though some of the joking is under the layers of overly reverential and oftentimes wooden translations down the ages, Chan's new account reveals an acerbic wit and dry humour that makes the point of a Mencian parable stick in the memory. Such an effective use of didactic humour, she shows, remains an influence on modern humour in the Chinese cultural sphere.

Similarly, the second chapter of the book unpicks the amusing detail in both verbal humour and characterisation that was established as a pattern in the late-Imperial Chinese narrative. Antonio Leggieri identifies a deeply satirical commentary that critiques social malpractices of the time and ridicules grotesque characters who abused power in times now safely past. These lively depictions of selfish and deceptive characters who get their comeuppance in the best farcical tradition are scattered like pearls embroidering the highly discursive narrative structure—and comic names often help identify them. Sadly, the best man rarely gets the right girl: and at such points, the novella's tone shifts from biting satire to a world-weary and ironic acceptance of the ways of the world. What strikes us here is the rapport between humourist and audience that made this a popular novel for its circle of readers. Leggieri argues that humour is probably the best-kept secret of Chinese fiction: although it has accompanied it from the beginning, like the wit of Mencius and other sages, it has so often been overlooked in critical commentaries.

Moving beyond classical China, the next four chapters present case studies from Japanese and Balinese culture in which tradition continues to shape modern-day humour. The themes here are humour as play and relief from life stress and humour's role in building social cohesion. Each of the four studies reveals the enduring beliefs and customs that underlie much of today's popular humour in these societies. Nengah Arnawa's study of traditional forms of verbal humour in Balinese culture today reveals links between humorous word-play in personal exchanges and in the more professional performances of the *wayang-kulik* or shadow puppet plays with their quick-fire banter between puppets. Balinese conventions of politeness and respect privilege subtlety over aggressive humour, resulting in complex patterns of word substitution and matching. These word-plays depend upon close linguistic knowledge, illustrating the role of humour in reinforcing affiliation and cohesion amongst a community. Arnawa's dissection of several *wayang-kulik* dialogues in particular also shows that, using this technique, the traditional clowns are able to give voice to satirical social comment without offence.

Exactly the same functions are embodied in the ancient Japanese staging of ritual laughter that annually celebrates departed ancestors on Ishigaki island to the south of Japan which is the subject of the next chapter. Here, as Makiko Takekuro's careful observation and recording of events shows, local knowledge and preoccupations are highlighted for catharsis by group laughter as the traditional mock-ancestral masked couple conducts its vaguely menacing dialogue with local residents. Despite the supernatural eeriness, the vital role of this pair is to unlock laughter and relieve tension so that local cultural values and regional identity can be invoked and celebrated in the usual concluding group dance. Confirmation of identity and belief system through humour is also the subject of Sachiko Kitazume's study of the cartoons of Michiko Hasagawa. Created during the postwar period until the mid-70s, these cartoons remain hugely popular, displayed in the Museum dedicated to the artist's work, translated into English and widely published. Kitazume shows that their structures and themes depend on two important and traditional beliefs that are still influential today: belief in the innate goodness of humankind, as originally argued by Mencius and still embedded in Japanese cultural morals today; and the Confucian dogma (endorsed by Prince Shōtoku Taishi 聖徳太子 in the sixth century CE) that evil should be punished and good deeds rewarded. Effectively, the modern characters and plots of this highly entertaining form of popular culture serve the same didactic purpose laid out by Mencius.

The final chapter in this group examines the humour of an art form that is often thought of as scarcely altered from its original form and texts, despite nowadays being offered in large and comfortable theatres and even made available online and in video recordings: the art of Japanese *rakugo*. M.W. Shores focusses on the relationship between performer and modern-day audience in order to unpick the detailed way in which rapport is built and distance associated with the past overcome. *Rakugo* is categorised alongside other *koten* 古典 (classical, traditional) performing arts and its transition to modernity depends on achieving a careful balance between what remains unchanging (such as the prescribed stories and presentation conventions) and what is relevant to today's modern and largely urban audiences. This overview should not spoil the story by revealing the secrets of Shores' conclusions, but his insights derive from both his own observations and personal interviews with practicing *rakugoka* artists (including one of Japan's most successful pioneering woman in this field). In this way he is able to demonstrate how conscious the artists themselves are of this challenge and how each goes about meeting it in a particular way.

Humour and cultural evolution

The clash between traditional and evolving modern attitudes to humour is the focus of the next two chapters, one set in South Korea and the other in Taiwan. Both deal with work-related conversational humour, with a particular focus on Confucian-based relationships and politeness in communication. Detailed observation of personnel in several companies and settings both inside and out of the office allow HeeSun Kim and her co-author, Barbara Plester, to draw conclusions about the range of purposes served by humour. Some of these are positive, saving face, according respect (particularly to older serving if not senior employees); but some are designed as reprimands, such the sarcastic use of honorifics, and do not signal politeness but promote distance, for example, between a speaker and a junior who has not acted appropriately. Humour can be unwelcome as well as welcome, and invariably in the settings studied, its use was subject to the Confucian values of hierarchy, respect and politeness. Korean workplaces are tightly bound by politeness rules that constrain humour usage, especially towards managers. The authors note that this strongly contrasts with much Western research that stresses the positive value of humour as a tool to help subordinates contest and challenge managers and organisational decisions (for example, in New Zealand, see Holmes and Marra 2002; Plester and Orams 2008).

Wei-Lin Melody Chang and Michael Haugh's chapter on verbal humour in contemporary Taiwanese conversation stresses that contemporary humour practices do not emerge out of the blue: they are shaped by intersecting societal, cultural and political forces over time to become what we observe today. In fact, Taiwanese cultural rules about humour today demonstrate this particularly well since they have been affected by multiple cultural influences, not only traditional Chinese humour practices but also those of modern Mainland Chinese culture, of Hong Kong and Japan. The result is evident in clear generational differences in conversational humour in Taiwan. The examples selected from everyday conversations reveal that although both younger Taiwanese (in their early 20s) and older Taiwanese (in their late 50s and early 60s) engage in light or mild forms of teasing (*cháoxiào* 嘲笑 or *cháofèng* 嘲諷), younger people also tend to engage in harsher forms of teasing (*tiáokǎn* 調侃 and *kāiwánxiào* 開玩笑) (see also Chang and Haugh 2020). These are avoided by older Taiwanese who favour word-play, drawing on the longstanding tradition of punning in classical Chinese humour (as demonstrated in Leggieri's chapter). This exploits the fact that many older Taiwanese regularly speak both Mandarin Chinese and Taiwanese Hokkien and are aware of Japanese influences on Taiwan from the first half of the twentieth century and so enjoy speaking Taiwanese Hokkien with code-switching into Mandarin Chinese, for example. The chapter goes further to examine some selections of humorous conversation from novels and short stories published in Taiwan from the 1960s to the 1990s to investigate whether the same time-linked difference exists between the two types of humour. These fictional representations of real-life conversations similarly reflect a generational change of habit from practicing more Confucian-influenced, politer forms of humour such as word-play and gentle teasing to quite acerbic teasing and sarcasm. The authors offer their findings as a possible model for future research into fiction as source material for humour studies.

As cultural change comes about, conventions about humour also slowly evolve and, in the cases studied, it seems to be becoming possible for people to use humour of all kinds in a more individualistic, openly critical way with and about others. The final pair of chapters in the book focusses on popular TV comedy series in Hong Kong and the Mainland and brings the narrative of humour and its cultural context up to date with contemporary developments. The theme in these chapters is the subversive nature of humour as it is deployed in ways that seem to challenge standing cultural conventions. In Ying Cao's chapter on a humorous TV reality show, humour and teasing are of vital importance to the four (real-life) women friends who are the stars. Although their teasing is by no means gentle, Cao shows that, nevertheless, it is deployed in order to build friendship and is, therefore, in psychological terms, a type of affiliative humour conforming to Confucian tradition. Questioning whether perhaps Chinese culture possesses a so-far hidden history of female groups employing aggressive but friendly humour with each other, the author also poses the question, whether methodological approaches developed in English can fully accommodate analysis of humour and teasing in Chinese contexts. The celebrity actors in this series live by and with their humour and the chapter brings them vividly to life, as well as providing insights into the linguistics of teasing, as it focusses on their daily conversational exchanges and travels together. Although the humour here is sharply acerbic, even aggressively critical, it serves to bind the group together and builds harmony between the group and also between them and their audiences.

Turning to Hong Kong, in a tribute to its linguistic and cultural richness, Marjorie Chan analyses some of the aspects of humour in the 2017 TV series, *Budong Sajiao de Nüren* 不懂撒嬌的女人 (*Women who don't know how to* sajiao—where *sajiao* means "to act cute, to be flirtatious"). The series was also cleverly marketed as *My Unfair Lady*, playing on the title of the famous 1964 film version of George Bernard Shaw's 1913 play, *Pygmalion*. Set in Hong Kong, the comedy series adopts the lens of a modern office and its denizens to comment humorously on both traditional gender roles and tensions between local and Mainland Chinese cultures. It explores the personal and business relationships of the company staff, both in Hong Kong, Taiwan and on the Mainland. Chan's expert and amusing study probes how the series uses humour in language, situation and character. It begins by examining the ubiquitous play upon names among the six main characters whereby proper names are often combined with prefixal forms and kinship terms, and nicknames are used as terms of address with special (often derogatory) implications. The humour employs a wide range of devices, including physical comedy and sight gags, irony, hyperbole, mock apophony and other word-play. It also exploits the use of code-switching between other dialects and languages, modulations of speech tempo and tone of voice (e.g., in "doing" *sajiao*). In this way, its humour is very traditional, reflecting the history of cultural practice as well as the natures of the rich array of Chinese languages available to the modern-day Hongkonger. As the professional and love lives of the characters unfold, however, humour intersects with gender-driven issues such as envy, admiration, scorn and jealousy, and the resulting depiction of women's roles in love, life and professional responsibility is decidedly modern. The chapter identifies a range of knotty societal issues that are brought to the fore under this guise of humour and laughter. As Chan concludes, these issues are treated seriously in a satirical social critique, but the overall tone of the humour is nevertheless warm-hearted. It rises above real-world problems and accepts human foibles for what they are. In a real sense, this is a case study of *youmo* 幽默 at its best.

Conclusion

In any society and age, humour provides relief and entertainment. It also challenges power and the status quo. This book offers a series of case studies of humour's interplay between power and challenge, between social status and rebellion, and entertainment and instruction. It focusses on important cultures in Asia but does not pretend to be exhaustive in any sense. It demonstrates the influence of tradition even in very modern forms of humour such as cartoons, TV and office chit-chat. While many of the forms and modes examined have reinvented themselves under modern social conditions, the evidence is that the influence of age-old tradition dies hard in humour-related practices and accepting that is important if present day humour is to be successfully understood, particularly by outsiders. The authors collected here aim, above all, to highlight the importance of understanding the nexus between humour and a wide range of localised cultural values in the present era of globalised communication. In the process, we hope to have both entertained and provided food for thought with our discussions, as well as paid richly deserved tribute to the artists and peoples of important cultures in the Asian region.

Notes

1 This author has contributed three books on the topic, one on Japan (Milner Davis 2006) and two coedited with Jocelyn Chey on humour in Chinese cultures (Chey and Milner Davis 2011; Milner Davis and Chey 2013). Other significant volumes focussing on specific historic periods are Paulo Santangelo (2012); Christopher Rea (2015); Steinmüller and Brandstadter (2016); and Ping Zhu et al. (2019). Xiaodong Yue (2018) examines the psychology of humour in the Chinese context. On Japan, the pioneering work is Marguerite A. Wells (1997), followed by Milner Davis (2006). For Taiwan, Laura Chao Chih Liao (1998). Indonesia and South Korea lack overview studies to date.
2 In this book, Taiwan indicates the geographical and political entity known as the Republic of China and as China, Taiwan; Hong Kong is the Hong Kong Special Administrative Region of the People's Republic of China (PRC); China is the PRC (sometimes also referred to as Mainland China).
3 For example, the excellent comparative study of humour-use in Singapore, Israel and America by Nevo et al. (*Journal of General Psychology*, 2001); Joel Sherzer's early study of Balinese verbal humour (*Language in Society*, 1993).
4 Humour's impact in geopolitics is reviewed by Dittmer in his report on how it builds collegiality at Model UN Assembly exercises (Dittmer 2013); see also Zelizer (2010) on humour and peace-building.
5 The Advertising Standards Board for Australia did note that while many Hindus are vegetarian, vegetarianism is not a requirement of that faith and ruled at first that the depiction of Lord Ganesh was "simply symbolic of the Hindu faith and his inclusion is part of the message of an inclusive multi-faith meal" (Morgan 2017). Nevertheless, the ad was, in fact, dropped. An independent review reversed the original decision, finding that additional material in the ad showed that the Hindu religion was treated less respectfully than Islam, for example. A reference to "the elephant in the room" singled that deity out for his physical characteristics while Allah remained undepicted (Sawatzky 2017).

6 For an account of the older Chinese Theory of the Humours, which still informs the practice of Traditional Chinese Medicine, see Tiquia (2011).
7 For an English translation, see Sample (2011); and for discussion, Qian (2011) and Sohigian (2007).
8 For an account of this interesting Institute, see Ikhwan Hastanto (2021).
9 Hofstede's original work (Hofstede 1980, expanded upon in Hofstede 2011) on defining and measuring cultural values has been extended by Schwartz (1992, 2021). Both scales relate well to studying broad cultural variations in attitudes to humour.
10 Schwartz acknowledges the important difference between cultural values, which can be compared across cultures, and values that are held to a greater or lesser extent by individuals. Accordingly, he developed two different but related sets of value dimensions (see Schwartz 2021).
11 On the evolution of *manzai*, see Katayama (2008: 214–215).
12 For Confucian concepts of humour, see Xu (2011); for Aristotelian *eutrapelia*, see Screech (2015, Chapter 1) and Morreall (1989).

References

Allport, Gordon. W. 1937. *Personality: A psychological interpretation*. New York: Henry Holt.
Arika, Noga. 2007. *Passions and tempers: A history of the humours*. New York: ECCO.
Bakhtin, Mikhail. 1968. *Rabelais and his world*. Trans. Helene Iswolsky. Cambridge MA: MIT Press. 1968.
Cai, Huajian, Zihang Huang and Yiming Jing. 2019. Living in a changing world: The Change of culture and psychology. In D. Matsumoto and H. C. Hwang, eds., *Oxford handbook of culture and psychology*. 786–801. 2nd ed. Oxford: Oxford University Press.
Cai, Shenshen and Emily Dunn. 2020. *Xiangsheng and the emergence of Guo Degang in contemporary China*. London: Palgrave Macmillan.
Chang, Wei Lin Melody. and Michael Haugh. 2020. The metapragmatics of "teasing" in Taiwanese Chinese conversational humour. *European Journal of Humour Research*, 8: 7–30.
Chen, Guo-Hai, David Watkins and Rod A. Martin. 2013. Sense of humor in China: The role of individualism, collectivism, and facework. *Psychologia*, 56: 57–70. doi: 10.2117/psysoc.2013.57
Chen, Hsueh-Chih, Yu-Chen Chan, Willibald Ruch and René T. Proyer. 2013. Laughing at others and being laughed at in Taiwan and Switzerland: A cross-cultural perspective. In J. Milner Davis and J. Chey, eds., *Humour in Chinese life and culture: resistance and control in modern times*. 215–230. Hong Kong: Hong Kong University Press.
Chey, Jocelyn. 2011. *Youmo* and the Chinese sense of humour. In Jocelyn Chey and Jessica Milner Davis, eds., *Humour in Chinese life and letters: Classical and traditional approaches*. 19–47. Hong Kong: Hong Kong University Press.
Chey, Jocelyn and Jessica Milner Davis, eds. 2011. *Humour in Chinese life and letters: Classical and traditional approaches*. Hong Kong: Hong Kong University Press.
Condren, Conal. 2020. The study of past humour: Historicity and the limits of method. In Daniel Derrin and Hannah Burrows, eds., *The Palgrave handbook of humour, history and methodology*. 19–41. London: Palgrave Macmillan.

Dittmer, Jason. 2013. Humour at the Model United Nations: The Role of laughter in constituting geopolitical assemblages. *Geopolitics*, 18 (3): 493–513. doi: 10.1080/14650045.2012.742066

Dore, Margherita, Laura Vagnoli, Francesca Addarii, Elena Amore and Rosanna Martin. 2021. The positive effect of humour and amateur dubbing on hospitalised adolescents. In Elisabeth Vanderheiden and Claude-Hélène Mayer, eds., *The Palgrave handbook of humour research*. 441–457. London: Palgrave Macmillan/ Springer Nature.

Goel, Vinod and Raymond J. Dolan. 2001. The functional anatomy of humor: Segregating cognitive and affective components. *Nature Neuroscience*, 4: 237–238.

Heintz, Sonja and Willibald Ruch. 2019. From four to nine styles: An update on individual differences in humor. *Personality and Individual Differences*, 141: 7–12.

Hofstede, Geert. 1980. *Culture's consequences: Comparing values, behaviors, institutions, and organizations across nations*. Thousand Oaks CA: Sage.

Hofstede, Geert. 2011. Dimensionalizing cultures: The Hofstede model in context. *Online Readings in Psychology and Culture*, 2 (1). https://doi.org/10.9707/2307-0919.1014

Holmes, Janet and Meredith Marra. 2002. Having a laugh at work: How humour contributes to workplace culture. *Journal of Pragmatics*, 34 (12): 1683–1710.

Ikhwan Hastanto. 2021. The science of telling jokes: Indonesia's first comedy institute. *The Jakarta Post*, 11 March. At: https://www.thejakartapost.com/life/2021/03/11/the-science-of-telling-jokes-indonesias-first-comedy-institute.html (accessed 27 September 2021).

Jiang, Tonglin, Li Hao and Hou Yubo. 2019. Cultural differences in humor perception, usage, and implications. *Frontiers in Psychology*, 10: article 123. doi: 10.3389/fpsyg.2019.00123

Katayama, Hanae. 2008. Humor in *manzai* stand-up comedy: A historical and comparative analysis. *International Journal of the Humanities*, 6 (1): 213–223.

Kuipers, Giselinde. 2015 [2006]. *Good humor, bad taste: A sociology of the joke*. Berlin and New York: Mouton de Gruyter.

Liao, Laura Chao Chih. 1998. *Taiwanese perceptions of humor*. Taipei: Crane.

Liao, Laura Chao Chih. 2003. Humor versus *huaji*. *Journal of Languages and Linguistics*, 2: 25–46.

Martin, Rod A., Patricia Puhlik-Doris, Gwen Larsen, Jeanette Gray and Kelly Weir. 2003. Individual differences in uses of humor and their relation to psychological well-being: Development of the Humor Styles Questionnaire. *Journal of Research in Personality*, 37 (1): 48–75. https://doi.org/10.1016/S0092-6566(02)00534-2

Milner Davis, Jessica. 2013. The cultural context of humour: Overview and introduction. In J. Milner Davis and J. Chey, eds., *Humour in Chinese life and culture: Resistance and control in modern times*. 1–21. Hong Kong: Hong Kong University Press.

Milner Davis, Jessica, ed. 2006. *Understanding humor in Japan*. Detroit MI: Wayne State University Press.

Milner Davis, Jessica and Jocelyn Chey, eds. 2013. *Humour in Chinese life and culture: Resistance and control in modern times*. Hong Kong: Hong Kong University Press.

Mobbs, Dean, Micheal D. Greicius, Eiman Abdel-Azim, Vinod Menon and Allan L. Reiss. 2003. Humor modulates the mesolimbic reward centers. *Neuron*, 40 (5): 1041–1048.

Moran, Joseph M., Gagan S. Wig, Reginald B. Adams Jr., Petr Janata and William M. Kelley. 2004. Neural correlates of humor detection and appreciation. *NeuroImage*, 21 (3): 1055–1060.

Morgan, Riley. 2017. Calls to ban "insulting" lamb ad featuring Ganesha dismissed by standards bureau. *SBS News online*, 19 September. At: https://www.sbs.com.au/news/calls-to-ban-insulting-lamb-ad-featuring-ganesha-dismissed-by-standards-bureau (accessed 6 April 2021).

Morreall, John. 1989. The rejection of humor in Western thought. *Philosophy East and West*, 39 (3): 243–265.

Mullan, Kerry and Christine Béal. 2021. The use of humour to deal with uncomfortable moments in interaction: A cross-cultural approach. In Vanderheiden, Elisabeth and Claude-Hélène Mayer, eds., *The Palgrave handbook of humour research*. 41–66. London: Palgrave Macmillan/Springer Nature.

Murata, K. 2014. An empirical cross-cultural study of humor in business meetings in New Zealand and Japan. *Journal of Pragmatics*, 60 (1): 251–265.

Nagashima, Heiyō. 2006. *Sha-re*: A widely accepted form of Japanese word-play. In Jessica Milner Davis, ed., *Understanding humor in Japan*. 75–83. Detroit MI: Wayne State University Press.

Nevo, Ofra, Baruch Nevo and J. L. S. Yin. 2001. Singaporean humor: A crosscultural, cross-gender comparison. *Journal of General Psychology*, 128 (2): 143–156. doi: 10.1080/00221300109598904

Noonan, Will. 2011. Reflecting back, or what can the French tell the English about humour?, *Sydney Studies in English*, 37. http://openjournals.library.usyd.edu.au/index.php/SSE/article/view/5321

Pearce, Philip L. and Anja Pabel. 2015. *Tourism and humour*. Bristol UK: Channel View Publications. doi: 10.21832/9781845415105

Plester, Barbara and HeeSun Kim. 2021. Risky business: Humour, hierarchy, and harmony in New Zealand and South Korean workplaces. In Elisabeth Vanderheiden and Claude-Hélène Mayer, eds., *The Palgrave handbook of humour research*. 245–262. London: Palgrave Macmillan/Springer Nature.

Plester, Barbara A. and M. Orams. 2008. Send in the clowns: The role of the joker in three New Zealand IT companies. *HUMOR: International Journal of Humor Research*, 21: 253–281.

Qian Suoqiao. 2011. Discovering humour in modern China: The launching of the *Analects Fortnightly Journal* and the "Year of Humour" (1933). In Jocelyn Chey and Jessica Milner Davis, eds., *Humour in Chinese life and letters: Classical and traditional approaches*. 191–217. Hong Kong: Hong Kong University Press.

Rea, Christopher. 2015. *The age of irreverence: A new history of laughter in China*. Oakland CA: University of California Press.

Rea, Christopher. 2013. Spoofing (*e'gao*) culture on the Chinese internet. In Jessica Milner Davis and Jocelyn Chey, eds., *Humour in Chinese life and culture: Resistance and control in modern times*. 149–172. Hong Kong: Hong Kong University Press.

Ruch, Willibald, ed. 2007. *The sense of humor: Explorations of a personality characteristic*. Berlin: De Gruyter.

Ruch, Willibald and Rene T. Proyer. 2009. Extending the study of gelotophobia: On gelotophiles and katagelasticists. *Humor: International Journal of Humor Research*, 22: 183–212. doi:10.1515/HUMR.2009.009

Rucynski, John Jr. and Caleb Prichard, eds. 2020. *Bridging the humor barrier: Humor competency training in English language teaching*. Lanham MD: Lexington Books.

Sample, Joseph. 2011. Contextualizing Lin Yutang's essay "On humour": Introduction and translation. In Jocelyn Chey and Jessica Milner Davis, eds., *Humour in Chinese life and letters: Classical and traditional approaches*. 169–189. Hong Kong: Hong Kong University Press.

Santangelo, Paulo, ed. 2012. *Laughing in Chinese*. Rome: Aracne Editrice.

Sawatzky, Robert. 2017. Australian lamb ad banned after review. *Campaign India*, 24 November. At: https://www.campaignindia.in/article/australian-lamb-ad-banned-after-review/441252 (accessed 14 May 2021).

Schnurr, Stephanie and C. K. Chan. 2009. Politeness and leadership discourse in New Zealand and Hong Kong: A cross-cultural case study of workplace talk. *Journal of Politeness Research Language Behavior Culture*, 5 (2): 131–157. doi:10.1515/JPLR.2009.009

Schnurr, Stephanie and Angela Chan. 2011. When laughter is not enough. Responding to teasing and self-denigrating humour at work. *Journal of Pragmatics*, 43 (1): 20–35.

Schwartz, Shalom H. 1992. Universals in the content and structure of values: Theory and empirical tests in 20 cultural groups. In M. Zanna, ed., *Advances in experimental social psychology*, 25. 1–65. New York: Academic Press.

Schwartz, Shalom H. 2021. A repository of Schwartz Value Scales with instructions and an introduction. *Online Readings in Psychology and Culture*, 2 (2). doi: https://doi.org/10.9707/2307-0919.1173

Screech, Michael A. 2015. *Laughter at the foot of the cross*. Chicago: University of Chicago Press.

Seidel, Jamie. 2017. Meat and Livestock Australia lamb ad faces Advertising Standards Bureau inquisition over depiction of religious deities. *Adelaide Advertiser*. 5 September.

Sherzer, Joel. 1993. On Puns, comebacks, verbal dueling, and play languages: Speech play in Balinese verbal life. *Language in Society*, 22 (2): 217–233. https://www.jstor.org/stable/4168431

Sohigian, Diran John. 2007. Contagion of laughter: The rise of the humour phenomenon in Shanghai in the 1930s. *positions: east asia cultures critique*, 15 (1): 137–163.

Steinmüller, Hans and Susanne Brandstadter, eds. 2016. *Irony, cynicism and the Chinese state*. London and New York: Routledge.

Takekuro, Makiko. 2006. Conversational jokes in Japanese and English. In J. Milner Davis, ed., *Understanding humor in Japan*. 85–98. Detroit MI: Wayne State University Press.

Tiquia, Rey. 2011. The *Qi* that got lost in translation: Traditional Chinese Medicine, humour and healing. In Jocelyn Chey and Jessica Milner Davis, eds., *Humour in Chinese life and letters: Classical and traditional approaches*. 37–47. Hong Kong: Hong Kong University Press.

Tunnisa, Dzakia, Murni Mahmud and Kisman Salija. 2019. Investigating teacher's sense of humor in Indonesia. *International Journal of Language Education*, 3 (2): 99–114. doi: 10.26858/ijole.v3i2.10201

Van Leest, Hyung-a Kim. 1991. Political satire in Yangju *Pyŏlsandae* mask drama. *Korea Journal*, 31 (1): 87–109.

Warren, Bernie, ed. 2007. *Suffering the slings and arrows of outrageous fortune: International perspectives on stress, laughter and depression.* Leiden: Brill.
Wells, Marguerite A. 1997. *Japanese humour.* Basingstoke UK: Macmillan.
Wells, Marguerite A. 2006. Satire and constraint. In Jessica Milner Davis, ed., *Understanding humor in Japan.* 193–217. Detroit MI: Wayne State University Press.
Wells, Marguerite A. and Jessica Milner Davis. 2006. Farce and satire in *kyōgen.* In Jessica Milner Davis, ed., *Understanding humor in Japan.* 127–152. Detroit MI: Wayne State University Press.
Wickberg, Daniel. 1998. *The senses of humor: Self and laughter in modern America.* Ithaca NY: Cornell University Press.
Xu, Weihe. 2011. The classical Confucian concepts of human emotion and proper humour. In Jocelyn Chey and Jessica Milner Davis, eds., *Humour in Chinese life and letters: Classical and traditional approaches.* 49–71. Hong Kong: Hong Kong University Press.
Yue, Xiaodong. 2011. The Chinese ambivalence to humor: Views from undergraduates in Hong Kong and China. *Humor: International Journal of Humor Research*, 24 (4): 463–480. doi: 10.1515/humr.2011.026
Yue, Xiaodong. 2018. *Humor and Chinese culture: A psychological perspective.* London and New York: Routledge.
Zelizer, Craig. 2010. Laughing our way to peace or war: Humour and peacebuilding. *Journal of Conflictology*, 1 (2): 1–9. http://journal-of-conflictology.uoc.edu/joc/en/index.php/journal-of-conflictology/article/view/vol1iss2-zelizer.html
Zhu, Ping, Zhuoyi Wang and Jason McGrath, eds. 2019. *Maoist laughter.* Hong Kong: University of Hong Kong Press.

2 Humour as rhetorical discourse in ancient Chinese philosophy
The Works of Mencius

Shirley Chan

Introduction

Commonly perceived as an art of persuasion for the purpose of changing thought and action at social, political and individual levels, rhetoric plays a significant role in different cultures through the representation of the power and impact of language (Vickers 1988; Jensen 1987). Recent scholarship generally accepts that rhetorical practices are universally shared, though with culturally specific experiences and conceptualisation (Lü 1998). In their artistic use of oral and written expression, Chinese rhetorical experience, expressions and conceptualisation offer a body of knowledge and practice that deserves attention and investigation. Classical and traditional texts show a rhetorical tradition that can be both diverse and unique in depicting human experience via the formulation and use of language and symbols, including irony, humour and satire. This chapter will contribute to the study of such humorous techniques in rhetorical discourse in the ancient Chinese philosophical text *Mengzi* 孟子 (*The Works of Mencius*, translated by Legge 1990).

While the ancient Greeks' practice and tradition of rhetoric have been well recognised and studied, it is only in recent years that scholars have started to pay attention to its counterparts in ancient China, revealing that Chinese contemporaries of the ancient Greeks used rhetorical strategies (van Els and Sabattini 2012).[1] As a technique in persuasive rhetorical discourse, humour in ancient philosophy remains even more understudied. Humour and philosophy are often regarded as incompatible, since the latter is considered serious rather than funny or amusing. In other words, neither philosophers themselves nor scholars of philosophy have taken humour seriously because it has not been considered serious business.[2] Nevertheless, this view has changed in recent years, with scholars arguing that philosophy might even be the discipline where humour is the most appropriate (Morreall 1984: 305).

While hard to define, it is generally accepted that the essential quality of humour and its sub-categories is funniness, which appeals to the sense of incongruity.[3] Although the English word "humour" was not translated into

Chinese until 1923 (as *youmo* 幽默, by Lin Yutang 林語堂, 1895–1976), taking in their broad definition, humour or the quality of humour have never been absent from Chinese life and letters.[4] The Han historian Sima Qian 司馬遷 (145?–86? BCE) introduced the pragmatic functions of humour in ancient China when he explained the reason for including biographies of humourists (*huaji* 滑稽) in his influential *Shiji* 史記 (*Records of the Grand Historian*): humour, he said, "is useful in resolving disputes and conflicts through subtle and pointed words" (*tan yan wei zhong, yi ke yi jie fen* 談言微中, 亦可以解紛).[5] Lin Yutang introduced and promoted the concept of humour to modern China by transliterating the term as *youmo* 幽默 (*you* 幽, meaning dim, dark, quiet and subtle that leads to a hidden deeper level, and *mo* 默, meaning silent and mute.) Lin explained that the whole process of *youmo* did not simply end with laughter but invited a deeper reflection on the humanistic or philosophical outlook on life (Chan 2011: 74). This same modern scholar argued that humour was actually of serious national importance:

> Any country's culture, literature, or thought needs to be enriched by humour. If a people do not have this enrichment of humour, their culture will become more hypocritical with each passing day, their lives will be closer and closer to cheating, their thought pedantic and outdated, their literature increasingly withered and their spirit increasingly obstinate and ultraconservative.
>
> (Trans. Sample 2011: 189)

Indeed, humour has a long history in ancient Chinese philosophy and has demonstrably served its overall serious purpose, despite its non-seriousness.[6] This study assumes that the pragmatics of humour in philosophical discourse lies chiefly in its serious functions of persuasion and motivation.

Unlike Daoists, who are well-known for their rejection of solemnity and social conventions and for being funny and elusive in richly imaginative expressions and fantasy, Confucians traditionally emphasise the practice of propriety and observance of social conventions. This could quite easily mean that in the Confucian view, humour is often considered inappropriate or distasteful.[7] The same could be said of the Legalists, who advocate a philosophy of administration that adheres strictly to laws to control human impulses and behaviour, and for whom humour could be something that turns all too quickly into a significant liability. It is not surprising, therefore, that humour in these two latter streams of teaching has largely been overlooked.[8]

Humour and laughter reflect the historical situation of a society. To grasp its deeper social significance, humour must be analysed and interpreted in each unique historical and cultural context. Through a close reading of textual passages from the Warring States period in China, when political persuasion was desperate and highly competitive, this study attempts to exemplify the use of humour to convince or influence particular readers. It elicits the features of humorous discourse in *The Works of Mencius*, considering the historical context, target reader(s) and the Confucian concept of humour. The questions we might ask are, what was the significance of humour in *The Works of Mencius*, who was it significant for and how were the humorous effects achieved?

Mencius, his times and his work

Mencius (372?–289? BCE) lived one hundred years after Confucius (551–479 BCE), in the mid-Warring States period (475–221 BCE), a critical period of transition. The feudal Zhou dynasty (c. 1046–256 BCE) had disintegrated into a multistate system of vassal states, each growing in independence. Power struggles between rival families and rival states developed into continuous warfare that intensified both in scale and frequency from the fourth century BCE until the land was unified by Qin Shihuangdi (259–210 BCE), the first emperor of Qin. Marked by political turmoil and violence, this was also a time of cultural and intellectual vigour when different schools of thought flourished. Power and competence were the major qualities feudal lords sought as they competed to attract talented and skilled advisers and officials who constituted the new *shi* 士 (gentry scholar) class. Originally trained to serve in administrative capacities, the aristocratic scholars who formed the *shi* class studied in order to occupy positions of rank, and then further developed into a bureaucratic scholarly elite, leading to noble lineage being de-emphasised. In competition with other contemporary ideas, strategists, advisors and master philosophers, therefore, had to devise engaging, interesting and convincing conversations aimed at providing solutions for social conflict. *The Works of Mencius* was compiled during this period, when members of the *shi* class were actively seeking employment of their talents and knowledge by feudal lords. During this troubled period, "masters"—many from the *shi* class—articulated various political ideas aimed at rescuing people from chaos and suffering. One of these master thinkers was Mencius, who identified himself as a follower of Confucius (for a very traditional portrayal of Mencius, see Figure 2.1 by an unidentified Chinese artist, taken from an early Western scholarly book on China and for a portrait of a typical member of the *shi* class by a modern artist, see Figure 2.2).

The Works of Mencius is traditionally attributed to Mencius and his disciples and followers. The text we have today was not written by a single hand; it was a collaborative effort undertaken during Mencius' life and in the decades after he died by people who shared an interest in advocating his teachings. The target readers of *The Works of Mencius* were mainly feudal lords/government officials, and the *shi* class from different backgrounds. The purpose of the text was not so much to present a historical Mencius as to acclaim his teachings triumphantly and exalt the intellectual group associated with them, through the voice of the master philosopher. The

Figure 2.1 A traditional portrayal of Mencius, from *Myths and Legends of China*, by E. T. C. Werner (London and Bombay: Harrap, 1922, accompanied by "Thirty-two Illustrations In Colours By Chinese Artists").

Source: P-D art from: https://commons.wikimedia.org/wiki/File:Mencius.jpg.

term "Mencius" in this present study refers to the ideas, words and acts of Mencius as the author(s) and editor(s) of *The Works of Mencius* understood or intended to portray them; it refers to the philosophical ambitions the author(s) would have wished to convey and how they might have been able to achieve those purposes. In other words, it addresses the fact that Mencius' rhetorical perspectives and humour discourse were embedded in what were purported to be his very serious philosophical views.

Seeking to advocate the teachings of Confucius, Mencius promoted what he referred to as *wangdao* 王道 (the kingly way), which meant ruling through

Figure 2.2 This modern portrayal of a *shi* gentleman wearing his customary robes conveys the earnest dedication to scholarly pursuits and self-improvement that characterised the class. Such high-mindedness also exposed it to satirical attack if members failed to live up to their ideals.

Source: Reproduced with kind permission of the artist, Gengle Jushi Yunong 耕樂居士雨農 (Han Yong 韓勇).

moral inspiration rather than by coercion or military power; it also meant that the government should provide welfare to the people to allow them to become economically self-sufficient. Like Confucius, Mencius maintained that self-cultivation was the primary means to a better society, based on his view of human nature. He believed in the potential goodness of human nature and that, as humans, we have the tendency to become good through education. Self-cultivation, therefore, was intended to develop the four cardinal virtues: *ren* 仁 (benevolence), *yi* 義 (righteousness), *li* 禮 (propriety) and *zhi* 知 (wisdom). In his writings, Mencius debated social issues and human activities with his contemporaries. For example, he criticised the Mohists, who devoted their efforts to attacking Confucian practices of observing rituals and giving impartial care to all. He also denounced the doctrines of Yang Zhu 楊朱 (440–360 BCE), who believed that one should keep one's nature intact, and thus advocated inaction in human affairs. He refuted the view that human nature was ethically neutral, and that moral cultivation was a matter of external imposition reshaping human predispositions.

In the texts, Mencius is shown as illustrating his points about social and political practices unequivocally, and always appears to have successfully influenced his audience (and readers) through persuasion, whether in conversation with a king or his contemporary opponents. His readers were presented with a mix of rhetorical techniques: irony, satire, wit, metaphor and analogy. Humour came into play when these rhetorical devices effectively communicated the playful state of the thinker/writer or that he sought to induce such a state in others (i.e., readers), while indirectly yet effectively ridiculing and deriding the social ills or moral failures of his time. His readers shared the humour when they made both connection and contrast between reality and ideal, between the moral and the immoral, and between what Mencius upheld and what he disapproved of in his philosophical discourse. The techniques and structures of double reference, contrast and unresolved antithesis in the jokes and other forms of metaphors served to initiate measurement and judgement that took aim at general human failings.

Humour elicits interpretations whose subtlety creates suspense and genial empathy that would be impossible to achieve through any other form of invective. In Mencius' philosophical discourse, therefore, humour was more than just being comical or amusing, it served the ultimate purpose of setting forth and defending Mencius' philosophical ideas and bringing morality to life for readers who shared the same concerns about social issues and human well-being. This purpose of philosophical discourse might well have appealed to Joseph Addison (1672–1719), who asserted that "true humour consists of truth, good sense, and wit and mirth" and noted that it requires "the direction of the nicest judgement by so much as it indulges itself in boundless freedom" (quoted by Szécsényi 2007: 83–84). On the other hand, we will also see examples of humour where Mencius was not afraid to be absurd—that is, incongruous—and to use tales and stories that might appeal to the community that included the ruling class and the *shi* class.

Accordingly, the theory proposed by Lord Shaftesbury (Anthony Ashley Cooper, 1671–1713) might be more appropriate to describe such humour, one that works within his concept of *sensus communis* (communal sensibility) in the tradition of the Roman Stoics: humour with feelings that are communal, social and capable of cooperation with the rational and consequently morally beneficial, rather than with feelings of fear and suspicion of laughter.⁹ One modern scholar, discussing Shaftesbury's ideas on humour and laughter, has described his approach as a more cheerful and open relaxation that connects hearts rather than heads (Szécsényi 2007: 87–90). I am not implying that there is any direct connection between Shaftesbury and Mencius. However, based on this positive understanding of humour, I would argue that Mencian humour, displayed in *The Works of Mencius*, serves the purpose of criticising social issues while enabling civil, reflective, and open-to-truth conversation.

Finally, apart from considering the historical background of specific target readers and the philosophical ideas that shaped the humorous discourse, this study will take account of the concept of humour within the Confucian tradition from which *The Works of Mencius* emerged. In opposition to the widely shared idea that humour should be absolutely free to bring laughter or to disregard all seriousness, proper humour, as seen from the Confucian perspective, cannot be separated from the sphere of humanity and the sense of propriety (Xu 2011). Humour in *The Works of Mencius* is moderate, subtle and didactic, and its nature and components will be discussed in the following sections.¹⁰

Instructing through jokes and humour

One of the features of the humorous discourse in *The Works of Mencius* is criticism of faults and follies through satirical jokes. This technique is used to illustrate funny points, linking humour inextricably to irony or satire, for instance, criticism of *shi* scholars for their phoniness and superficiality. Coming from humble origins and with practical advancement and high social status very much on their minds, the *shi* easily became targets, as is evident in this story of a man from the state of Qi:

> 齊人有一妻一妾而處室者, 其良人出, 則必饜酒肉而後反。其妻問所與飲食者, 則盡富貴也。其妻告其妾曰:「良人出, 則必饜酒肉而後反; 問其與飲食者, 盡富貴也, 而未嘗有顯者來, 吾將瞯良人之所也。」蚤起, 施從良人之所之, 遍國中無與立談者。卒之東郭墦間, 之祭者, 乞其餘; 不足, 又顧而之他, 此其為饜足之道也。其妻歸, 告其妾曰:「良人者, 所仰望而終身也。今若此。」與其妾訕其良人, 而相泣於中庭。而良人未之知也, 施施從外來, 驕其妻妾。

> A man of Qi lived with his wife and his concubine. Whenever he went out, he would take his fill of wine and meat before he came home. When his wife asked him with whom he had eaten and drunk, it was always with wealthy and honourable people. His wife informed his concubine, saying, "When our good man goes out, he is sure to come back having partaken plentifully of wine and meat. When I ask with whom he ate and drank, they are all, it seems, wealthy and honourable people. And yet no people of distinction ever come here. I will spy on our good man and see where he goes".

Accordingly, she got up early, and secretly followed her husband. Through the whole city, no one stopped by or talked with him. At last, he came to those who were sacrificing among the tombs beyond the outer wall on the east, and he begged for what they had left over. Not satisfied, he looked about and went to another party—and this was the way in which he was replete. His wife returned home and said to his concubine, "It was to our husband that we looked up in hopeful contemplation, with whom our lot in life is cast—and now these are his ways!" At this, along with his concubine, she reviled the husband, and they wept together in the middle hall. In the meantime, the husband, knowing nothing of all this, came in with a jaunty air, acting proudly towards his wife and concubine.

(Legge 1990: "Lilou II", modified)[11]

The story takes a surprising turn when the wife and the concubine find out that their husband has tricked them—he has met no people of high status and has actually been begging for food from those sacrificing to the dead. While the wronged women weep together and revile their deceiver, readers would see the humorous picture of an over-confident man so used to his life of self-deception that he has become complacent about his own false and ingratiating behaviour. The satirical ridicule is intensified when he continues to boast in front of his wife and concubine without realising they have found out the truth. The man is addressed several times as *liangren* 良人, a term that means "husband" but whose literal meaning is "good man".[12] This double meaning would elicit from readers an amused smile at the irony that the "good man" looked upon by his family for so long not only as a husband but also as a respected citizen, a Confucian superior man, *junzi*, has turned out to be just a pretentious petty man. Stories such as that of the man of Qi were tied to narratives and experiences familiar to the *shi* class and exemplified a theme central to *The Works of Mencius*—mockery of hypocritical and pedantic scholar-officials. The joke served as a powerful means to influence and inspire as it created a connection allowing readers to imagine how they would have acted if they had been the man of Qi. By relating to the experience of the characters in the story, readers engaged in the process of building meaning and purpose not only based on their personal experiences but also helping them better understand others. Another example of such storytelling follows.

Moral cultivation was a major concern in Mencius' discussions. To illustrate how one should proceed with self-cultivation, Mencius employed an allegorical tale when asked about the nature of the heart-mind (*xin* 心) and its relation to *haoran zhi qi* 浩然之氣 (fully developed spiritual energy):[13]

宋人有閔其苗之不長而揠之者, 芒芒然歸。謂其人曰:『今日病矣, 予助苗長矣。』其子趨而往視之, 苗則槁矣。天下之不助苗長者寡矣。以為無益而舍之者, 不耘苗者也; 助之長者, 揠苗者也。非徒無益, 而又害之。』

There was a man of Song who was grieved that his growing crop was not taller, and so he pulled it up higher. Having done this, he returned home, looking very stupid, and said to his people, "I am tired today. I have been helping the crop to grow tall." His son ran to look at it and found the crop all withered. There are few in the world who do not deal with their passion-nature as if they were assisting the crop to grow tall. Some indeed do consider this to be of no benefit to them and let it alone—they do not weed their crop. Those who assist it to grow tall, pull their crop higher. What they do is not only of no benefit to nature but also injures it.

(Legge 1990: "Gong Sun Chou I")

Fundamentally deceitful, just like the man of Qi, this man from the state of Song (who may well have been a *shi* who owned some land) sought a shortcut in the process of growing his crop without realising the crucial role of nature. The act of pulling at the crop in order to make it taller had several serious philosophical implications: it was a random act that was not part of the natural process of growing; metaphorically, growing the crop symbolised the process of cultivation; the man's interference by pulling at the crop signified that he had not attained a sincere manifestation of human nature nor acquired a natural tendency towards such a process. Mencius emphasised the importance of genuineness and commitment in moral cultivation, which involved interaction between the moral feelings of *xin* and development of *qi*. He argued against the idea proposed by Gaozi 告子 (c. 420–350 BCE) that righteousness was simply an external act and used the story of the man of Song to disprove the excessive utility of artificial, external forces in cultivation. What makes this short allegory funny is its ironic focus on human folly: it presents a vivid picture of the man returning home, exhausted after having spent the whole day pulling up the crop. Oblivious to his own stupidity, the man appears to have felt proud of his foolish act, which not only made him sick and tired but also, ironically, turned out to have done more harm than good to the crop. More significantly, the joke serves to show the foolishness of those who are generally insincere because they try to take shortcuts when attending to everyday business, and, metaphorically in this context, also to moral cultivation.[14]

Comic irony and mockery of human weakness are also used in another episode in which someone in a position of authority tells Mencius that he could not immediately abolish duties and taxes but that he could lighten them and would get round to ending them the following year. Mencius responded with a tale about stealing:

孟子曰:「今有人日攘其鄰之雞者, 或告之曰:『是非君子之道。』曰:『請損之, 月攘一雞, 以待來年, 然後已。』如知其非義, 斯速已矣, 何待來年?」

Mencius said, "Now there was a man who stole a chicken from his neighbour every day. 'Such is not the way of a good man', he was told.

'Well, then I'll reduce the rate', he replied. 'I'll steal one every month, and next year I won't steal anymore.' If you know that the thing is unrighteous, then use all despatch in putting an end to it—why wait till next year?".

(Legge 1990: "Teng Wen Gong II")

Mencius drew an analogy between collecting high taxes and stealing from people to make his readers aware that reducing tax was not good enough, it was like stealing one chicken a month instead of one every day. The moral is that one should have a total commitment to good and stop doing what is wrong immediately and completely. The comparison between levying taxes and regulating moral behaviour implies an intuitive perception of the disgraceful and immoral nature of theft and its humour lies in its ability to "speak truth to power". The (government) officer is compared with a chicken thief who cannot resist stealing—this image of a selfish and greedy thief was the antithesis of the ideal Confucian ruler. The allegorical narrative offered light-hearted and gentle mockery of a generally corrupt government that made itself rich and powerful by exploiting and stealing from its people. The philosopher used the same witty and humorous comparison in the well-known episode in which King Xuan of Qi asked permission to shorten the ritually mandated mourning period. When Gong Sun Chou defended this request by saying it was better than doing away with it altogether, Mencius' response was that this was like saying, "Do it gently!" to someone twisting his elder brother's arm (Legge 1990: "Jinxin I").

Like Confucius, Mencius attached importance to ritual practice and the rules of propriety (*li* 禮). At one point, someone called Wu Lu was asked for advice about what priority should be accorded to the observation of rituals and food and that of rituals and sex. Unable to advise, he enquired of Mencius (Legge 1990: "Gaozi II"). Mencius was mindful that for argument's sake, choosing between rituals and sex or food was not feasible: rituals were highly significant in Confucian teaching, while sex and food were essential parts of human nature and natural desires.[15] That one should act only to satisfy natural desires was dangerous; acts must be appropriate to rules of propriety or ritual. To Mencius, the logical answer had to depend on establishing an appropriate frame of reference and equivalence between the two.[16] He then gave the argument a twist by posing rhetorical questions:

紾兄之臂而奪之食, 則得食; 不紾, 則不得食, 則將紾之乎? 踰東家牆而摟其處子, 則得妻; 不摟, 則不得妻, 則將摟之乎?

If, by twisting your elder brother's arm and snatching what he is eating, you can get food for yourself, while if you do not do so you will not get anything to eat, will you so twist his arm? If, by climbing over your neighbour's wall and dragging away his virgin daughter, you can get a wife, while if you do not do so you will not be able to get a wife, will you so drag her away?

(Legge 1990: "Gaozi II")

Instead of levelling direct criticism at elevating an essential part of life (food and sex) above ritual, Mencius moved the argument forward in a more conversational way by means of comparisons with lively examples of everyday ill-doing. This oriented the practice of rituals to a position of advantage by posing questions with obvious answers such as whether one would twist one's elder brother's arm in order to get food, or would drag away a young woman in order to have a wife. The over-dramatisation and personification of the abstract idea of observing ritual as being such juvenile ill-doing is a humorous and surprising denouement.

Using humour to advise the powerful

Like many other philosophers portrayed in early Chinese texts, Mencius is presented as an advisor to feudal lords. In his conversations with these rulers, Mencius used a question-and-answer style to convince those superiors who had sought his advice on topics such as the appropriate exercise of power, expansion of territory, how to attract a greater population and so on.

When King Xuan from the state of Qi asked how to expand his power and territories, Mencius began his response by asking a seemingly odd question: whether it was true that the king had saved the life of an ox that was about to be slaughtered as a sacrifice. Upon learning that the king had felt affection for the ox, Mencius affirmed that the king had the ability to be a good king, just as easily as "lifting a feather" (Legge 1990: "Liang Hui Wang I").[17] One might find it difficult, or even funny, to see how kindness to animals could be a relevant issue, to judge from the hypothetical that Mencius posed. Underlining his question was his ironic criticism of a king who cared more for animals than for his people. The case of the ox highlighted that the king's failure in government was not because of lack of passion but because of his failure to fully act on that passion. Only by realising the potential within himself for compassion for his people and for governing the state with benevolence, and by handling state-to-state relations on the basis of virtue, could a ruler win popular support and subsequently become a true king whose rule would be inclusive and boundless.[18]

On the other hand, Mencius was also confident that if the king intended to expand his territory by armed force, that would be a case of "doing what you do to seek for what you desire, [which] is like climbing a tree to seek for fish" (*Yi ruo suowei qiu ruo suo yu, you yuan mu er qiu yu ye* 以若所為求若所欲, 猶緣木而求魚也). Here, Mencius caught the attention of the king, who was naturally eager to find out why what he desired would not work. Mencius did not engage with the "why" question, but, rather, what the king heard from Mencius was that it would be even worse than climbing a tree to seek a fish: "If you climb a tree to seek for fish, even though you do not get the fish, you will not suffer any subsequent calamity. But doing what you do to seek for what you desire, and doing it moreover with all your heart, you will assuredly afterwards meet with calamities" (*Yue: Dai you shen yan. Yuan mu qiu yu, sui bude yu, wu hou zai. Yi ruo suowei, qiu ruo suo yu, jin xinli er wei zhi, hou bi you zai.* 曰: 「殆有甚焉。緣木求魚, 雖不得魚, 無後災。以若所為, 求若所欲, 盡心力而為之, 後必有災。」, Legge 1990: "Liang Hui Wang I").

The use of hyperbole, together with declarative sentences in the above conversation with King Xuan, amplified the effect of the message. The story ended with the king deferring to Mencius and approving of his views. The king's remark at the end of the conversation is noteworthy: "I am stupid, and not able to advance to this. I wish you, my Master, to assist my intentions. Teach me clearly; although I am deficient in intelligence and vigour, I will try to put your instructions into effect" (*Wang yue: Wu hun, buneng jin yushi yi. Yuan fuzi fu wu zhi, ming yi jiao wo. Wo sui bu min, qing changshi zhi.* 王曰:「吾惛, 不能進於是矣。願夫子輔吾志, 明以教我。我雖不敏, 請嘗試之。」, Legge 1990: "Liang Hui Wang I"). We can easily picture how an ambitious ruler seeking to follow Mencius' advice would be humbled by his instructions. A sensibility of humour could also be seen in this statement, from the perspective of the *shi* class who might have enjoyed high status by assisting the ruler through their words and ideas. Might Mencius or a member of the *shi* class like him thus have even been encouraged to use more humour in any future advice to his superiors? We don't know. Nevertheless, the request of the king(s) to receive instruction and assistance from Mencius, as presented in the stories, provided a rhetorical discourse framework of legitimacy in which Mencius' arguments rested.

One further example of the rhetoric of humour is the following passage, a well-known conversation in which Mencius criticised the way of governing of King Hui of the state of Liang:

梁惠王曰:「寡人之於國也, 盡心焉耳矣。河內凶, 則移其民於河東, 移其粟於河內。河東凶亦然。察鄰國之政, 無如寡人之用心者。鄰國之民不加少, 寡人之民不加多, 何也?」孟子對曰:「王好戰, 請以戰喻。填然鼓之, 兵刃既接, 棄甲曳兵而走。或百步而後止, 或五十步而後止。以五十步笑百步, 則何如?」曰:「不可, 直不百步耳, 是亦走也。」

King Hui of Liang said, "Small as my virtue is, in the government of my kingdom I do indeed exert my mind to the utmost. If the year be bad on the inside of the river, I remove as many of the people as I can to the east of the river and convey grain to the country in the inside. When the year is bad on the east of the river, I act on the same plan. On examining the government of neighbouring kingdoms, I do not find that there is any ruler who exerts his mind as I do. And yet the people of the neighbouring kingdoms do not decrease, nor do my people increase. How is this?" Mencius replied, "Your majesty is fond of war—let me take an illustration from war. The soldiers move forward to the sound of the drums; and after their weapons have been crossed, on one side they throw away their coats of mail, trail their arms behind them, and run. Some run a hundred paces and stop; some run fifty paces and stop. What would you think if those who run fifty paces were to laugh at those who had run a hundred paces?" The king said, "They should not do so. Though they did not run a hundred paces, they also ran away".

(Legge 1990: "Liang Hui Wang I")

The king believed he had exhausted himself on behalf of his state and therefore must be a good king compared to others; he could not understand why he failed to attract more people to his state. We could imagine that the king was expecting Mencius to express sympathy if not admiration for his dedication to state affairs. Mencius neither praised nor ridiculed the king. Instead, he asked if there was any difference between fleeing 50 paces and fleeing 100 paces from the battlefield. The king admitted there was little difference, since both were essentially an attempt to escape. Mencius used this illustration to make the king realise that his own state was not doing any better than other states. Mencius maintained that ruling should be carried out in a kingly way, and that what King Hui was doing was not good enough. The power of this analogy is such that the proverbial phrase "those who run fifty paces laugh at those who run a hundred paces" (*yi wushi bu xiao baibu* 以五十步笑百步), equivalent to the English saying "the pot calling the kettle black", is commonly used in China even today. It mocks those who are blind to their own shortcomings and mistakes but still laugh at others with the same failings.

The rhetorical device being used here can be summed up by Bertrand Russell's observation that "the point of philosophy is to start with something so simple as not to seem worth stating, and to end with something so paradoxical that no one will believe it" (Russell 1918: 53). The same approach is also embedded in the Incongruity Theory often cited in humour studies, referring to the element of surprise arising from a conflict between what is predicted or expected and what actually occurs in the text/conversation.[19] We have seen how all of Mencius' conversations start with an ambiguity or inappositeness, for example, a question with an answer misleading the audience/readers followed by an explanation and a punchline that resolved the conflict.

Asking seemingly irrelevant questions not only resolves the conflict created by incongruity but is also a skilful form of persuasion. Drawn into answering Mencius' apparently simple questions, readers are won over to his side and so attend to his discourse and its concluding punchline. The following passage is another example of this persuasive technique using humour and incongruity:

孟子謂齊宣王曰:「王之臣有託其妻子於其友, 而之楚遊者。比其反也, 則凍餒其妻子, 則如之何?」王曰:「棄之。」曰:「士師不能治士, 則如之何?」王曰:「已之。」曰:「四境之內不治, 則如之何?」王顧左右而言他。

Mencius said to King Xuan of Qi, "Suppose that one of your Majesty's ministers were to entrust his wife and children to the care of his friend, while he himself went into Chu to travel, and that, on his return, he should find that the friend had let his wife and children suffer from cold and hunger—how ought he to deal with him?" The king said, "He should cast him off." Mencius proceeded, "Suppose that the chief criminal judge could not regulate the officers under him, how would you deal with him?" The king said, "Dismiss him." Mencius again said, "If within the four borders of your kingdom there is not good government, what is to be done?" The king looked to the right and left and spoke of other matters.

(Legge 1990: "Liang Hui Wang II")

Here Mencius does not directly instruct the king on governing. Instead, he asks the king a series of questions about someone who fails to perform their duties, first as a friend and then as a criminal judge. As the king answers the questions, he is subtly led on by Mencius, only to have his answers dismissed by the philosopher. The last question forms the punchline of the humorous rhetorical technique we have examined, when Mencius draws an analogy to a king who failed to rule his state properly. The king is then embarrassed: evidently, Mencius' logical series of questions hit all the right emotional buttons to win his point.

The nature of this type of conversation formed a dialectic set within Mencius' presupposed discourse by which he engaged his audiences, drew their attention to and persuaded them to reflect on specific topics. Through engagement and response to Mencius' questions, audiences took a conscious, active role in the discourse. At this point, one can observe some parallels between Mencius' questioning and answering and what Hegel referred to as the Socratic Method. The conversation first brings a person to reflect on their duty by exploiting an occasion that might either have happened spontaneously or was brought about by the teacher. As Hegel points out (1892–1896: B.1):

> By going to the work-places of tailors and shoemakers, and entering into discourse with them, as also with youths and old men, Sophists, statesmen, and citizens of all kinds, he [Socrates] in the first place took their interests as his topic—whether these were household interests, the education of children, or the interests of knowledge or of truth. Then he led them on from a definite case to think of the universal, and of truths and beauties which had absolute value, since in every case, from the individual's own thoughts, he derived the conviction and consciousness of that which is the definite right.

In Mencius' case, it is his conversations with kings about soldiers, a chief criminal judge, a friend or other rulers that inspire readers by drawing on concrete experiences of state affairs and/or political ideology. Although Mencius appears to have been an advisor to the king, in order to bring others, including the king himself, to reflect, he represents himself as being in ignorance and reverses roles, asking the king questions as if the ruler is supposed to be teaching him. When the person addressed then comes forward with an opinion, Mencius, like Socrates, resorts to question and answer in order to instruct to good effect. Thus, he achieves his natural aim of leading kings through thought and reflection to the true good. Dogmatism and self-assertion are replaced in the questions and replies by humour and wit; and, what is more, when readers smile at the absurdity, the logical incongruities and surprise reversals, they also defer to Mencius' philosophy. In this way, as in similar examples to be found in storytelling and jokes, the concrete experience (of an individual) becomes shared common knowledge at the moment when all parties both within the narrative and outside it as audience/readers reach the same conscious understanding and manage to relate or extend the particular case to universal principles.[20] As in Socrates's philosophy, Mencius' ideas were adduced through people's own thoughts and admissions (Hegel 1892–1896, B.1.c):

> Socrates thus put questions in the intent that the speaker should be drawn on to make admissions, implying a point of view opposed to that from which he started. That these contradictions arise because they bring their ideas together, is the drift of the greater part of Socrates' dialogues; their main tendency consequently was to show the bewilderment and confusion which exist in knowledge. By this means, he tries to awaken shame, and the perception that what we consider as true is not the truth, from which the necessity for earnest effort after knowledge must result.

Using humour to criticise contemporary teachings

There are similar examples of the use of wit and humour in Mencius' criticism of other philosophers who he believed exercised a corrosively negative influence. He described Yang Zhu, for example, as an egotist: "Though he might have benefited the whole kingdom by plucking out a single hair (from his body), he would not have done it" (*ba yimao er li tianxia, bu wei ye* 拔一毛而利天下, 不為也). He also accused the Mohists of believing in charity that was so impractically impartial that "if, by rubbing smooth his whole body from the crown to the heel, he could have benefited the kingdom, he [a Mohist] would have done it" (*moding fangzhong li tianxia* 摩頂放踵利天下, 為之) (Legge 1990: "Jinxin I"). These examples of powerful and entertaining humorous hyperbole illustrate the extreme contrast between the Mohist doctrine and Yang Zhu's. As Mencius saw it, both harmed the way of the right principle. "Plucking out a single hair from the body" and "rubbing smooth the whole body" both entail so much overstatement that the exaggeration becomes wildly absurd, creating comic effect. For generations of readers, the playful exaggeration in many of Mencius's descriptions succeeded in evoking strong feelings and even hostility towards these two doctrines and their followers; for example, the Yangzhu school was normally taken to have an image of selfishness, while the Mohists were ridiculed for their impracticality in advocating impartial love.

Elsewhere, Mencius objected to certain views of human nature that were current in his day. For example, he expressed disapproval of Gaozi, who proposed that human nature was what constituted human life (Legge 1990: "Gaozi I"). Mencius responded with a swift and humorous *reductio ad absurdum*: "Very well, since dogs, oxen, and humans are all the same in being alive—therefore, dogs, oxen and humans have the same nature?" (Legge 1990: "Gaozi I"; Van Norden 2019). He himself argued that what distinguished human beings from animals were the innate but latent moral tendencies in their hearts (Legge 1990: "Gong Sun Chou II"). For Mencius, it was this essentially moral nature of the heart, even if it appeared to be only slight, that defined human nature (Legge 1990: "Li Lou II"). The true gentleman retained this distinguishing feature while the petty man lost it. Gaozi's theory failed to acknowledge what made a human being truly *human*, and by humorously equating human beings with dogs and oxen, Mencius established unanswerably that this led to absurdity and contradiction.

Over the last two millennia, Mencius' precepts marked by humour and with pragmatic and/or didactical functions gradually made their way into Chinese society, despite the prevailing general literary negativism towards humour in classical Confucianism (Xu 2011: 66–67). The meanings presented through the fables and stories in *The Works of Mencius* and their style of humorous instruction have been elaborated in other written works, and even re-created widely as idiomatic expressions, common metaphors and popular expressions. Used in daily conversation, literature or other forms of writing, these idiomatic expressions ultimately derive from *The Works of Mencius* but now present figurative meanings with either the literal meaning of their original use attached or new suggested connotations. Because of the exaggeration of some of these well-known expressions and/or their associated stories, the idiomatic expressions, when used properly, possess all the dramatic effects of comic irony and heightened contrast and are thus consciously humorous remarks. The saying, "I will go forward against thousands and tens of thousands of people" (*sui qianwan ren, wu wang yi* 雖千萬人, 吾往矣) in *The Works of Mencius* describes how a person's sense of uprightness could make them feel fearless in doing what is right, so that they have the strength to battle against thousands and thousands of people. But this statement about a rather solemn moral commitment is now widely used by Chinese people to refer broadly to how under extreme adversities one persists in carrying out one's own mission regardless. Depending on the context, such exaggerated courageousness can easily be smiled at as inappropriate or even absurd. Similarly, the phrase, "not plucking one's hair" (*yimao buba* 一毛不拔) used by Mencius to ridicule Yang Zhu's philosophy of naturalism as selfish inaction, is now often used satirically with the meaning of "extreme stinginess", not with its original more solemn import. The story of the man from Qi has now been turned into a popular expression *Qi ren zhi fu* 齊人之福 (literally, a fortune enjoyed by the man of Qi) that mocks a man who enjoys having many wives or lovers. Someone who knows the original story would laugh at how such a man could have attracted any woman, let alone many. On the other hand, the term 大丈夫 (the Great Man), which normally refers to the concept of the Mencian morally great man, is sometimes used for more subtle self-irony. For example, when someone suffers a great drawback in their life, they might quote Mencius' saying: "To be above the power of riches and honours to make dissipated, of poverty and mean condition to make swerve from principle, and of power and force to make bend—these characteristics constitute the great man (*Fugui bu neng yin, pinjian bu neng yi, weiwu bu neng qu. Ci zhi wei da zhangfu.* 富貴不能淫, 貧賤不能移, 威武不能屈。此之謂大丈夫)" (Legge 1990: "Teng Wen Gong II"). Far from being unfaithful to the spirit of their original, I would argue that these speech habits are precisely in the true Mencian humour tradition. Being able to use these idiomatic expressions and others from *The Works of Mencius* provokes an ironic tone and creates a comic effect while serving the pragmatic purposes of communication, a combination much practised by the master himself.

Conclusion

Various techniques and structures contribute to a humorous sensibility in the text of *The Works of Mencius*. They create connection and contrast between reality and the ideal and between the moral and the immoral. Humour arises when social realities are mocked and ridiculed. There is also the funniness associated with incongruity resulting from false expectations, as exemplified by the stories of the man of Song and the man of Qi, as well as the funniness presented in the dialogues above between Mencius and the lords, where an opening scenario builds tension that is then released by an unexpected explanation or reversal of expectations. Release may take the shape of a smile when the ruler is finally convinced, or when he is embarrassed at his failure to grasp Mencius' political theories. The narratives would undoubtedly be far less humorous if such tensions were resolved with violence—if, for instance, the king became angry with Mencius and punished him for his incrimination. However, the humorous twists to the jokes and question-and-answer sequences are benign and gentle despite the seriousness of the topics, and Mencius himself is revealed as a surprisingly witty and understated philosopher.

Metaphor, analogy, irony and exaggeration are all embedded in the highly effective storytelling, questioning and answering that formed part of Mencius' method or mode of philosophical enquiry. Wrapped in the softening context of jokes and conversations, these devices are special ways of communication that serve to make plain the didactic purpose and to render more agreeable and pleasing what might otherwise be punitive expressions of criticism. The underlying assumption of Mencius' humorous discourse is that his audience shared the same knowledge and/or cognitive framework and would reflect on and relieve their own tension by following the stories, each of which ends with Mencius winning his argument. Much of this humour is suggested rather than stated. The humorous rhetoric is used to invite thought and judgement and to engage readers and audience in what is both an effective and an affective way. As we have seen, the stories and conversations provide an astute means of persuasive argument, showing the pragmatic value of humour (embodied in metaphor, satire, irony and wit) to challenge dominant social views and the political order. As noted above, some of the examples have been so profoundly influential that the figures and jokes associated with them have become eponymous with vice, or are bywords for caution, used in writing and daily conversation by Chinese people over the centuries and in the present day.

Despite the conventional view that overlooks such aspects of *The Works of Mencius*, the text contains good examples of humour as a unique form of communication that also constitutes one of the finest pragmatic strategies in rhetorical discourse in philosophy. If, as this study has modestly attempted to show, philosophers like Mencius help their readers to understand their ideas and promote creative problem-solving by engendering trust and reducing conflict through rhetorical techniques, then humour can indeed be said to serve a pragmatic, serious and valuable function in interpreting life and in shaping flexible and tolerant human attitudes. The Mencian humour tradition, being used, reused, and deployed in a myriad different contexts, has continued to influence modern practices in rhetoric and everyday life in Chinese culture and shows little sign of ceasing to do so.

Notes

1 Studies on Chinese rhetoric were carried out from the early 1950s, with pioneering studies such as Crump and Dreher's short papers, "Peripatetic rhetors of the Warring Kingdoms". These have been followed by books and articles published between the 1960s and the present, motivated by the pragmatic needs of studying non-Western languages (van Els and Sabattini 2012).
2 Most philosophers, from ancient Greece to the twentieth century, have been negative in their assessments of humour. Sceptical of the practical, real-world application of rhetoric, which he viewed as a superficial, deceptive method of communication, Plato was also the most influential critic among them of laughter, an emotion he regarded as overriding rational self-control. He advised the Guardians of the state to avoid laughter: "for ordinarily when one abandons himself to violent laughter, his condition provokes a violent reaction" (Morreall 2016).
3 George Meredith's influential 1877 celebration of the English tradition of humour, for example, was one "in which comedy combined emotion with intellectual wit or incongruity" Chey (2011: 21). It follows that this broad definition of humour includes "sub-categories such as jokes, wit, satire and other forms of mirthful expression" (Chey 2011: 23). In philosophy and psy-

chology, the dominant theory of humour is Incongruity Theory. Arising in the eighteenth century, it holds that the cause of laughter is "the perception of something incongruous—something that violates our mental patterns and expectations" (Morreall 2016). This approach has been taken by many philosophers and psychologists, including Immanuel Kant, James Beattie and Arthur Schopenhauer. While some Western theories of humour are considered useful and applicable to some Chinese examples, as later discussion will show, it is not the intention of this chapter to delve into the topic of Chinese humour vis-à-vis Western theories, e.g., superiority, relief, play and incongruity theories (for further details, see Morreall 2016).

4 This is evident from the highly developed technical vocabulary in ancient Chinese texts, such as *xue* 謔 (joking), *xie* 諧 or *huaji* 滑稽 (glib or laughable), *ji* 譏 (to ridicule), *chao* 嘲 (derision). The closest older Chinese term is *huaji* 滑稽, which intertwines the concepts of humour, wit, subtlety and funniness, which are the characteristics of humour, as can be recognised in the two characters *hua* or *gu* 滑 (fluent, glib, subtle and smooth) and *ji* 稽 (recrimination and discussion) (Chan 2011: 74).
5 Sima Qian, "Huaji liezhuan", in *Shiji*, no. 66, juan 126.
6 Christoph Harbsmeier, for example, lists examples of humour in some early Chinese philosophical texts, although he does not provide detailed accounts (Harbsmeier 1989; see also Chan 2011).
7 For example, the *Shiji* names Zhuang Zhou as someone who attacked Confucian social conventions by being a humourist: "*bi Ru xiao ju, ru Zhuangzhou deng, you huaji luansu* 鄙儒小拘, 如莊周等, 又滑稽亂俗" (Sima Qian 1982: Vol 7, page 2348).
8 Lin Yutang was reluctant to accept that Mencius' works qualified as what he termed humour, preferring to class it as cerebral wit. He wrote (1934: 434–438): "*Kongzi ji mo, Mengzi you neng huixie baichu, yu dong jia qiang er lou qi nüzi, shi ling shi shidafu suo buxie chu yu kou de, qi ren yi qi yi qie zhi yu, yi da you fengci qiwei, ran Mengzi yi jin yu yu ti, bu jin yu youmo* 孔子既歿, 孟子猶能詼諧百出, 逾東家牆而摟其女子, 是令時士大夫所不屑出於口的, 齊人一妻一妾之喻, 亦大有諷刺氣味, 然孟子亦近於鬱剔, 不近於幽默 (After Confucius' death, Mencius was able to display a style full of funniness or [what is called in Chinese] *huixie* 詼諧. His tale of 'dragging off the neighbour's daughter and marrying her' is something that even today scholars would not tell; his story of the man from Qi and his wife and concubine is full of irony. Yet Mencius' style is closer to wit, not humour)". Lin does not explain how he reached the conclusion that there is no humour in *The Works of Mencius* other than asserting that "Mencius's works have more reasoning and less feeling" (理智多而情感少故也) and as a result are "not deserving of discussion". In the same essay, Lin comments on the Legalist philosopher Han Feizi's work as "examples of a college professor's style of humour in that they were calculated and lacking in spontaneity". See also Sample (2011: 175–176) for discussion of Lin's specialised concept of humour. This study shows that, contrary to what Lin suggests, Mencius employed rich rhetorical devices including humour as we now understand the term in his philosophical debate and argumentation.
9 The Roman Stoics understood *sensus* communis as "sense of public weal and the common interest, love of the community or society, natural affection, humanity, obligingness …" (Earl of Shaftesbury 1999: 48).
10 For limitation of space, only characters and English translation (from Legge 1990) are given throughout this chapter.
11 The English translations of Mencius in this chapter are mainly adopted or modified from Legge (1990). For limitations of space, romanisation is omitted from lengthy quotations.

12 For example, the "Da Ya" 大雅 in the *Book of Songs* has: "*wei ci liangren, fu qiu fu di* 維此良人，弗求弗迪 (Here is the good man, but he is not sought out nor is he employed)". "Tian zi fang" 田子方 in the *Zhuangzi* 莊子 has: "*Xizhe guaren mengjian liangren* 昔者寡人夢見良人 (A long time ago, I dreamt that I saw a good man)". The term *junzi* 君子 (the superior man) at the end of the story in *The Works of Mencius* also suggests that *liangren* carries the double connotation of husband and good man.

13 Q*i* 氣 is an all-embracing term for a broad range of interrelated qualities, natural, biological, emotional, spiritual, etc., that constitute life and material things. *Haoran zhi qi* has been often translated as "flood-like" *qi*. In this particular conversation, *qi* refers to spiritual energy related to the cultivation of the heart-mind of righteousness, although understandably, it did not entirely exclude biological and emotional attributes.

14 *Cheng* 誠 (sincerity and integrity) is viewed in the Confucian teaching as fundamental to the learning of sagehood and self-cultivation, as revealed in the *Great Learning* 大學 and the *Doctrine of the Mean* 中庸.

15 *Gaozi yue: Shi se, xing ye* 告子曰: 食色，性也 (The philosopher Gao said, biol-have] food and sex is part of nature" (Legge, 1990: "Gaozi I").

16 孟子曰: 於答是也何有？不揣其本而齊其末，方寸之木可使高於岑樓。金重於羽者，豈謂一鉤金與一輿羽之謂哉？取食之重者，與禮之輕者而比之，奚翅食重？取色之重者，與禮之輕者而比之，奚翅色重？ Mencius said, "What difficulty is there in answering these enquiries? If you do not adjust them at their lower extremities but only put their upper parts on the same level, a piece of wood an inch square may be placed higher than the pointed peak of a high building. Gold is heavier than feathers; but does that saying refer on the one hand to a single clasp of gold, and on the other to a wagonload of feathers? If you take a case where eating is of the utmost importance and observing rules of propriety is of little importance, and compare these things, why stop at saying merely that eating is more important? So, taking the case where gratifying the appetite of sex is of the utmost importance and observing the rules of propriety is of little importance, why stop at merely saying that gratifying the appetite is the more important?" (Legge 1990: "Gaozi II").

17 King Xuan explained that he "could not bear [the ox's] frightened appearance, as if it were an innocent person going to the place of death", to which Mencius responded that the king's conduct was "an artifice of benevolence". Then follows Mencius' well-known saying: "So is the superior man affected towards animals that, having seen them alive, he cannot bear to see them die; having heard their dying cries, he cannot bear to eat their flesh. Therefore, he keeps away from his slaughterhouse and cook-room" (Legge 1990: "Liang Hui Wang I"). For Mencius, benevolence began with not bearing to see any living creature suffer and this feeling should extend to the people, as in King Xuan's case.

18 Elsewhere Mencius gave the example of the alarm and distress someone seeing a child in danger of falling into a well would feel so that they would immediately rescue the child. Mencius considered this feeling of commiseration (*ceyin zhi xin* 惻隱之心), similar to being unable to bear (*buren* 不忍) to see the suffering of the ox, to be the beginning of benevolence.

19 See Note 3.

20 It is assumed that the original target readers of *The Works of Mencius* were mainly the *shi* gentry scholars and the ruling class, who would have possessed the knowledge necessary to understand the text and the sub-texts. Canonisation of the text apparently greatly expanded its readership, with layers of scholarly commentary added over the centuries, especially after the Southern Song era (1127–1279), philosopher Zhu Xi (1130–1200) included it in his *Four Books* as one of the foundation pillars of Confucian education.

References

Chan, Shirley. 2011. Identifying Daoist humour: Reading the *Liezi*. In J. Chey and J. M. Davis, eds., *Humour in Chinese life and letters: Classical and traditional approaches*. 73–88. Hong Kong: Hong Kong University Press.

Chey, Jocelyn. 2011. *Youmo* and the Chinese sense of humour. In J. Chey and J. M. Davis, eds., *Humour in Chinese life and letters: Classical and traditional approaches*. 19–47. Hong Kong: Hong Kong University Press.

Earl of Shaftesbury, Anthony Ashley Cooper. 1999 [1777]. *Characteristics of men, manners, opinions, times*. Lawrence E. Klein, ed. Cambridge and New York: Cambridge University Press.

Harbsmeier, Christoph. 1989. Humor in ancient Chinese philosophy. *Philosophy East and West*, 39 (3): 289–310.

Hegel, G. W. F. 1892–1896 [1805–1806]. *Hegel's lectures on the history of philosophy. Part one: Greek philosophy. First period, Second division*. Trans. E. S. Haldane. At: https://www.marxists.org/reference/archive/hegel/works/hp/hpsocrates.htm (accessed 8 April 2020).

Jensen, J. V. 1987. Rhetorical emphasis of Taoism. *Rhetorica: A Journal of the History of Rhetoric*, 5 (3): 219–229.

Legge, James (trans.). 1990. *The Works of Mencius*. Available as *Mengzi, Chinese Text Project*. At: https://ctext.org/mengzi (accessed 25 April 2020).

Lin Yutang. 1934. *Lun youmo* 論幽默 (On humour). *Lunyu banyuekan* 論語半月刊 *(Analects Fortnightly)*, 33 (16 January): 434–438.

Lü, Xing. 1998. *Rhetoric in ancient China, fifth to third century BCE: A comparison with classical Greek rhetoric*. Columbia, SC: University of South Carolina Press.

Morreall, John. 1984. Humour and philosophy. *Metaphilosophy*, 15 (3/4): 305–317.

Morreall, John. 2016. Philosophy of humor. In Edward N. Zalta, ed., *The Stanford encyclopedia of philosophy* (Winter 2016). At: https://plato.stanford.edu/archives/win2016/entries/humor/ (accessed 22 June 2020).

Russell, Bertrand. 1918. *The philosophy of logical atomism*. London: Allen and Unwin.

Sample, Joseph C. 2011. Contextualizing Lin Yutang's essay "On humour". In J. Chey and J. M. Davis, eds., *Humour in Chinese life and letters: Classical and traditional approaches*. 169–189. Hong Kong: Hong Kong University Press.

Sima Qian 司馬遷. 1982. *Shiji* 史記. 10 vols. Beijing: Zhonghua shuju.

Szécsényi, Endre. 2007. Freedom and sentiments: Wit and humour in the Augustan Age. *Hungarian Journal of English and American Studies (HITEAS)*, 13 (1/2): 83–84. At: www.jstor.org/stable/41274384 (accessed 6 May 2020).

van Els, Paul and Elisa Sabattini, eds. 2012. Introduction: Political rhetoric in early China. *Extrême-Orient Extrême-Occident*, 34: 5–14.

Van Norden, Bryan. 2019. Mencius. In Edward N. Zalta, ed., *The Stanford encyclopedia of philosophy* (Fall 2019). At: https://plato.stanford.edu/archives/fall2019/entries/mencius/ (accessed 12 May 2020).

Vickers, Brian. 1988. *In defence of rhetoric*. Oxford: Clarendon Press.

Xu, Weihe. 2011. The classical Confucian concepts of human emotion and proper humour. In Jocelyn Chey and Jessica Milner Davis, eds., *Humour in Chinese life and letters: Classical and traditional approaches*. 49–71. Hong Kong: Hong Kong University Press.

3 Humour in the *huaben* novellas of the Ming Dynasty
The *Guzhang Juechen* 鼓掌絕塵 in context

Antonio Leggieri

Up to the present day, "humour" is still far from being an essential keyword in the research field of the late-Imperial Chinese narrative. Whether it is the four great master novels (*si da qi shu* 四大奇書), or the shorter *huaben* 話本 (novella, short story) pieces of the time, discourse on humour has traditionally occupied a rather marginal place, and its essential presence in these legendary works has always appeared too elusive to be conceptualised in any systematic and organic way. Nonetheless, exceptions do indeed apply! Some of the full-length novels, especially among those produced during the Qing 清 dynasty (1644–1911), show in selected passages a surprisingly mature and at times bitter sense of humour which can be understood and appreciated by Chinese and Western readers alike. Such is the case for *Rulin waishi* 儒林外史 (*Unofficial history from the forest of literati*, 1750), and—maybe less evidently—for *Jing hua yuan* 鏡花緣 (*The Flowers in the mirror*, 1827), two works which, though having satire as their primary focus and concern, do nonetheless reveal in some episodes a sophisticated sense of (mostly verbal) humour. In the former, humour provides a warm and gentle contrast to the aggressive satire of certain passages.[1] In the latter, we see a ruthless ridicule of the literati and their extreme and pointless exegesis of the Confucian classics.[2]

If we take a short step backwards in time, the masterpiece *Honglou meng* 紅樓夢 (*The Dream of the red chamber*, first printed in 1791 but dating much earlier) has recently been studied in relation to humour, although we cannot by any means call it a humorous work. Even the erotic *Rou pu tuan* 肉蒲團 (*The Carnal prayer mat*, 1657), defined by authoritative voices as "a sexual comedy",[3] is at best only a comedy in the Dantesque or Shakespearian sense of the word (i.e. something with a sad beginning but a happy ending), with some grotesque elements interspersed here and there and a strong moral message that serves to justify all the debauchery going on in the rest of the text. In the following pages, we will look at a text from the same period that lacks an established critical apparatus and that will hopefully help shed light on some lesser-known aspects of Chinese fiction. A question that cannot be answered here is how well such humour travels in translation, but I have reported all the passages in the original text with translations, in order to let specialist readers decide for themselves.

DOI: 10.4324/9781003176374-3

Background and nature of *Guzhang juechen*

Guzhang juechen 鼓掌絕塵 (*Clap your hands and rid yourself of dust*, hereafter *GZJC*) is a collection of four medium-length stories, first published during the Ming 明 dynasty (1368–1644). Each story unfolds over 10 *hui* 回 (chapters), giving the text a total length of 40 chapters. Its foreword pins down rather precisely the era in which it was finished (and probably started circulating): it bears the date *Chongzhen Xinweisui zhi Yuandan* 崇禎辛未歲之元旦 (First Day of the Xinwei Year of the Chongzhen Era, therefore 1631). Respecting the praxis of writers of that time, its author and compiler conceal their identities behind artsy, bombastic pseudonyms.[4] The text is signed by one Gu Wu Jinmu Sanren 古吳金木散人 (Idle man of metal and wood from Old Wu), and, apart from him, more people seem to have collaborated in the book. The names of Bihu Xiansheng 閉戶先生 (Master of the closed house) and Chicheng Linhai Yisou 赤城市臨海逸叟 (Old Man at leisure close to the sea from Chicheng) appear in the introductions. The former signs the *tici* 題辭 (foreword), and the latter is featured as author of the opening *jueju* 絕句 (a form of regulated poetry with seven syllables for each line). They also signed the *xu* 序 (preface) to the work and the introduction to each section.

The four ten-chapter stories or sections are named respectively, *Feng* 風 (Wind), *Hua* 花 (Flowers), *Xue* 雪 (Snow) and *Yue* 月 (Moon), and each tells a different story, although some recurring macro-themes can be traced throughout the work. As if the reader did not have enough names to remember already, different reviewers with extravagant pseudonyms appear for each section. Readers might well be disappointed to notice that the title of each section apparently bears no connection to the corresponding story. There is in fact a slight connection, visible in the introductions to each section, which are written in a much higher style, closer to *wenyan* 文言 (literary language), than the rest of the book.

The reason for the titles of the four sections most surely derives from the idiom "*feng hua xue yue* 風花雪月 (literally, wind, flowers, snow, moon)", which describes an idyllic scene, perfect for a romantic encounter. Already by the time *GZJC* came out, this idiom could, by extension, indicate the romantic encounter itself, especially one in narrative and drama. Here we can quote the Ming prince, Zhu Quan 朱權 (1378–1448), himself a playwright and scholar of drama, who used precisely this idiom to define a plot revolving around romantic love, one of the twelve *ke* 科 (themes) of the *zaju* 雜劇 (variety plays of that era).[5] If we want to find the term in a temporally (and thematically) closer setting to *GZJC*, it was used in the fifteenth story of the 1628 *Chuke pai'an jingqi* 初刻拍案驚奇 (*Slapping the table in amazement, 1st volume*) by Ling Mengchu 凌濛初 (1580–1644) where it describes a scholar's dissipated way of living.[6] This connotation, which pairs the romantic encounters and idyllic landscape with a rather carefree approach to life, might have urged Patrick Hanan to describe this work as "the earliest work of the romantic-erotic kind" (1981: 161) among all the *huaben* collections that appeared after Feng Menglong 馮夢龍 (1574–1646) published his three volumes, collectively known as *Sanyan* 三言 (*The three [collections of] stories*), between 1620 and 1627.

Hanan's definition follows his own major division of *huaben* stories into those dealing with romantic and those with heroic themes; judging by the details provided, he does not seem to be wrong. However, the four *huaben* pieces we are concerned with contain much more nuanced storylines within each. Some of the intricate plots will be explored below, but for the moment, we can borrow the summary given by Chinese scholar Hu Shiying of the four sections (1980: 504)[7]:

風集演巴陵書生梅萼與歌伎韓玉姿婚姻故事。
花集記汴京婁祝與俞生、林生將兵征韃靼事。
雪集記蘇州文荊卿與李若蘭婚姻事。
月集記金陵人張秀報恩遭難事。

Feng tells the story of the marriage between Baling 巴陵 county scholar Mei E 梅萼 and entertainer Han Yuzi 韓玉姿.

Hua tells the story of Lou Zhu 婁祝, Yu Canjiang 俞參將, and Lin Yaoru 林燿如 from the city of Bianjing 汴京, who organise a successful expedition against the Tartars.

Xue tells the story of Wen Jingqing 文荊卿 from Suzhou 蘇州, and his wedding with Li Ruolan 李若蘭.

Yue tells the story of Zhang Xiu 張秀 from Jinling 金陵, and his misfortunes in trying to repay a debt of gratitude.

As noted above, we can pin down some common and recurring themes throughout the stories. Most evidently, both the *Feng* and *Xue* sections deal with love and marriage, and indeed they have been viewed more than once as the precursors of the many *Caizi jiaren* 才子佳人 (*Brilliant scholar and beautiful maid*) stories that were published during the Qing dynasty.[8] However, as one can imagine, all ten-chapter stories have plenty of room for secondary plots to emerge, unfold and, in the end, influence the main one in different ways. An example is the *Hua* story, in which readers are challenged to witness, one after another, a series of what Plaks has defined as non-events. In discussing the relationship between events and non-events, he notes that, in contrast to the accepted European tradition of the event being the narrative unit, "the Chinese tradition has tended to place nearly equal emphasis on the overlapping of events, the interstitial spaces between events, in effect on non-events alongside of events in conceiving of human experience in time". This creates what he describes as "a thick matrix of non-events: static description, set speeches, discursive digressions, and a host of other non-narrative elements" (Plaks 1977: 315).

In accord with this pattern, in the *Hua* story, a character called Xia Fang 夏方 steals a horse from Lou Zhu 婁祝, who in turn manages to retrieve it only a couple of chapters later; the protagonists then attend a lengthy song-and-dance performance in a pavilion, put on by two female entertainers (with song lyrics quoted entirely, one might say for the purpose of augmenting the sense of realism, or more cynically, to lengthen an otherwise short and uneventful storyline); Xia Fang is robbed while his young son, Xia Hu 夏虎, exposes a scam about a talking statue of the Buddha in a monastery; Lou Zhu is seduced by a fox spirit, and so on. The final resolution is also triggered by what would surely pass as a non-event or an unrelated subplot: Prime Minister Wei 韋 is miraculously cured by the medical use of the bladder of a strange and exotic animal (*huojing niu* 火睛牛, literally, a fire-eyed bull) which Lou Zhu has provided him with; and, as an act of gratitude, Wei appoints him and his friends to various official positions. This finally ends with the characters leading a victorious expedition against the Tartars, but not after many awkward moments. One is depicted in Figure 3.1 where the protagonists engage in an inconsequential shooting competition.

All the stories tend to present seemingly insignificant or unrelated plot devices at their beginnings and then tie up virtually all the loose ends by the end of the last chapter. This kind of narration inevitably slows down the pace of the stories, and therefore might not be suitable for the reader who is looking for fast-paced narrations, or for psychological introspection. Simply put, the stories in *GZJC* are modelled after the slightly older *huaben*, but with more things happening (both events and non-events). A positive side of this is that *GZJC* would go on to create a new niche in the Chinese literary tradition: that of the medium-length multi-chapter story.

Humour and satire in *GZJC*

Little more than a page is dedicated to *GZJC* in one influential book on Chinese satire, *Jing yu Jian: Zhongguo Fengci Xiaoshuo Shilüe* 鏡與劍: 中國諷刺小說史略 (*The Mirror and the sword: A brief history of the Chinese satirical novel*). The authors do nevertheless comment on the *Yue* story, arguing as follows (Qi and Chen 1995: 117):

> 《鼓掌絕塵》的月集是一篇諷刺狂文，其諷刺對象不是凌濛初筆下的愚人愚行，而是一些社會地位較高，甚至像魏忠賢這樣的大人物，作品具體描寫了魏忠賢專政時期，朝中文臣武職都來趨附他的權勢，乾兒義子遍天下，為首便是江西道御史崔呈秀 [...]
>
> The *Yue* story in *GZJC* is a crazy satirical story, the object of its satire is different from the foolish characters and actions from Ling Mengchu's pen. The text satirises important persons with high social status, even aiming at important people such as Wei Zhongxian. The text describes in detail the era in which Wei Zhongxian exercised tyrannical power, when civil and military officials in the court tried to curry favour with him, and he had plenty of adoptive children, headed by Cui Chengxiu, Censor of the Province of Jiangxi [...]

44 Antonio Leggieri

Figure 3.1 Original plate from *Guzhang Juechen* 鼓掌絕塵 (*GZJC*), 1631 (facsimile, edited by Jinmu Sanren 金木散人, Taipei: Tianyi Chubanshe, 1985, p. 96). Illustration and caption echo the shooting competition in the title of Chapter XVIII (part of the *Hua* story), "*Wei Chengxiang dongguan da Kaiyan, Sheng Zongbing xiting xiao bishe* 韋丞相東館大開筵, 盛總兵西廳小比射 (Prime Minister Wei gives a big feast in the eastern guestroom, Commander Sheng has a small shooting competition in the western outer hall)".

This commentary focusses on the most immediately evident piece of satirical humour—and indeed the most widely discussed in the rather scarce critical literature on *GZJC*—the appearance of the tyrannical Ming dynasty court eunuch Wei Zhongxian 魏忠賢 (a historic figure, 1568–1627). Despite this, Wei is no more than a cameo in one short fragment of the *Yue* story (Chapter 36, to be precise); his parable starts and finishes in the same

Humour in the huaben *novellas* 45

Figure 3.2 Original plate, *Guzhang Juechen* 鼓掌絕塵 (*GZJC*), 1631 (facsimile, edited by Jinmu Sanren 金木散人, Taipei: Tianyi Chubanshe, 1985, p. 132). Illustration and caption echo part of the title of Chapter XXXVI (part of the *Yue* story): "*Zao yange jiansheng ming dun, bian Fengyang jianhuan quan qing* 遭閹割監生命鈍, 貶鳳陽奸宦權傾 (The imperial students are castrated, and their lives reduced; the treacherous official whose power reaches all under Heaven is banished to Fengyang)". The treacherous official being banished is none other than Wei Zhongxian 魏忠賢.

chapter, with his demotion and confinement in the city of Fengyang 鳳陽, as shown in Figure 3.2. Moreover, his description is neither concrete, specific nor detailed, i.e. *juti* 具體, as the brief comment above claims. Hanan's remark that Wei Zhongxian "makes an appearance" (1981: 162) is a much more accurate characterisation of the presence of this historical figure in Chapter 36.[9] He is in fact depicted as a mostly one-dimensional character, interested solely in power and enjoying being indulged by his adoptive sons. In addition, the episodic structure of the *Yue* story must be taken into account. To put it in another critic's words, "[i]ts structure resembles the beads on a rosary, it does not have one fixed protagonist from start to finish, but it is made up of a series of characters and stories in succession, in which every chapter tells a different episode" (Cai 1987: 206). This makes it difficult if not impossible for any character to be depicted in great depth. Although Wei's presence is thus limited, he has attracted the attention of quite a number of critics of the novel[10] and he deserves our attention, too.

As with other characters in the rest of the *Yue* story, Wei Zhongxian comes to the forefront only in a single chapter. His story intermingles with that of one of the many main characters who turn out to be completely disposable, in this case, Chen Zhen 陳珍, who decides to travel to the capital and take part in the imperial examination, exactly when the feared Wei is in power. As soon as he arrives, Chen Zhen is met with a rather singular edict issued by Wei's lackey on the powerful eunuch's birthday. Before this, however, the chapter opens with Chen Zhen burying his father and making up his mind finally to redeem himself, move to the capital with his mother and wife, and take the imperial exam. The narrating voice tells all this before revealing that our characters are indeed heading to the capital during Wei's tyrannical rule, which allows an instance of bitter humour to appear at the first mention of the powerful eunuch (keywords here and elsewhere in bold):

卻說此時，正是東廠太監**魏忠賢**當權的時節。京師中有人提起一個魏字兒，動不動拿去**減了一尺**。

Let us also say that at that time, palace eunuch Wei Zhongxian was in power, set up there by the secret eunuch society. If anyone in the capital dared to mention his surname [in order to impeach him or denounce him], he would immediately **lose a *chi***.

The *chi* 尺 is an ancient measurement unit, roughly equivalent to 25 to 30 centimetres, and its use allows the narrator to avoid getting extremely literal in his description of beheading. Instead, he goes for this more veiled allusion. It has a double application, since the verb *jian* 減 literally means "to subtract" or "to reduce", and consequentially the removed *chi* could also allude to (or mirror) the eunuch's removed genitalia.

The theme of writing a forbidden or taboo name, together with the removing of body parts, is reprised and expanded upon in the passages that follow.[11] After Cui Chengxiu, lackey and favourite adopted son, comments how drawn (*qingjian* 清減) the eunuch looks on his birthday, the great man laments how tiresome and time-consuming the construction of the shrines dedicated to him has been:

崔兒，你不知道麼。近日為起陵工，那些官兒，甚是絮煩。你一本，我一本，你道哪一個不要在咱爺眼裡瞧將過去？那一件不要在咱爺手裡抓將出來？晝夜討不得個自在，辛苦得緊哩！

Cui, my child, you do not know [about] this! These days, in order to start building the shrines, all the other magistrates are really wearing me out! You write a text, I write a text, which one does not have to be seen and approved by me? Which one does not have to be passed by my hands? I am busy day and night, and I am working extremely hard!

This is a wonderful case of satire playing its role as a reflection of reality. History informs us about the countless *shengci* 生祠 (shrines to a living person) in honour of Wei Zhongxian which appeared during his rule, a common practice in Ming China. Two targets for the satire are visible here: first, that the physical work of the scholar-officials building the shrines should result in Wei himself also being tired; second, that although historically the eunuch is described as illiterate, in this fictionalised version, he has accepted the task of approving by his own hand each memorial written about him. The combined effect is to ridicule his egotism.

Moreover, we go on to read that when Cui wants him to rest and take better care of his precious body, Wei reveals his own plan to ease the pressures on him:

魏太監道：「咱爺常是這樣想，只是那些眾孩兒們，如今還吃著天啟爺家俸糧，教咱爺難開著口哩！咱爺倒想得一個好見識，卻是又難出口。」崔呈秀道：「殿爺權握當朝，鬼神欽伏，威令一出，誰敢不從？有甚麼難出口處？」魏太監道：「崔兒，講得有理。咱爺思量要把那些有才學的，監生也使得，生員也使得，選這樣二三十名，著他到咱爺裡面效些勞兒，倒也便當。」崔呈秀道：「殿爺見識最高，只恐出入不便。」魏太監道：「崔兒，這個極易處的事，一個個都著他把雞疤閹割了進來就是。」崔呈秀道：「殿爺，恐那些生員和監生，老大了閹割，活不長久哩！」魏太監道：「崔兒，你不知道。咱爺當初也是老大了閹割的，倒也不傷性命。只是一件，那有妻小的卻也熬不過些。」這崔呈秀欣然領諾。

The Eunuch Wei said: "I always thought about that [that I should take care of myself], but you know, all of those kids of mine, they are still eating from the Tianqi Emperor's bowl, and therefore it's hard for me to open my mouth! I have had a good idea, but I do not dare say it". Cui Chengxiu replied: "Dear father, you have power over the Empire, even Gods and Demons bow down in admiration, who would dare disobey your edict?" Wei answered: "Cui, my child, you are right. I thought of taking some people with erudition, students in the literary academy or candidates who already passed the local-level exams, select twenty or thirty of them, and making them work for me: that would be great!" Cui Chengxiu praised him: "Father, you have the best ideas! But it would not be convenient for them to get in and out of the court." Wei the Eunuch answered: "My son, this can be easily solved: before they enter [the court], we castrate each and every one of them!" Cui answered: "Father, I am afraid that, these people being already adults, they will not have much longer to live if we castrate them!" Wei replied: "My son, you are wrong here. Even I was castrated when I was an adult, and this has not damaged my longevity. The only problem is that the people with wives and kids would be a bit more reluctant to go on with this." Cui Chengxiu agreed wholeheartedly.

Satire flirts here with grotesque themes concerning the human body. Many studies of Wei Zhongxian as a literary character in fiction that was published immediately after his downfall stress the way in which he—and eunuchs in general—reconstruct their identities to become potent palace servants after their castration. It is not uncommon for such fiction to feature accounts of eunuchs who even grew back their penises after gaining high position (McMahon 2014: 1–28). This paradigm is however inverted in *GZJC*: Wei's intention in the passage above is to make the scholars become like himself, rather than to recover the body part he has lost. This certainly echoes the novella's introduction to Wei as a character (quoted above), which claimed that everyone who offended him would lose a *chi*.

At the beginning of Chapter 36 of *GZJC*, history must be summoned once more to help the reader: Wei Zhongxian was in fact the object of many denunciations carried out by the rival Donglin 東林 faction of the eunuchs, who attempted to impeach him on the basis of his growing power and influence. This is why it is said that every document in which the surname Wei 魏 appeared would have been dangerous. In this aspect, Wei Zhongxian is almost equating himself to the emperor, whose name was never used in official documents because it was considered taboo. Conversely, Cui Chengxiu is depicted as having another moment of comically extreme submission to his adoptive father when it is revealed that, together with a gown, he has presented him with a night pot inscribed with the characters of his own name, *Cui* 崔, *Cheng* 呈, *Xiu* 秀. Not only is the name written but also it appears on a very humble utensil designed to receive his adoptive father's excreta.

This text works as humour because overall it violates some of the readers' expectations while at the same time meeting and even exaggerating others. From a purely humorous standpoint, it features evident incongruities that produce a humorous result from their grotesque or degrading comparisons. Cui's concept of presenting a chamber pot as a gift is already quite unique, but even more so is the sudden appearance of the object by itself, inscribed with his name. The inclusion of a scatological element in a joke or in a passage does not need to have a precisely contrasting and serious element, since its transgressive connotation is already so strong that by default it evokes— and clashes with—an imaginary non-scatological context, in the same way that Raskin noted for sexual triggers operating in jokes (1985: 152). But this moment is made much more comic if we oppose it to the previous account regarding documents bearing Wei's name.

On the other hand, Chapter 36 is also concerned to satisfy the reader's supposed expectations. Invective directed towards a historical character, especially one not well-known among historians and readers outside a particular area, does not age specially well (nor does it travel well in translation, even with lots of footnotes). In fact, without knowing something about Wei Zhongxian's life and deeds, a contemporary reader might easily miss all the traits highlighted here. For this reason, it is likely that the author of *GZJC* imagined his own "humour community", a group of readers well informed about Wei's misdeeds and probably still cheering at his demise.[12]

However, linguistic analysis of this humour does not get us very far. The scene in which Wei is depicted as seriously proposing to have twenty to thirty young students and candidates castrated does not rely on any predictable script opposition as defined by Attardo (1991: 293–347) for the General Theory of Verbal Humour (GTVH). Instead, it adopts the principle of caricaturing some selected traits of one particular existing script regarding the palace eunuch. In fact, based on the many historical and fictional accounts of Wei's life, one can construct a mini-script of the GTVH kind around him, revolving around two main traits: being a eunuch and being a tyrannical usurper of imperial power. *GZJC* satisfies and exaggerates both these traits; therefore, there is no violation of the script. If, instead, we attempt to analyse the passage from the point of view of global expectations—i.e., humour resulting from a violation of what the world is supposed to be—then we would become entangled in a moral debate about the legitimacy of having to be castrated in order to advance in a bureaucratic career, which is far from funny.[13] Therefore, it seems better to say that the humour here is caused by a contrast between what has already happened (*GZJC* was published three years after Wei's suicide) and a plausible extrapolation from that into what might have happened, judging by the tyrannical behaviour of the eunuch. If we consider that Wei's actions in *GZJC* are not implausible nor inconsistent for the real-life eunuch that he represents, his behaviour can even be seen as an example of appropriate incongruity.[14] If, instead, the text had presented us with a "married with (biological) kids" version of the same character, we would still have perceived his incongruity with his real-life counterpart, but there would be no relation between the two, no *appropriateness* to be found in the incongruity, and therefore the character would not have deserved the humorous attention that he has always received.

This kind of analysis applies not only to Chapter 36 of our text, but also, in a synecdochic way, to the whole *Yue* story; and similarly to the whole text. In fact, one critic has seen the whole text as a miscellanea of different social malpractices of the time, with each chapter describing and satirising a different aspect (Cai 1987: 206). However, the issue raised by scholars such as Cai as to whether the satire in *GZJC* might have inspired other texts such as *Unofficial history of the literati* remains open and deserves its own separate study. Suffice it to say that rather than tracing a direct thread of influence between the two works, the most probable hypothesis is that both books drew from widespread images and stories about the Imperial exams and less-than-stellar candidates.

Humour on the micro-level

Mischievous and mean-minded characters as satirical targets not only populate the fourth story in *GZJC*, but, as one might expect, antagonists and people with low moral standards are present in all four tales as they wander around the empire. The story in which such less-than-ideal characters predominate is the ten-chapter *Hua* story (Chapters 11–20). Its recurring theme is an expansion of "what goes around comes around". To be more precise, it can be summarised as "swindlers will be swindled" (Li and Miao 1985: 142). The swindlers are embodied in Xia Fang 夏方 and his son Xia Hu 夏虎, who travel under false names, before being tricked into believing that a Buddha statue can talk (and eventually revealing the scam). Within this general narrative is an isolated but rich case of verbal-visual humour, in which father and son try and disguise their identities after stealing a horse. It is virtually impossible to translate its wit fully, since it has to do with the formal aspects of some Chinese characters, but nevertheless, an elementary knowledge of Chinese suffices to appreciate this clever and witty renaming:

> 夏方遂改口回答道:「小可姓**秋名万**,小兒便喚做**秋彪**。」
>
> **Xia Fang** opened his mouth as if trying to correct his previous remarks, and replied: "My humble name is **Qiu Wan**, and this is my child, called **Qiu Biao**".

This can be explained as follows. When Xia Hu was renamed Qiu Biao, he just exchanged the surname Xia 夏 (summer) for Qiu 秋 (autumn), and the second name Hu 虎 (tiger) for Biao 彪 (young tiger). His father by comparison modified his second name from Fang 方 (upright) to Wan 万 (ten thousand). As emerges clearly, when the two characters *wan* and *fang* are put next to each other, they share a striking resemblance, making the pun visual rather than verbal.[15] Nevertheless, the author must have worried that his audience was not the brightest, because he felt the need to explain the pun a few pages later, when an exchange happens between the three main characters, Lou Zhu 婁祝, Yu Canjiang 俞參將, and Lin Yaoru 林燿如:

> 林二官人驚訝道:「那人姓甚名誰?」婁公子道:「名喚夏方。」林二官人想了一想,呵呵大笑道:「是了,小弟前日交易的時節,那人說是姓**秋名万**,敢就是此人改名, 賣與小弟的了。」婁公子道:「俞兄,端的不差。你想,夏與秋一理,方與万相同,這再不消講起。」
>
> Lin the Second Official asked, surprised: "Who was this person?" Sir Lou replied "His name was **Xia Fang**". Lin thought about it for a second, and laughing wholeheartedly, answered: "All right, when I came into contact with him, he said his name was **Qiu Wan**, I dare think that

it is the same person with a different name who sold me [this horse]". Lou added: "Brother Yu, he is not wrong. Think about it, **Xia** (summer) and **Qiu** (autumn) are the same principle [they are both seasons], and **Fang** is similar to **Wan**, it goes without saying".

Apart from this isolated case of a visual pun, *GZJC* exhibits many more traits of verbal humour, especially in the form of exaggerated and colourful expressions. The book is said to incorporate some aspects of the Wu 吳 (Suzhounese) dialect (Snow et al. 2018: 143–166). However, given the nature of the Chinese written language in which the correspondence between sound and symbol is not as direct as in alphabetical languages (and it is indeed possible to read the same text aloud in Mandarin and in Cantonese, or in Suzhounese, without losing meaning), one can only see a flickering shadow of that. What is more evident to the common reader are original expressions, rich in local colour, and inserted into the dialogue. These colourful expressions are mostly uttered by the lowly and secondary characters who swarm over the pages of all four stories; in these cases, humour is superimposed on texts or narrative events which do not constitute laughing matters in and of themselves. Two good examples occur in Chapter 21, when the young protagonist of the *Xue* story, Wen Jingqing 文荊卿, is advised by his uncle and adoptive father to leave his house, quit drinking wine, and concentrate on his studies. Offended, Wen decides instead to leave the house immediately, without communicating his decision to the rest of his family, but entrusting all his discontent to a poem. His servant advises against this, to no avail:

大官人不肯去見員外, 也聽你主意, 只待安童去稟個明白, 免得日後員外尋訪大官人蹤跡不著, 到把安童名字告到官司, 那時做個逃奴緝獲將來, **便是渾身有口, 也難分剖**。

If you, Young Sir, do not want to go see [your uncle] the Master, please at least wait for me to go explain the situation to him. This will avoid [the consequence] that, in the next [few] days, when he comes looking for you, he will report me to the authorities [after not finding you], and that when they finally catch this runaway servant, **even if I had mouths all over my body, it would be difficult for me to explain everything**.

After Wen moves out, his uncle reads his poem of discontent and, furious, exclaims:

哎, 畜生, 畜生! 看你久後, 若是還有個與我相會的日子, **只怕你掏盡湘江水, 難洗今朝一面羞**。

Oh, you brute, you brute! Let me see how you will get on in the future, if there is ever a day in which we meet again; **even if you had to use up all the water from the Xiang River, it will be hard to wash away today's shameful deeds**.

Exaggerated images like these often invoke the realm of fantasy. Mouths all over the body and using up an entire river in washing are both impossibilities and are presented as absurd hypotheses inside the text in order to prefigure a future scenario. Thus, it is plausible to assume that they are uttered to incite laughter from the characters inside the text themselves, before doing so outside it. In this aspect, they are different from Wei Zhongxian's earnest remarks about castrating candidates, which provoke only the reader's laughter.

Exaggeration is not the only device used to convey this sort of verbal humour; double entendre is also used, albeit more sparingly. Double entendre is commonly defined as a word or expression having a double meaning, with one of them often being sexual in nature. This allows for a good deal of transgressive joking by implication rather than by outright statement. Chapter 24 provides us with the example best matching this definition. In Li Ruolan's 李若蘭 household, the maidservant Qiong'e 瓊娥 (literally, beauty) discovers another maidservant, Chougu 丑姑 (literally, the ugly girl, both names comically revealing the girls' appearances) having an affair with a shepherd boy. Qiong'e exclaims:

> 你兩上做得好事，卻瞞我不得了。小姐著你來喚牧童採花，原來你到被牧童先採了花去。
>
> Oh, you two messed up big time, and you cannot hide from me! The Mistress sent you to **pick some flowers** with the shepherd boy, and here you are, being "**plucked like a flower**" by him instead.

Little explaining is needed to grasp this humour, since the verb *caihua* 採花, besides its literal meaning, to pick flowers, offers a sexual connotation, just as it does in English. This is here made even more explicit by the expression *huanghua* 黃花, repeated several more times in the text, which describes both a daylily and a virgin girl. Undoubtedly, *GZJC*'s humour community both in the time of its author and down the ages would understand this double entendre.

An example of more sophisticated humour at the micro-level is embodied in a folly-and-consequence episode of the same story.[16] In Chapter 25, the Li household wants to arrange a marriage for Chougu, the protagonist of the aforementioned scandal with the shepherd boy. In order to earn a more substantial profit, Li Yue 李岳, a relative of the Li family from a southern village, chooses to contact two matchmakers and decides to trick them by showing them the other maid, Qiong'e (the pretty one), as a prospective bride. The ruse is successful, as outlined in the story as follows:

> 只見次日吳婆同了一個奶娘，竟來與老夫人、小姐相見，假以小姐姻事為由。你看這老夫人，只道這兩個婆子果是來與女孩兒說親的，這兩個婆子又只道是老夫人曉得其中緣故的，那裡曉得是李岳的計策，使這兩個婆子來看瓊娥的。好笑兩家都坐在瞌睡裡，這奶娘不住眼把瓊娥上上下下

仔細看了一會,見他生得幾分顏色,便也喜歡,遂起身與吳婆別了夫人、小姐。

And on the next day, there she was, Mrs Wu [the matchmaker] together with a wet nurse [from the prospective groom's family], arrived to meet old Mother Li and her daughter [Li Ruolan] on the pretext of talking about her [Li Ruolan's] wedding. Look at this old mother, she thought that these two were there to propose a husband to her daughter [Li Ruolan]. These two also thought that the old mother knew why they were there [to see the maidservant]. They could not possibly know that it was all part of Li Yue's plot, who wanted to let the two of them have a look at Qiong'e. Just when the two [Mother Li and Li Ruolan] were having a nap, the wet nurse went to have a good look at Qiong'e and noticed with pleasure that she was extremely pretty. Therefore, she soon got up and, together with Mrs Wu, said goodbye to both mother and daughter.

That same evening (and not without some comic animosity between the two matchmakers), Chougu steps into the sedan chair, ready to be married off. Since she must remain veiled until after the ceremony has been performed, the substitution is not spotted until it is too late. Together with the underlying comical situation of a substitute prospective bride, a couple of episodes of verbal humour can also be detected here, for example (again, bold text indicates key phrases discussed below):

眾人仔細一看,見是**三分不像人,七分不像鬼的模樣**,都說是調了包兒。便喚那原與吳婆去看的奶娘來一認,也說**哪裡是這樣一副嘴臉**。原來那李岳得了那一塊銀子,四個彩緞,與嫂嫂作別一聲,竟往南莊走去。這鄉宦人家,待要告官爭訟,見這邊也是個宦家,只得忍著氣,把那吳婆凌辱了一場,方才休息。

Everyone, upon seeing her in detail [revealed], perceived that **for three parts out of ten, she did not look like a human person, and for seven out of ten she did not look like a ghost**, and they understood that the bride had been replaced. Even the wet nurse who had gone with Mrs Wu to look at her, upon seeing Chougu, exclaimed, "**Where in the world could she have [got] this face?**" Li Yue had already taken his share [of the profit], a piece of silver and four lengths of coloured satin, so he said goodbye to the old woman and went back to the southern village. The groom to be, a village official, wanted to take everyone to court, but, upon seeing that she too came from a family of officials, could only bottle up his rage, insult Mrs Wu for a while and suck it up.

The matchmaker's plot is reported in detail so that its surprise is ruined for us, because the plot is too transparent. However, the pleasure of reading this section of the story comes from being in the know and witnessing the build-up that ultimately leads to the characters' astonishment. In reading about the matchmaker preparing his plan, we anticipate that the groom and the wet nurse (and anyone else) are going to receive some sort of shock. When this happens, our expectations are confirmed and our suspense and arousal resolve into relief.[17] Moreover, the overemphatic way that the expected shock is verbalised without any accompanying enlightenment (first on the part of the people witnessing the ceremony and then the wet nurse) contributes to the fulfilment of our expectations.

The "three parts A, seven parts B" proportion is commonly used in the Chinese language to put together two contrasting but coexisting qualities. An example still used today is *sanfen zui qifen xing* 三分醉七分醒 (three parts drunk, seven parts sober). In the present instance, the highly precise fractions and double negatives serve to exaggerate the calculations made by the observers while trying to work out what they were looking at. The effect is to underline their slow-wittedness, compared with the reader's privileged position. "Three tenths not a person and seven tenths not a ghost" hints at something much more monstrous by telling us what the servant *does not* look like. This proportion can also be seen as a parodic reversal of the three *hun* 魂 and the seven *po* 魄, the two types of vital entities (one is tempted to call them "souls") which compose the source of life and return respectively to heaven and earth at the moment of death.

The story of a man being tricked into marrying an ugly wife after a matchmaker has been shown and has accepted a pretty one is a highly amusing theme. In fact, it provided a model for a variant in the first story of a later collection of short stories, *Wusheng xi* 無聲戲 (*Silent operas*), by Li Yu 李漁 (1611–1680?). This later tale is called *Chou langjun pa jiao pian de yan* 醜郎君怕嬌偏得豔 (*An ugly husband fears a pretty wife but marries a beautiful one*), and in this version, roles are inverted so that the mother of a wife-to-be is tricked into choosing an ugly man for her daughter after a matchmaker shows her a handsome one.[18] As in *GZJC*, the joke is an amusing but satirical comment on human folly.

Humour on a macro-level

GZJC is a book of the past, and also a book in which the past plays a fundamental role. This is frequently evoked with the recurring adage *guren dao* 古人道, "as the ancients would say", or its variant *guren shuo de hao* 古人說得好, "the ancients said it well". In addition, it is evoked in the constant intertextual references to previous works or authors that emerge when characters are in discussion. *GZJC* in fact engages in a continuous dialogue with the past; its author is aware of the tradition he is addressing and he shares that background with his audience. Thus, he can afford to leave some references unexplained while using them to advantage when describing humorous situations. However, another type of meta-dialogue also happens during the stories, that between the events narrated and the voice of the narrator commenting on them. Literary history is full of examples of such literary sabotage,[19] in which the narrative voice intervenes to comment on the characters' words or actions in a way which disrupts or belittles them. *GZJC* presents many of these comments that sabotage or belittle the characters' behaviour. Some are very visible, for example, when it is pointed out in the *Feng* story that even Daoist monks contradict their own words with their actions, but there are also more subtle ways in which the text "plays" with itself.

One aspect of how the narratorial voice works at cross-purposes with the main story appears in the introduction to the *Feng* story. Here, the narrating voice rehashes the age-old theme of marriage as a predestined union in which mortal men have no say (*yiduan qiyi hunyin, bu jia renwei, shi you tianyi* 一段奇異姻緣, 不假人為, 實由天意); but then the following story disrupts this maxim by recounting how Du Kaixian 杜開先 elopes with his beloved Han Yuzi 韓玉姿. One critic notes that this is the way the text works to promote a progressive view and fight against a backwards, feudal tradition (Miao 1993: 218–222). However, it is the narrative voice and not the text that has the last say, because at the end of the story, Han Yuzi can only live with Du Kaixian as his concubine. While this has been labelled weak storytelling (by Li and Miao 1985), I suspect that this was the author's intention all along. His viewpoint is one that endorses the divine comedy of human folly.

More instances in which the narrator intervenes inside the story are comments on trades and professions, as in Chapter 26, when the young man Wen Jingqing pretends to be a doctor in order to sneak into Li Ruolan's house and cure her from a persistent illness. He is depicted as babbling on about some medical principle or other and convincing the patient's mother, who, "hearing these proper principles, of course, believed in them" (*tingle zhe yipian zhengjing daoli, ziran ken xin* 聽了這一篇正經道理, 自然肯信). Nothing strange in this, until the narrative voice informs us that Wen Jingqing has only learnt the medical terms in order to fool his pretended patient's family. In addition, not many lines afterwards, we are presented with the arrival of an astrologer who is asked to predict Li Ruolan's future. We witness some more technical and specialistic terms, pertaining this time to the world of astrology, before the narrator glosses his account with the explanation that, "[i]t turns out, these sentences are the fundamental secrets of success of every astrologer" (*yuanlai, zhejiju que shi xingjia de rumen jueqiao* 原來, 這幾句卻是星家的入門訣竅). The satirical implication is clear: astrologers are charlatans, and anyone with a quick tongue can pass for one. The same is true for doctors.

Another way in which the narration sabotages itself is by alluding to a story and slightly changing one element of it for a comical effect. At the beginning of the *Feng* story, we are introduced to Du Kaixian's literary talent, which is improbably said to rival the two greatest Chinese poets, Li Bai and Du Fu. Such ironical comment appears as early as the first chapter:

此兒不可藐視, 開口成詩, 一字不容筆削。即李、杜諸君無出其右, 豈非天才也耶?

This child should not be despised, he is able to recite fully formed poems as soon as he opens his mouth, with no single character needing correction. Peerless, like the Great Li and Du, how can he not be a talent?

Mirroring this, in the first chapter of the *Xue* story, great poets are once again evoked in comparison to a young talent—but this time for his drinking capacity, not for his literary skills. One character remarks to the young man, Wen Jingqing:

相公，嘗酒便嘗了一甕，若是沽飲，須得幾百十甕才夠來。這樣的酒量，還比李白、劉伶高幾倍哩！

Sir, you already had a whole jar of wine just for tasting, if you decided to buy, I am afraid that no less than a hundred jars would suffice for you. This capacity for liquor is many times greater than even Li Bai and Liu Ling [two Tang dynasty poets renowned for their fondness for wine].

This protagonist's drunken state is shown in Figure 3.3, where the intoxicated student dreams of the God of Literature bringing him the good news. The whole *Xue* story can be seen as reflecting the *Feng* story in more than one way. In terms of plot, it concerns a male protagonist falling in love and exchanging poems with his love interest, then introducing himself into her house, having sex with her, and eventually marrying her. The author deliberately uses the same structure but alters some of its elements so as to enforce a parody of the classical love story and its happy ending "from the inside".

Register humour is also used to convey parody and satirical comment. A sudden and inappropriate rise in the communicative register quite often occurs in *GZJC*, usually to narrate or describe less than high-class moments or characters. The book is full of poems on high themes, describing the beauty of flowers and of pretty girls. But this is often completely subverted, for example, in Chapter 23, where an entire formal poem is incongruously used to describe the appearance of a newly arrived shepherd boy whose scalp is infected with ringworm (tinea favosa, a severe fungal infection):

頭如芋子，頂似梨花，
一陣風飛來玉屑，三竿日現出銀盔。
幾莖黃毛，挽不就青螺模樣；
一張花臉，生將來粉蝶妝成。
鬧哄哄逐不去腦後蒼蠅，
氣呼呼撇不盡鼻中蚯蚓。
這正是啞園公同胞的嫡派親兄弟，
新下南莊小牧童。

A head like a taro, a scalp looking like pear blossoms,
a gust of wind that flies over fragments of jade, a sun as tall as three bamboos shines on his silver-like hat.

Humour in the huaben *novellas* 57

How much fuzz cannot grow on his clam-shaped [scalp];
an opera-mask face, naturally painted at birth.
No matter how he moves, he cannot drive away the flies on the back of his head,
no matter how angry he gets, he cannot expel the worms from his nose.
This is the blood brother of the deaf courtyard guardian,
The new shepherd boy from the southern village.

Figure 3.3 Original plate from *Guzhang Juechen* 鼓掌絕塵 (*GZJC*), 1631 (facsimile, edited by Jinmu Sanren 金木散人, Taipei: Tianyi Chubanshe, 1985, p. 132). Illustration and caption echo the student's dream in the title of Chapter XXI (part of the *Xue* story), "*Jiuchisheng zuihou kan sitong, Zitongjun mengzhong chuan xixun* 酒癡生醉後堪絲桐, 梓童君夢中傳喜訊 (After getting drunk, a student both infatuated and intoxicated with wine strums the lute; The God of Literature brings good news in a dream)".

Further instances of such subversive parody can be noticed in some cases of coincidence. Coincidence is not really in and of itself a humorous device, and certainly not when used in any extended way, because it helps tear down the structure of a story and destroys any willing suspension of disbelief that the reader may have. However, its use can also be intended to provoke laughter through a kind of self-parody. Coincidences are extremely common in many other stories of the same era, and they usually take the shape of "people recognising other people", or "people knowing other people that in turn know other people", often from a foreign land or region. Such is the case in the *Feng* story referred to above, where Du Kaixian runs away with Han Yuzi, only to reunite with his actual father who had abandoned him when he was only a child and had in the meantime opened a hostel (Chapter 7). And of course, it is only by coincidence that, attending the Imperial exam, he is reunited with both his adoptive father (who just happens to be an examiner), and also with his bosom friend Kang Ruping 康汝平. In other cases, the text demands even greater suspension of disbelief when it confronts the reader with a whole concatenation of coincidences such as make up both the *Hua* and *Yue* stories. The effect is to undermine its own seriousness and to invite laughter.

Conclusion

Humour, being a subtle narrative technique, runs throughout the entire history of Chinese narrative. One might argue that it is in fact the best-kept secret of Chinese fiction, having accompanied it since its inception but being so often overlooked or misinterpreted in critical appraisals. Scholars looking for humour in the late-Imperial times often turn to jestbooks and closet dramas, but there is no doubt that highly enjoyable instances of humour can be observed and analysed in narratives too. According to specialists, the *huaben* stories were already past their prime by the end of the Ming dynasty, but it was precisely then that their countless writers were obliged to experiment in order to say something new and exciting for their readers, and humour offered a rewarding medium. We might agree that *GZJC* is not necessarily among the best texts (whatever that means) to come out of this period. Nevertheless, we must admit that its four medium-length stories keep the promise that is highlighted in the book's preface: it is in fact true that the text "bears no interest in stirring people's hearts, but has the intention of ridiculing the world" (*wuyi liaoren, youxin chaoshi* 無意撩人, 有心嘲世). Although its characters and events are mostly filtered through the largely unmerciful and unsympathetic lens of satire, *GZJC* is nonetheless also a precious source for analysing how a gentler style of humour is successfully constructed. It is certainly one that goes beyond the jokes found in common jestbooks by carefully intertwining its humour and narration.

Notes

1 For an analysis of humour in *Unofficial history from the forest of literati,* see Di Toro (2020: 459–480).
2 For an analysis of humour in *Flowers in the* mirror, see Huang (1991: 353–399).
3 For example, Hanan's preface to his translation of Li's works (Li 1990: 13).
4 According to Hanan, "Shi Chengjin, born in Yangzhou in 1659, was the first writer in the history of the vernacular story to sign his work with his own name" (1981: 209).
5 Zhu's description is quoted in Wu Mei (2004: 124).
6 Ling's original sentence is: "*Guangyin ru xiju, Chen xiucai feng hua xue yue le qi ba nian, jiang jiasi nongde ganjing kuaile* 光陰如隙駒, 陳秀才風花雪月了七八年, 將家私弄得乾淨快了". It can be translated into English as: "Time sped by. After seven or eight years of *such a dissipated way of life*, Scholar Chen's family fortune was almost all gone" (Ling 2018: 298, my italics and bolding).
7 Unless otherwise stated, all translations in this chapter are by the author. Given limitations of space, only characters and English translation are given throughout this chapter.
8 Lin (2015: 78–82) argues that *GZJC* inspired many *Caizi jiaren* novels.
9 More detailed, albeit fictionalised, descriptions of Wei Zhongxian's life in texts contemporary with *GZJC* can be found in a series of condemnatory novels sparked by his demise, the *Wei Zhongxian Xilie Xiaoshuo* 魏忠賢系列小説 (*Wei Zhongxian series of novels*), mostly published soon after his fall from power and subsequent suicide. For a detailed study of them, see Wu (2009: 42–55).
10 For example, Qi Yukun and Chen Huiqin wrote about *GZJC* almost exclusively because of the Wei Zhongxian passage. Cai (1987) mentions it as well, as does the article by Li and Miao (1985) on *GZJC*.
11 For discussion of the connection between name taboos and humour in classical China, see Shirley Chan in this volume.
12 This concept of a "humour community" is taken from Simpson (2003: 60ff), who in turn bases his discussion on Carrell's notion of discourse communities (1997).
13 Roberts (2019: 52), who in turn relies on Noël Carroll (2014).
14 This concept was formulated by Oring (1992: 1–15), who later expanded it (2003: 16–28).
15 Incidentally, the *GZJC* copy preserved in Dalian (which ends at Chapter 14) reports the character *wan* 万 in its complete form, 萬, which makes the pun slightly less intelligible for the Chinese readers (visible on page 210 of the Dalian edition scanned and made available online by the Institute for Advanced Studies on Asia of the University of Tokyo, Japan).
16 For a longer discussion of folly and consequence stories in *huaben*, see Hanan (1981: 59–68).
17 See Roberts (2019: 93–06) and his analysis of release theories.
18 The story is available in English in Li Yu 李漁 (trans. Patrick Hanan, 1990).
19 Such sabotage is also termed metanarrative disruption by Attardo (1991: 96ff).

References

Attardo, Salvatore. 1991. *Humorous texts: A semantic and pragmatic analysis*. Berlin and New York: Mouton De Gruyter.
Cai Guoliang 蔡國梁. 1987. *Ming Qing Xiaoshuo Tanyou* 明清小説探幽 (*A research on the obscure works of Ming and Qing fiction*). Hangzhou: Zhejiang Wenyi Chubanshe.

Carrell, Amy. 1997. Humor communities. *HUMOR: International Journal of Humor Research*, 10 (1): 11–24.

Carroll, Noël. 2014. *Humour: A very short introduction*. Oxford: Oxford University Press.

Di Toro, Anna. 2020. The scholars, *chronique indiscrète or neoficial'naja istorija*? The challenge of translating eighteenth-century Chinese irony and grotesque for contemporary Western audiences. In Daniel Derrin and Hannah Burrows, eds., *The Palgrave handbook of humour, history, and methodology*. 459–480. Cham: Palgrave Macmillan.

Hanan, Patrick. 1981. *The Chinese vernacular story*. Cambridge and London: Harvard University Press.

Hu Shiying 胡士瑩. 1980. *Huaben Xiaoshuo Gailun* 話本小說概論 (*An introduction to huaben fiction*). Beijing: Zhonghua Shuju.

Huang Kewu 黃克武. 1991. *Jing Hua Yuan zhi youmo—Qing zhongye Zhongguo youmo wenxue zhi fenxi* 鏡花緣之幽默—清中葉中國幽默文學之分析 (Humour in *Flowers in the Mirror*: An Analysis of Chinese humorous literature of the Mid-Qing period). *Hanxue Yanjiu*, 9 (1): 353–399.

Jinmu Sanren 金木散人. 1985. *Guzhang Juechen* 鼓掌絕塵 (*GZJC*). Taipei: Tianyi Chubanshe.

Li Luo 李落 and Miao Zhuang 苗壯. 1985. *Xiang yun jinping zhi mei, Wei gong Liangshan zhi shui:* Guzhang Juechen *shilun* 香韻金瓶之梅,味共梁山之水:《鼓掌絕塵》試論. (A perfume akin to the *Plum in the Golden Vase*, a flavour akin to the *Water of Mount Liang:* A tentative discussion of *GZJC*). *Mingqing Xiaoshuo Luncong*, 2: 138–152.

Li Yu 李漁. 1990. *Wusheng xi* 無聲戲 (*Silent operas*). Trans. Patrick Hanan. Hong Kong: Chinese University of Hong Kong Press.

Lin Yiqing 林宜青. 2015. *Guzhang Juechen Yanjiu* 鼓掌絕塵研究 (*Research on GZJC*). New Taipei: Hua Mulan Wenhua Chubanshe.

Ling Mengchu 凌蒙初. 2018. *Pai'an jingqi* 拍案驚奇 (*Slapping the table in amazement*). Trans. Shuhui Yang 楊曙輝 and Yunqin Yang 楊韻琴. Seattle, WA: University of Washington Press.

Liu Shide 劉世德, Chen Guanghao 陳廣浩, and Shi Changlun 石昌淪 (ed.). 1990. *Guben Xiaoshuo Congkan* 古本小說叢刊 (*A Collection of ancient novels*). Beijing: Zhonghua Shuju.

McMahon, Keith. 2014. The potent eunuch: The story of Wei Zhongxian. *Journal of Chinese Literature and Culture*, 1 (1–2): 1–28.

Miao Zhuang 苗壯. 1993. *Guzhang Juechen* 鼓掌絕塵. In Zhou Juntao 周鈞韜, Ouyang Jian 歐陽健 and Xiao Xiangkai 蕭相愷, eds., *Zhongguo Tongsu Xiaoshuo Jianshang Cidian* 中國通俗小說鑒賞辭典 (*A Dictionary of evaluation of Chinese popular fiction*). 218–222. Nanjing: Nanjing Daxue Chubanshe.

Oring, Elliott. 1992. *Jokes and their relations*. Lexington: The University Press of Kentucky.

Oring, Elliott. 2010 [2003]. *Engaging humor*. Urbana and Chicago: University of Illinois Press.

Plaks, Andrew, ed. 1977. *Chinese narrative: Critical and theoretical essays*. Princeton, NJ: Princeton University Press.

Plaks, Andrew. 1987. *The Four masterworks of the Ming novel: Ssu ta ch'i-shu*. Princeton, NJ: Princeton University Press.

Qi Yukun 齊裕焜 and Chen Huiqin 陳惠琴. 1995. *Jing yu Jian: Zhongguo Fengci Xiaoshuo Shilüe* 鏡與劍: 中國諷刺小説史略 (*The Mirror and the sword: A brief history of the Chinese satirical novel*). Taipei: Wenjin Chubanshe.

Raskin, Victor. 1985. *Semantic mechanisms of humor*. Dordrecht: D. Reidel.

Roberts, Alan. 2019. *A Philosophy of humour*. Cham: Palgrave Macmillan.

Simpson, Paul. 2003. *On the discourse of satire: Towards a stylistic model of satirical humour*. Amsterdam and Philadelphia, PA: John Benjamins.

Snow, Don, Zhou Xiayun and Shen Senyao. 2018. A Short history of written Wu, Part I. *Global Chinese*, 4 (1): 143–166.

Wu, H. Laura. 2009. Corpses on display: Representations of torture and pain in the Wei Zhongxian novels. *Ming Studies*, 1: 42–55.

Wu Mei 吳梅. 2004. *Zhongguo Xiqu Gailun* 中國戲曲概論 (*Introduction to Chinese drama*). Ed. Feng Tongyi 馮統一. Beijing: Zhongguo Renmin Daxue Chubanshe.

4 Linguistic devices in traditional forms of Balinese humour

Nengah Arnawa

Humour and the Balinese linguistic background

To begin this study of examples of traditional Balinese oral humour, it is useful to outline some background to the complex linguistic conventions of Indonesian languages, specifically those found in the island province of Bali. In 2020, the Language Center Office of the national Ministry of Education and Culture noted that Indonesia had 718 regional languages. This may increase in the future because recording and identification of regional languages are still ongoing. Of the present number, there are 14 regional languages with speakers equal to or exceeding 1,000,000, namely Javanese (84,300,000), Sundanese (34,000,000), Malay (13,040,00), Batak (7,045,000), Madurese (6,770,000), Minangkabau (5,530,000), Betawi (5,000,000), Bugis (5,000,000), Acehnese (3,500,000), Balinese (3,300,000), the Makassar language (2,130,000), the Sasak language (2,100,000), the Lampung language (1,834,000) and the Gorontalo language (1,000,000).

The Balinese language is used by over 3.3 million speakers who live in Bali Province as well as other provinces such as West Nusa Tenggara, Lampung, Southeast Sulawesi and others. The existence of the Balinese language outside the Province of Bali is related both to historical-cultural factors and to the government's transmigration policy. As a regional language, Balinese functions as a marker of identity and a social language for members of the Balinese tribes, and as a language in the realm of Hindu tradition, culture and religion. It also supports the Indonesian language and acts as a means of creativity.[1] One of the many creative functions of Balinese is to form humour.

Sociolinguistically, the Balinese language has a number of different speech levels called *anggah-ungguhing basa*. These have been identified and classified from various perspectives. Generalising from these various views, there are three levels, namely Balinese *alus* (high variety), *kepara* (general variety) and *kasar* (low variety). Balinese *alus* is used to show respect for speech participants in relation to both traditional and modern social status. Traditional social status reflects caste which is static because it derives from *purusa* (lineage). The concept of *purusa* relates to the patrilineal kinship

DOI: 10.4324/9781003176374-4

system which is determined based on the father or male line. In Balinese customary law, *purusa* has a broader meaning because it includes both men and women who have been given the status of men (Suwitra-Pradnya 2017). Women being accorded the status of *purusa* occurs in *nyentana* marriages (where women propose to men). *Purusa* lineage in the traditional Balinese stratification has four levels of caste, from high to low, namely: *brahman, ksatria, wésia,* and *sudra*. The *brahman, ksatria* and *wésia* castes are often classed together as the *triwangsa* group.

The Balinese *alus* language is used when the *sudra* caste speaks with a caste-member of the *triwangsa* group. Furthermore, modern social status is a dynamic hierarchy which also relates to one's position or office at any given time in a government organisation, for example, governor, regent, *camat* (head of the district); or in a customary organisation such as *bendésa* (customary leader), *patajuh* (deputy customary leader), *panyarikan* (customary secretary). Because respect is also shown to guests and strangers, the Balinese *alus* variety is used with them. Apart from relating to the participants, the use of Balinese *alus* also relates to speech events and topics. In traditional and religious activities or when discussing something that is purified and sacred, the *alus* variety of Balinese must be used. Given such sociolinguistic facts, the *alus* variety of Balinese is quite rare and even more rarely used for humour.

In Balinese, humour is largely an oral tradition that is widely found in *satua* or folk tales (fairy tales). Bali *satua* generally use Balinese *kepara* (general variety), sometimes mixed with Balinese *kasar* (low variety). In *satua*, these varieties are considered the most natural. This linguistic practice can be interpreted as reflecting the social fact that humour in Bali, as in many other places, is widely used in relations between equals, in relaxed and intimate settings and when topics are far from things that are holy and sacred. However, the message behind use of Balinese humour can often be serious, for example, conveying moral advice and even social criticism. This tradition of oral humour has been passed down from generation to generation. Balinese humour is found in both *kesusastraan Bali purwa* (classical Balinese literature) and in *kesusastraan Bali nyar* (modern Balinese literature), in the forms of *paribasa* (proverbs) and *satua* (folk tales). There have been many attempts to inventory this oral tradition of humour. Bagus (1976) and Kardji (1991) both carried out an inventory of *satua Bali sané banyol* (funny Balinese folk tales), such as those classified by the names of their leading characters, *I Belog, Pan Balang Tamak, I Bungkling* and others. Tinggen (1988) and Simpen (1980) inventoried *paribasa Bali* (the Balinese proverb) which covers a range of humorous linguistic constructs, such as *cecimpedan* (children's riddles in Balinese), *bladbadan* (a form of sound play with meaning transposition), *wewangsalan* (a kind of rhyme only two lines) and *cecangkitan* or *raos ngémpélin* (a puzzle based on ambiguity of meaning). In current developments, the oral forms of Balinese humour widely used in traditional theatre performances, such as *drama gong* (traditional

Figure 4.1 A traditional nightime *wayang kulit* performance by Cenk Blonk with audience members of all ages, Jembrana District, Bali, August 2011.

Source: News-video still, Pemerintah Daera Kabupaten Jembrana (Jembrana District Government), 25 August 2011, at: https://images.app.goo.gl/qXouuL6aBh5SEcKX8, accessed 13 July 2021.

drama accompanied by a Balinese orchestra, where each character has their own live dialogue), *séndratari* (drama that combines dance moves with dialogue, also with musical accompaniment, but where the dialogue between its characters is carried out indirectly via the puppeteer as intermediary), *bondrés* (Balinese comic performing art using masks and a Balinese orchestra), and finally *wayang kulit*. This last is Bali's famous traditional shadow puppet theatre which today is not only performed live (see Figure 4.1) but also widely available in short films posted on YouTube and elsewhere.

The presence of humour in Balinese is also reflected in the availability of several terms related to the actions of using this oral tradition, such as *magegonjakan* (conversations that are not serious are usually punctuated with humour), *makedékan* (joking), *magegiakan* (laughing out loud), *mabebanyolan* (funny stories)—all meaning "joking with laughter". The prevalence of humour in Balinese society has encouraged local television stations to broadcast regular *balé kedék* ("a vehicle for laughter") which reflect the various forms of Balinese humour. This study concentrates on the linguistic forms of humour that are common to all these oral, written and performative contexts.

Methodology

This study of *bebanyolan* (a general term for Balinese humour) uses a linguistic anthropological approach (Duranti 1997). It focusses on the uniqueness of the way that humour is implemented through linguistic tools such as lexical items, phrases and other grammatical constructions (Arnawa 2017b). Examples were collected from various written sources such as a collection of *paribasa Bali* (Balinese proverbs) and a collection of *satua banyol* (funny folk tales); and from recordings of Balinese traditional art performances such as *wayang kulit, drama gong, séndratari* and *bondrés*. From the *paribasa Bali* collection, 37 pieces of data were obtained; the *satua banyol* collection yielded 23 examples; *wayang kulit* 8, *drama gong* 6; *sendratari* 4 and from *bondres* 18 were obtained.[2]

These data were collected applying the document recording method with each item recorded in a single unified context (Sudaryanto 1993; Gunarwan 2002). A selection was made from the whole corpus and, for validation purposes, the selection was triangulated by Balinese language and literature experts. After analysis using the anthropological linguistic approach, four linguistic constructs emerged as the most frequent vehicles for humour. In the following sections, discussion is organised according to these four traditional constructs.

Four traditional Balinese joking constructs

Cecimpedan

The first construct to be examined is the *cecimpedan*. Morphologically, the term comes from the root *cimped* (guess) to which is added the suffix {-an} and *dwipurwa* (reduplication of the first syllable) so that the word becomes *cecimpedan* which means guessing (Simpen 1980). Reflecting this morphological process, *cecimpedan* is in fact a Balinese puzzle, generally played by children but also by adults for fun. The game involves two people or groups in opposition to each other. Each group takes turns asking questions to the opposing group. Assessment is given based on the accuracy of the answers within a certain time duration. Semantically, there are two varieties of *cecimpedan*, one of which has onomatopoeic and the other associative patterns, and both use Balinese *kepara* (general variety) (Arnawa 2017a; 2019). *Cecimpedan* onomatopoeia is constructed using the abbreviation principle by keeping the end syllable as a rhyme to give interpretive support. An example is: *Apa cing dag?* (What is cing dag?).[3]

The phrase *cing dag* is an abbreviation of the two words *cicing* (dog) and *undag* (stairs) combined but maintaining the final syllable. Maintaining the final syllable in Balinese is a characteristic of colloquial variety or those speech levels that are generally used in casual and intimate conversation. Colloquial variety is mostly in the form of *kepara* but is sometimes mixed with *kasar* (low variety), depending on the level of familiarity of the participants. The higher the level of familiarity, generally the more frequent the insertion of *kasar*-variety vocabulary. In this case, following the principle of rhyme similarity, the meaning of the *cecimpedan*, *Apa cing dag?*, can be arrived at when it is paraphrased as *Cicing medem di undag* (Dog sleeping on the stairs). Interpreting the meaning of *cecimpedan* onomatopoeia in this way involves inductive logic based on phonetic motivation (Sumarsono

2007). *Cecimpedan* onomatopoeia are generally used and enjoyed by children under ten years of age, although they are not necessarily meant to evoke humour. The idea is merely a cognitive-linguistic game played in an atmosphere of intimacy and joy. So, what is cheerful and joyful is located in the atmosphere of the game, rather than in the structure of *cecimpedan* onomatopoeia.

On the other hand, *cecimpedan* associative are used by children of any age and including adults. They are generally constructed using whole words (without abbreviations) in an interrogative sentence. The formation of *cecimpedan* associative involves associating ideas with other people, events or things. Linkage of ideas occurs because of the match between one idea and another (Alwi et al. 2001). Interpretation of *cecimpedan* associative involves declarative reasoning and often causes a humorous reaction. Their challenging nature is shown by some examples collected from written data sources (Simpen 1980; Tinggen 1988) and shown below:

1. *Apaké jemuh belus, émbonin tuh?*
   What is it: wet in the sun, dry in the shade?
2. *Apaké medil bataran kena cunguh?*
   What is it: shoots at the floor, hits the nose?
3. *Apaké macelep ka sisi?*
   What is it: to go into the outside?
4. *Apaké majujuk éndép, nyongkok tegeh?*
   What is it: when standing, short, when crouching, high?
5. *Apaké majujuk medem, medem majujuk?*
   What is it: when standing, asleep, when sleeping, standing up?
6. *Apaké ulung betén alihin ba duur?*
   What is it: falls below but sought above?
7. *Apaké celepang kekeh, pesuang kisut?*
   What is it: when put in, stiff, when removed, withered?
8. *Apaké songné cukcuk, jitné égol-égol pesu putih keprat-keprit?*
   What is it: the hole is poked, her arse is swaying, bringing out something white?

Syntactically, *cecimpedan* in this format are constructed using the question word *apa* (what?). In Balinese, the vowel /a/ in the open final position is pronounced /ə/ so it is read as [apə]. Balinese language has six question words, namely *apaké* (what), *nyén* or *sira* (who?), *kuda* (how much?), *dija* (where?), *ngudiang* or *ngéngkén* (why?), and *pidan* (when?). The common usage of *apaké* (what is it?) in *cecimpedan*, as exemplified above, reflects the fact that generally the question being asked is, what is something.

Semantically, however, these eight individual *cecimpedan* are differently constructed. *Cecimpedan* 1-6 use contradictory logic that creates an imbalance of reason and thus rely on incongruity as their source of humour. *Cecimpedan* 1 (What is it: wet in the sun, dry in the shade?) contains logical contradictions. For example, the verb-form *jemuh* (dried) should correspond to *tuh* (dry) but is paired with *belus* (wet); and conversely, the verb-form *émbonin* (shaded) should correspond to *belus* (wet) but is paired with *tuh* (dry). The clever answer to *Cecimpedan* 1 is *lengar* (bald). By analogy, if *lengar* (bald) is dried in the sun, it will eventually get wet with sweat, whereas if it is shaded, the wet sweat will become dry. It is this game of conflicting logics that causes laughter.

Like the first example, *Cecimpedan* 2 (What is it: shoots at the floor, hits the nose?) takes advantage of logic drift. The noun *bataran* (floor) connotes the lower part of the house, while the noun *cunguh* (nose) is found on the upper part of the human body. On this basis, semantically *Cecimpedan* 2 asks what is something that hits the floor (bottom) but also hits the nose (top). To that question, the answer is *entut* (fart). The sound of a fart is analogous to the sound of a gunshot (shoot) and since the anal canal always faces downward, the "shot" will hit the *bataran* (floor). And when the *entut* comes out, Balinese people will cover their noses due to the unpleasant smell. This clever logical displacement from the realm of the warrior to that of the body and its natural functions is what triggers humour.

Cecimpedan 3 (What is it: to go in outside?) turns on the verb *macelep* which in Balinese means "to enter". Something or someone who has entered something is supposed to be inside, as in *macelep ke kamar mandi* (going into the bathroom), meaning the person is in the bathroom. However, this *cecimpedan* reverses that logic, requiring that something is into but is also out. The unexpected and witty answer is *kancing baju*, "a (shirt) button". A button on the shirt works by being inserted into the buttonhole until it comes out behind. The logic here plays with displacement of perspective so as to focus on the flat fabric of the shirt that possesses an "inside" and an "outside" rather than on an expected three-dimensional container such as a building or a room. This unexpected shift creates incongruity and surprise which are essential ingredients of humour.

Cecimpedan 4 (What is it: when standing short, but when crouching high?), presents two logical contradictions with the verb-form *majujuk* (standing) paired with the adjective *endep* (short), and the verb *nyongkok* (squats) paired with the adjective *tegeh* (high). Any creature will generally appear taller when standing than when crouching; but here that logic is reversed. The answer to *Cecimpedan* 4 is a dog, or maybe a cat or a monkey. The rationale for this is that when the four-legged beast stands up, its head, back and tail are on a horizontal line, whereas if it squats, the head, back and tail are in a vertical line or at least a diagonal one. Thus, the horizontal position causes the dog's head to be closer to the ground than the higher distance in the vertical position.

In *Cecimpedan* 5 (What is it: when standing asleep, but when sleeping standing up?), the logical paradox is generated by the word pairs *majujuk–medem* (standing–sleeping) and *medem–majujuk* (sleep–standing). Many Balinese interpret this *cecimpedan* as almost pornographic because it suggests an erect penis. However, this is not actually correct: the answer is the *telapak batis* (the soles of the feet). Isn't it the case that when a person is asleep, the soles of their feet are vertical to the floor (i.e., they are standing up) and conversely, when the person is standing, the feet are horizontal (i.e., asleep)? In Balinese, there are several *cecimpedan* which can be interpreted as sexually suggestive, but none of them have any explicitly sexual aspect. However, the possibility of these multiple interpretations can also cause laughter before the right answer is arrived at. For example, *Apaké nyemumuk selem, yén kebitang ngenah barak, yén celek makejengan*? (What is it: has a black mound, when opened looks red, if it is plugged in, twitches?). Balinese people are generally ashamed to guess this one because it seems to refer to sexual matters. Balinese people consider such humour to be unethical and therefore inappropriate to be conveyed in public. Thinking in sexual terms, the answer could be the vagina and its mucus lining, but the true meaning of the *cecimpedan* is *sumi matunjel* (a mound of burnt straw), because a burning mound of straw will look black, if it is opened, it will reveal red embers, and if it is plugged into an electrical current, it will shock the plug. That is the true, perfectly innocent answer, not at all related to sex. The wittiness in these two examples of *cecimpedan* occurs in two stages. First, the cuteness occurs when the *cecimpedan* construct is spoken. In this phase, the audience's mind seems to be focused on the phonography or pattern of the words and appreciating it which causes laughter. The next cuteness happens after the meaning is explained, which turns out to have nothing to do with the expected sexual meaning. This humour is caused by the participants' success in tricking the audience's logical predictions and expectations.

Returning to the list above, the sixth *cecimpedan* (What is it: fall below, sought above?) introduces a logical contradiction between *ulung betén* (to fall under) and *alihin ba duur* (sought above). If something falls, naturally the search for it must be made down below in the vicinity of where it fell, not sought above that point. But the answer is actually a common everyday experience summed up in one word: *tuduh* (the roof is leaking). When it rains and the roof leaks, water droplets must fall on the floor but residents or construction workers will look for and find their source up on the roof of the house. This simple resolution of the conundrum posed by the *cecimpedan* surprises and satisfies at the same time, creating laughter.

Based on semantic-cognitive processes, *Cecimpedan* 1–6 are all constructed using logical deviations and paradoxes that are perfect illustrations of humour based on incongruity theory, one of the three most widely recognised principles in humour. This theory emphasises that humour occurs when there is a mismatch between natural logic and a given objective, event or situation (Mulder and Nijholt 2002; Gibson 2019). Giving the correct answer to resolve this perception of logical incompatibility succeeds time and again in tricking the participants' thought-processes, causing laughter from the audience.

The semantic-cognitive process of *Cecimpedan* 7 and 8 is different from that of 1-6: these do not use contradictory logic. Both, however, are applications of the relief tension theory of humour. Conceptually, this theory sees humour as a spontaneous release of tension due to various causes (Morreall 2016) such that humour can be used to reduce physical and emotional tension. Many people perceive both *Cecimpedan* 7 (What is it: when put in stiff, when removed withered?) and *Cecimpedan* 8 (What is it: the hole is poked, her ass is swaying, bringing out something white?) as sexually suggestive. For people who think this way, both are interpreted as relating to a husband and wife (or man and woman) having sex. This interpretation perhaps arises because of the natural drive of the human libido, whereas the true meaning of *Cecimpedan* 7 is not related to sexual activity at all: it is simply *naar tebu* (to eat sugarcane). Aren't pieces of sugar cane stiff and hard when you put them in your mouth and doesn't the wilted bagasse get removed from the mouth after the sugarcane is chewed? The answer tricks those who are attracted to sexual thoughts.

In the same way, the meaning of *Cecimpedan* 8 is *anak nepung* (woman making flour). In the past, Balinese women made flour by pounding rice in a hollow mortar with a pestle. The process is as follows. First, the rice is put into the hollow mortar. Then the rice is pounded with the pestle and during this crushing process, the woman who is doing the pounding sways her hips and bottom. Lastly, during the pounding process, some white flour usually leaks out. So, this *cecimpedan* does not relate to the sexual act and its emissions. The semantic logic of both these *cecimpedan* employs an analogy that rests on the physical similarities of processes that could perhaps apply to the sexual act but more exactly matches a purely innocent explanation (Arnawa 2016).

Bladbadan

The second frequently occurring traditional humour construct found in the data examined here is that known as *bladbadan*. This is a Balinese proverb which is used in intimate and informal situations, very rarely in official speech events. *Bladbadan* are generally used for joking. Morphologically, the term comes from the root word *badbad*, plus the infix {-el-} and the suffix {-an}, forming the word *beladbadan*. Then by a syncope process with the phoneme /e/, *beladbadan* becomes *bladbadan* (Ginarsa 2009). Since in lexical semantics, the word *badbad* means "being drawn from a spool like a thread" (Warna 1978), *bladbadan* can be interpreted as a Balinese proverb form having an elongated morphological construction. Lengthening is done by changing words into phrases. Reflecting this process of elongation, *bladbadan* has three elements, namely: *giing/bantang* (frame), *arti sujati* (denotative meaning) and *suksemanyané*, its associative meaning.

The following saying about a person called Ni Luh Sari is a good example (quoted from Arnawa 2017b):

> *Ni Luh Sari sesai pesan majempong bebek*
> Ni Luh Sari often has the crown of a duck
> Ni Luh Sari often sulks

In this example, *bladbadan* applies to *majempong bébék* and its three elements are as follows:

> Frame: *majempong bébék* (crested duck)
> Denotative meaning: *jambul* (feathery outgrowth on a bird's head, i.e., crest)
> Associative meaning: *ngambul* (sulking)

The denotative meaning of *majempong bébék* is "a crest" or *jambul*, which is linked with *ngambul* via an association process that rests on phonetic and rhyme similarities between the two words. Reflecting these three elements, *bladbadan* is a semantic transposition process with phonetic, lexical and syntactic emotive devices supported by morphological principles (Arnawa 2017b). The logic applied in the semantic interpretation process is an inductive analogy that rests on the similarity of form and sound between denotative and associative meanings (Sumarsono 2004).

In contrast to *cecimpedan* where humour arises from logical deviations, *bladbadan* is very much tied to its broader context of speech, and cannot be used independently or out of context. Speech interaction context greatly determines the intensity of humour in general, as Ortega (2013) has noted. This concept seems very relevant to *bladbadan* as can be seen in the dialogue shown in Table 4.1, taken from a *wayang kulit* episode performed by the well-known Balinese puppeteer Cenk Blonk (the artistic name of I Wayan Nardayana, b. 1966). Cenk Blonk is also the name of his contemporary shadow puppet show, originating from his hometown of Tabanan in Bali. It is named for two of the traditional clown figures (*punakawan*) in *wayang kulit*, Cenk and Blonk. As well as giving live performances, Cenk Blonk has many video recordings available on YouTube and his *wayang kulit* is one of the most popular in Bali today.

The dialogue presented for analysis in Table 4.1 does not feature Cenk and Blonk but a different *punakawan* pair called Délem and Sangut, who are present in every Balinese *wayang kulit*. Their dialogue occurs within the narrative of how the hero, Rama, has had his wife, Dewi Sita, kidnapped by the King of Alengka, resulting in war. The two clowns describe a plan to arrest Rama himself, introducing several *bladbadan* as they exchange quick-fire questions and answers. Délem is a fat man with an ugly goitre. He is the dominant protagonist of the pair, while Sangut is a thin man with a fickle, changeable character. The difference in character between the two clowns

Table 4.1 Sangut and Délem discuss the kidnapping of Rama

Délem:	*Cenek, jeg jemak I Rama ajak ka Buléléng tanggun danginé*[1]
	In short, catch Rama and take to the east end of Buleleng
Sangut:	*Dija?*
	Where?
Délem:	*Diculik*
	Kidnapped
Sangut:	*Suud diculik?*
	After being kidnapped?
Délem:	*Ajak lantas ke Nusa Dua tanggun dajané*[2]
	Then take him to the north end of Nusa Dua ...
Sangut:	*Dija?*
	Where?
Délem:	*Ditanjung*
	Kicked
Sangut:	*Suud diculik jak ditanjung?*
	After being kidnapped and kicked?
Délem:	*Ajak lantas ke dauh kota Negarané*[3]
	Then, take him to the west of Negara town
Sangut:	*Kénkén?*
	How?
Délem:	*Dicekik*
	Strangled
Sangut:	*Suud diculik, ditanjung, kén dicekik?*
	After being kidnapped, kicked, and strangled?
Délem:	*Cara montor sing misi mesin*[4]
	Like a motorcycle without an engine
Sangut:	*Kénkén?*
	How?
Délem:	*Séda*
	Dead

Source: From a video recording of a performance by Wayang Cenk Blonk of the episode *Sura Bhuta Gugur*, or *The Death of Sura Bhuta* (at: https://www.youtube.com/watch?v=eZgI6Q3K42E&t=1097s, accessed 8 May 2019).

is often used to show off their wit and humour. These two puppets are shown in Figures 4.2 and 4.3; the first is pictured from the audience's point of view in front of the shadow screen on which the puppets appear, and the second reveals the scene behind the screen showing the hands of the puppeteer controlling the two puppets.[4] The dialogue in Table 4.1 is shown with numbers attached in bold to individual words to indicate the presence of *bladbadan* and corresponding to their analyses in Table 4.2 There are four *bladbadan* in this short excerpt in Table 4.1. They all play on names of places and objects, as is described in the list of elements provided in Table 4.2 and discussed below.

The main narrative of this extract is that Rama will be *diculik* (kidnapped) by Alengka troops, then *ditanjung* (kicked), then *dicekik* (strangled) until he is *séda* (dead). These four verbs of violent action are expressed using the *bladbadan* construction, causing laughter in the audience at the incongruity between the seriousness of the threatened action and the playful way

Table 4.2 Key to *bladbadan* in Table 4.1

1. Frame:	*Buléléng tanggun danginé*
	east end of Buleleng
Denotation:	*Désa Culik*
	Culik Village
Association:	kidnapped
	diculik
2. Frame:	*Nusa Dua tanggun dajané*
	north end of Nusa Dua
Denotation:	*Désa Tanjung*
	Tanjung Village
Association:	*ditanjung*
	being kicked
3. Frame:	*dauh Kota Negara*
	west of Negara City
Denotation:	*Desa Cekik*
	Cekik Village
Association:	*dicekik*
	being strangled
4. Frame:	*montor sing misi mesin*
	motorcycle without engine
Denotation:	*sepéda*
	bicycle
Association:	*séda*
	die

Figure 4.2 Délem (on the left) and Sangut, two of the many *punakawan* or clown characters in traditional *wayang kulit*, as they appear on the shadow screen for an audience.

Source: Photography by Nengah Arnawa at a live performance in Bali in 2019.

Figure 4.3 The *punakawan* characters, Sangut (on the left) and Délem as they appear from behind the shadow screen. Note the hands of the puppeteer as he cleverly manipulates the puppets with their detailed colouring.

Source: Photography by Nengah Arnawa at a live performance in Bali by the puppeteer, Cenk Blonk, in 2019.

in which the words are arrived at. The verb *diculik* (abducted) is introduced by the phrase *Buléléng tanggun danginé* (the east end of Buleleng). At the east of Buleleng is Culik Village. The name *Culik* is then transposed into the verb *diculik* (abducted), resulting in a construction of *Bladbadan* 1. The verb *ditanjung* (kicked) is similarly introduced with a location phrase, *Nusa Dua tanggun dajané* (the north end of Nusa Dua). At the north end of Nusa Dua is Tanjung village whose name is interpreted as the verb-form *ditanjung* (kicked) to produce *Bladbadan* 2. The verb *dicekik* (strangled) is expressed via another location phrase, *dauh Kota Negara* (west of Negara town). Here is Cekik village whose name of *Cekik* is interpreted as the verb-form *dicekik* (strangled), arriving at *Bladbadan* 3. Finally, the word *séda* (dies) is expressed via the phrase *montor sing misi mesin* (motorcycle without engine) which has the denotative meaning of *sepéda* (bicycle). Such a noun can be used as a basis to arrive at *séda* (to die) because of their rhyming similarity in this *Bladbadan* 4.

Given the quite serious narrative content of the extract above, the four *bladbadan* used in it introduce a number of humorous elements. As noted above, the speakers are two stereotypical clowns who invite the audience to laugh at them, creating elements of both superiority and incongruity. They themselves try to laugh at Rama, the princely character whose predicament is being talked about, by looking down on him and using him as the subject of a quick-fire question and answer session. Additionally, *Bladbadan* 1–4 all use clever word-play and manipulation of logic to prevent the concept of

Rama's abduction and death from being taken too seriously. Instead, they direct the audience's attention to the interplay of rhyming congruence and apparent incongruity as they set up the logic of their associative meanings.

Despite the strong implementation of superiority in the four examples above, not all *bladbadan* are developed using that theory, as is shown by the following examples taken from a printed collection (Srawana 1978: 34).

Example 5.

Apang paturu malawar gerang, paturu cager (literally, so that both are scarred, dried anchovies, just as faithful i.e., So that both are as faithful as dried anchovies sticking to each other).

Example 6.

Yen ane luh luas, da ja mara madamar di langit, bulanan, kadong kone onggol-onggol cina malakar kedelé, tahunan, apang ane muani nu satia (literally, if women travel for lights in the sky, let alone for months, although Chinese onggol-onggol is from soybeans, for many years the male will remain faithful, i.e., if the wife is away for months or years, the husband will remain faithful).

The *bladbadan* in Example 5 can be described in Table 4.3 and Example 6 contains two *bladbadan* (6a and 6b), described in Table 4.4.

Table 4.3 Key to *bladbadan* in Example 5

5. Frame:	*malawar gerang*
	making lawar from dried anchovies (lawar is a traditional Balinese dish made with coconut)
Denotation:	*sager*
	a dish of dried anchovy with coconut seasoning
Association:	*cager*
	faithful

Table 4.4 Key to *bladbadan* in Example 6

6a. Frame:	*madamar di langit*
	lights in the sky
Denotation:	*bulan*
	moon
Association:	*bulanan*
	monthly
6b. Frame:	*onggol-onggol Cina malakar kedelé*
	Chinese onggol-onggol made from soybeans
	[onggol-onggol is a Balinese snack made from sago]
Denotation:	*tahu*
	tofu
Association:	*tahunan*
	years

The purpose in using *Bladbadan* 5 and 6 is for people to remind each other to remain *cager* (trustworthy enough to maintain their faithfulness), even if they travel or part ways for *bulanan* (many months) or even *tahunan* (many years). In *Bladbadan* 5, *malawar gerang*, the adjective *cager* is expressed through the denotative meaning *sager* (i.e., *lawar* made from dried anchovies). Because of the rhyming similarity, the noun *sager* is interpreted as the adjective *cager* (trustworthy enough to maintain faithfulness). In Example 6a, the adverb *bulanan* (for many months) is expressed in the *bladbadan madamar di langit* (lights in the sky), for which the denotative meaning is *bulan* (the moon), associated with *bulanan* (for many months). The same semantic process occurs in Example 6b, where the adverb *tahunan* (for many years) is expressed through the *bladbadan ongol-ongol Cina malakar kedelé* with its denotative meaning of *tahu* (tofu i.e., made from soybeans) which is then associated with *tahunan* (for many years).

Paying due observance to equality of relations between the speech participants, using any of these three *bladbadan* is an effort to reduce the seriousness or formality of speech so that the atmosphere becomes more relaxed and less tense. On this basis, using *bladbadan* such as Examples 5 and 6, is a form of coping humour which is an application of the relief theory of humour. Thus, both in structure and use, *bladbadan* humour does not rest on only one particular humour theory.

Wewangsalan

Morphologically, *wewangsalan* derives from the root word *wangsal* (ward), which lexically means *arena* (Ginarsa 2009). In ancient times, the *arena* (or ward) was often used as a gathering place for Balinese people to chat. From the word *wangsal*, the word *wewangsalan* is formed through the morphological process of *dwipura* (reduplication of the front part of the word) and the addition of the suffix {-an}. The word is interpreted as an expression making fun of someone and pragmatically, *wewangsalan* are often used to mock or insult someone (Aridawati 2014). Ridicule or satire expressed through the construction of humour helps avoid tensions in social relationships and is found in most human societies, although some (like Japan) have stringent rules about when and where it can be appropriately used. In the Balinese data collected, *wewangsalan* occurred very frequently. In its pragmatic aspect, this witty humour is based on the relief of tension theory of humour, although it also employs superiority theory. The structure of *wewangsalan* is identical to that of traditional Balinese poetry consisting of only two lines, consisting of one line called *sampiran* and a second containing the meaning, with straightforward poetical rhyme between the two, AA (Pusat Bahasa 2001). The following examples from Simpen (1980: 28) illustrate these qualities:

Example 1.

Asep menyan majegau;   Myrrh, incense, agarwood [all tree-names];
nekep lengar aji kau   covering baldness with a coconut shell

Table 4.5 Rhyming in *Wewangsalan* 1 and 2

1. asep	→ nekep	end rhymes /e/ plus /p/
majegau	→ kau	rhymes at end with diphthong /au/ consonants /g/ and /k/ are sounds produced by the same articulation
2. buangit	→ lengit	rhymes at end with the syllable—*ngit*
kaligangsa	→ gasa	rhymes at end with the syllable—*sa*

Example 2.

Buangit kaligangsa;	Buangit [tree-name], kaligangsa [tree-name];
magaé lengit ngamah gasa	work lazily, eat strongly

The first line of each *wewangsalan* is the *sampiran* which is generally more concerned with form than meaning: even its morpho-syntactic aspects are often neglected. The focus of *sampiran* is on the aspect of rhyme which will be used as a basis for giving meaning. The second line gives the interpretive meaning of each *wewangsalan* which rests on its rhymes with the first line. Semantically, the concept of meaning based on resonance applies to *wewangsalan*. Thus, the interpretation of its meaning rests on a phonetic device and it is this phonetic-semantic likeness that triggers laughter.

Wewangsalan 1 makes fun of people with *sirah lengar* (bald heads). For the Balinese, *sirah lengar* is identified with the coconut shell and covering a bald head with a coconut shell is considered completely futile work: it may hide the ugliness but it still looks bad. *Wewangsalan* 2 is used to make fun of those people who are lazy about work but still have strong appetites for eating. The entailment of both *wewangslan* rests on the following types of rhymes as shown in Table 4.5. Based on such rhymes, *wewangsalan asep menyan majegau* is interpreted by its audience as *nekep lengar aji kau* (cover the bald with coconut shells) and *wewangsalan buangit kaligangsa* as *magaé lengit ngamah gasa* (lazy to work, [but] so strong).

While in *cecimpedan*, humour arises because of a contradictory internal logical structure, and in *bladbadan* as we have seen it emerges from a broader context of use, in *wewangsalan,* it stems from the relation between *sampiran* and a meaning that rests on rhyme. Rhyme in *wewangsalan* can be formed through the processes of assonance and/or alliteration. Assonance is rhyme caused by the repetition of vowels, while alliteration repeats consonants (Kridalaksana 1993): both are used in the following Examples 3 and 4 (from Simpen 1980: 29).

Example 3.

Délem Sangut Merdah Tualén	Délem, Sangut, Merdah, Tualén [four Balinese *punakawan* puppets]
medem bangun ngamah dogén	sleep and awake, always eating

Table 4.6 Rhyme and interpretation in *Wewangsalan* 3 and 4

3. Délem	→	*medem*; repeating vowels /e/ and consonants /d, m/
Sangut	→	*bangun*; consonant /ŋ/ and vowel /u/
Merdah	→	*ngamah*; vowel /a/ and consonants /m, h/
Tualén	→	*dogén*; repeating vowels /é/ and consonants /n/
4. gamongan	→	*omongan*; repeating vowels /o, a/ and consonants /m, ŋ, n/
kladi	→	*dadi*; repeating vowels /a, i/ and consonants /d/
jahé	→	*gaé*; repeating vowel /a, é/

Example 4.

gamongan kladi jahé	lempuyang, taro, ginger [three Balinese tubers]
omongan dadi gaé	talk can be made

The construction of the *sampiran* in these two *wewangsalan* does not pay attention to the morphosyntactic rules of Balinese language. The sole concern is for rhyme as the foundation for semantic interpretation. In both *wewangsalan*, the *sampiran* is only a group of words. In *Wewangsalan* 3, it is a collection of names of clowns in *wayang kulit* and *Wewangsalan* 4 simply groups names of different tubers. Assonance and alliteration between the *sampiran* and its interpretation can be described for both cases as shown in Table 4.6.

Evidently, the force of the humour in *wewangsalan* once again lies in the *sampiran's* relationship with its interpretive meaning, resting on the harmony of rhyme. In all four examples of the relationship between *sampiran* and interpretive meaning involves assonance, because the vowel is the centre of sonority in the rhymes involved. In fact, the construction of any *wewangsalan* always involves vowel rhymes, whether accompanied by consonant rhymes or not. Phonologically, the appearance of assonance in each *wewangsalan* construct is triggered by the nature of the vowel as a syllable centre and, as Staroverov describes (2016), in sonority theory, each word has loudness peaks located on the vocoid. Because of this, the relationship between the *sampiran* and the meaning of *wewangsalan* always involves assonance, either with or without alliteration, as is demonstrated in the following two examples from Tinggen (1988: 25).

Example 5.

Cekcek poléng temisi bengil	Black lizard, dirty snail
desek ngeréng yén gisi nengil	Urge to scream unless it's held still

Example 6.

Sintok pulasari	[herbs and spices in Balinese]
baang acepok nagih sesai	granted once, ask many times

Table 4.7 Sonority in *Wewangsalan 5*

Sampiran	Interpretation	Sonority
cekcek	desek	/e/
poléng	ngeréng	/é/
temisi	gisi	/i/
bengil	nengil	/i/

Table 4.8 Sonority in *Wewangsalan 6*

Sampiran	Interpretation	Sonority
sintok	acepok	/o/
pulasari	sesai	/i/

The peak of sonority in *Wewangsalan 5* lies in the vowels /e, é, i/, as is shown in Table 4.7. Meanwhile, in number 6, the peak of sonority lies in the vowels /o, i/, also shown in Table 4.8.

Pragmatically, Example 5 is used to make fun of a woman's behaviour: if she is teased or pressed by a man, she will *ngeréng* (shout out loud), but if she accepts being held tight, she will *nengil* (be silent). *Wewangsalan 6*, however, ridicules someone who insists on repeating a request that has already been granted.

Cecangkitan

The final traditional humour construct found in the data examined here is the *cecangkitan*, often also called *raos ngémpélin*. Morphologically, *cecangkitan* comes from the root word *cangkit* meaning "lexically tricky" and the term is applied to words that have ambiguous meanings (Warna 1978). The word *cecangkitan* is formed through the process of *dwipura* (repetition of the front part of the word) together with the addition of the suffix {-an}. A *cecangkitan* is made using words, phrases, clauses or sentences that are ambiguous and its alternative name reflects that ambiguity: *raos ngémpélin* is an ambiguous speech. *Cecangkitan/raos ngémpélin* are generally used to make fun of someone or something and to joke around. In traditional performances, *cecangkitan* are often used by the clown characters to arouse laughter in the audience, as is illustrated in Table 4.9. This extract is another episode from the same *wayang kulit* script performed by Cenk Blonk quoted earlier. The two *punakawan* characters speaking, Tualén and Merdah, are complaining about the cost of education. These two clown characters are illustrated in Figure 4.4. Tualén is an old man who has an ugly face with black skin, but a wise attitude. In contrast, Merdah is a female character who is very tolerant and can interact well with anyone.

In this excerpt, the phrase *dana BOS* means "school operational assistance funds". However, Tualén cleverly interprets *dana BOS* as being "funds for the boss". This difference in entailment results from the ambiguous

Table 4.9 Tualén and Merdah discuss the cost of education

Tualén:	*Biaya pendidikan mahal, sekolahé onya bisnis.*
	Education costs are expensive, schools are all doing business
Merdah:	*Bisnis?*
	Business?
Tualén:	*Guru ngaé les, guru ngadep buku, ngadep pakaian seragam …*
	Teachers hold private lessons, sell books and uniforms …
Merdah:	*Kadén suba ada dana BOS?*
	Aren't there BOS funds already? [BOS are governmental school funds]
Tualén:	*Dana Bos kan bosé maan dana …*
	BOS funds are for the boss …

Source: From a video recording of the episode *Sura Bhuta Gugur* (*Death of Sura Bhuta*), performed by Cenk Blonk (at: https://www.youtube.com/watch?v=eZgI6Q3K42E&t=1097s, accessed 8 May 2019).

grammatical construction of the phrase *dana BOS*. First, the phrase itself is an acronym, the abbreviation of *bantuan operasional sekolah* (school operational assistance) funds. This is a Government of Indonesia program designed to reduce the financial burden on parents of students. Second, the phrase *dana BOS* can nevertheless be interpreted as meaning funds for boss(es). Both these semantic interpretations are possible because in

Figure 4.4 Merdah (on the left) and Tualén, two of the many *punakawan* or clown characters in traditional *wayang kulit*, as they appear on the shadow screen for an audience.

Source: Photography by Nengah Arnawa at a live performance in Bali by the puppeteer, Cenk Blonk, in 2019.

the Indonesian language system, word order is an important syntactical device (Kentjono 1984). Thus, word order in any phrase can indicate the origin of something, as in the phrase *orang Bali* which means "people from Bali"; but it can also mean the possessive, as in the phrase *baju Putu*, which means "Putu's clothes" or "clothes for Putu". This grammatical ambiguity is used by the puppeteer to arrive at the two different interpretations and is exploited to produce humour by being linked to a discussion that is a social critique of corrupt education officials.

Cecangkitan like this are generally used in casual verbal speech between participants who already know each other, who are close or intimate. The purpose of its use is to joke and generate laughter on shared themes. Some frequently used *cecangkitan/raos ngémpélin* quoted by Simpen (1980: 53) are:

Example 1.

Lasan mati padang idup apang joan tanema

Example 2.

Tain cicing déngdéng goréng jaen

Example 3.

Cara janiné, anaké nganten makejang beling malu

Example 4.

Batuné ento Culik-Culik bis makeber

Example 5.

Dalangé ento joh-joh pesan kupahan

In *Cecangkitan* 1, there are three words as sources of ambiguity, namely *lasan*, *padang* and *joan*. Viewed as a monomorphemic word, *lasan* means "lizard", but viewed as polymorphemic, then the word derives from the root *las* meaning "sincere", plus the suffix {-an} to express a superlative. Based on this morphological process, *lasan* means "more sincere". The same double interpretation occurs with the word *padang*. Viewed as monomorphemic, it means "grass", but viewed as polymorphemic, *padang* comes from the root *pada*, which, in acquiring the suffix {-ang} becomes *padaang* and, undergoing a process of unifying vowels, becomes *padang* which means "being compared [with]". Likewise with *joan*: when viewed as a monomorphemic word, *joan* means "pole". However, when viewed as polymorphemic, *joan* comes from the word *joh* "far", plus the suffix {-an} and so becomes *johan* and since the phoneme /h/ weakens or causes lenition, it becomes *joan* which means "a bit far". Given such morphological explanations, this *cecangkitan* contains rich ambiguity, yielding the following two possible interpretations, a and b:

a More willing to die than live and at the same time be buried far away.
b The lizard is dead, the grass is alive, but the pole is buried.

In the first interpretation, the speaker chooses to die rather than live; whereas in the second, speakers can be inferred to want to live still because the dead are lizards. The ambiguity is often used to joke and evoke laughter.

Ambiguity in *Cecangkitan* 2 lies in the polysemic word *déngdéng*. Its two meanings are "drying" and "beef jerky". The interpretive meaning of this *cecangkitan* is determined purely by intonation so that if the intonation is emphasised at the end of the word *déngdéng*, it forms the clause *tain cicing déngdéng* (dog turds in the sun). But, if the stress is applied at the end of the word *cicing*, it forms the phrase *tain cicing* (dog turd). Applying different intonation in this way gives this *cecangkitan* two syntactic contour variants, a and b, with ambiguous implications as follows:

a *Tain cicing déngdéng//goréng jaen*
  Dog turds are dried in the sun, fried delicious
b *Tain cicing//déngdéng goréng jaen*
  Dog turds, *déndéng* [jerky] is dried in the sun and fried delicious

For contour a, what is fried is *tain cicing* (dog turd) that has been dried in the sun. For contour b, what is fried is *déngdéng* (beef jerky), while the mention of dog shit is just a trick or distraction. Appreciating the ambiguity of the two possible meanings triggers laughter for the audience.

In *Cecangkitan* 3, ambiguity resides in the adverb, *malu*. This is a polysemic word with two meanings, namely "in front of" and "beginning". Given these semantic relationships, the phrase *beling malu* can be interpreted both as "early pregnancy", that is, pregnant before marriage, and as "pregnant in the front", that is, showing a pregnant stomach, which is of course at the front of the body. In Balinese culture, becoming pregnant too early has a negative connotation because it does not conform to accepted ethics and religious norms. Saying a woman is "pregnant early" can cause a dispute to arise because such an allegation relates to honour and self-esteem. But the second interpretation, being pregnant in front of the body (i.e., showing a baby bump), avoids this threat of tension. The ambiguity of this *cecangkitan* can be summarised in the following two interpretations:

a These days, everyone gets married because they get pregnant early.
b These days, everyone gets married and is pregnant in front.

The ambiguity of *Cecangkitan* 4 derives from the homonym, *culik-culik*. The homonymy of this word is caused by morphological factors. In Balinese, the word *culik* means "poke" and *culik-culik* means "pokes", due to the reduplication process. So, *culik-culik* is a polymorphemic word. However, in the Balinese language, the word *culik-culik* also exists as a monomorphemic form meaning "the name of a crow-like bird". As with *Cecangkitan* 2, the ambiguity here arises from giving a pause in utterance. The pause can be given at the end of either the word *ento* or *culik-culik*, so that the syntactic contour is formed as follows:

a *Batuné ento//culik-culik bisa makeber*
   The stone//*culik-culik* (bird) can fly
b *Batuné ento culik-culik//bisa makeber*
   The stone is poked//can fly

In the first syntactic contour(a), those flying are *culik-culik* (birds); but in (b), what can fly is the stone after it has been poked or pushed. This second interpretation reflects a superstitious belief.

Ambiguity in *Cecangkitan* 5 arises from the polysemic reduplication of *joh-joh*. *Joh-joh* can mean "far away" which collocates with a place, but it can also be interpreted as "far away", collocated with time or frequency. Thus, this *cecangkitan* can be interpreted either way, as follows:

a The puppeteer is very far away
b The puppeteer rarely performs

In fact, the first interpretation is a form of praise implying that the puppeteer is very famous (so, remote from the speaker and hearer). Conversely, interpretation b is a form of ridicule implying that the puppeteer is not very popular and does not sell well in society. The contradictory nature of these two interpretations causes humour.

In general, the forms of Examples 1–5 reveal that the principal instrument for creating humour is vagueness of meaning. This is a natural result of the abstractness of language and several linguistic factors can trigger the appearance of vagueness of meaning. However, in these *cecangkitan* two factors dominate, namely variety of word form and phonetic factors (as noted by Sumarsono 2004). The various aspects of words and their forms include the semantic relations between homonymy and polysemy (Gan 2015). Polysemic words have more than one meaning and, homonymy arises as we have seen when two different words have the same form but each has a different meaning (Arnawa 2008). As noted above, words like *lasan, padang*, and *joan* in the first *cecangkitan*, *déngdéng* in the second, and *cuulik-culik* in the fourth are all homonymic, giving rise to multiple interpretations that cause laughter. The usage of words such as *malu* in number 3 and *joh-joh* in number 5 is ambiguous because of polysemy, but both homonymy and polysemy can cause ambiguity and *cecangkitan* happily combine the two. Apart from these lexical factors, semantic deception is also an effective source of humour in *cecangkitan*. It is supported by phonetic factors, namely pressure and pause, which produce different syntactic contours. This can be seen most clearly in *Cecangkitan* 2 and 4, where differences in intonation, such as pauses, pressure and tone, are reliable phonetic tools for producing imprecise interpretations. *Cecangkitan* are designed to be deliberately ambiguous as a way of generating humour.

The social functions of *bebanyolan* in Balinese culture and conclusions

Bebanyolan, or "humour" in Balinese, is a highly popular genre of folk entertainment. There are many Balinese artists today who are known as *tokoh banyol* (humorous figures, or comedians). They include masters such as I Nyoman Subrata, alias Petruk (b. 1949) and I Wayan Tarma, alias Dolar (1954–2016) in the *drama gong*; I Made Mundra alias Sakuni (aged 62) in the *séndratari*; the puppeteer I Wayan Nardayana alias Cenk Blonk (b. 1966) and in the modern theatre, Puja Astawa (b. 1974) and many others. In Balinese culture, however, humour has never been merely empty entertainment but often serves other social functions. Because humour is a basic element in social interaction between humans, it is often used for very practical purposes, for example, to reduce tension and to avoid conflict. It is known to be an effective means of strengthening social relationships and bonds so as to improve group cohesiveness (Romero and Cruthirds 2007; Martin et al. 2003). While this concept of course applies universally, Balinese people are particularly closely connected by social bonds so that providing the experience of togetherness is often a priority. The institutions known as *banjar* and *témpékan* provide empirical evidence of how strong the notion of community is for the Balinese people and their framework of customs and culture. *Banjar* is the grouping of families within a traditional village in Bali which has autonomy, while *témpékan* is a smaller part of the *banjar* and does not have autonomy. Together, the two structures are responsible for law and religion and serve to cement custom and cultural observance. At even the smallest traditional gatherings and interactions overseen by the *banjar*, humour is frequently expressed spontaneously. Humorous remarks within these customary events are facilitated by the fact that, in general, participants are very familiar with each other and enjoy the intimacy of exchange.

Bebanyolan, in its many forms, is thus an important part of the Balinese oral tradition. It can be found in fairy tales and folk games as well as in traditional art performances. Balinese humour is often packaged in unique linguistic forms, including those examined in this study, *cecimpedan*, *bladbadan*, *wewangsalan* and *cecangkitan* or *raos ngémpélin*, all of which rely on semantic play (as illustrated above). With *cecimpedan*, intention and meaning are manipulated through a contradictory logic and hidden in interrogative sentences. If participants in a verbal exchange of *cecimpedan* can find the right answer, humour and laughter are sure to break out. Like other forms of riddle and joke around the world, the humour of *cecimpedan* rests chiefly on incongruity theory which sees laughter as generated by the appropriate resolution of a conflict of logic (Mulder and Nijholt 2002; Balmores-Paulino 2018; Oring 2016). However, some of the samples discussed above, such as in *Cecimpedan* 7 and 8, also reflect the relief theory of humour which sees humour as a means of reducing tension via a positive emotional charge that reduces tension and anxiety (Morreall 2016; Mulder and Nijholt 2002; Suyasa 2010). *Cecimpedan* 7 and 8, as noted, do not use antonymy relationships between words nor contradictory logic, although like the other examples, they focus on lexical play as a trigger for humour. They carry out semantic manipulation via reference and collocation, but particularly with sexual connotations. As discussed above, these connotations have the effect of "steering" the audience to think that the phrases involved are about the taboo topic of sex and therefore causing tension. The surprise, then, is that the answers to both *cecimpedan* are practical and innocent! Thus, even in these two relief theory examples, words are manipulated and the meaning of the words is hidden while laughter appears when the unexpected answer is revealed.

The traditional form of *bladbadan* is also a semantic and lexical game. The context-bound nature of this form has been noted above and this dependency on context is what gives rise to humour in *bladbadan*. The lexical manipulation in the examples discussed is carried out by changing the word constructions to be longer and by transposing the lexical semantics. However, observing the context in which these *bladbadan* examples are typically used, they can be seen as implementing the superiority theory of humour (Raskin 2008) in which speakers want to laugh at others. This use of humour aligns with the aggressive humour style (identified by Martin et al. 2003; Chen and Martin 2007) whereby humour is used to mock and belittle others, amusing the audience. However, not all *bladbadan* are aggressive, as the discussion of Examples 5 and 6 demonstrated. In these, the position of those involved is equal: participants exchanging these *bladbadan* want to remind each other of the importance of life-partners being equally faithful. Using *bladbadan* to address this sensitive topic is an effort to overcome the seriousness of the situation in which the conversation takes place. Thus, use of *bladbadan* in this context is an effort to reduce tension and reflects the relief theory of humour. This in turn aligns with the affiliative style of humour use (see Martin et al. 2003), where laughter is evoked through spontaneous expressions designed to promote tolerance between participants and maintain social relationships (Yue et al. 2014).

In the case of *wewangsalan*, banter is also conveyed spontaneously to maintain intimacy and relieve tension. In Examples 1 and 2 discussed above, an affiliative style of humour is used to address what would otherwise be embarrassing topics—someone trying to conceal their baldness and someone who is lazy about work but has a strong appetite. In Balinese society, a person with this second kind of character is often identified with I Cupak, a traditional figure in Balinese folklore who is lazy but greedy and eats a lot, someone to be mocked. Nevertheless, the choice of semantic topic and the pragmatic aspect of exchanging this humour reveal that this type of *wewangsalan* also reflects superiority theory in which laughter is conveyed in an aggressive style to criticise others. The clever construction of the *wewangsalan* form serves to make the criticism more palatable and less socially disruptive.

The final form discussed here, *cecangkitan* or *raos ngémpélin,* rests on ambiguity with polysemic and/or homonymic words at the centre of the game. As we have seen, the homonymic or polysemic word is played with in different intonations so that it represents different meanings. That difference becomes a trap for the participants and it is in this trap that the humour of the joking lies. While this form is commonly used for jokes, it is rarely used in serious situations and therefore also represents an affiliative style of Balinese joke, serving to reduce tension and maintain close and intimate social relationships.

Cecimpedan, bladbadan, wewangsalan and *cecangkitan/raos ngémpélin* are all Balinese forms of humorous jokes that are based on semantic and lexical play. Their principal differences are structural but as the analysis has shown, they all rely on ambiguity and contradictory logic to produce humour and laughter. They more often play an affiliative and bonding role in society than an aggressive and critical one, but nevertheless serve as an outlet for social critique and the discussion of serious topics. Their importance to Balinese culture and its people is immense and their clever wit deserves to be better known outside their homeland.

Notes

1 This is officially recognised by Regional Regulation No. 1/2018 (at: https://jdih.baliprov.go.id/produk-hukum/peraturan-perundang-undangan/perda/24561 accessed 13 July 2021).
2 Sources are given below when each example is quoted and discussed.
3 Cited in Tinggen (1988); also in Winaya (2007).
4 Traditionally, audiences only viewed *wayang kulit* from the front of the stage, but today, a second audience may be seated at the rear. The rear view shows more of the puppet figures' artistically coloured carving, and of course, the strings by which the puppeteer controls them.

References

Alwi, Hasan, et al. 2001. *Kamus Besar Bahasa Indonesia (Bahasa Indonesian dictionary).* Jakarta: Balai Pustaka.
Aridawati, Ida Ayu Putu. 2014. *Makna Sosiokultural Peribahasa Bali dalam Seni Pertunjukan Drama Gong Lakon Kalung Berlian* (The sociocultural meaning of Balinese proverbs in the performing arts *drama gong* "Diamond Necklace"). *Jurnal Jnana Budaya,* 19 (2): 167–182.
Arnawa, Nengah. 2008. *Wawasan Linguistik dan Pengajaran Bahasa (Linguistic insights and language teaching).* Denpasar: Plawa Sari.
Arnawa, Nengah. 2016. *Interpretasi Pragmatis Analogis Metafora Bahasa Bali (Pragmatic and analogical interpretation of Balinese metaphor). Jurnal Kajian Bali,* 6 (1): 59–80.

Arnawa, Nengah. 2017a. *Cecimpedan*: Semantic-cognitive process in Balinese children. *Theory and Practice in Language Studies*, 7 (11): 974–983.

Arnawa, Nengah. 2017b. *Bladbadan: Dinamika Semantik dan Pragmatik dalam Bahasa Bali* (Bladbadan: *Semantic dynamics and pragmatics in Balinese*). Denpasar: Pustaka Larasan.

Arnawa, Nengah. 2019. Personification in *cecimpedan*: The semantic structure of the tradition of Balinese children. *Revista Opcion*, 35 (89): 896–912.

Bagus, I Gusti Ngurah. 1976. *Satua-Satua Bali Sane Banyol ring Kesusastraan Bali* (*Funny stories in Balinese literature*). Singaraja: Balai Penelitian Bahasa.

Balmores-Paulino, Rosel S. 2018. An exploration of the schema and function of humor. *Israeli Journal for Humor Research*, 7 (2): 43–63.

Chen, Guo-Hai and Martin, Rod A. 2007. A comparison of humor styles, coping humor, and mental health between Chinese and Canadian university students. *HUMOR: International Journal of Humor Research*, 20 (3): 215–234.

Duranti, Alessandro. 1997. *Linguistic anthropology*. Cambridge: Cambridge University Press.

Gan, Xiaoli. 2015. A study of the humor aspect of English puns: Views from relevance theory. *Theory and Practice in Language Studies*, 5 (6): 1211–1215.

Gibson, Janet M. 2019. *An introduction to the psychology of humor*. New York: Taylor and Francis.

Ginarsa, Ketut. 2009. *Paribasa Bali* (*Balinese proverbs*). Denpasar: C. V. Kayumas.

Gunarwan, Asim. 2002. *Pedoman Penelitian Pemakaian Bahasa* (*Language usage research guidelines for Bahasa Indonesian*). Jakarta: Pusat Bahasa, Departemen Pendidikan Nasional.

Kardji, I Wayan. 1991. *Antug-Antugan: Pupulan Satua Banyol Jaruh* (*Mixed up: A collection of pornographic folktales*). Denpasar: Fakultas Satra Universitas Udayana.

Kentjono, D. 1984. *Dasar-Dasar Linguistik Umum* (*Fundamentals of general linguistics*). Jakarta: Faculty of Science–University of Indonesia.

Kridalaksana, Harimurti. 1993. *Kamus linguistik* (*Linguistic dictionary*). Jakarta: Gramedia Pustaka Utama.

Martin, Rod A., Patricia Puhlik-Doris, Gwen Larsen, Jeanette Gray and Kelly Weir. 2003. Individual differences in uses of humor and their relation to psychological well-being: Development of the Humor Styles Questionnaire. *Journal of Research in Personality*, 37 (1): 48–75. doi:10.1016/S0092-6566(02)00534-2.

Morreall, John. 2009. *Comic relief: A comprehensive philosophy of humor*. Malden, MA: Wiley-Blackwell.

Morreall, John. 2016. *Laughing all the way. Your sense of humour. Don't leave home without it*. Melbourne, FL: Motivational Press.

Mulder, M. P. and Anton Nijholt. 2002. *Humor research: State of the art*. Enschede, Netherlands: Center for Telematics and Information Technology, University of Twente.

Oring, Elliott. 2016. *Joking asides: The theory, analysis, and aesthetics of humor*. Boulder, CO: Utah State University Press.

Ortega, M. Balén Alvarado. 2013. An approach to verbal humor in interaction. 5th International Conference on Corpus Linguistics. *Procedia Social and Behavioral Sciences*, 95: 594–603. At: https://www.sciencedirect.com/science/article/pii/S1877042813042079 (accessed 9 July 2021).

Peraturan Daerah Provinsi Bali Nomor 1 Tahun 2018 tentang Bahasa, Aksara, dan Sastra Bali (Regional Regulation of Bali Province No. 1, 2018, concerning Balinese language, script, and literature). 2018. At: https://jdih.baliprov.go.id/produk-hukum/peraturan/katalog/24561 (accessed 2 June 2018).

Pusat Bahasa, Departemen Pendidikan Nasional. 2001. *Kamus Besar Bahasa Indonesia* (*Dictionary of Bahasa Indonesian*). Jakarta: Balai Pustaka.

Raskin, Victor (ed.). 2008. *The primer of humor research*. Berlin and New York: Mouton de Gruyter.

Romero, Eric J. and Kevin W. Cruthirds. 2007. The use of humor in the workplace. *IEEE Engineering Management Review*, 34 (3): 58–69.

Simpen, I Wayan. 1980. *Basita Paribasa* (*Balinese proverbs*). Denpasar: Upada Sastra.

Srawana, I Gede. 1978. *Mlancaran ka Sasak* (*Traveling to Sasak*). Denpasar: Yayasan Saba Sastra Bali.

Staroverov, P. 2016. Washo onsets and the revised sonority theory. *Open Linguistics*, 2: 471–499.

Sudaryanto. 1993. *Metode dan Aneka Teknik Analisis Bahasa* (*Methods and language analysis techniques for Bahasa Indonesian*). Yogyakarta: Duta Wacana University Press.

Sumarsono. 2004. *Filsafat Bahasa* (*The philosophy of Bahasa Indonesian*). Jakarta: Grasindo.

Sumarsono. 2007. *Pengantar Semantik* (*Introduction to semantics*). Yogyakarta: Pustaka Pelajar.

Suwitra-Pradnya, Ida Bhagawan Istri. 2017. *Purusaha dan Predana dalam Agama Hindu dan Hukum Adat Bali* (*Men and women in Hinduism and Balinese customary law*). Tabanan: Pustaka Ekspresi.

Suyasa, P. T. Y. S. 2010. Identifying types of humor: Funny, funny, and funny. Paper presented at Temu Ilmiah Nasional Psikologi, Jakarta, August 2010. At: https://www.researchgate.net/publication/260751019 (accessed 2 July 2021).

Tinggen, I Nengah. 1988. *Anaka Rupa Paribasa Bali* (*Forms of Balinese proverbs*). Singaraja: Rhika Dewata.

Warna, I Wayan. 1978. *Kamus Bali—Indonesia* (*Balinese—Indonesian dictionary*). Denpasar: Dinas Pengajaran Provinsi Bali.

Winaya, Pande Ketut Kaca. 2007. *Paribasa Bali: Apang Cening Nawang* (*Balinese proverbs: So that you know*). Denpasar: Yayasan Sanggar Seni Dananjaya dan Perpustakaan Agama Hindu.

Yue, Xiao Dong, Katy Wing Liu, Feng Jiang and Neelam Arjan Hiranandani. 2014. Humor styles, self-esteem and subjective happiness. *Psychological Reports*, 115 (2): 517–525.

5 Pluri-modal poetic performance of banter

The *Angama* ritual on Ishigaki Island in Japan

Makiko Takekuro

Introduction

After the scorching sunsets, the shades of nightfall in a quiet neighbourhood on one of Japan's southernmost islands. Out of nowhere, one hears somebody playing a nostalgic melody on a *sanshin* サンシン 三線 (a traditional Okinawan fiddle with three strings, like a shamisen). In the dark, a group of people is parading down narrow residential streets, performing loud music. Some, regaled in colourful costumes, are portraying an ancestral couple and descendants in a ritual called *angama* アンガマ (Yaeyaman performance). They soon vanish from the street into a house. There, a crowd is standing in the garden, surrounding the drawing room. No permit or invitation is required to enter the home, where the doors and windows are wide open. The host's relatives and neighbours, and strangers all go inside. The descendants and the visitors sit quietly in the drawing room and observe the ancestral couple pray at the Buddhist altar, worship ancestors of the household, and congratulate the family on this special occasion. When banter starts, the room suddenly comes to life, erupting with laughter and hand clapping. Why are people laughing at this sacred event?

On Ishigaki Island in Okinawa Prefecture (see Figure 5.1 for the map of location), people celebrate the *sōron* ソーロン 祖霊/旧盆 (Bon festival) festival every summer. Similar to Halloween in Ireland, Canada, and the United States or Día de Muertos in Latin American countries, it is a memorial rite to commemorate the dead and communicate with ancestors' spirits. Among the many festive elements during this commemoration, *angama*, a spectacle unique to this region, takes place. *Angama* refers to a traditional ritual performed by young members of a community association, who visit designated houses and institutions (e.g., restaurants, hotels, nurseries and senior nursing homes). The youth take up ritual chants, sing, dance and perform humorous skits by dramatising the roles of ancestors and exchanging banter with the audience. This chapter describes the humorous performance of banter characteristic of the *angama* ritual.

In recent years, research into humour has increasingly focused on interaction studies and pragmatics. For instance, Japanese humour studies

DOI: 10.4324/9781003176374-5

Pluri-modal poetic performance of banter 89

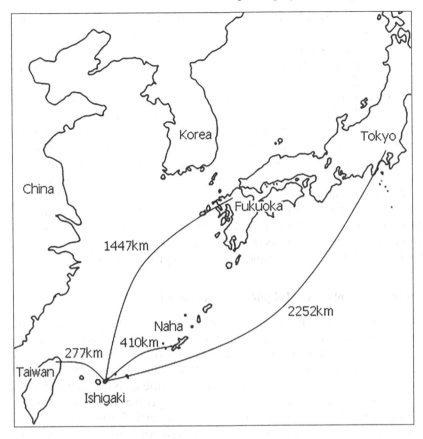

Figure 5.1 Map showing the location of Ishigaki Island and distances to major cities of Japan.

Source: Designed by Motoki Saito, reproduced by permission.

have ranged from the analysis of traditional arts and stand-up comedy to everyday conversations (Katayama 2008; Matsumoto 2009; Murata 2014, 2015; Okamoto 2009; Ōshima 2006, 2013; Stadler 2019; Stocker 2006; Takekuro 2006; Tanaka 2018). The literature shows the significance of humour in social life, as well as the interconnectedness of language and culture. Despite the variety of empirical research, performative aspects of humour have not been given much consideration. Most linguistic studies of humour have concentrated on referential meaning. Only a few studies of Japanese humour have paid attention to modalities other than language, such as body, surrounding objects and environments, although they are in fact inseparable from the way humour enhances its performative effects (Hosoma 2011; Okamoto 2009; Okamoto et al. 2008). Moreover, previous research on Japanese humour has addressed data primarily collected from the Greater Tokyo Area and the Kansai Region or has analysed humour in business settings and media broadcasts. Naturally occurring expressions of humour enjoyed by diverse people in different parts of Japan remain relatively unexplored.[1]

This study reveals the complexities in the humorous performance of banter that has long transcended generations during an annual ritual in a small community on Japan's periphery. Such banter is considered here as a poetic performance (Bauman and Briggs, 1990), embedded in the community's sociohistorical context. To capture the dense layering of language and other semiotic domains in *angama*'s banter, it draws on the concept of "pluri-modality" (Kataoka 2018), which emerged from poetics research. By paying attention to verbal, gestural and non-verbal elements as inherent aspects of pluri-modal poetics (cf. Kataoka 2012; McNeill 2005), the cultural meanings of such poetic performances can be discussed as anchored in the context of the present, which itself is embedded in the reproduction of a ritual frame.

Humour as a pluri-modal poetic performance

In anthropology, folklore and related disciplines, research into performance has enriched our understanding of cultural production. The idea of performance emphasises cultural forms of process and practice. Here, performance is not viewed as a mere reproduction of written or verbal texts exemplifying a certain worldview. It comes to life through socioculturally and historically anchored interaction among people. Bauman (1986) and Bauman and Briggs (1990), who highlighted an artistic and poetic conception of performance as verbal art, considered performance as a communicative event in which the audience expresses their evaluation or aesthetic response. In this sense, the artful use of language in performance enacts "the poetic function, and the essence of spoken artistry" (Bauman 1986: 3). Whether it takes the form of oratory, a performable text, or an everyday interaction, poeticity permeates the conduct of social life. Performance and poetics are socially constitutive and efficacious, and they are both realised only by the joint interaction of many participants, not solely by leading performers.

Humour embodies these characteristics of performance. Beeman (2000) defines humour as "a performative pragmatic accomplishment involving a wide range of communication skills including, but not exclusively involving, language, gesture, the presentation of visual imagery, and situation management" (103). In humour, the presence of an audience matters greatly, as one of humour's purposes is to convey a sense of enjoyment to others, most commonly manifested as a physical display of pleasure, such as smiles and laughter. This study treats humour as a poetic performance that entails verbal and non-verbal stylistics as well as significant audience responses during its dynamic processes.

While verbal texts are still the primary objects of the analysis in this study, insights into the role of humorous performance in a ritual cannot be excluded. The analytical perspective of humour performance must be extended from language into the spheres of kinesics, surrounding environments of the event, and/or symbols. The notion of "pluri-modality" (Kataoka 2018) is relevant to the present study's direction. Pluri-modality comes from Kataoka's prolonged research into poetics. While much of multimodal analysis is geared towards determining the interplay among several modes of communication, such an analysis tends to emphasise ongoing achievements *in situ*, largely disregarding cultural preferences and assumptions. However, he found that more research into tangible and intangible prerequisites is necessary via speaking and via behaviours such as dressing, dancing and musicking to understand the community-based poetic practice. This awareness urged him to adopt the term "pluri-modality" and to explore which elements of cultural performances could be constructed, maintained and naturalised in poetic performance, and how.

Kataoka's studies (2017, 2018) demonstrate the expansion of the analytical perspective of poetic performance including conceptual, somat and physical phenomena. He maintains that poetics and performance are mutually constructive through discursive recursivity or what Bourdieu (1977) calls "*habitus*, systems of durable, transposable dispositions, structured structures predisposed to function as structuring structures, that is, as principles of the generation and structuring of practices and representations" (72). Thus, both verbal elements and non-verbal, bodily and environmental representations concurrent with each other must be incorporated into poetics research. Drawing on poetics and related research in the disciplines of anthropology, discourse analysis and gesture studies (Du Bois 2014; Friedrich 2001; Hymes 1994, 1996; Jakobson 1960; McNeil 1992, 2005; Silverstein 1985; Tedlock 1977; Tannen 1989), Kataoka (2018) proposed the following six broad categories into the analytical scope of pluri-modal poetic performance: sound (e.g., alliteration/rhyme, homophone, sound symbolism and onomatopoeia), language (e.g., linguistic [lexical, morphological, syntactic, semantic pragmatic], textual, discursive, meta-/paralinguistic and prosodic), body (e.g., gaze, gesture, posture, multi-party body formation, scripted/improvisational performance and proxemics), thought (e.g., mental image, theorisation, cognitive constrains/preference and ethnoscience), artefact (e.g., music, sculpture, architecture, art forms, commercial products and visual design) and environment (not necessarily related to human intention or capacity: e.g., climate, fractal structures, birds' flying formation and snowflake patterns). With these broader scopes and enormous research potential, he suggested that poetics research could offer promising paths towards an integrated study of language and semiotic signs. The concept of pluri-modality is thus foundational to this study considering humour as a poetic performance and seeking to expand the analytical perspective of such poetic realisation.

The *angama* ritual on Ishigaki Island

Ishigaki is the main island in the Yaeyama archipelago, and one of the southernmost territories of Japan. Historically, Ishigaki was under the influence of the various power centres including the Ryukyu Kingdom, the Satsuma Domain, the Japanese central government, and the American Occupation. Although the influence of the mainland has been significant for centuries, many cultural events of this island are unique from those in mainland Japan. One such event is the *sōron* festival, held on 13–15 July, lunar calendar.

Similar to the *Bon* in mainland Japan, *sōron* is a festival dedicated to the dead and to ancestors, whose spirits are believed to visit the present life for three days. To welcome these spirits, people light lanterns and offer food, drinks and flowers on an altar, until the ancestors depart on the third day. Despite its religious nature, a cheerful atmosphere prevails, primarily owing to the *angama* ritual, a unique spectacle of the Yaeyama archipelago.[2] There are various views about how and when *angama* began and developed but details remain unclear (cf. Karimata 1993; Kishaba 1976; Sakamoto 2020). Today, *angama* is performed in eight districts on Ishigaki by young members of a community association impersonating the ancestors' spirits.[3] Every evening during the *sōron* period, around 20 performers visit 3 or 4 designated houses as well as places such as restaurants, hotels, nurseries and senior nursing homes within their districts. The young people chant, pray, dance and exchange banter with their audience.

Angama features two leading characters: the male, *ushumai* ウシュマイ 爺 (old man), and the female, *nmī* ンミー 婆 (old woman), portraying an ancestral couple (shown in Figure 5.2). Typically, a pair of males play the roles, dressed in a dark coloured *yukata* or summer kimono, with their faces covered with wooden masks and carrying a leaf fan in their hands. The mask features vary from district to district, but *ushumai's* mask usually has one tooth and *nmī's* none at all.[4] The missing teeth in their masks are not only characteristic of great age but also draw people's attention and become a commonly discussed subject of the banter, particularly among children.

Accompanying the ancestor couple are their descendants, called *fāmā* ファーマー 花子/子孫 (children and grandchildren), who play Yaeyama folk music, sing and dance. They wear colourful *yukata* and thin flip-flop sandals. The *fāmā's* faces are fully covered with cotton towels and sunglasses, and they wear huge straw hats adorned with red or pink artificial flowers.[5]

The performers' appearances have much to do with the premise of the ritual. In *angama*, the characters represent the spirits of the dead and are hence "invisible". Even with the heavy humidity and high temperatures that remain at this time after sunset, the performers are covered from head to toe, barely avoiding heatstroke, in order to retain the invisibility of the imagined spirits.[6] Their ironic appearance, dressed in a mixture of Yaeyaman and Japanese tradition combined with modern fashion, is too salient to escape anyone's attention. Humour often raises a discrepancy between assumption and reality and the gap between the performers' presumed disguise and

Pluri-modal poetic performance of banter 93

Figure 5.2 Ushumai and *nmī* performing *angama*, Ishigaki Island, 2017.
Source: Photography by Makiko Takekuro.

their showy appearance provides a solid instance of humour. Being overtly conspicuous while pretending to be invisible establishes *angama* at the outset as a funny and humorous event.

Humour performance during banter

The data in this study were collected during fieldwork in 2017 and 2019. In those two summers, I was able to videotape fourteen *angama* performances at houses and institutions but only one, performed at a nursery home by a group of children, was entirely conducted in the Yaeyama languages. My analysis is based on video-recorded exchanges of banter as well as personal interviews with some performers and islanders in standard Japanese.[7] I will first address the rules of communication that are widely shared in the *angama* ritual of any district. Following that, analysis of the banter directed at adult and child audience members, respectively, will reveal that despite some differences in poetics, all the humour performances serve to narrate local cultural values in a manner that is easy to understand, entertaining for everyone and confirms the strength of regional identity.

Communication rules in angama

Among the numerous stated and unstated customs regarding the ritual, I identified three noteworthy rules of communication in *angama*. First, *angama* is conducted in Yaeyaman languages.[8] Those who perform as the ancestral couple begin practicing chants and songs one or two weeks before the *sōron* period, because most of the youth no longer speak the Yaeyaman languages daily. As many performers confess, memorising the chants and songs is not so challenging, but holding a substantial conversation in Yaeyaman is. Despite their lack of knowledge and their practising, as a matter of principle, they are expected to use these local languages in the banter and question-answer sequences with the audience, even if they cannot predict the questions. Occasionally, some islanders ask questions in fluent Yaeyaman to test if the young performers properly respond. The performers who cannot understand and speak Yaeyaman fluently tend to avoid such people, standing away from them during the banter. Typically, at the beginning of the banter, one of "ancestors" either declares a code-switch from Yaeyaman to Japanese or requests permission to use standard Japanese, asking *Hyōjungo de ii kane* 標準語でいいかね? (Is standard Japanese okay?) This way, the performers feel freer to engage in the banter, as does the audience, many of whom do not understand Yaeyaman languages either.

The second remarkable rule is that those who play the roles of ancestors should use a falsetto tone, because dead spirits should be portrayed differently from living humans in all aspects, including their voices. Just as their appearance signals the "invisible" identity, their voice must also indicate their spiritual existence. To commit to such roles, performers are expected to vocalise in an extremely high pitch, not only in reciting the prayers but also in the banter. While listening to questions from the audience, the ancestral couple sends constant backchannelling in the falsetto. In their responses, they try to maintain the pitch, although it usually lowers a little. Their shrill voice sounds funny and bizarre enough to make the audience laugh. The third rule is that answers in the banter must be quick and clever—many islanders described this as *tonchi de kaesu* 頓智で返す (provide a quick-witted answer). Those who perform as the ancestral couple are responsible for creating an exciting atmosphere at the event and entertaining the audience. Providing straightforward and serious answers to the audience's questions would ruin the evening and defeat the purpose of *angama*. The performers are expected to use their wits and intellect as much as possible.

Some rules exist for the audience as well. When asking questions, questioners should hide their faces so that they are not visible to the "dead"

Pluri-modal poetic performance of banter 95

spirits. A local myth suggests that if their faces are seen by the dead, they will be taken to the other world. Humour in the *angama* ritual is thus not only linguistically construed but also perceived as part of the comprehensive performance. Many of the tourists and migrants I interviewed at the *angama* site did not understand some of the expressions used in the banter but they still enjoyed the atmosphere and found the entire event hilarious. Overall, everyone's engagement in the fictitious scenario creates a unique and entertaining atmosphere to enjoy the humour.

The next section will analyse actual examples of performances. Differences exist between performances catering to adults and those targeted for children, but collectively such humour performances provide community members and visitors of all ages with opportunities to learn moral lessons and remind them of their cultural values.

Locally based humour among adults

During *angama*, adult islanders particularly enjoy locally based humour that depicts their everyday lives and cultural values within the region. Such humour evidently helps people sense a shared belonging to the same community and unites their regional traditions and cultural values, as is evidenced from the next two examples.

Example 1, collected in 2017 within a residence where numerous neighbours were gathered as shown in Figure 5.3, involves an entertaining question from a male islander. Having listened to prior exchanges between the

Figure 5.3 *Angama* taking place in a family home, Ishigaki Island, 2017.
Source: Photography by Makiko Takekuro.

ancestral couple and others, the man had been considering whether to ask a question. He finally made a decision, received a towel from someone, wrapped it around his head, and hid himself behind others' backs. Absorbed in the fictional world of the *angama* ritual, he began to call out for *ushumai's* attention.

Example 1

Context: The man (B) managed to draw the attention of *ushumai* (U) and *nmī* (N) and began to talk about his band called Ishigaki Store. Pseudonyms are used for all names in this and the following examples. Transcription conventions used in the numbered lines here and in other examples that follow are: . = falling intonation;? = rising intonation; , = slight fall indicating continuity; (( )) = scenic description by the observer; (1) = pause of one second and so on. Terms in bold indicate key expressions discussed.

01. B: *yo, ushumai nmī yo, ishigaki shōten no yo,*
        Hey, *ushumai* and *nmī*, you know, Ishigaki Store
02.   *ishigaki shōten no yo, bando yo, wakaru?*
        Do you know the band called Ishigaki Store?
        ((*Ushumai* pauses for a while))
03. B: *ishigaki shōten wakaru sa?*
        Do you know Ishigaki Store?
        ((SILENCE))[9]
        ((*Ushumai* was thinking and stayed silent))
04. B: *ushumai to nmī ni yo, narau koto ga aru te yo,*
        I want to learn from *ushumai* and *nmī*
05. B: *shitsumon suru surukara, narashōri yo,*
        Let me ask, ask you a question, so please teach me,
06. U: *yo.*
        Oh.
07. B: *sekai de tsūyou suru yo,*
        In order to be,
08. U: *ai.*
        Yeah.
09. B: *ātisuto ni naru ni wa,*
        A world-class musician,
10. B: *nani ga hitsu yō desu ka?* ((people chuckling))
        What would I need?
11. U: *sekai de tsūyō suru ātisuto.*
        A world-class musician.
12. B: *un. gusō demo, tsūyō suru ātisuto.*
        Yeah, a great musician in another world, too.
13. U: *gusōdemo nee, kore yo, nanda,*
        Also in another world. That is, well ...
14.   *Ishigaki shōten, shimazō sa,*
        Ishigaki Store needs island sandals,
15. B: *uba?*
        What?
16. U: *shimazōri.*
        Island sandals.

17. B: *shimazōri.*
              Island sandals.
18. U: *un, utteru shimazōri de yo,*
              Yeah, island sandals that are sold,
19. B: *shimazōri?*
              Island sandals?
20. U: *shimazōri de yo,*
              With island sandals.
21. B: *namae o* [inaudible] *anji?*
              We shall [sell] our name, is that right?
22. U: *ōo.*
              Yeah.
23. B: *waraji na,*
              With straw sandals,
24. U: *uri yo, doko ni utteru ka, zōri yo,*
              As for where the sandals are sold,
25. B: *shima shōri yo,*
              Island sandals,
26. U: *minami.*
             In Minami.
27. B: *minami?*
             In Minami?
28. U: *taira.* ((The audience laughed a lot))
              At Taira.
29. B: *taira.*
             At Taira.
30. U: *un.*
             Yeah.
31. B: *taira shōkai?*
              At Taira Store?
32. U: *un.*
             Yeah.
33. B: *anji? uri, ikuraka ya?*
              Really? Then, how much?
34. U: *uri yo, gusō dewa, sengohyaku en.*
              In heaven, they cost 1,500 yen.
35. B: *sengohyaku en. anji?*
              1,500 yen? Really?
36. U: *minami dewa ne, nisen en.*
              In Minami, they are 2,000 yen.
37. B: *nisen en, anji?*
              2,000 yen? Really?
38. U: *un.*
             Yeah.
              ((The performers began to hold their *sanshin*))
39. B: *rainen wa yo,*
              Next year,
40.   *sekaishinshutsu suru kara yo,*
              We will expand our activities overseas
              ((The performers started to play music))
41.   *ōen shintsuke yo,*
              Cheer us up!

Typical of speech between adult islanders, the man's regular insertion of the sentence-final particle *yo* (bolded in the lines above) at the end of the intonation unit helps create a rhythmic tempo and flow, as in lines 1, 2, 4, 5 and 7. Initially, *ushumai* was not in sync with the man because in the crowd, he could not hear him well, as indicated by a frequent gesture of placing his hand to his ear and pausing between utterances. At the end of line 7, the man changed his tone of voice and segued to his question, marking it with the polite form of honorifics *desu* in line 10. Throughout their exchange, this was the only place where an honorific was used. Generally speaking, the use of *desu* sounds too formal and unnatural and is therefore interpreted among islanders as rather playful in their interactions. As a professional musician and entertainer who had recorded several CDs and toured in mainland Japan, this man was both trying to be funny and genuinely wondering how to become internationally known.[10] In line 10, the audience around him chuckled. One obvious reason is that they thought it too unrealistic to assume international success, even though the band had already gained some popularity on the small island. But another reason was the man's sudden use of the honorific form of address that made the question sound out of place.

In line 11, when *ushumai* rephrased the man's speech from line 7, saying, "*sekai de tsūyō suru ātisuto* (a world class musician)", the man added in line 12, "*gusō* (another world)", a key dialectic word in the *angama* ritual which *ushumai* acknowledged by repeating it in line 13. These turns clarify that the speakers were sharing the same footing (cf. Goffman 1981) and seeking a punchline. In line 14, *ushumai* told the man to buy *shima zōri (shōri)* 島ぞうり (literally, island sandals; i.e., flip-flops) and the audience laughed. Hereafter, *ushumai* continued to lead the banter, aided by his frequent use of sentence-final particles such as *yo, sa* and *na* that create a rhythm. Meanwhile, several uses of "*anji?* (really?)" as a response to *ushumai* in the man's speech reveal his surprise at *ushumai's* idea and in lines 17 through 31, he simply repeats *ushumai's* turns. In line 28, when *ushumai* referred to the store in their district where "island sandals" (or flip-flops) could be purchased, the audience laughed the most. They may have expected to hear the name of some special shop, whose sandals could possibly launch the band towards world-class fame, but the store *ushumai* mentioned was actually very ordinary, intensifying the absurdity of the idea of sandals helping achieve a world-class band.

Ushumai's sense of humour betrayed people's expectations of providing dialogue that was within the ordinary range of conventional ideas and this brought laughter to the audience. Further, in exchanging practical information about the price of the sandals, the two speakers maintained the humorous banter at an everyday level until the remaining performers took up their musical instruments, sending a cue to both performers and audience about the ending. Immediately after the man made his final absurd remark about "*sekai shinshutu* (advance to the world)" in line 40, the loud sound of the *sanshin* fiddles marked the end of the banter. Throughout their interaction, both speakers shared quick turn-taking, witty inventions, repetitions and finally musical cues. All these elements and the fine balance between the two participants served to provide symmetrical and poetic effects to the interaction, creating a true humour performance.

The next example involves participants from a different community association but exhibits a similar interactional pattern in its humour. This encounter was videotaped in a restaurant filled with tourists during the summer of 2017. Since tourists do not know how the banter should go, the community association had arranged for skilled questioners to be present. According to the performers (whom I interviewed later), they intended to introduce the tourists to some basics of the ritual and had therefore planned in advance to ask a question about *ushumai's* teeth, the most common topic in *angama*. Although prior to the banter, they had discussed how to lead the performance and make the exchange funny, they did not prepare a script. In Example 2, a skilled questioner (Q), tied a towel around his head and carried a thin tree branch in order to conceal his identity from *ushumai* (U). Again, the performers created a fictitious foundation for the ritual, even though it was probably not completely understood by most of the audience.

Example 2

Context: The questioner began to address *ushumai* in a falsetto tone. Terms in bold indicate key expressions discussed. Shading indicates repetition and parallelism and underlining indicates onomatopeia.

01. Q:	*ushumai jīchan ga yo,* Speaking of *ushumai,*	
02. U:	*ōo.* Yeah.	
03. Q:	*ha.* [Your] teeth!	
04. U:	*ha.* [My] teeth	
05. Q:	*hā ga yo,* Your teeth are,	
06. U:	*ha.* My teeth	
07. Q:	*zenbu nukete nai ka ne?* They are all gone, aren't they? ((*Ushumai* sighed, making a face))	
08. Q:	*ushumai jīchan ha ga nai sa ne?* Ushumai, you have no teeth, do you?	
09. U:	*nande yo, hā ga naika tte yo?* Are you asking me why I have no teeth?	
10. Q:	*ōo.* Yeah. ((*Nmī* found a little boy in a woman's arms. *Nmī* tried to hold him but he refused and started crying. The audience laughed.))	
11. U:	[inaudible] *yo,*	

(Continued)

12. Q: ōo.
Yeah.
13. U: [inaudible] *yo*,
14. Q: ōo.
Yeah.
15. U: [inaudible] *yo*,
[inaudible]
16. Q: ōo.
Yeah.
17. U: *mukāshi kara no, sensō no toki ni yo*,
Long ago, during the war,
18. Q: ōo.
Yeah.
19. U: *sensō no toki ni yo*,
... during the war,
20. Q: *nichiro sensō ōo*,
The Russo-Japanese War.
21. U: *ano, tā ya hata ni, tā no hata kara*,
Well, from the, the field over there,
22. Q: ōo.
Yeah.
23. U: *amerikagun ga yo*,
Came the American soldiers,
24. Q: ōo.
Yeah.
25. U: *teppō o yo*.
With guns.
26. Q: *teppō?*
Guns!
27. U: *mottekitotte yo*,
They carried guns with them,
28. Q: ōo.
Ah.
29. U: *ano ushumai to nmī no ie ni yo*,
To *ushumai* and *nmī*'s [our] house,
30. Q: ōo.
Oh.
31. U: *dadadada tte, uttekita wake yo*.
They fired guns like "DUDUDUDU"!!
32. Q: *hohoho*.
Wow ...
33. U: *ushumai to nmī yo*,
Ushumai and *nmī* [We],
34. Q: *hō*.
Yeah,
35. U: *fāmā kakaete yo*,
Held our children
36. Q: *fāmā kakaete*,
Held your children ...
37. U: *migi ni hidari ni ashi ni yo*,
To our right and left arms, on our legs.
38. Q: *un*.
Yeah ...

39. U:		*kakaete yo*,
		We held them,
40. Q:		*ōo.*
		Oh ...
41. U:		*nigeta wake yo.*
		And we ran away from the soldiers.
42. Q:		*ōo. ōo. ōo.*
		Oh no ...
43. U:		*ushiro kara yo,*
		From the back,
44. Q:		*ōo*
		Oh ...
45. U:		*amerika* ((holding a leaf vertically))
		The American army
46.		<u>*dodododododododo*</u> *tte yo*
		Fired at us like "DUDUDUDUDUDUDUDU".
47. Q:		*kanpō shageki*,
		Bombarded by warships!
48. U:		*kanpō shageki* *de yo,*
		Bombarded by warships!
49. Q:		*un.*
		Yeah.
50. U:		*soremo yo,*
		Again,
51. Q:		*un.*
		Yeah.
52. U:		*ushumai yo, hā de yo,*
		I stopped the bullets, using my teeth,
53.		<u>*kāāppe*</u>,
		Like "Kapow"!
54. Q:		*hoi,*
		Hey!
55. U:		<u>*kāāppe*</u> *tte yo,*
		Like "Kapow"!
56.		*kizuitara, hā nuketotta sa.*
		When I realised it, my teeth were gone.
		((The audience laughed))
57.		*fāmā mamoru tameni* *yo,*
		To protect our children
58. Q:		*fāmā mamoru tameni*,
		To protect your children
59. U:		*fāmā mamoru tameni*,
		To protect our children
60. Q:		*un.*
		Yeah.
61. U:		*minna yo, hā o, suteta sa.*
		I sacrificed all my teeth.
		((The audience laughed))
62. Q:		*sōo.*
		I see.
		((The speakers exchanged some more words. When Q thanked *ushumai*, the music resumed))

In this example, humour performance was achieved through voice quality, repetition, parallelism, rhythm, onomatopoetic words, gestures and body posture while making use of objects such as a mask and a leaf. Though this cannot be adequately described on paper, both *ushumai* and the questioner vocalised a shrill pitch throughout the banter. The particle *yo* (bolded above) was also salient in *ushumai's* speech. It appears in nearly every intonation unit to which the questioner responded with a short backchannel. These two, the particle and the backchannel, contributed to the fast-forward tempo, as if they were beating cadence together.

In addition, this exchange included many instances of repetition and parallelism (cf. Jakobson 1960) between both intra- and inter-speakers, as indicated in the shaded sections in lines 7–8, 17 and 19 and 37. In the shaded sections of lines 25–26, 35–36, 47–48, and 57–59, the two speakers simply repeated one another's utterances. To convey the content of their story as clearly as possible, they relied on repetition and parallelism so that the information could be better understood. Onomatopoetic words were effectively used along with high-pitched voices. For example, when describing the sound of guns in war, *ushumai* heightened his pitch and said *dadadada* and *dodododododododododo* in lines 31 and 46, also holding a leaf fan vertically in the posture of a shooting gunman. He also used one more onomatopoetic word, *kāāāppe*, in lines 53 and 55, to express how he caught bullets with his teeth. His higher pitch in line 55 marked a climax of the humorous narrative and immediately afterwards produced a vivid contrast with his dramatically lowered voice. The onomatopoeia combined with the high pitch climaxed in the punchline, followed by the lowered voice in relief of tension. In the middle of line 56 when he said "*kizuitara* (when I realised it)", his voice was no longer in falsetto. He sounded stunned, as expressed by a lack of the sentence-final particle *yo* after the word *kizuitara*. The repeated use of *yo* in the previous turns clarified the rhythmic collapse created by the non-use of the particle, strengthening the effect of the punchline.

In terms of the content of the humour, *ushumai* incorporated the story of war into his narratives of Yaeyaman life. He discussed World War II as if it was acceptable and not too threatening, presumably because this region was not affected by ground warfare, although it was damaged by air raids and naval gunfire. Despite being under American rule in the post-war period, on Ishigaki Island, people's feelings were not as bitter as on Okinawa (Main) Island. In addition, the audience consisted of post-war generations of adults, many of whom were tourists from mainland Japan. The performers evidently deemed that the memory of war could be narrated as an unrealistic and comical story. What *ushumai* emphasised was the value placed on family, the importance of life, and the sacrifice that the previous generations had made. Since the *sōron* is a ritualistic period in which people pay tribute to the dead, moral lessons delivered through the banter typically do include cultural concepts, such as remembering the former generations and respecting regional values. This banter was no exception.

Pluri-modal poetic performance of banter 103

The examples in this section illustrate two characteristics of humour in banter among adult islanders. First, the banter never stagnates but rhythmically progresses in short turns with the constant insertion of the sentence-final particle *yo* and quick turn-taking. The duration of the banter is usually no longer than three minutes. In Example 1, after a punchline was expressed at 2 minutes and 40 seconds, the music immediately signalled the end. In Example 2, the banter was shorter, lasting only one and a half minutes. Humour in banter does rely on not only what the primary performers say but also on how all participants speak, including questioners and musicians, each playing a role in determining the rhythm and seeking the proper timing for questioning, turn-taking, repeating, commenting, gesturing and musicking. Impressively, these tasks are shared among islanders without prior rehearsal; although, as noted in Example 2 above, some options may be determined in advance when tourists are present. Second, humorous material is limited to local matters and ancestral worship. In Example 1, such materials include the native islander musician and his band, island sandals, the store in their district and the afterlife. In Example 2, the wartime experience on Ishigaki Island and family ties were the primary topics. In other words, the examples demonstrate how resources for linguistic humour in *angama* rarely extend outside the insular life of the participants and how banter with an adult audience reveals this tendency to think and focus on local life.

Children are more fun than fiction

The banter with children exhibited different patterns of humour from the banter with adults. According to performers I interviewed in several community associations, when they perform the roles of the ancestral couple, they endeavour to keep their own pace and performance style, regardless of the audience. Many admitted, however, that laughter does not occur as much with children. Instead, something unexpected always tends to happen which often leads the audience to laugh. Two examples reveal that children, unlike adults, do not back channel or intentionally ask funny questions. Neither does the banter with children proceed in a fast-forward tempo. However, children's innocence in questions and replies produces plenty of laughter among the adult audience.

The next example comes from the annual *angama* visit to a daycare centre, where more than forty children and their parents, guardians and teachers were gathered (see Figure 5.4). As soon as a teacher elicited questions, a boy raised his hand, stood up, and started asking *ushumai* about his teeth. As this is the most common topic in *angama*, adult islanders must have heard countless versions of the story of *ushumai's* teeth in their lifetimes, and so have some of the children; but it is still often discussed, particularly in banter with small children.

104 Makiko Takekuro

Figure 5.4 Performance of *angama* at a daycare centre on Ishigaki Island, 2017.
Source: Photography by Makiko Takekuro.

Example 3

Key: A = the boy questioner; B, C, D, E, F and G = unidentified children; U = *ushumai*; T = Teacher

01. A:	*utamai,*
	Ushumai,
02.	*nande sono ha ippai aru n desu ka?*
	Why do you only have many teeth left?
	((The audience laughed. The teacher puts up her index finger, showing one.))
03. U:	*ha ippon, ī shitsumon na, un.*
	One tooth. That's a good question.
04.	*demo yo, shitsumon no mae ni yo,*
	But before I answer that
05.	*onamae o oshiete kure yo*
	Will you tell me your name?
06. A:	*Yamashiro Takuya desu,*
	Takuya Yamashiro,
07. U:	*Yamashiro Takuya kun,*
	Takuya Yamashiro,
08. A:	*budōgumi san desu,*
	I'm in class Grape,
09. U:	*budōgumi san, nansai desu ka?*
	Class Grape! How old are you?
10. A:	*yon sai desu,*
	I'm four years old.
11. U:	*yonsai, haha, jōtō danā.*
	Ah, you're four! Great!
	((*Ushumai* patted the boy's head with a leaf))

12.	*nande ushumai wa haga ippon kana?*
	Why do you think I only have one tooth?
13. B:	*mushiba, mushiba dakara.*
	Bad teeth! Because you had bad teeth!
	((The audience laughed))
14. A:	*ojīchan dakara*
	Because you are old!
15. U:	*sō, atatteiru, atatte wa iru.*
	Yes, yes, that is also true.
	((The audience laughed))
16.	*ushumai to nmī **na**, mukāshi kara **yo**,*
	From long ago, *Nmi* and I
17.	*amāi mono ga **yo**, tōttemo suki de **yo***
	Have had a very sweet tooth.
18.	*oi mite, butsudan ni **yo**,*
	Hey, look at the altar.
19.	*kūgāshi, ammāāi okashi **na**,*
	See *kūgāshi*, sweet candy
20. C:	*kūgāshi tte nanī?*
	What is *kūgāshī*?
21. U:	*kūgāshi?*
	Kūgāshī?
22.	*kūgāshi, kore **nā**,* [pointing] *kore,*
	Kūgāshī? It's this [pointing]. This is it.
23. D:	*a sugu chikaku no omise ni mo aru yo*
	I've seen it at the store near here.
	((The audience laughed))
24. U:	*omise ni mo aru?*
	Seen it at the store?
25.	*ā itte shimae. nmī **na**, dāisuki de **yo**,*
	I'll tell you what. We love them!
26.	*ato **na**, chokorēto.*
	And chocolate!
27. D:	*chokorēto daisuki*
	I love chocolate.
28. U:	*chokorēto minna suki?*
	Do you all like chocolate?
29. All:	*hāi*
	Yes.
30. U:	*minna suki da **na**.*
	Looks like everyone likes it.
31.	*minna suki? chokorēto mo.*
	Does everyone also like chocolate?'
32.	*uā **na**, kore mo na, daisuki de,*
	Oh, I love it, as well,
33. A:	*aisukurīmu mo suki desu ka?*
	Do you also like ice cream?
	((The audience burst into laughter))
34. U:	*aisukurīmu mo suki dakedo **yo***
	I like ice cream, too.
	((*Ushumai* was chuckling, turning his back to the children))

(Continued)

35.		*daisuki **sa**,*
		I love ice cream
36.		*de, hai, aisukurīmu mo suki de **na**,*
		Yes, I like ice cream and
37.		*amāāāi mono ippai tabeta ato,*
		After I ate a lot of sweets,
38.		*sonomama kuku tte **yo**,*
		I slept like "zzz ..."
39.	E:	*hamigaki shite nain desho?*
		You didn't brush your teeth?
40.	U:	*atari. a onamae nante yū no?*
		That's right! Ah, what is your name?
41.	F	*goto kana desu.*
		My name is Kana Goto.
42.	U:	*kana chan? kana chan atari **na**, hai.*
		Kana? Yes, Kana, you are right!
43.	F:	*yon sai desu.*
		I'm four years old.
44.	U:	*hamigaki **yo**, hamigaki.*
		Brushing your teeth, brushing your teeth.
45.	G:	*itsumo yatteru.*
		I always do.
46.	U:	*ushumai to nmī **na**,*
		Nmī and I,
47.		*shinakattara dōnaru no kanā?*
		What happens if we don't brush our teeth?
48.	All:	*ū baikin*
		Um, germs!
49.	H:	*shinakattara baikin ga dete kara **yo***
		Germs would come out, if we didn't,
50.		*ha ga nakunaru*
		We'd lose our teeth,
51.	U:	*ā mō deta. hai.*
		Yes, that's it.
52.		*mushiba ni nattekara, bōro boro **na**,*
		After my teeth had decayed,
53.	U:	*nukete, ippon dake nokotetta kara,*
		They all fell out but one, so
54.		*ima wa **yo**, goshi goshi shite,*
		Now, it's like "scrub-a-dub"!
55.		*kirēni kirēni shitete **yo**,*
		I treasure this by carefully brushing it,
56.		*ima ippon dake shika nokotte nai **sa**.*
		Now I only have this one tooth.
57.	T:	*wakatta?*
		Got it?
58.	U:	*wakari mashita ka?*
		Did you all understand?
59.	A:	*hai arigatō gozaimashita*
		Yes. Thank you very much.

Compared to the previous examples with adults, the banter at the daycare consisted of much longer turns by *ushumai* and it is not so balanced. Although tempo and rhythm cannot be fully represented in the written format, the lack of sentence-final particles in the children's utterances, together with long turns by *ushumai* made their exchanges more like ordinary classroom discussion than the earlier examples of poetic humour performance. Similar to the other performers who played the role of *ushumai*, this person also frequently used the sentence-final particles *yo*, *sa* and *na* at the end of an intonation unit—as indicated in the excerpt by bolding—but the absence of back channelling from the children eliminated much of the rhythmic contour in the overall interaction. Moreover, the children received the *ushumai's* story at face value and did not respond with wit as the adults did in Examples 1 and 2. The children responded to *ushumai's* questions quite literally, as they usually would in a school setting. According to the teachers, the children were too stunned and alarmed at the presence of dead ancestors to be able to associate the whole ritual with humour. As a result, the exchange lacked any interplay of wits and appeared more like a regular classroom scene than a humorous performance.

However, the children's spontaneous comments were worthy of attention. For example, in line 1, the boy spoke with a lisp, calling *ushumai utamai*, his postalveolar fricative becoming a dental plosive. In line 2, he said *ippai* (many) instead of *ippon* (one) to describe the number of teeth in *ushumai's* mask. Since the word choice of *ippai* was incorrect, the teacher was anxious to make him realise the mistake by demonstrating "one" with her index finger. These incidents brought mild laughter among the adults in the audience. There was further laughter when another child responded to *ushumai* in line 13 about why he had lost his teeth. Conventionally, a question about bad teeth in an *angama's* mask is responded to with a standard answer that carries a moral lesson. Thus, when the question about *ushumai's* lack of teeth was raised, the adult audience expected that *ushumai* himself would tell a moral story in response. However, before he said anything, this child immediately revealed the punchline in line 13. In line 15, *ushumai*, being in a fluster, admitted that this second child had answered correctly, which made the audience laugh further. Then, in illustrating how the ancestral couple had themselves developed bad teeth, *ushumai* mentioned several kinds of sweets, including a confectionery offering called *kūgāshi* which was on the altar and also chocolates, from lines 19 through 32. The children could not see where this story was heading and interrupted with random comments about sweets, although their comments were by no means utterly irrelevant. In line 23, a girl commented that she had seen a similar offering in a nearby store, whereas the first boy asked *ushumai* in line 33 whether he also liked ice cream in addition to chocolates, which made many adults burst out into laughter. Faced with the children's gravity and genuine curiosity, *ushumai* himself finally could not help but chuckle (in line 34). He had to turn his back to the children to hide his laughter and took some time to recover his straight-faced composure. Some children were so innocently oblivious to *ushumai's* intentions that their own reactions became funny, and ultimately, the main provider of humour could not refrain from laughing like the audience.

The last example to be discussed here formed part of the *angama* visit to an individual's house. The descendants of the ancestral couple being represented sat on the floor on one side of the living room, while more than 30 relatives and neighbours were on the other, all watching the couple and the host near the altar in the middle of the room. When the ancestral couple finished chanting, a boy began to call out to *ushumai*. In this example, it seems that humour and laughter occurred not so much because of what the ancestral couple literally said or did but because everyone was sharing the same space and experience together.

Example 4

Context: *Ushumai* (U) tried to find his way towards the voice of the boy (Y), although he could neither hear nor see since his ears were covered with a towel and eyes with a mask. N = *nmī*; C = another child

01. Y:		*ushumāāi*
		Ushumaaaai!
02. U:		*hai.*
		Yes.
03. Y:		*usshumāāi.*
		Ushumaaaai.
04. N:		*hai, ushumai hai.*
		Yes, *ushumai*, yes.
05. U:		*hai ushumāi tte yonda no wa dare kana?*
		Yes, who called me?
06. Y		*ushumāāi.*
		Ushumaaaai.
07. U:		*hai.*
		Yes.
		((An adult said "Here, here, here"))
08. U:		*hai hai hai hai*
		Yes, yes, yes, yes.
09. Y:		*ushumāāāi.* ((The audience laughed))
		Ushumaaaaaai!
10. U:		*haai.*
		Yes!
11. Y:		*ushumāāi. Ushumāāi*
		Ushumaaaai! Ushumaaaai!
		((*Ushumai* stood in front of the boy.))
12. U:		*namae nani? namae nani?*
		What's your name?
13. Y		*osada yūto.*
		Yuto Osada.
14. U:		*yūto? hai yūtō* ((People laughed.))
		Yuto. Yes, Yuto!

15. Y:		*ushumāi* ((People laughed.))
		Ushumaai!
16.		*angama no ouchi wa doko desu ka?*
		Where is the home of *angamas*?
17. U:		*angama no ouchi wa tengoku ni arimasu*
		Well, the home of *angamas* is in heaven.
		((The audience laughed.))
18. C:		*dōyatte iku no?*
		How do you get there?
		((*Ushumai* put his hand to his ear.))
19.		*dōatte iku no?*
		How do you get there?
20. U:		*dōyatte iku ka?* ((People laughed.))
		How do I get there?
		((*Ushumai* looked at *Nmī*.))
21.		*dōyatte tengoku ni kaeru ka yo,*
		Well, how do we go back to the heaven?
22.		*kita no wa īkedo dōyatte kaeru ka wa,*
		We got here but how do we go back?
23.		*ima kangae chū*
		We're thinking about it right now.
		((People burst into laughter.)) (3)
24. U:		*yūto ima nansai?*
		Yuto, how old are you?
25. C:		*yon.* ((Yuto showed four with his fingers.))
		Four.
26. U:		*yon? ushumai mo yonsai*
		Four years old? Me, too!
		((*Ushumai* made the same gesture as Yuto and the people around them laughed.)) (5)
		((As Yuto shrugged, the audience burst into laughter.))
27. U:		*yūto orikō danā, yō,*
		Yuto, you are such a good boy.
28.		*saigo ni isshoni odori yarōna,*
		Let's dance together at the end, okay?
		((Yuto nodded.))
29. U:		*saigoni na,*
		For the last time!
		((Yuto nodded.))
30. U:		*mattero yo,*
		Hold on a second
31. C:		*arigatō gozaimashita.*
		Thank you very much.

This exchange is also filled with self- and allo-repetition (repetition of words of another, both types indicated by shaded text) as well as with parallelism. In lines 1 through 11, the boy's voice became louder, his penultimate vowel *a* longer, and the audience's laughter greater. When *ushumai* finally stood in front of the boy, the boy shouted again. *Ushumai* imitated the boy's loud voice, shouting back the boy's name in line 14, to which the boy reacted by calling *ushumai* one last time. Watching the two engage repeatedly in calling out to one another, the audience erupted with laughter. Subsequently, to answer the question posited by the boy in line 16, *ushumai* partially repeated the boy's words in a normal voice, not falsetto, and then told him that his home was in heaven. Although his answer was within the *angama's* assumptions, the audience cracked up when *ushumai* gave a straightforward answer to the boy, who looked half-convinced and half-suspicious of the whole story. Further, when answering the genuine and highly practical question from the boy in lines 18 and 19, *ushumai* lowered his voice and looked at his partner *nmī* with puzzlement, giving the audience another opportunity to laugh.

Unlike a stand-up comedy duo performance (*manzai* 漫才),[11] typical in western Japan, *ushumai* and *nmī*, do not engage very often in collaborative conversational humour, regardless of the district on Ishigaki. In this case, *nmī* remained silent and returned no response to *ushumai's* gesture. This meant that *ushumai* had to invent an answer by himself—but he escaped doing that by claiming that the two of them were still thinking about it. By this time, the audience found everything laughable, including *ushumai's* obvious lie about his age and the boy's expressive look in line 26, and was in a mood to respond with more laughter. In this example, therefore, the laughter initially triggered by the boy's act of repetition turned into the audience's realisation of sharing a time and space in which laughter was appropriate, thus contributing to creating and enjoying a festive atmosphere.

In a performance involving children, the linguistic content of the humour can be rather ordinary, because children do not perceive and return quick wit responses in the same way as adults. Therefore, the performers often employ various interactional resources rather than language, such as exaggerated facial expressions and gestures, ritualistic objects, their surroundings and exploit the atmosphere of the audience to convey conventionalised humour that four to six-year-old children can find improbable and funny. Humour in banter with children depends on their genuine gravity and the firmness of their faith in the *angama*'s fiction. Since children often say or do the unexpected, they can be relied on to produce intriguing reactions beyond the adults' expectations. Simply by being children, they are sometimes more humorous than any fictitious performance.

"Think local, act local" in the pluri-modal performance of banter

These examples have illustrated comedic differences that depend on the audience. However, the chief performers' interactional patterns and their fundamental stances towards the ritual remained constant. Looking further at what underlies humour in *angama*'s banter, two perspectives will be useful: the pluri-modal poetics of humour and the participants' commitment to local values and identity.

Overall, humour in the banter was realised from an interplay among various modes of communication, performances and artefacts. Whether or not the audience reacted, the performers in each example tried to maintain their own rhythm through instances of self- and allo-repetition, parallelism, and stress of sentence-final particles at the end of intonation units, as well as occasional insertions of Yaeyaman tokens. In the banter with adults, in particular, short utterances by either of the ancestral couple gave the audience time to backchannel or respond using words of repetition or parallelism, which contributed to forming a rhythm with a good tempo. In the flow of the banter, performers and sometimes the audience too exchanged quick-witted remarks. Before revealing the punchline, however, the performers dropped the use of sentence-final particles and stopped backchannelling while introducing new gestures, onomatopoetic words or wordplays. The humorous punchline was revealed when they lowered the pitch of their voices, evoking laughter. The sound of instruments interrupted that laughter, indicating an end to the banter.

Behind these linguistic moves, there also existed the performers' attempts to perform the role of the *boke* (a funny person or jokester such as a stand-up comedian) in order to maximise the co-present audience's excitement and the festive atmosphere of the whole event. The same kind of pluri-modal poeticity can also be seen in other performing arts such as American Jazz, African–American Spirituals or evangelical preaching. All these contain pluri-modal elements of improvised participation by audience members, call and response, and set cues for drawing to an end. Far from being limited to a manipulation of linguistic referencing, banter is a poetic performance that is only realised when pluri-modal elements are integrated.

Most of what an audience hears in banter in fact reflects a repetition of past performances (Bakhtin 1981; Tannen 1989), even though a spontaneous wit is deemed crucial for verbal exchanges in *angama*. Despite an unspoken rule that performers' answers must be quick-witted and display a sense of humour, the contents and resources for their humour do not extend outside traditionally discussed matters, such as stories about the other world and moral lessons or details about their insular life. For instance, when children asked questions, these were either about the couple's age or lack of teeth, to which the couple responded with predictable answers. Since quick wit is less necessary in banter with children, the performers devote themselves to creating an unlikely scenario such that even the small children can grasp its absurdity. Simultaneously, they do not forget to include moral education, particularly the importance of greetings, acquiring good lifestyle habits, listening to adults' wisdom, respecting elders and ancestors, as well as learning the cultural knowledge of *angama*. To questions received from adults, the performers' answers mostly involved the couple's life stories from another world or trivial matters regarding daily life on the island that would sound familiar to most of the local residents. Regardless of the audience, the resources for linguistic humour in *angama* mostly consist of previously discussed matters or their own insular life.

Today's *angama* illustrates aspects of contemporary identity ambivalence (cf. Bhabha 1994) on the island. Some people recall that *angama* used to be performed in Yaeyaman languages. Today's young performers, albeit with the benefit of an intensive language learning rehearsal before the event, are mostly comfortable conducting the question-answer sequences in standard Japanese with only occasional insertions of Yaeyaman tokens. This provides some people over 70 years of age who are more familiar with Yaeyaman languages with cause for complaint. Ironically, using standard Japanese in this way helps attract more tourists and migrants who come from other regions, who not only observe but also partake in and promote this regional event. Under these circumstances, it seems all the more important that the performers' fundamental stance of placing emphasis on passing down traditions in a relaxed and fun atmosphere remains constant. In this way, humour in these performances, conducted by performers principally for an audience from a similar background and observing the same principles annually, serves ultimately to confirm and maintain local cultural values and regional identity.

Limitations and implications

In this study, I have explored the poetics of banter performance in the ritual called *angama* on Ishigaki Island, paying close attention to the question-answer sessions between the performers and the audiences. The findings suggest that various semiotic elements in the ritual combine to make the entire humour performance effective. Specifically, communicative practices in a space with ritualistic decorations and offerings as well as people's roles, clothing and even the climate and environment, constitute improvised, pluri-modal poetics of banter. These poetics of banter lead to the reproduction of cultural values and a firm ritual framework. Through community-based humour for adults and stylised humour for children, a sense of belonging is obtained and local values and cultural practices are passed on to the next generation.

Although the *angama* ritual on Ishigaki Island has undergone and continues to undergo language shift and language loss in a community which is in itself an interesting research topic, the focus of this study was only on the poetics of *angama*'s humour. Into this analysis, I have incorporated insights gained from ethnography which provide a certain amount of insight into people's values and social relations. Basing pragmatics studies of humour not solely on language but also on the pluri-modality of interaction accessible through ethnography, scholars may be able to gain a deeper insight into the cultural and historical meanings of the way that humour extends importance to people's lives. Such an approach is not only timely and applicable to this small island but can also be replicated in any culture that uses humour, as Japan does, to pass on traditions and heritage.

Acknowledgements

This study was supported by a Grant-in-Aid for Scientific Research C (Project No. 17K02747) of the Japan Society for the Promotion of Science. I would like to thank members of several community associations who granted me interviews and allowed me to videotape their performances. A segment of this paper was presented at the 2nd Symposium of the Japanese Association of Sociolinguistic Sciences in September 2020 and at the 17th International Pragmatics Conference in July 2021. I greatly benefited from comments made by Katsuro Nawa. I am also grateful to Jessica Milner Davis for her comments and suggestions. All remaining weaknesses are my own responsibility.

Notes

1 Some works available in English (Abe 2006; Gerber 2011) have dealt with ritual performances of laughter in rural Japan.
2 Broadly speaking, *angama* has two versions: the *Bon* 盆 *angama* and the *Shitwi* 節 *angama*. While the former *angama*, focused on ancestor worship, is performed throughout the Yaeyama region, the latter *angama*, conducted merely to pray for a good harvest, is passed down in a few communities such as the west side of Iriomote Island. In this study, I use the term *angama* to refer to the former version.
3 In the literature, it is described that a group typically consists of people of ages 2–80 (Ōyama 2005). In 2017 and 2019, I watched 14 *angama* performances altogether, all of which were performed by teenagers and young adults in their 20s and 30s.
4 According to a myth, *ushumai* offered his teeth one by one to a monster each time it attacked his descendants, whereas *umī*, who was blessed with many offspring, lost all of her teeth, giving up one each time she delivered a child.
5 There is no record available of the historical development or transformation of their outfits. It would require careful investigation, but as some residents told me, the resemblances in their costumes to those used in Nishimonai's *bon* dance of the dead in Akita Prefecture and in the Hanagasa dance in Yamagata Prefecture seem to suggest that the outfits in *angama* may not be inherently Yaeyaman inventions.
6 Even a family member might find it difficult to identify their own kin in the group. I once overheard a woman complain that she could not recognise her own daughter because of the unidentifiable outfits.
7 None of the performances analysed in this study involve overlapping participants with other performances.
8 All those I interviewed mentioned *yaeyama hōgen* (Yaeyama dialect) as the language in which *angama* should be performed. However, as many scholars note, what people in Yaeyama may call "dialects" are, technically speaking, Ryukyuan languages that are indigenous in Okinawa (Shimoji and Pellard 2010; Anderson and Heinrich 2014; Heinrich et al. 2015; Hammine 2019). Since the Yaeyama archipelago consists of ten inhabited islands and several islets,

there are numerous such languages. Even within Ishigaki Island, neighbouring districts have their own linguistic varieties that can be mutually unintelligible. My data in this chapter contains standard Japanese with a few tokens of Yaeyaman languages, though it is hard to distinguish which varieties they are within the Yaeyaman group. On this point, I would like to express my gratitude to an anonymous reviewer of an earlier version of this chapter, who commented on these issues.
9 I have omitted material here for the sake of space.
10 According to the band's website, they were serious about becoming world famous.
11 See Chapter 1 for a short account of this Japanese comic form.

References

Abe, G. 2006. A ritual performance of laughter in Southern Japan. In J. Milner Davis, ed., *Understanding humor in Japan*. 37–50. Detroit, MI: Wayne State University Press.

Anderson, M. and P. Heinrich. 2014. *Language crisis in the Ryukyus*. Newcastle upon Tyne: Cambridge Scholars Publishing.

Bakhtin, M. 1981. *The dialogic imagination: Four essays*. Austin, TX: University of Texas Press.

Bhabha, H. 1994. *The location of culture*. New York, NY: Routledge.

Bauman, R. 1986. *Story, performance, and event: Contextual studies of oral narrative*. Cambridge: Cambridge University Press.

Bauman, R. and C. Briggs. 1990. Poetics and performance as critical perspectives on language and social life. *Annual Review of Anthropology*, 19: 59–88.

Beeman, W. O. 2000. Humor. *Journal of Linguistic Anthropology*, 9 (1–2): 103–106.

Bourdieu, P. 1977. *The logic of practice*. Trans. R. Nice. Palo Alto, CA: Stanford University Press.

Du Bois, J. W. 2014. Towards a dialogic syntax. *Cognitive Linguistics*, 25 (3): 359–410.

Friedrich, P. 2001. Lyric epiphany. *Language in Society*, 30: 217–247.

Gerbert, E. 2011. Laughing priests in the Atsuta Shrine Festival. In Hans Geybels and Walter van Herck, eds., *Humour and religion: Challenges and ambiguities*. 55–65. London: Bloomsbury Academic.

Goffman, E. 1981. *Forms of talk*. Philadelphia, PA: University of Pennsylvania Press.

Hammine, M. 2019. Our way of multilingualism-translanguaging to break a chain of colonialism. In C. A. Seals and V. I. Olsen-Reeder, eds., *Embracing multilingualism across educational contexts*. 100–125. Wellington, NZ: Victoria University Press.

Heinrich, P., S. Miyara and M. Shimoji. 2015. *Handbook of the Ryukyuan languages*. Berlin: Mouton de Gruyter.

Hosoma, H. 2011. "Performative awareness" of the Tsukkomi role in Manzai talks and skit performances. *IEICE Technical Report*, 111 (190): 83–86.

Hymes, D. 1994. Ethnopoetics, oral-formulaic theory, and editing texts. *Oral Traditions*, 92: 330–370.

Hymes, D. 1996. *Ethnography, linguistics, narrative inequality*. London and Bristol, PA: Taylor and Francis.

Jakobson, R. 1960. Linguistics and poetics. In T. Sebeok, ed., *Style in language*. 350–377. Cambridge, MA: MIT Press.

Karimata, Keiichi 狩俣恵一. 1993. *Yaeyamashotō no angama to takaikan* 八重山諸島のアンガマと他界観 (*Angama* and the view of the other world in the Yaeyama archipelago). *Bulletin of Kokugakuin Junior College*, 11: 101–135.

Kataoka, K. 2012. Toward multimodal ethnopoetics, *Applied Linguistics Review*, 3 (1): 101–130.

Kataoka, Kuniyoshi 片岡邦好. 2017. *Gengo/shintai hyoshō to media no kyōbōteki jissen ni tsuite—baraku Obama jōingiin ni yoru 2008nen minshutō tōin shūkai enzetsu o daizai ni* 言語／身体表象とメディアの共謀的実践について—バラク・オバマ上院議員による 2008 年民主党党員集会演説を題材に— (The collusive practice of textual and bodily representation and the media: Focusing on Senator Barack Obama's victory speech at the Iowa Caucus Night in 2008). *Japanese Journal of Language in Society*, 20 (1): 1–16.

Kataoka, K. 2018. Poetics, performance, and pluri-modality: From Asia-Pacific perspectives. Paper presented at Sociolinguistics Symposium 22, University of Auckland, 27–30 June 2018.

Katayama, H. 2008. Humor in *manzai* stand-up comedy: A historical and comparative analysis. *International Journal of the Humanities*, 6 (1): 213–223.

Kishaba Eijun 喜舎場永珣. 1976 [1940]. *Iriomotejima no sichi to angama odori hoka* 西表島の節祭りとアンガマ踊他 (Southern Islands: *Sichi* and *angama* dances on Iriomote Island). Tokyo: Yaeyama Bunka Kenkyūkai.

Matsumoto, Y. 2009. Dealing with life changes: Humor in painful self-disclosures by elderly Japanese women. *Ageing and Society*, 29: 929–952.

McNeill, D. 1992. *Hand and mind*. Chicago, IL: University of Chicago Press.

McNeill, D. 2005. *Gesture and thought*. Chicago, IL: University of Chicago Press.

Murata, K. 2014. An empirical cross-cultural study of humor in business meetings in New Zealand and Japan. *Journal of Pragmatics*, 60 (1): 251–265.

Murata, K. 2015. *Relational practice in meeting discourse in New Zealand and Japan*, Tokyo: Hituzi Syobo.

Okamoto Masashi 岡本雅史. 2009. *Kaiwa koozoo rikai no tame no bunseki tani: jissen: manzai taiwa no maruchi moodaru bunseki* 会話構造理解のための分析単位: 実践: 漫才対話のマルチモーダル分析 (Units of analysis for understanding conversational structure: A case study: Multimodal analysis of *manzai* dialogues). *Journal of the Japanese Society for Artificial Intelligence*, 23 (4): 552-558.

Okamoto, M., M. Ohba, M. Enomoto and H. Iida. 2008. Multimodal analysis of manzai dialogue: Toward constructing a dialogue-based instructional agent model. *Journal of Japan Society for Fuzzy Theory and Intelligent Informatics*, 20 (4): 526–539.

Ōshima, K. 2006. *Rakugo* and humour in Japanese interpersonal communication. In J. Milner Davis, ed., *Understanding humor in Japan*. 99–110. Detroit, MI: Wayne State University Press.

Ōshima, K. 2013. An examination for styles of Japanese humor: Japan's funniest story project 2010 to 2011. *Intercultural Communication Studies*, 22 (2): 91–109.

Ōyama Nobuko 大山伸子. 2005. *Yaeyamashotou no dento geino* 八重山諸島の伝統芸能 (Traditional performances on Yaeyama islands). *Creating Music Culture*, 36: 49–53.

Sakamoto Kaname 坂本要. 2020. *Okinawa no nenbutsuka to chondarā: angamā to shima eisā* 沖縄の念仏歌とチョンダラーーアンガマーと島エイサー (Chants and *chondarā* in Okinawa: *Angama* and island *eisā*). *Bukkyō Keizai Kenkyū*, 49: 45–61.

Shimoji, M. and T. Pellard. 2010. *An introduction to Ryukyuan languages*. Tokyo: Research Institute for Languages and Cultures of Asia and Africa.

Silverstein, M. 1985. On the pragmatic "poetry" of prose: Parallelism, repetition, and cohesive structure in the time course of dyadic conversation. In D. Schiffrin, ed., *Meaning, form, and use in context: Linguistic applications.* 181–199. Washington, DC: Georgetown University Press.

Stadler, S. 2019. Laughter and its functions in Japanese business community. *Journal of Pragmatics,* 141: 16–27.

Stocker, J. F. 2006. *Manzai:* Team comedy in Japan's entertainment industry. In J. Milner Davis, ed., *Understanding humor in Japan.* 51–75. Detroit, MI: Wayne State University Press.

Takekuro, M. 2006. Conversational jokes in Japanese and English. In J. Milner Davis, ed., *Understanding humor in Japan.* 85–98. Detroit, MI: Wayne State University Press.

Tanaka, H. 2018. Solo or shared laughter in coparticipant criticism in Japanese conversation. *East Asian Pragmatics,* 3: 125–149.

Tannen, D. 1989. *Talking voices: Repetition, dialogue and imagery in conversational discourse.* Cambridge: Cambridge University Press.

Tedlock, D. 1977. Toward an oral poetics. *New Literary History,* 8 (3): 507–519.

6 Themes, cultural context and verbal exchanges in the cartoons of Machiko Hasegawa

Sachiko Kitazume

Introduction

Much Japanese humour remains unknown to the rest of the world and thus unappreciated outside the country. This is not just on account of the language barrier. Muramatsu (1997) attempted to explain why Japanese people themselves appear humourless in the eyes of many Westerners. He argued that one big difference between Japan and many other societies is that the Japanese do not employ humour as a lubricant in public communication, but exercise it only in private, intimate circles. Nevertheless, humour is publicly available in Japan, including printed cartoons in the newspapers and animated cartoons on television. One much-loved example is a popular comic strip called *Sazae-san* サザエさん, written and illustrated by Machiko Hasegawa 長谷川町子 (1920–1992) from 1946 to 1974. The narrative centres around Sazae サザエ, a good-natured, cheerful, but careless heroine. Its popularity is such that the strip holds the Guinness World Record for the longest-running animated television series in the world (Anime News Network 2013). Its celebrated status in Japan suggests that examining the comic story of *Sazae-san* will likely provide insight into what kind of humour appeals most readily to a Japanese audience.

As a useful contrast, this chapter will also discuss *Ijiwaru Baasan* いじわるばあさん (*Granny Mischief*), another strip written and illustrated by Machiko Hasegawa from 1966 to 1971 (Hasegawa 2001).[1] The main character here is a mean and mischievous old woman whose principal concern is to cause problems and trouble to those around her: a character type directly opposite to the good-natured, cheerful, but scatterbrained Sazae. Strangely enough, this old woman has also become a popular figure, even in the face of her spiteful antics. The themes, cultural contexts and verbal exchanges of the two comic strips will be analysed to hypothesise why both this malicious woman and her kind-hearted counterpart have become endearing humorous heroines.

DOI: 10.4324/9781003176374-6

Methodology

To introduce the examples of humour found in *Sazae-san* and *Ijiwaru Baasan* (*Granny Mischief*), pragmatic analysis will be used, employing the "Twist theory" proposed by myself (Kitazume 2008; 2010a; 2010b). This will reveal the mechanisms of humour in four-panel cartoons and clarify its essence as well as its functions. The pragmatic analysis will argue that in interpreting humour, implicature (in the Gricean sense) plays an important role; especially when, as is common with humour in the form of strip cartoons, a reader has to interpret a hidden meaning between successive panels. Linguistic analysis will also confirm the importance of context when interpreting a four-panel cartoon; especially in understanding Japanese humour in which the context of culture plays a key role.

The following section reviews some competing theoretical approaches to the analysis of humour and outlines what I have called "Twist theory". It argues the importance of this mechanism in humour, particularly in that of the cartoons of *Sazae-san*. I will then review the definitions of "implicature" and "conversational implicature" by Grice (1975) and the notions of "text" and "context" proposed by Halliday (1985), as well as those of "conventional context", "context of situation" and "context of culture". The chapter then outlines the nature and background of the source material, the Japanese comics, *Sazae-san* and *Ijiwaru Baasan* (*Granny Mischief*) and introduces the English version of *Sazae-san*, *The Wonderful World of Sazae-san*. For accessibility in presenting the source material, the English versions of the cartoons are used, accompanied by the original Japanese speech balloons. The comic stories of *Granny Mischief* are then discussed, relating this lady's popularity to the morals embodied in contemporary Japanese culture. Finally, some conclusions are drawn about popular themes in Japanese humour, as illustrated by these two comic creations.

Frames, scripts and "Twist theory"

Many authorities have attempted to identify the essential device at the heart of humour. For example, Koestler (1964: 1–3) contended that both humour and creativity are based on bisociation; that is, connecting two frames of references in an unusual way so that they can create either a new theory in science or a humorous situation. Raskin (1985: 99–147) proposed a semantic analysis of humour named Semantic Script-based Theory of Humor (SSTH), taking a rather similar position that humorous elements are a result of a partial overlap of two different and, in a sense, opposite scripts. Attardo (2001: 22) developed Raskin's SSTH into the more widely accepted General Theory of Verbal Humor (GTVH).

Other researchers place greater emphasis on the context in which language is interpreted, proposing different explanations for the mechanisms of humour. Minsky (1975; 1980) uses the term "frame" for a data structure used to represent stereotypical situations. He argues that the different forms of humour can easily be assimilated within the notion of "framing". Fauconnier (1997: 125–126) attempts to explain the mechanism of humour by introducing cognitive processes that include "frames" and "mapping". Coulson (2001) affirmed the importance of frame-based inferences in language interpretation, claiming that the process of frame-shifting is nowhere more evident than in jokes.

None of these frame-based interpretations, however, work in many examples of humour, as I have argued elsewhere (Kitazume 2010b: 99–120). Here I provide two short examples, both recognisably humorous linguistic constructs:

1 She makes coffee that tastes like cham … poo.
2 A doctor fills out a death certificate and signs his name under the heading "Cause of death".

In No. 1 above, the reader can activate a "good coffee" frame to guide his or her construction of the meaning of the first of two possible scripts, "She makes good coffee that tastes like champagne". However, the second script, "She makes bad coffee that tastes like shampoo", is not constructed by any recognisable frame, because it is highly unusual for coffee to taste like shampoo. Considering that "frame" is the term for a data structure used to represent commonly encountered, stereotypical situations (Minsky, 1975; 1980), the second interpretation of "cham" as "sham" (poo) cannot be generated by what might be called a "bad coffee" frame. Thus, the key to this joke must lie elsewhere. In example No. 2, the doctor's mistake of signing his name under the heading "Cause of death" is highly unlikely and therefore unconvincing, because common knowledge tells us that doctors have a set format for signing a death certificate. Again, the key to this humorous critique of medical malpractice must lie elsewhere.

Elsewhere, I have suggested (Kitazume 2010b: 119–120) that humour is in fact created out of the incongruity between a prototypical and recognisable scenario and a ludicrous one. While the former scenario can easily be interpreted using common sense, the latter can only be interpreted by a twisted or altered interpretation that is not supported by ordinary logic. Thus, in order to interpret humour, we must make a pragmatic approach using notions such as implication and context. The interpretation of humour requires a special way of interpretation that is different from interpreting bona fide communication, because humour involves this "twist". Accordingly, "Twist theory" argues that "the essence of 'humour' is a 'twist'. The 'twist' is a minor alteration, which, in effect, transforms a 'prototypical' scenario into a 'ludicrous' one. The dynamics of this drastic change triggered by a minor alteration produce laughter" (Kitazume 2010b: 23–24).

Consideration of "Twist theory" leads to the question of why we should seek to overturn context, logic and stereotypical knowledge about something in order to create humour. Pragmatics assumes that human beings are constantly trying to interpret utterances based on the stereotypical knowledge and context in which the sentences are uttered. The intention of a humourist however is to offer a temporary freedom or relief from these set boundaries, because humour shows us that any prototypical assumption that we have made about something can easily be transformed into a ludicrous one with only minor alterations (Kitazume 2010b: 23–24).

Implicature and context in humour

An important element of humour is that the most conspicuously intended meaning of a writer or speaker is always hidden so that a reader or hearer must recover the implicit meaning (or implicature) in order to understand and enjoy the humour. Researchers have proposed a variety of views on this notion making it necessary to clarify the meanings of implicature used in this paper.

Grice's theory of implicature introduces the following linguistic terms, "the verb *implicate* and the related nouns *implicature* (cf. implying) and *implicatum* (cf. what is implied)" (1975: 43–44). He argues that what is *said* is "closely related to the conventional meaning of the sentence uttered" (1975: 44). Conventional meaning is limited (strictly speaking) to what is meant conventionally by the sentence and does not include whatever else the speaker may have been trying to convey. Thus, if one says (a) "He is an Englishman; he is, therefore, brave", the conventional meaning is that (b) his being brave is a consequence of his being an Englishman. The meaning of "therefore" generates the implicature of (b). (Other words triggering conventional implicatures are: but, even, too, still, yet, already, again, stop, start, know and regret.)

Contrasting with the conventional implicature, Grice (1975: 45-51) coins the term "conversational implicature" as being essentially connected with certain general features of discourse. For example, A is standing by an obviously immobilized car and is approached by B and the following exchange takes place: A: "I am out of petrol". B: "There is a garage round the corner". B implicates that the garage is, or at least may be open. B tries to give information relevant to A's statement and A will receive a conversational implicature that the garage is open and he can get petrol. According to Grice (1975: 45–47), conversational implicatures arise because in communicating, people expect to obey what he terms the Cooperative Principle and also the subcategorised Maxims of Conversation: Quantity, Quality, Relation and Manner. All of these play a central role in predicting conversational implicatures. Despite this, Raskin (1985) and Attardo (2001) both note that humour disobeys such Gricean principles, as will be confirmed in the following sections of this chapter.

Another important feature in the interpretation of language is the notion of context, which is especially important in the interpretation of humour.

Halliday (1985: 5–6) explains Malinowski's theory of "context of situation" as follows:

> Up to that time [i.e., the 1920s], the word 'context' in English had meant 'co-text'; that is to say, the words and the sentences before and after that particular sentence that one was looking at. Malinowski needed a term that expressed the total environment; including the verbal environment, but also including the situation in which the text was uttered. So ... he coined the term CONTEXT OF SITUATION. By 'context of situation', he meant the environment of the text.

Halliday (1985: 46) goes on to argue that "context of situation, however, is only the immediate environment. There is also a broader background against which the text has to be interpreted: its CONTEXT OF CULTURE". An interesting feature of "context" is pointed out by Verschueren when he argues that the relationship between text and context using the terms "structure" or "linguistic structure" to refer to "text" and "context" in Halliday's definition: "Structure and context ... are not independent from each other; for one thing, every utterance becomes part of the context as soon as it has been produced; together, structure and context define the *locus* of meaning-generating processes" (Verschueren 2008: 16).

Louw and Cilliers (2014: 22) analyse the notion of context into various forms such as "physical context", "social context", "cultural context", etc. This study is not concerned however with the various forms of context in detail. Rather it focusses on the importance of context (in Halliday's general sense) in the interpretation of humour, and on three connections of context: the linguistic context (the lexical items that come immediately before and after any word in an act of communication), the situational context and the cultural context. These are the aspects which will be highlighted in the following discussion of the source material.

Sazae-san (*The Wonderful World of Sazae-san*) and *Ijiwaru Baasan* (*Granny Mischief*)

The post-war comic strip *Sazae-san* was first written and illustrated by Machiko Hasegawa in 1946 for the *Fukunichi Shinbun* フクニチ新聞, a Japanese local paper, and was later also published by the respected national daily *Asahi Shinbun* 朝日新聞 until Hasegawa retired and ended the comic in 1974. A television animation of the strip began airing in Japan in 1969 and is still running today, holding the Guinness World Record for the longest-running animated television series in the world. The animation has 7,000 short episodes and constantly ranks high in the Japanese TV rankings (Anime News Network 2013).

Discussion of these strips will be complemented below by discussion of three strips appearing as Figures 6.4, 6.5 and 6.6, taken from *Granny*

Mischief at, respectively, pp. 29, 37 and 96, which correspond to pp. 30, 41 and 113 of the original Japanese version, *Ijiwaru Baasan* (Hasegawa 1998, Vol. 1). All the cartoons have been published and republished in Japanese, also translated into English and copies are held in the Hasegawa Machiko Art Museum 長谷川町子記念館 (with its website at: https://www.hasegawa-machiko.jp/).[2] The artist was greatly honoured in her lifetime, receiving the Order of the Precious Crown (4th class) in 1990 and the People's Honour Award in 1992.

As previously outlined, the form of the cartoon is a four-frame strip with speech balloons contained within the frame but without captions. Sazae, the main character in the popular comics, is depicted as a cheerful, light-hearted housewife whose carelessness often causes trouble and embarrassment to herself and to people around her. Most cartoon episodes are based on the daily activities of a large family group consisting of Sazae's family and the related Isono 磯野 family. The background to the family situation is that Sazae is a very "liberated" independently minded woman and her mother was worried that she was not ladylike enough to attract a husband, but she eventually married Masuo マスオ, a very earnest and calm man, and they have a son, Tarao タラオ. They live together with Sazae's family, the Isono's. Namihei 波平, Sazae's father, is the patriarch of his family; Fune フネ, Sazae's mother, is a calm lady, trusted by all her family; and the other children are Katsuo カツオ, Sazae's mischievous little brother; and Wakame ワカメ, Sazae's little sister, an honours student whose hobbies are reading and fashion. All these names are comically unusual in that they all relate to the sea. For example, Sazae means a shellfish, Masuo, a spring salmon; Tara, a codfish; Nami (in Namihei) is a wave; Fune, a ship; Katsuo, a bonito; and Wakame, a kind of seaweed.

The popularity of Sazae-san is embodied in bronze statues of the two families located in Sakura-Shinmachi Town 桜新町 in Tokyo, where Machiko Hasegawa used to live. On the pavement of a street named for the heroine, Sazae-san Street サザエさん通り, the bronze statues are placed as if they were real citizens of the town: I saw them there in 2014![3] Far away from Tokyo in Kyushu, the southernmost of the four major Japanese islands, Fukuoka City also has a street called "Sazae-san Street" and an "Isono Square" 磯野広場, commemoratively showing that this is where Machiko Hasegawa originally worked out her ideas for her manga stories.

Humorous narrative in Sazae-san

As source material for the exploration of humorous narrative in Hasegawa's cartoons, three examples, Figures 6.1–6.3, have been selected from *The Wonderful World of Sazae-san*, the English version of *Sazae-san*. They are taken from volumes 12 (Hasegawa 2004b), 6 (Hasegawa 2003) and 11 (Hasegawa 2004a) of *The Wonderful World of Sazae-san*, which correspond respectively to volumes 43 (Hasegawa 1995b), 21 (Hasegawa 1994) and 40

Themes, cultural context and verbal exchanges 123

(Hasegawa 1995a) of *Sazae-san*, the original Japanese version (see List of References for further details). All English translations are by Jules Young and Dominic Young. Figure 6.1 depicts a typical humorous sequence involving Sazae and illustrating her daily life. Its humour will be analysed using the "Twist theory", with reference to the frame and context of the language and situations represented.

The first panel in Figure 6.1 shows a number of people including the heroine Sazae waiting in an orderly line for a bus, representing the prototypical scene and script of "Queue up for a bus". In the second panel, a young man in hippie clothes with a cigarette dangling from his mouth cuts into the

Figure 6.1 The Wonderful World of Sazae-san, Vol. 12, p. 68 (originally published as *Sazae-san*, Vol. 43, p. 98).

Source: Reproduced with kind permission of the Hasegawa Machiko Art Museum.

line, creating a prototypical scene of "Queue jumping". Given that Sazae's character includes a strong sense of justice, predictably she cannot ignore this misbehaviour. In the third panel, she accuses the lady in front of her of letting the queue-jumper in, and uses the derogatory term for a young counter-culture male, "punk": "Are you letting a punk like that jump the line?". This scene represents a prototypical script of "A verbal battle" or a quarrel over public behaviour. The lady responds in an unexpected way, saying "That's my son. He just went to buy cigarettes".

This response alters the prototypical scene of "Queue jumping" into a ludicrous scene of Sazae's carelessness in completely misunderstanding the situation and unintentional rudeness in calling the other lady's son a "punk". Her sense of justice is instantly 'twisted' to become the weakness in her character which is her quick-tempered personality, carelessness and rudeness. The twist lies in a hidden difference between two similar-looking situations: a young man cutting into the line and a young man just coming back into the line he had left. Short-tempered Sazae jumps to the wrong conclusion by failing to think about the context of the situation in which the young man joins the queue. Since neither she (nor the reader) has witnessed the original state of the line, she (and we) fail to bring out this alternative interpretation of the situation and are therefore surprised and, in Sazae's case, embarrassed by the new information provided. This humour clearly exemplifies the theory proposed above that the essence of humour is a twist which is a minor alteration that transforms a "prototypical" scenario into a ludicrous one (Kitazume 2010b: 23–24).

It is also important to note that every panel in Figure 6.1 becomes part of the context as soon as it has been produced by the artist or processed visually by the reader, in the same way as Verschueren's (2008: 16) observation that "every utterance becomes part of the context as soon as it has been produced". Each stage of the four-panel cartoon adds something new and vital to the context: the prototypical scene of "Queue up for a bus" becomes the context in which the next prototypical scene of "Queue jumping" is interpreted. Then this scene, becomes in the next panel the context for interpreting the next prototypical scene of "A verbal battle". In the last panel, all the prototypical scenes related to "Queue jumping" depicted in the first three panels are completely twisted, resulting in a ludicrous scene of "Embarrassment" that leaves the impetuous Sazae without words to explain herself.

The character flaw on which this cartoon is based is that Sazae is a woman who cannot think deeply about things but too readily accepts surface appearances. This characteristic seems to reside in the genes of Sazae's family, as is demonstrated by humorous scenes involving her parents in the next example (Figure 6.2).

The first panel in Figure 6.2 shows Sazae's mother, Fune, at home reading a description of a new cosmetic, which the caption reveals as saying, "It removes wrinkles and makes your skin so fair you'll look like a different

Themes, cultural context and verbal exchanges 125

Figure 6.2 The Wonderful World of Sazae-san, Vol. 6, p. 100 (originally published as Sazae-san, Vol. 21, p. 71).

Source: Reproduced with kind permission of the Hasegawa Machiko Art Museum.

person". In the second panel, she happily puts on the beauty cream, evidently hoping to reduce her wrinkles and to have fairer skin. These two panels represent a prototypical scene of "Beauty (cosmetic treatment)" for an elderly lady who wishfully believes in the efficacy of the cosmetics. The third panel adds another scene to the preceding context. Her husband Namihei sniffs at the written claims about the efficacy of cosmetics, saying, "Huh! A lot of nonsense". This brings in another script, the "Inefficacy of cosmetics", to the preceding context of "Beauty (cosmetic treatment)". His remark in this third panel implies his hard-edged, sceptical way of thinking and low regard for his wife's judgement.

Despite Namihei rejecting his wife's efforts as nonsense, the last panel illustrates his private turn-around, showing him saying "That stuff is just a placebo" while happily putting hair tonic on his bald head. This scene alters the previous prototypical scene by transforming it into the complete opposite. Namihei's image as a man of "Hard-edged skeptical way of thinking" (the implicature from his earlier remark) is transformed into that of a man of "Wishful thinking" (implicature from his action, although not his words) who is making exactly the same fruitless efforts as his wife, wishing to have more hair and using a placebo. The "twist" which distinguishes the two similar actions is the alteration in the context of the situation. This happens whether one judges the similar actions from an objective or a subjective viewpoint. When Namihei thinks objectively of the efficacy of cosmetics as it applies to his wife, he displays a "Hard-edged way of thinking", while when it comes to his own self-interest, he becomes a man of "Wishful thinking". The character flaw on which this "twist" turns is hypocrisy and double standards on the part of the dominant patriarch. The humour created by their revelation engages the reader on the side of the wife, who despite her vanity, is at least honest in her thinking.

Figure 6.3 depicts another humorous story about the ways of Sazae's family and twists in behaviour.

In the first panel of Figure 6.3, Namihei asks his daughter Wakame, "What day is it today?" She simply replies, "Don't know", playing with a cat and paying no attention to him. Namihei interprets his daughter's apparently unfeeling response as a sign that she is unaware that it is in fact Father's Day and in the second panel, he tries to remind his son Katsuo of this important fact by saying, "It's Father's Day!", expecting a warmer response from him. To this, Katsuo just says, "Really?" These panels present a prototypical scene of "Cold attitude to Father", not untypical at the time of growing social change from a traditional patriarchy to a more democratic style of family life in Japan.

The narrative does not end there, however. Faced with an apparently indifferent attitude from his family, Namihei arrives at the implicature that his family is not going to celebrate Father's Day. When this cartoon was drawn in 1963, Japanese society was already witnessing times of change from a dominant and controlling patriarchy to a democratic family style. Interpreted in the context of culture, this cartoon's lament by the father that "It's a sign of the times" implies that Namihei cannot expect to get the respect or even the affection that he used to receive from his family anymore. So, in order to forget his loneliness, Namihei decides in panel three to comfort himself by going to a food stall to have a cup of sake and grilled chicken skewers. This represents a prototypical scene of the "Loneliness" felt by the patriarchal father, based on the implicature from the first two panels that seemed to express his family's indifferent attitude to him.

The last panel, however, reveals the hidden "twist": secretly, his family is actually planning to have a big surprise party with a large cake, a sea bream

Themes, cultural context and verbal exchanges 127

Figure 6.3 The Wonderful World of Sazae-san, Vol. 11, p. 111 (originally published as *Sazae-san*, Vol. 40, p. 126).

Source: Reproduced with kind permission of the Hasegawa Machiko Art Museum.

(traditionally served at festivals) and many presents for their father. The difference between the prototypical scene being planned for of "Father's celebration party" and the ludicrous actual scene of "Father's celebration party without father" is the key absence of the father, who has misunderstood the loving family plans to have a surprise party for him as cold-heartedness. This misunderstanding "twists" a happy celebration party into a disappointing one. The result is humorous but also touching, because the family's goodwill turns out to be in vain, disappointing both Namihei and his family.

128 Sachiko Kitazume

Surveying the examples so far considered, it is possible to summarise across the three narratives: the author, Machiko Hasegawa, depicts Sazae's family as mostly good-natured people who possess small drawbacks that cause many small troubles, misunderstandings, embarrassment, irritation and nuisance. Their undoubtedly good intentions are often defeated by all too human minor failings. In general, then, a "twist" by which a scene of good-natured people ends up turning into a scene of trouble, embarrassment and irritation is evidently a well-appreciated type of humour among the Japanese reading public. It can safely be assumed that the long-lasting popularity of this particular comic is associated with the Japanese culture of "belief in the innate goodness of humankind", originally argued by Mencius 孟子 (4th–3rd c. BCE; see Chan 1963: 49-50) and still embedded in cultural morals today. When this common view of human nature as fundamentally good but flawed is confirmed by a narrative that suddenly "twists" one prototypical aspect of human life into its complete opposite by a small alteration in viewpoint or interpretation, humour is the result.

Humorous narratives in **Ijiwaru Baasan (Granny Mischief)**

After the success of *Sazae-san* series, Hasegawa went on to publish *Ijiwaru Baasan* (*Granny Mischief*), which proved to be just as popular. Here the main character is a mean, mischievous and greedy old woman whose chief interest is to cause problems and trouble to those around her—her family, friends and neighbours. Strangely enough, this woman has also become a favourite figure with Japanese people, in spite of her mean antics. This malicious woman's popularity might seem to contradict the assumption above, that good-natured, cheerful but scatterbrained heroines are the most endearing to the Japanese readers. If it does, then the hypothesis that Mencius's values still characterise popular taste in humour in Japan might prove unsound. To probe this further, three examples of *Granny Mischief* cartoon strips will be examined, selected from the English language edition published in 2001, translated by Jules Young and Dominic Young, and corresponding to the original cartoons published in *Ijiwaru Baasan*, Vol. 1 (Vol. 24 of *Machiko Hasegawa's Collected Works*, 1998).

Figure 6.4 provides a good introduction to the typically greedy and self-interested nature of this anti-heroine, Granny Mischief, although her true nature is not revealed at the outset.

The first panel of Figure 6.4 shows a young lady with an apron crying, "My lovely Siamese cat is lost". In response, Granny advises her to put up a notice. This presents to the reader the prototypical scene of "A lost cat" and "Kind advice" on how to find it. The second panel shows the cat-owner following the Granny's advice and putting up a notice offering a reward of 1,000 yen to the finder. Granny even helps her, with a bottle of glue in her hand. The reader of the cartoon receives an implicature that Granny is showing kind helpfulness to the sad lady. The third panel is dated several

Themes, cultural context and verbal exchanges 129

Figure 6.4 Granny Mischief, 2001, p. 29 (originally published as *Ijiwaru Baasan*, Vol. 1, p. 30).

Source: Reproduced with kind permission of the Hasegawa Machiko Art Museum.

days later and shows Granny suggesting that the reward be raised to 2,000 yen—confirming that all three panels represent a prototypical script of "Granny's kindness" in helping a neighbour in need.

In the last and fourth panel, however, we discover to our surprise that the cat is actually in the hands of Granny herself—she has found or perhaps even stolen it and is keeping it hidden. The implicature now for the reader is that Granny's seemingly kind suggestions stem from her greediness, expecting to get higher and higher rewards for restoring the cat. Thus, the scene of "Granny's kindness" presented in the first three panels is unpredictably "twisted" into its reverse in the scene of "Granny's greediness" in the last

130 *Sachiko Kitazume*

Figure 6.5 Granny Mischief, p. 37 (originally published as *Ijiwaru Baasan*, Vol. 1, p. 41).

Source: Reproduced with kind permission of the Hasegawa Machiko Art Museum.

panel. Granny is not only lustful but also mischievous, constantly planning some prank or other, causing embarrassment, trouble and nuisance to others. The victim of the prank, however, is not always the people around her, as the following example demonstrates.

The first panel in Figure 6.5 shows Granny coming out of the cold bathroom in winter, representing a prototypical scene of "Cold winter". In the second panel, Granny rushes to get her feet under her *kotatsu* こたつ (foot warmer), implying that she wants to warm herself and showing a prototypical scene of "Warm *kotatsu*", a familiar scene in Japan. The third panel, however, shows her astonished face with her hair all blown upwards, signifying a prototypical scene of "Astonishment". The last panel shows an active electric fan under the Kotatsu, gushing out a warm blast of air. The speech bubble then reveals that Granny remembers that it was she herself who set the fan under the *kotatsu* as a mischievous trick to surprise others: "Oh yes, I'd forgotten it was a trap I'd set". The implicature from this final panel is that while Granny intended to surprise others, the victim of the trap is "twisted" to become herself. It implies the ludicrous scene of "A failed trap" that rebounds on its setter, or the familiar trope from folk literature of the robber robbed. The reader's reaction to this "twist" is relief and satisfaction to know that the trickster sometimes becomes a victim of her own mischief.

The moral justification of this clever humour makes it very acceptable to a Japanese audience, because it exemplifies the deeply embedded Japanese cultural theme of "rewarding-good-and-punishing-evil". The moral code proposed by Confucius 孔子 (551–471 BCE) was vigorously promoted by Shōtoku Taishi 聖徳太子 (574–622 CE), who made it one of the seventeen articles in the "Seventeen Article Constitution" 十七条憲法 issued in 604 CE.[4] Prince Shōtoku was such an influential regent that his portrait appeared on the front of the 10,000 yen bill issued by Bank of Japan from 1958 to 1986. From the beginning of the seventh century down to the present, this moral has been rooted in Japanese culture as the basic code of personal conduct.

As exemplified in these two cartoon strips, Granny has a nasty, disruptive personality and enjoys causing embarrassment, trouble and nuisance. Why then is *Granny Mischief* so popular? The previous examples from *Sazae-san* supported the argument that Japanese culture turns upon the assumption that people are—or should be—good in nature so that the humorous "twist" from a scene of good-natured people to a scene of trouble, embarrassment and irritation is a favourite type of rule-breaking humour among the Japanese reading public. Granny, however, is a vicious character causing trouble to people around her. Indeed, Granny is such a notoriously mischievous old woman that her own neighbours tend to evaluate her in that context. Both in the cartoon narrative and on the part of the readers, everyone suspects when she starts to do something that she is likely to be planning mischief: this defines her stock character or stereotype. Nevertheless, the next cartoon shown in Figure 6.6 reveals an unexpected personality aspect for Granny.

In the first panel, Granny is checking what is going on outside her back door. The second panel shows her checking further into the garden and the third depicts her coming back and checking inside the house. These three panels sequentially build up a prototypical scene of "Examining the house closely"—which might be for a very innocent reason. However, the reader, who knows Granny's character, will be suspicious about her intentions and watchful for whatever mischief she might be planning this time.

The last panel definitely brings a surprise rather than confirmation of this prediction: we find her secretly feeding a starving, stray dog. In addition,

132 Sachiko Kitazume

Figure 6.6 Granny Mischief, p. 96 (originally published as *Ijiwaru Baasan*, Vol. 1, p. 113).
Source: Reproduced with kind permission of the Hasegawa Machiko Art Museum.

the speech bubble reveals her as saying, "If people see me doing this, it'll ruin my reputation as Granny Mischief". The implicature here is that she herself knows her reputation as a nasty person, rejoices in it and cannot bear to have it overturned. Thus, she cannot openly show the milk of human kindness. The humour lies in this surprise "twist" from what is predictable (her getting up to mischief) to learning that, despite her reputation, she is sometimes forced to act as a normally generous human being. Granny's sympathy with the vulnerable animal in fact complies with the Japanese moral tenet of "belief in the innate goodness of humankind".

To sum up, while Figure 6.4 shows Granny as a greedy old woman causing trouble to her victims, Figure 6.5 reveals her as a victim of her own mischievous trap—punishment she deserved but escaped in Figure 6.4. Figure 6.6 goes further to show that despite her faults, she possesses hidden kindness but is obliged to live up to her reputation as the mischievous Granny. At a deeper level then, she is the victim of her own character stereotype, ashamed of showing the little bit of human kindness inside her, which she intentionally tries to conceal in order to live up to her reputation as *Granny Mischief*. What is more, this comic strip series allows us to experience a triumphant feeling of superiority over the old woman with the proud face, by seeing her made a victim of her own mischief. From these insights, it is safe to assume that the Japanese audiences love this kind of humour in which becoming the victim of Granny is "twisted" from applying to people around Granny to Granny herself. There is comic relief in finding out that someone gets what they deserve (while not being seriously hurt). In short, the popularity of this old woman is surprisingly closely associated with the cultural context of belief in "rewarding-good-and-punishing-evil".

Conclusion

In order to explore what kind of humour enjoys popular appeal in Japan, this study has analysed two contrasting popular comic strips written and illustrated by Machiko Hasegawa. Close examination of the narratives, scenes and verbal exchanges has demonstrated that the same cultural context of morality underlies the popularity of both contrasting heroines, the good-natured Sazae and the ill-natured Granny. In the daily lives of Sazae, her family and their neighbours as shown in the three strips considered, the problem or source of the comic conflict is that nobody is perfect. Sazae and her husband are good-natured, cheerful but careless; her parents are optimistic people but suffer from wishful thinking. In terms of humorous narrative, each four-panel strip reveals a "twist" that transforms an implied prototypical scene of good-natured people into a scene of minor troubles, embarrassment and irritation. I argue that humour is created in these cartoon narratives when a very small alteration of implied meaning instantly changes a scene illustrating "belief in innate goodness of humankind" into the opposite result.

In the strips featuring *Granny Mischief*, the main character is quite opposite to Sazae and her family: a malicious and greedy old woman who is proud of her nasty reputation. Her popularity contradicts any assumption that only a good-natured and cheerful heroine like Sazae can be endearing for most Japanese readers. However, a closer study of *Granny Mischief* reveals that even this woman possesses hidden kindness and shows that she is on occasion made to suffer from what she has done to other people. In short, this counter-narrative to the first one about a loveable cartoon heroine confirms that the popularity of the second also derives from being based on the morals of Confucius and Prince Shōtoku which are deeply embedded in Japanese culture (and shared with other cultures around the world), the belief in "rewarding-good-and-punishing-evil".

In each of Hasagawa's four-panel strips, these moral lessons are conveyed by careful shaping of the comic narratives and dialogue. This study has shown the important role played by commonly accepted, prototypical scenes and scripts that lead to certain implicatures which, sometimes after lengthy reinforcement, are then overturned or transformed by a simple "twist" into unforeseen contradictions of the implied meanings. It argues that, when appreciated in the light of the associated cultural contexts, it is these "twists" which surprise and delight the reader, giving rise to humour.

Notes

1 An earlier version of this chapter was presented as a paper in 2014 at the 26th International Society of Humor Studies Conference in Utrecht, The Netherlands.
2 I would like to express my sincere thanks to the Hasegawa Machiko Art Museum, Setagaya City, Tokyo, for kind assistance and for permission to reproduce the figures in this article.
3 A similar tribute is paid to Cervantes' Don Quixote and Sancho Panza, whose life-size statues are found on the street of the author's hometown in Spain, Alcalá de Henares, where the 20th conference of the ISHS was held in 2008.
4 For more detail on Shōtoku Taishi and the Seventeen Article Constitution and its debt to Confucius, see http://www.duhaime.org/LawMuseum/Law Article-1182/604-The-Seventeen-Article-Constitution-of-Japan.aspx (accessed 31 March 2021).

References

Anime News Network. 2013. Guinness certifies Sazae-san as longest running animated show, 5 September 2013. At: http://www.animenewsnetwork.com/news/2013-09-05/guinness-certifies-sazae-san-as-longest-running-animated-show (accessed 5 May 2014).
Attardo, Salvatore. 2001. *Humorous texts: A Semantic and pragmatic analysis.* Berlin: Mouton de Gruyter.
Chan, Wing-Tsit. 1963. *A source book in Chinese philosophy.* Trans. and comp. Wing-Tsit Chan. Princeton, NJ: Princeton University Press.
Coulson, Seana. 2001. *Semantic leaps: The role of frame-shifting and conceptual blending in meaning construction.* Cambridge: Cambridge University Press.
Fauconnier, Gilles. 1997. *Mappings in thought and language.* Cambridge: Cambridge University Press.
Grice, H. Paul. 1975. Logic and conversation. In P. Cole and J. Morgan, eds., *Syntax and semantics 3. Speech acts.* 41–58. Cambridge, MA: Academic Press.
Halliday, M. A. K., and Ruqaiya Hasan. 1985. *Language, context, and text: Aspects of language in a social-semiotic perspective.* Oxford: Oxford University Press.
Hasegawa Machiko 長谷川町子. 1994. *Sazae-san* サザエさん. Vol. 21. Tokyo: Asahi Shinbun Publishing.
Hasegawa Machiko 長谷川町子. 1995a. *Sazae-san* サザエさん. Vol. 40. Tokyo: Asahi Shinbun Publishing.
Hasegawa Machiko 長谷川町子. 1995b. *Sazae-san* サザエさん. Vol. 43. Tokyo: Asahi Shinbun Publishing.

Hasegawa Machiko 長谷川町子. 1998. *Ijiwaru baasan* いじわるばあさん (*Granny mischief*). Vol. 1. In *Hasegawa Machiko zenshu* 長谷川町子全集 (*Collections of Machiko Hasegawa*), Vol. 24. Tokyo: Asahi Shinbun Publishing.

Hasegawa, Machiko. 2001. *Granny mischief*. Trans. Jules Young and Dominic Young. Tokyo: Kodansha International.

Hasegawa, Machiko. 2003. *The wonderful world of Sazae-san*. Trans. Jules Young and Dominic Young. Vol. 6. Tokyo: Kodansha International.

Hasegawa, Machiko. 2004a. *The wonderful world of Sazae-san*. Trans. Jules Young and Dominic Young. Vol. 11. Tokyo: Kodansha International.

Hasegawa, Machiko. 2004b. *The wonderful world of Sazae-san*. Trans. Jules Young and Dominic Young. Vol. 12. Tokyo: Kodansha International.

Kitazume, Sachiko. 2008. A Visual study of laughter and humor. Paper presented at 20th Conference of the International Society for Humor Studies, Alcalá de Henares, Spain.

Kitazume Sachiko 北爪佐知子. 2010a. *Warai to yūmoa no shikakuteki kousatsu* 笑いとユーモアの視覚的考察 (A Visual study of laughter and humor). In Yūmoa Saiensu Gakkai ユーモア・サイエンス学会 (Academic Association of Humor Science) ed., *Warai no kagaku* 笑いの科学 (*Science of laughter*). Vol. 2: 63–71. Kyoto: Shoraisha.

Kitazume, Sachiko. 2010b. *How to do things with humor*. Tokyo: Eihosha.

Koestler, Arthur. 1964. *The act of creation*. Hutchinson, KS: Hutchinson Press.

Louw, M., and Du Plooy-Cilliers, F. 2014. *Let's talk about interpersonal communication*. 4th ed. New York: Pearson.

Malinowski, B. 1923. The problem of meaning in primitive languages. Supplement 1. In C. K. Ogden and I. A. Richards, eds., *The meaning of meaning*. 295–336. International Library of Philosophy, Psychology and Scientific Method. London: Kegan Paul.

Minsky, Marvin Lee. 1975. Frame system theory. In P. N. Johnson-Laird and P. C. Watson, eds., *Thinking: Readings in cognitive science*. 355–376. Cambridge: Cambridge University Press.

Minsky, Marvin Lee. 1980. Jokes and the logic of the cognitive unconscious. *AI Memo*, No. 603, November 1980. Cambridge, MA: Massachusetts Institute of Technology. At: https://web.media.mit.edu/~minsky/papers/jokes.cognitive.txt (accessed 15 December 2021)

Muramatsu. M. 1997. Japanese humor: An Oxymoron?. *Japan Update*, July 1997. Tokyo: Keizai Koho Center.

Raskin, Victor. 1985. *Semantic mechanisms of humor*. Dordrecht: Reidel.

Verschueren, Jef. 2008. Context and structure in a theory of pragmatics. *Studies in Pragmatics*, 10: 14–24. Tokyo: The Pragmatics Society of Japan.

7 The *makura* of *rakugo*, tradition and modernity

M.W. Shores

> I try as much as possible to make my *makura* about "now" and "today". I do this to show that [we] storytellers aren't people who simply recite classics—we watch the same news that audiences do, and we have similar feelings. But it's imperative that the contents of a *makura* tie into that day's story, whether it's a classic or a new composition.
>
> —Katsura Ayame III[1]

Introduction

Makura マクラ, 枕 (lit. pillows) are used by practitioners of *rakugo* 落語—Japan's traditional comic storytelling art—as embedded warm-up segments to help their audiences settle in, provide context for the stories about to be told, and prime them for laughter.[2] While there are numerous elements and approaches to *makura*, all have something in common: they are intended to make the audience feel welcome, get in the mood to listen to *rakugo*, and to set the tone for the story that is to come. Most stories in the repertoire call for *makura* and without one of quality, *rakugoka* 落語家 (storytellers; also, *hanashika* 噺家) can hardly get started on the right foot. This study will briefly introduce *rakugo* as a traditional form of humour still popular today, consider its elements including *makura*, then turn to a detailed analysis of *makura*'s elements and functions. Several *makura* in translation are discussed in order to understand why they are important and how they help the old art of *rakugo* stay fresh and relevant to modern audiences.

Rakugo

Rakugo is Japanese comic storytelling. It is a one-person art traditionally performed by men—originally outdoors and then, from around the turn of the nineteenth century, in dedicated venues—but today women are included in the ranks of professionals. There are roughly 900 *rakugoka* based in Tokyo and Osaka, and about 60 (less than seven percent) of these are women. *Rakugoka*, most of whom belong to *rakugo* guilds, wear kimono and narrate stories in both *yose* 寄席 (play-houses) and non-traditional venues. The art is

DOI: 10.4324/9781003176374-7

performed by the *rakugoka* while kneeling on a plush cushion and she or he may choose from hundreds of stories in the repertoire. To be precise, there are two distinct traditions—Kamigata and Edo/Tokyo—thus two repertoires with some overlap. *Rakugoka* employ only two-stage properties, a folding fan and a hand towel. These two items can become virtually anything that one can imagine, from tobacco pipes and wallets to smart phones and X-ray film.

Rakugo is comprised of hundreds of old tales and a growing number of new stories. Since the art is orally transmitted, there are no formal scripts. Masters train pupils in apprenticeships that typically last two or three years. Most early-career *rakugoka* struggle to make a living, but, once a performer establishes herself and gains a dedicated fanbase, the art can be lucrative. *Rakugo* is alive and well today, but one cannot say that all Japanese people go to shows, or even know much about the art—some are hardly aware that the art exists. Some young people view *rakugo* as a holdover from past generations, an art that their parents or grandparents loved. However, today artist numbers are at an all-time high, many performers are active on social media and more younger people are finding new interest in this "hoary" art.

Unlike in Japan's traditional theatre arts (e.g., *nō* 能, *kyōgen* 狂言, *kabuki* 歌舞伎, and *ningyō jōruri* 人形浄瑠璃 i.e., *bunraku* 文楽 puppet theatre), language in *rakugo* constantly undergoes change. This is to be expected of an oral tradition in which each new generation of *rakugoka* must determine what to retain, update, or do away with. There is a perception that *rakugo* stories—that is *hondai* 本題 (stories proper)—over time remain unchanged, but this is not the case. With each generation, each teller, and indeed each telling, *rakugo* changes. As long as *rakugoka* do not depart too far from what is recognised as the "story", they enjoy flexibility about how to present the material. If at some point part of the story is no longer funny or is deemed inappropriate (e.g., mocking people with disabilities), it inevitably gets reworked or cut. Language is updated so that stories set in the distant past remain fresh and modern. But, because *rakugo* is categorised alongside other *koten* 古典 (classical, traditional) performing arts, a misperception remains that *rakugo* is unchanging and therefore too old-fashioned for contemporary audiences to enjoy without being bookish connoisseurs. Importantly, *makura*, the first of three structural components (the other two being *hondai* and *ochi* オチ, 落ち, lit. drop, or punchline), help dispose of such notions and are greatly responsible for *rakugo*'s continued popularity.

Makura

The term *makura* does not belong to *rakugo* alone. It is used in other arts as well. In traditional poetry, one finds devices such as *makura kotoba* 枕詞 (pillow words) and *uta makura* 歌枕 (poem pillows). Typically placed at the beginning of a poem, *makura kotoba* were fixed epithets that served to amplify feelings, imagery and other features. *Uta makura*, as Edward Kamens elucidates, were once booklets containing lexical terms that served as "foundations of poetry", or focal points of "reference" and "reliance". *Uta makura* later came to refer to poetic place-names, "elements upon which the structure of a poem rests" (Kamens 1997: 5). The word *makura* also denotes the head, top, or beginning of a work, as is the case for the preludes in traditional musical genres such as *jiuta* 地歌 and *koto* 琴 music. In *gidayūbushi* 義太夫節, the musical narrative of *ningyō jōruri*, *makura* refers to the aphoristic verses heard at the beginning of each act. The word was used to refer to the introductions before main performances or stories by at least 1711 (Ōno et al. 2002: 1216).

Scholars have spent a good deal of time analysing *hondai* and *ochi*, but *makura* have been rather neglected. This is surprising since *makura* are almost always employed to custom tailor the performance to the audience and bridge the present day to the world of the story. *Makura* are what keep this oral tradition immediately relevant to each woman and man who buys a ticket and takes their seat before the stage. Still, scholars tend to mention them only in passing. One obvious reason for this is that *makura* are topical and fluid in nature, often cut short or eliminated for television and radio broadcasts. Amateur videographers also edit out *makura* before uploading *rakugo* videos to YouTube and other video-sharing platforms. When it appears in print, *rakugo* rarely comes with *makura*. *Rakugo* is not only performative but also intimately communicative—house lights stay on to accommodate this—so one can understand why many deem *makura* irrelevant beyond the live performance. There is no doubt that *makura* are designed and modified for each different live audience (indeed, some artists view them as *himitsu no hanashi* 秘密の話 (secret, private conversations); however, this does not mean they are superfluous, as my personal conversations with individual *rakugoka* confirm.

A primary function of *makura* is to put a human face on the art. *Rakugoka* aim to present themselves via *makura* as relatable and to put the audience at ease. *Rakugo* has become one of Japan's "distinguished" traditional performing arts, but *makura* help keep it grounded. They show listeners that it is not in fact as lofty as some (particularly Tokyo intellectuals in the first half of the twentieth century) have tried to make it out to be. For example, one such wrote that *rakugo*, as an art of laughter, constitutes "the salt of life" and that this is evidenced by the art being featured in respectable anthologies (Noma 1933: i).

Makura help convey the message that *rakugo* is accessible and can be enjoyed by experts and novices alike. While there is certainly a methodology to these prologues, they are equally driven by personal taste. Some *rakugoka* approach *makura* as something to be kept short and engaging, something to help audiences quickly settle in and get in the mood for *rakugo*. They believe *makura* should be kept succinct—five to ten minutes—because audiences attend in order to listen to *hondai*, not to openings. Some disagree. *Makura* are, in their mind, what allow artists to put their individual stamps on the art. They feel that their fans are coming to hear *them*, so, if it feels right and the audience seems happy, they are entitled to continue their *makura* for as long as they wish. Indeed, some *rakugoka* fill more time with *makura* than with *hondai*. Katsura Ayame III 三代目桂あやめ (b. 1964) stresses that *makura* are meant to be introductions: "If a *makura* is too impressive and the audience is still thinking about it during the story proper, the *rakugoka* has failed. *Makura* can be likened to appetisers at a multi-course meal: they're served to complement the main dish".[3]

Based on personal observations and analysis, there are nine prominent elements that *rakugoka* regularly incorporate into their *makura* (see Table 7.1). These are both structural and functional. After the initial greeting, there is no particular order that one needs to follow (or include), but Numbers 5 through 9 are most effective when they link to the *hondai*. Overlap is common and, given the personal nature of *makura*, *rakugoka* sometimes include items not on the list. For example, if the performance is taking place overseas or for an audience otherwise presumed to know little about *rakugo*, one might add an extended introduction to the art. These elements will be discussed in further detail below.

It should be noted that not all *rakugoka* require a list with so many elements. For some, it is simply a matter of whether one is able to capture an audience or not. In discussions with myself, Shōfukutei Tama 笑福亭たま (b. 1975) stated that he learned from his master, Shōfukutei Fukushō 笑福亭福笑 (b. 1949), that *makura* consist of three elements: *tsukami* つかみ (catch), *apuroochi* アプローチ (approach), and *honpen* 本編 (main part).[4] The *tsukami* captures the audience's heart; the *apuroochi* deepens the *rakugoka*-audience relationship; and the *honpen* consists of material that suggests or ties into the forthcoming *hondai*. These three are essentially aims, or actions. When presented with the nine elements introduced above, Tama suggested breaking them into two groups: Numbers 1, 5, 6, and 7 can be considered "representative techniques"; Numbers 2, 3, 4, 8, 9 are "desired results". Applied to his three-constituent *makura*, the *tsukami* encompasses the greeting {1} (and opening laughs), resulting in being able to "feel out" the audience {2} and break ice {3}; the *apuroochi* encompasses topical material {5}, *kobanashi* and jokes {6}, *rakugo* information {7}, resulting in rapport building {3} and establishment of artistic authenticity {4}. Finally, the *honpen* encompasses

Table 7.1 Selected *makura* elements

1.	Greet the audience
2.	"Feel out" the audience
3.	Break ice, build rapport
4.	Establish artistic authenticity
5.	Present topical material
6.	Tell *kobanashi* 小話, 小咄 (literally, short tales, make jokes)
7.	Instruct/teach audience about *rakugo* past and present
8.	Transport audience to a different time/place
9.	Set up a smooth transition into the hondai

anything from the list (including knowledge about the seasons, discussion of history, anecdotes about one's private life) that relates to the *hondai*, resulting in a smooth transition {9}. Like other *rakugoka*, Tama considers *makura* to be *rakugo*'s privileged, secret *naibu jijō* 内部事情 (internal affairs), meant only for the people attending a given live performance.

Ui Mushū has pointed out that some stories, namely those less comic and more dramatic, scary, or tense, are better with short *makura* or no *makura* at all (Ui 1965: 23–24). This in theory and in practice, keeps the audience at a distance, disallowing them the chance to get comfortable or warm to the performer. Kamigata *rakugoka* Katsura Fukudanji IV 四代目桂福団治 (b. 1940) recently presented the following brief and self-ridiculing *makura* before telling the heartrending tale *Nezumi ana* ねずみ穴 (*Mousehole*). The numbers inserted in curly brackets identify the corresponding *makura* elements listed in Table 7.1.

> I'm the last one [you have to listen to], so… {1, 2, 3} (*audience laughter*) Yeah, well, I've been at this a long time… {4} You can tell by looking at my hair, right? I'm "Kamigata" *rakugo* in the flesh.[5] {4, 6} (*laughter*) I've been doing this for more than a half-century… {4} I'm tired. {6} (*laughter*) This isn't necessarily an exhausting line of work though. After all, all I've done for fifty years is hold this fan here. {4} These days, I use it to prop up this old body of mine. {6} (*laughter*) *Rakugo* stories can be fun even if you just read them. Old classics, there are hundreds of them. {7, 8} But you know what? Some stories from beginning to end aren't a bit funny. You can't laugh no matter how hard you try. Rather, it would be rude if you did. {7, 8} Listening to those stories, you fall into a dark melancholy—the type of story that sends audiences home depressed. {6} (*laughter*) … I'm going to tell you one of those right now. {6, 9} (*laughter*)[6] (Terebi bangumi)

The story that Fukudanji IV follows this with concerns two brothers who receive an equal inheritance after their father's death. The older brother turns his share into a fortune through hard work; the younger squanders his away on alcohol, gambling, and geisha. Wishing to change his ways, the younger brother goes to the other to ask for financial help but gets only an insulting three copper coins. The pitiful story that plays out invites tears rather than laughter. Still, seasoned *rakugo* audiences know that *ninjōbanashi* 人情噺 (stories of human emotion) like this tend to end on a happy note. Fukudanji IV skilfully sets up *Nezumi ana* by keeping his *makura* short and maintaining a degree of distance and tension, saying just enough to let the audience settle in. He makes them laugh at his pithy self-deprecation, including personal matters such as his long career, aging and thinning hair, and assumes the role of lecturer when explaining that not all *rakugo* is meant to make audiences laugh. But he keeps it short because the *hondai* calls for that.

It is natural that *rakugoka* will have different approaches to winning over audiences. Some open deliberately with a slow tempo while others prefer

The makura *of* rakugo, *tradition and modernity* 141

to hit the ground running. An artist may be impelled to change *makura* delivery, based on the material or style of the *rakugoka* (or other variety act) ahead of them in the line-up. The audience's responsiveness also comes into play. Although not documented, this must surely have been the case since the early nineteenth century when telling stories to paying audiences in fixed venues became the norm. To gauge listeners today, some *rakugoka* get started before taking the stage: they listen to and/or watch monitors in the dressing room, and it is common to see them standing in the wings taking mental notes on the audience prior to their own sets.

Other factors that influence *makura* (and story selection) include anything from audience age and gender to that day's weather and current events. *Yose* managers try to help with this too, for example, by noting (on bulletin boards, etc.) when a large group is attending from a school, an aged care facility, or a business corporation. Despite their different approaches, most *rakugoka* would agree that one's goal should be to *kyaku o raku ni saseru* 客を楽にさせる or, to put the audience at ease—make them feel good. *Yose* are designed and decorated with this in mind, in fact. They are meant to look and feel like extensions of one's own home. One illustration of this is the framed calligraphy that one sees hung on the back walls of stages. Figure 7.1 shows an example on display at the Tenma Tenjin Hanjōtei in Osaka; written by Katsura Beichō III 三代目桂米朝 (1925–2015), it reads *raku* 樂 (ease, comfort).[7]

Figure 7.1 The stage at Tenma Tenjin Hanjōtei. Opened in 2006, this was Osaka's first formal *yose* of the post-World War II era.

Source: Photograph copyright Kamigata Rakugo Kyōkai 上方落語協会, reproduced with kind permission.

The nine elements of *makura*

Greeting the audience

The *rakugoka* greeting begins when she enters the stage and makes eye contact with members of the audience. She proceeds to downstage centre, takes her seat, kneeling on a plush cushion called a *zabuton* 座布団. She ceremoniously places her fan before her knees, places her hands behind it, then bows deeply to the audience. The placing of the fan marks the ritual of two worlds coming together, with a boundary maintained. Next, she thanks the audience for coming or makes some other formal acknowledgement or address. This is the *maeoki* 前置き (introductory remarks) and a scholar such as Nomura Masaaki does not consider this as part of the *makura* linguistically, but concedes that it is linked and can be viewed as one element (Nomura 1994: 66).

As noted above, it is crucial that *rakugoka* make a strong start and there are many ways to do this. Choosing language is at the forefront of the decisions to be made. There are inevitably those who use casual or even blunt language, but this is generally done to signal intimacy or otherwise to feed into the performer's persona whether it be devil-may-care, nonconformist, or pithy. Most use polite and honorific language from the start, however: the *-desu/-masu* です・ます (formal copula) form is prevalent and the humble equivalent *-de gozaimasu* でございます often replaces *-desu*. When thanking audiences, *rakugoka* use the honorific *-te itadaku* ていただく (receive) and *-te kudasaru* てくださる (give me) far more often than the polite *-te kureru* てくれる (give me) and *-te morau* てもらう (receive). As Chiyo Kyono points out, *-te kureru* and *-te morau* grammatically mark the speaker's construal of the event in referential usage while *-te itadaku* and *-te kudasaru* intrinsically carry interpersonal meanings in any speech act. Of special interest is that the honorific choice conveys substantial attention to the addressee's welfare (*ki o tsukau* 気を使う or, use mind/heart attention) (Kyono 2017: 51). This corresponds to *rakugoka* philosophy, which as a rule elevates audience and individual patron.

"Feeling out" the audience

Makura are devised so that *rakugoka* can get a feel for audiences and set the tone for what is to come, but it is often the case that they do not even decide which story they are going to tell until they are well into the *makura*. For example, if an audience has just come in from the summer heat and is fanning themselves with programmes, a *rakugoka* would be inclined to tell a story that literally has a chilling effect—like a ghost story. If an audience appears to be somewhat melancholy (or conversely, rambunctious), the *rakugoka* may wish to tell a story that takes listeners in a different emotional direction. Some *rakugoka* say the art is about capturing the audience, keeping them tied to a string and at the end, cutting them loose with the *ochi*. To do this efficiently, one needs time to feel out the audience during the *makura* and, as mentioned, sometimes backstage before even entering. Naturally, the artist continues reading the audience throughout the *makura* until the end of the performance.

Breaking ice, building rapport

Rakugoka are viewed as Japan's traditional funny women and men. While they no longer enjoy the following they once did, namely in the Meiji period (1868–1912), they are routinely guests on Japanese game shows and talk shows. Some host their own radio and TV shows and a handful have become national celebrities. Nevertheless, there is something that remains "lofty" about *rakugoka*, not necessarily because they call for it (though some do), but because scholars and critics have painted them with such a brush. Still, people who buy tickets to *rakugo* generally understand that *rakugoka* are in the business of making comedy—lofty or not—and expect them to say or do something funny. Predictably, making the audience laugh is the most common way for *rakugoka* to break the ice. This is accomplished in various ways, including feigning a stumble on the way (or giddily prancing) to downstage centre, using one-liners and self-deprecating humour, or giving a sheepish smile. *Gyagu* ギャグ (gags) can be useful too: Hayashiya Someta 林家染太 (b. 1975), who weighs more than the average Japanese man, often tells his audiences that he is the Anpanman of the *rakugo* world.[8] *Rakugoka* use *gyagu* as a *tsukami*, which helps endear them to the audience, drawing it closer.

Rakugoka also employ honorific language to win their audience. Considering that honorifics sometimes signal greater psychological distance, there is a risk that this could backfire, inhibiting ice-breaking and the building of rapport. Delivered appropriately, however, honorifics can signal heightened attentiveness to not impinging on the addressee's freedom of action (Kyono 2017: 28). This is what *rakugoka* aim for—to not impinge, but efficiently break ice and appeal to their listeners. Knowing that as performers they are in control of the show, *rakugoka* nevertheless aim to make audiences feel as though they are the ones who direct the trajectory of the exchange. This is one reason that, unlike stand-up comedians, *rakugoka* rarely direct questions at the audience. They rarely say things like, "How's everyone doing?" or "How many first-timers are in the audience tonight?" Asking questions impinges on what Suzuki Mutsu calls *kikite no shiteki ryōiki* 聞き手の私的領域 (hearer's private territory) (Kyono 2017: 32). They are, after all, money-paying customers and not being impinged on makes audiences feel in control, feel safe and helps them settle in, facilitating a strong start.

After breaking the ice, *rakugoka* work to build rapport. They may find fans in any given audience—and *rakugoka* rely on these people for easy laughs and moral support—but inevitably, there will be more first-timers who need to be won over. How to establish rapport? One expert believes that "by establishing who we are, we establish rapport or solidarity with others ... We display this by finding commonalities. This leads to a relationship" (Boxer 2011: 5–6). *Rakugoka* begin by introducing uncontroversial topics that everyone likely has in common, such as the weather or the stores and restaurants found on the way to the *yose* from the nearest train station. They then move into more personal but still amicable topics, such as family relationships and pets.

Katsura Zakoba II 二代目桂ざこば (b. 1947), known for the personal touch he puts on *makura*, frequently talks about life away from the *rakugo* stage, as in the following excerpt. In fact, most *rakugoka* will talk about themselves or backstage *episoodo* エピソード (episodes) to build rapport—it makes audiences feel as though they are being granted insider status.

> I was thinking about the people to whom I owe a great debt. {3, 5} Of course, one is [my master] Katsura Beichō. {4} I can hardly hold up my head before him. {3} I've been benefiting from his kind auspices from the time I was fifteen until this very day. {4} I'll probably have to grow up one of these days, but ... {6} (*audience laughter*) Yes, he really does look out for me. {3}
>
> Then I wondered, is there anybody in the world who can't raise their head to me? {3, 5} First thing I thought was, my wife and kids perhaps? Guess what. This isn't the case ... {6} (*laughter*) I'm the one who can't raise my head to *them*. {3, 6} (*laughter*) I don't get it. I don't know why. They just made it that way over time. {3, 6} (*laughter*) Yep ... If I had sons, I may have been able to do something about this, but no, I've got daughters. {3} And they always side with my wife. {6} (Nihon no wagei)

In her analysis of *makura* discourse flow, Miyamoto Kanako determines that *rakugoka* commonly go from presenting a subject or scenario to presenting the (typically humorous) outcome, then this is followed with more specific examples. She notes that *rakugoka* frequently use the sentence-ending particles *na* な and *ne* ね, which convey emphasis, invite agreement and establish common ground. Also common at the beginning of sentences is the utterance *ee* ... え え ..., which is similar to "uh ..." or "um ..." in English. Interestingly, *ee* ... is not simply used to fill silence, but tends to be employed to bridge audience laughter (or other responses) with the next segment (Miyamoto 2004: 34–35). *Rakugoka* are not only shrewd in reading audiences, but in building rapport through carefully selected language, timing and sociolinguistic techniques. This gives a sense of why *rakugo* apprenticeship entails more menial tasks such as waiting on one's master and learning proper etiquette and language than they do actual *rakugo* lessons. In theory, if one is able to look after one's master, who is impatient and overdemanding (or so the stereotype goes), one will be well-positioned to break ice and build rapport with money-paying customers.

Establishing artistic authenticity

In the excerpt above, Zakoba II pays tribute to his master, Katsura Beichō III. This practice is common in the *rakugo* world—both on stage and off—because of the hierarchical nature of the tradition even today. It is also a quick (and anticipated) way of establishing one's artistic authenticity. In order to be "authentic" in the *rakugo* world, one needs to undergo a formal apprenticeship with a master affiliated with a *rakugo* guild or prominent "*rakugo* family".[9] Thus, one often hears *rakugoka* naming or alluding to their master—or mentioning relationships with other prominent artists.

In the following excerpt from his performance recorded on 14 January 2015, Katsura Bunza V 五代目桂文三 (b. 1967) not only mentions his master Katsura Bunshi V 五代目桂文枝 (1930–2005) but also the amount of time that he lived with him:

> I used to live in the Nishinari-ku area of Osaka. {3, 5} My late master, Katsura Bunshi V, lived there. {4} Yes, Bunshi V was my master. {4} I lived with him for fifteen years. {4} And in that period of fifteen years, I had four and a half bikes stolen. {6} (*laughter*) Half because on one occasion somebody just stole the wheel. {6} (*laughter*) Quite a nuisance, really. {3, 6} (Uhuhu01)

Bunza V's case is remarkable since, traditionally, pupils stay with their masters for just two or three years. So, here, as well as laughter, the reaction from people in the audience, whether they are familiar with *rakugo* customs or not, would be, "Wow, this guy's the real deal. He spent so long with his master that he must be worth the price we paid for the ticket".[10]

Presenting topical material

Another way *rakugoka* put audiences at ease during the *makura* has always been by introducing topical material. An important difference with comedy in the West, however, is that most *rakugoka* rarely bring controversial political or social issues to the *rakugo* stage. Ayame III says that she makes a point of steering clear of religion and political views, or anything that might hurt others' feelings.[11] Performers do this because they wish to avoid potentially alienating anybody in the audience and thus bring in "harmless" material. Depending on the *rakugoka*, this might be about sports, celebrity gossip, popular culture and entertainment, or news stories that can safely be made fun of. In the following excerpt, Bunza V talks about the New Year and related topics:

> I hope you've been well. {1, 2} I'm sure you all have many things planned for the New Year. {2, 3, 5} With so much ahead, I hope that everything goes smoothly for you. {3, 5} That would make me very happy. {3} And I hope you enjoy your time here today, too. {3, 5} You often hear the

saying, *Ichi go ichi e* 一期一会 (one moment; one encounter). {5, 8} This is about enjoying the same space with others. {5} Not with your family, but those with whom you don't usually spend time. {5} I can't say for sure that you'll enjoy this particular space with me, but I hope that's the case. {5, 6} (*laughter*) (Uhuhu01)

Regardless of what topical material *rakugoka* introduce into the *makura*, the aim is always to present common ground. Despite being traditional entertainers with a perceived inexhaustible supply of historical knowledge and peerless savviness when it comes to Japanese culture, *rakugoka* draw audiences closer when they can show that they are like most other people. They think smartphones are incredible yet expensive, they marvel at—or lament—how convenient the world has become, they get excited about the Olympics coming to Japan, they rejoice about news of vaccines that could end a pandemic. Presenting such safely topical material helps *rakugoka* demonstrate that they have similar interests and concerns and allows them to reinforce their relationship with the audience.

Telling kobanashi *and other jokes*

Joke-telling is different in Japan than in countries like the United States, Australia and the United Kingdom. This is particularly the case in formal situations. As Makiko Takekuro writes, "In Japanese society, jokes are the least-expected verbal behaviour on formal occasions, but in the United States, sociocultural norms actually encourage people to exchange jokes on these occasions" (Takekuro 2006: 95). In the *yose*, people need not worry about whether it is the right time or place for a joke since here jokes and laughter are sanctioned as appropriate. Shōkichi Oda calls laughter-safe spaces *warai no ba* 笑いの場 (laughter places) (Oda 2006: 18). Members of *yose* audiences are themselves targeted with humour on occasion, but this is rare compared to Western stand-up comedy. Laughing at *oneself*, or one's own family or in-group is far more acceptable, as are jokes about harmless incongruencies, wordplay, and *oyaji gyagu* 親父ギャグ (dad jokes). Slapstick and scatological humour have long been popular, too. *Rakugoka* help audiences get into the right mental space to listen to *rakugo* stories by appropriately gauging and selecting their humour. Tasteful jokes not only serve the moment but also ultimately enable *rakugoka* to safeguard their livelihoods.

Japanese jokes are frequently anecdotal and dialogic. One such kind of "joke" is referred to as *kobanashi* and this is a regular fixture in *makura*. Ui Mushū calls *kobanashi* the "raw material and essence of *rakugo*" (Ui 1965: 169). Like *rakugo* stories, *kobanashi* build up to an *ochi*-style punchline, ending suddenly but satisfyingly. To illustrate, the following *kobanashi* might precede *rakugo* stories about ill-conceived schemes to quickly get rich (or happy). One can hear something like this quite often at a performance and the fine points may change with the performer:

If you want to be happy for a day, go to the barbershop. If you want to be happy for a week, get married. If you want to be happy for a year, build a house. If you want to be happy for a lifetime, be honest with yourself. If you want to be happy right now, listen to the *rakugo* story I'm about to tell you. {6}

Kobanashi can also be dialogue-heavy, similar to *rakugo* stories. The following *kobanashi* is sometimes heard before stories about looks being deceiving, overconfidence, or the fine arts:

A certain woman went to an art exhibition and called over the person in charge.
"Excuse me, curator? Curator! This piece here, it's a Renoir, right?"
"No, madam, this is a van Gogh".
"Oh goodness, it's a van Gogh? Well, the one next to it's clearly a Renoir, is it not?"
"No, this one is a Modigliani".
"Oh, my. Really? ... Ah, well, the one next to it, I know this one. No doubt about it. It's a Picasso".
"That ... is a mirror". {6}

There are hundreds of *kobanashi*, some of which can be traced to early collections such as *Konjaku Monogatarishū* 今昔物語集 (*Collection of Tales of Times Now Past*, ca. 1120) but are still relevant to today's *hondai*. Dialogue-heavy *kobanashi* allow *rakugoka* to set the tone for the *hondai* to come, but also within a short space to exploit social and linguistic boundaries (e.g., female and male, casual and polite, old and new). This is done not to push limits, per se, but for comic effect or parody and to get a feel for audiences, perhaps comparable to the way that *gei tarento* ゲイタレント (literally, gay talent, i.e., television personalities) "use more exaggerated, or strongly stereotypical, feminine forms than many SJ [standard Japanese]-speaking straight women do in situated practice" (Okamoto 2016: 27). When performing female characters, some *rakugoka* look like men doing poor impressions of women, but others take female roles quite seriously, pursuing a respectable degree of realism. Still, since most male *rakugoka* dress and look like men, the effect always has some degree of humour. The same can be said for female *rakugoka* performing as men. As mentioned earlier, some *kobanashi* are predetermined, so that when a seasoned *rakugo* fan hears them, she may be able to guess the story the *rakugoka* is going to tell before that begins.

Instructing/teaching the audience about rakugo *past and present*

Many *stories* in the repertoire—in both the Tokyo and Kamigata tradition—were polished in the Meiji period and are linked to stories told and/or published in generations prior to this. Consequently, today there is an increasing amount of content that listeners are unfamiliar with. But it is precisely for this, the traditional, that *rakugo* is valued. Traditional content can be to do with anything from kimono (and their numerous accessories), which were once worn every day but now usually only for special occasions, such as graduations and weddings. One can easily get lost in kitchens of yesteryear, too, where one wore outdoor footwear and found open wood and charcoal fires, water brought in from the well, altars to oven gods, and *sake* jugs called rabbits (*usagidaru* 兎樽). Needless to say, there were no refrigerators or other modern appliances in Japan's old kitchens. The dilemma is that *rakugo* is traditional and therefore valued, but difficult because traditional.

Keeping audiences in the know is not always a straightforward process. Katsura Beichō III felt that he and fellow artists are faced with a challenging task when it comes to getting audiences to follow *koten* material. One approach, he wrote, is to, "explain potentially difficult content before the story begins" (Katsura Beichō 2004: 185). Many agree, but others believe it is unfair to presume that audiences will not be able to understand *rakugo* content, complex or otherwise. Some include more explanation before or during a story—narrator asides are acceptable and common in *rakugo*—while others depend on listeners garnering understanding through context. In *makura*, *rakugoka* sometimes encourage audiences to study up if they would like to move from being *rakugo* admirers to aficionados. Sure enough, one can find countless books (many by *rakugoka* themselves) that make the tradition more accessible. One example is the *rakugo* introduction series by Katsura Shikō 桂枝光 (b. 1959). The first two titles are: *Chiri-tote-chin no ajiwaikata* ちりとてちんの味わい方 (*How to taste Chiri-tote-chin*), and *Atagoyama no noborikata* 愛宕山の登り方 (*How to climb Mt. Atago*) (Katsura and Doi 2007, 2008).[12] The former opens with a section on "What is *rakugo*?" and is followed by chapters on *rakugo* history, the two traditions (Kamigata and Edo [Tokyo]), ten popular *rakugo* stories, and Shikō's own career. Books like these also help elucidate a good deal of traditional subject matter.

In the following excerpt, Hayashiya Kikumaru III 三代目林家菊丸 (b. 1974) discusses sumō, which features in the story he is about to tell, *Kōsuke mochi* 幸助餅 (*Kōsuke's mochi*). Most Japanese people know at least a little bit about sumō wrestling because one can see it on television and other media throughout the year. In fact, top sumō wrestlers, similar to popular *kabuki* actors, remain celebrities in their own right. To transport listeners back to the world of Kōsuke, a patron of the wrestler Ikazuchi Gorōkichi (1802–1877), Kikumaru III starts with sumō in the present day, then discusses its history. He also introduces an interesting fact about the term used for sumō patrons, and this links to the story's protagonist.

> I'd like to tell you a story about sumō. {9} Sumō now takes place on a fifteen-day [tournament] system. {5} Long ago there were circuits in both Osaka and Edo and they wrestled on a ten-day schedule. {7, 8} The

highest-ranking wrestler today is called *yokozuna*, but before it was the *ozeki* who was at the top. {5, 7, 8} In any case, sumō wrestler patrons are referred to as "Tanimachi". Tanimachi is the name of a place in Osaka. {5, 7} Many years ago, there was a doctor who was absolutely obsessed with sumō. {7, 8} Whenever young wrestlers came in for examinations, he refused to accept any sort of payment. {7, 8} Rather, he was the one who gave *them* spending money. {7, 8} The doctor lived in Tanimachi, so this is what sumō patrons came to be called. {7, 8} Well, they say that sponsoring sumō wrestlers is sure way to burn bridges. {5, 9} After all, one could easily get carried away and use up their entire savings. {5, 9} This is just as true today as it was in yesteryear. {5, 7, 8, 9} (Sandaime Hayashiya)

Many in Japan view *rakugo* as "classical" and misperceive it as something abstruse, if not esoteric. Wishing to kill the stereotype that *rakugo* is old and stuffy, *rakugoka* aim to provide audiences with fresh context and imbue them with confidence that they will be able to follow the story to the end. More than this, *rakugoka* strive to make audiences feel as though they share common ground, that they already possess the knowledge needed to enjoy stories. This knowledge, as Cade Bushnell has written, extends even to being able to recognise "laughter relevant positions" (i.e., junctures when one can or should laugh during the sequence of the talk/performance) (Bushnell 2017: 90). I can myself remember many times not being able to comprehend and laugh at comic highpoints, only to later anticipate and delight in being able to join the laughter when listening to the same story on another occasion. By regularly attending *rakugo*, anyone—including non-Japanese people—can become a *rakugo* connoisseur. *Rakugoka* help facilitate this in the *makura*.

Transporting audience to a different time/place

The Kikumaru III excerpt above also serves to effectively transport its audience to a different time. Such a "transport" is often initiated with the words *Mukashi wa* 昔は (Long ago [as opposed to this day and age]), which functions similarly to the more literary *Mukashi mukashi, aru tokoro ni* ... 昔々、ある所に (Long, long ago, in a certain [unnamed] place ...). If the story to be told is an older, traditional piece, listeners are often able to mark the moment when the transport takes place, when time travel commences. There will be a clear verbal cue, such as *mukashi wa*, or the *rakugoka* may say something to the tune of, "X is the case today, but that surely wasn't so in yesteryear". Another approach is to recite old adages or poems that can be linked to the *hondai*.

In his *makura* for the story *Shibahama* 芝浜 (*Shibahama shore*), Katsura Mikisuke III 三代目桂三木助 (1902–1961) regularly recited the following verse by Matsuo Bashō (1644–1694). This helped transport his audience back to the Edo period (1600–1868) when *shirauo* 白魚 (whitebait) could still be caught in the Sumida River:

Akebono ya	あけぼのや	Early dawn
shirauo shiroki	白魚白き	Whitefish, whiteness
koto issun	こと一寸	Three centimetres long

The integration of traditional poetry and *makura* is especially appropriate in view of the opinion of Andō Tsuruo (1908–1969), who felt that Mikisuke III's *makura* were second to none. He wrote that the charm of *makura* can be likened to the poetic verses that often accompany Japanese paintings and other works of art, for example, a painting of *matsutake* 松茸 mushrooms might feature a verse about the autumn wind or something along those lines. Similarly, he believed, *makura* should not depart too far from the story about to be told (Andō 1966: 70).[13] As Lori Brau (2008) has noted, incorporating poetry and other material not only helps *rakugoka* transport listeners in time and space but also conveys knowledge and promotes cultural heritage. Whether or not they have cultural heritage in mind, *rakugoka* understand that poems, adages, and *kobanashi* are indispensable devices that help transport the audience and set the mood.

Setting up a smooth transition into the hondai

The three theoretical terms *jo*, *ha*, *kyū* 序破急 (prelude, breach, quick; or, introduction, development, conclusion) refer to tempo and progression in an artistic endeavour. They appear to have first been applied to the ancient arts *bugaku* and *gakaku* 舞楽, 雅楽 (court music, and dance) and are today commonly associated with the medieval theatre art *nō* and the teachings of the *nō* master, Zeami 世阿弥 (c. 1363–c. 1443). While much has been written about *jo*, *ha*, *kyū* in the context of *nō*, they also apply to other performing, fine and literary arts, including importantly *rakugo*. Here, the *makura* is the focused and purposeful *jo*; the *ha* is the *hondai*, which is more substantial, involved, and builds up both comic or dramatic tension and speed as the end nears; the *ochi* is the *kyū*—it promptly brings the story to an end. One could also apply *jo*, *ha*, *kyū* to the *makura* itself. In this case, the final laugh and quick transition into the *hondai* would be the *kyū* of the *makura*.

Rakugoka wish the audience to feel properly mirthful by the end of the *makura*. They want them to be laughing or at least eager to listen to the story approaching. To achieve a smooth transition of mood, good timing is essential. For instance, during the final laugh of the *makura*, *rakugoka* wait for the instant that the laughter begins to cease, so as to not be drowned out. They then wait a beat and issue a brief statement along the lines of, "And this is where our story today begins …", or "Long ago, people experienced very much the same thing; in fact, there was a one woman who …" and so the *hondai* begins. Effectively, it is at this stage that *rakugoka* get into character and raise the theatrical fourth wall.

Typically, *rakugoka* do not stop to announce the story's title or introduce characters unless they think it is necessary to aid listeners' enjoyment or understanding. Indeed, as already mentioned, seasoned *rakugo* fans do not appreciate spoilers. Nevertheless, it is customary for *yose* managers or *rakugoka* to post story titles near the entrance *after* shows. Audience members can then be seen gathering around, making comments, such as, "See, I was right!" or "Oh, that's what that story was!" This is one facet of *rakugo* fan culture, or being "professional spectators", which encompasses everything from collecting recordings and other artefacts to becoming deeply knowledgeable about "information about the repertory, the performers, and their performances" (Brau 2008: 212).

On the issue of timing, the term used in *rakugo* is *ma* 間 (lit. interval). *Ma* can be likened to the concepts of comic timing, beats, pregnant pauses, and suchlike which are also considered vital for the success of comedy in the West.[14] Some *rakugoka* gauge their delivery by always being mindful of the time it takes to get laughs. If they get a laugh in, say, ten seconds, their next bit should be prolonged, then a shorter one follows—good balance is key. *Rakugoka* are perhaps most often criticised (and criticise each other) on *ma*. One frequently hears comments like, "She has impeccable *ma*", or "He really hasn't grasped the concept of *ma* yet". In the *makura*, good *ma* are essential because they set the tone for the story ahead. If a performer's *ma* are off, the results can be devastating: they may lose the audience. At the end of the *makura*, for the typical comical story, *ma* need to be carefully gauged, punchy, quick, yet inconspicuous. The transition from *makura* to *hondai* needs to be premeditated yet effortless: it is a difficult technique to master which is why afficionados use it to judge expertise.

Often, there is an interesting and anticipated physical cue that the *hondai* will soon start or is beginning. *Rakugoka* remove their *haori* 羽織 (kimono jacket). *Rakugoka* do not simply take it off and put it on one side, however. The action used is quite stylistic. I had the pleasure of watching numerous times as Katsura Harudanji III 三代目桂春団治 (1930–2016), who was famous for this gesture, nimbly untied his *haori* cords, bringing his fingers to the tips of the sleeves, holding them out for a moment, then giving them a quick tug. The silk garment shot behind him, sliding down his back to the floor, where he easily tucked it away from the audience's view. It reminded me of a magic trick or the instantaneous costume changes (*hayagawari* 早替わり) popular in *kabuki* and *jōruri* puppet theatre. Harudanji III did this without glancing at his *haori* or pausing his speech. It was a tiny but compelling show within the show that helped sweep the audience from the *makura* into the *hondai* almost without them knowing it. Not all *rakugoka* time their *haori* removal with the commencement of the *hondai*. In fact, some do this at the beginning of their *makura* (particularly if they are hot). Some leave it on for the entire performance since some *rakugo* characters being portrayed, such as high-ranking samurai, monks and wealthy merchants, are simply more believable when wearing *haori*. (This does not apply to a woman or man in training who typically do not wear *haori* on stage both because they have not earned the right to it and because they remain busy with various menial tasks backstage.)

Analysis of three *makura*

I have selected *makura* by three *rakugoka* who have been professionals for between 20 and 30 years, all practitioners of the Kamigata tradition. I am choosing to highlight them both because there has been a streak of Tokyo-centrism in *rakugo* scholarship, and because they are remarkable performers. The first, Katsura Ayame III is the second woman who has succeeded as a professional on the Kamigata circuit. She performs both *koten* and original pieces, but more of the latter. She is also known for reworking *koten* stories to make them in her view better suited to a woman performer. Katsura Bunza V is a traditionalist in the sense that he performs primarily *koten* stories. He is known for specialising in more complex pieces, including stories with music, a hallmark of Kamigata *rakugo*. Finally, Shōfukutei Tama performs both *koten* and original stories and is known for being savvy and outspoken (especially on Twitter, @Gomaizasa) about politics and other current events—he is one of the few *rakugoka* who can boast of having graduated from a Japanese national university. I present these *rakugoka* in order of seniority, though they would appear in the reverse order at an actual show, that is, the highest-ranking performer comes last—she is the headliner.

Katsura Ayame III

Ayame III (see Figure 7.2) is counted among the pioneer women in the profession and as such receives a good deal of esteem. She began her apprenticeship with Katsura Bunshi V in 1982, one of the *shitennō* 四天王 (four greats) of post-World War II Kamigata *rakugo*, but first had to overcome an obstacle. Bunshi V initially was not interested in training a woman and tried to dampen Ayame III's enthusiasm. He asked her if she could drive and, as many Japanese 18 year olds would, she answered, no. Bunshi V told her that it would thus be impossible because he requires pupils to drive him. Ayame III quietly left, only to enrol herself in an intensive driver training course. She earned her driver's license in just two weeks then called on Bunshi V once more. After such an admirable display of determination, he could hardly turn her down (Katsura Bunshi 1996: 231–232).

Ayame III learned *koten* stories but, with Bunshi V's encouragement, soon began making them her own. She has also composed original stories that place women centre stage, such as *Seerusu uuman* セールス・ウーマン (*Saleswoman*), *Watashi wa obasan ni naranai* 私はオバさんにならない (*I'll Never be an Old Woman*), and many others. She is quoted as saying, "It's rare to see a woman in a line of work where getting older is a joy. I hope I can always continue doing what I love in the moment" (Yamada 2010: 104).

Figure 7.2 Katsura Ayame III performing *rakugo* on stage, recounting the story of the protagonist who eats *chiri-tote-chin* (i.e., pungently rotten tofu).

Source: Photograph copyright Katsura Ayame III 三代目桂あやめ, reproduced with kind permission.

When asked what she tells her own pupil about *makura*, she said: "I don't give much guidance on this because I feel it's a time for one to express their own sensibilities. What I do insist on is *ochi*. Just like in everyday conversations, nobody wants to hear someone drag out topics and end without punchlines".[15] In 2007, she presented the following *makura* before the *koten* story *Chiri-tote-chin* (*Twing-a-Twang*), which features entertaining scenes of drinking and eating, including one item that is beyond foul (see Figure 7.2). As she herself notes, she has adapted the story to better suit a woman *rakugoka*.

> AYAME III: (*Enters and bows*) I'm Katsura Ayame. {1} Time sure flies, doesn't it? {5} Can you believe that this year marks my twenty-fifth year in the profession? {2, 3, 4} (*audience applause*) Thank you. {3} So, that means I started my apprenticeship when I was three ... {6} (*laughter*)

Indeed. Back in those days people used to ask me quite a bit, "Are you all right? How's a woman supposed to survive in a world as strict as that?" {4} Well, the *rakugo* world *is* pretty strict. {7} If your master tells you something's white, then it's white. If he says, "That crow flying by is white, isn't it?" you've got to say, "Yes sir, it's white!" {4, 6, 7} (*laughter*) That's the kind world this is. It's been this way for a long time. We're all faced with it. You've just got to respect your master and seniors. {4, 7} Take for example, if your master or senior gives you a gift, the first thing you do is exuberantly accept it. This is a given. Even for little things. {4, 7} Say you're absolutely full and your senior says, "Here, have this croquette". You say, "Thank you!" {3, 4, 6, 7, 9} (*laughter*) These are the basics, no matter what. {7} People are becoming more straightforward recently though. {5} When drinking at an afterparty, my seniors will say something like:

Hey, everybody wants beer, right?

YES! {4, 6, 7, 9} (*laughter*)

That's it—there's no other option. {7} It's never:

Hey, everybody wants beer, right?

Sorry, I'll take a grape *shōchū* 焼酎 [distilled beverage made of barley, sweet potatoes, etc.] highball. {6} (*laughter*)

Whatever the hell that is. But people are becoming more straightforward these days. {5}

I get tipsy pretty easily when I drink. {3, 5, 9} Say I see a handsome younger *rakugoka* sitting over there and I decide to go have a seat next to him. {2, 3, 4, 6, 7} (*laughter*) I get up and jest, "Hey you, maybe I'll just have a seat right there on your lap!" {3, 6} (*laughter*) Up until a few years ago, they'd say, "Oh sis, you're just trying to make me blush, but okay!" Those days are gone. {6} (*laughter*) Today I say something like that and all they say is, "You're too heavy!" {6} (*laughter*) I tell you, it's hard to tell if young *rakugoka* have become more honest or if I'm just getting older. {3, 4, 5, 6} (*laughter*)

Now there are people in the world called *mono yorokobi* もの喜び— people who become animated no matter what they're offered. People like that make you feel good, don't they? For the next story, I'm going to tell you my own version of it—a woman's version. Usually it only has men, but I've made it a little sexier. I've added geisha and it's set in a teahouse... {7, 9} (Edward White)

Ayame III is on topic in this *makura*, considering that what is to come is a story with lots of eating and drinking. She carefully primes the audience for laughter and also says a great deal that establishes her authenticity as a professional *rakugoka*. As mentioned, this is something that most *rakugoka* touch on, due to the hierarchical nature of the art. Points are earned for paying tribute to those ahead of the speaker and it also pays to show the audience that one is struggling to make it in this very traditional sector. Women regularly spend more time than their male counterparts establishing their authenticity in *makura*, which has to do with the fact that women have only been formally accepted as professionals for fifty years. Some people still seem to doubt that women go through the same rigorous training as men, or that they could compete with them on an artistic level. Let there be no doubt—women do undergo a demanding apprenticeship, and many are in fact more accomplished *rakugoka* than some men. Because the playing field remains unequal, playing up authenticity may be one way for women to subvert the system. Edgy and challenging material is another one.

Katsura Bunza V

In 1991, Bunza V (see Figure 7.3) began his apprenticeship with Katsura Bunshi V, the same master that Ayame III trained with. Bunza V presented the following *makura* at his Hōjuji *yose* show on 14 January 2015. Although

Figure 7.3 Katsura Bunza V performing *rakugo* on stage.

Source: Photograph copyright Katsura Bunza V 五代目桂文三, reproduced with kind permission.

there are now two formal *yose* in western Japan (Osaka and Kobe), and several in Tokyo, *rakugoka* numbers are so high today that they are obliged to create opportunities for themselves outside fixed venues. There are many ways to go about this, but the most common is to establish a dedicated fan-base that will ultimately help *rakugoka* produce their own shows. A case in point is the show which Bunza V puts on every year at the temple Hōjuji in Wakayama, south of Osaka in the Kansai region. Audiences are not large, but they regularly fill the main hall of the small temple past capacity and the atmosphere is merry. Shows like this are designed to be less formal and *rakugoka* can count on local fans—usually their biggest supporters—coming to every show. Close relationships are forged and consequently *makura* become much more personal in nature and longer. Audiences want to hear *rakugo* stories, but they also wish to spend as much time as possible "schmoozing" with their favourite artist.

Bunza V presented the following *makura* prior to the *koten* story *Imodawara* (*Sack of Potatoes*), which features feckless thieves who plot to rob a well-to-do merchant. As one may predict, it includes humorous discussion of his personal experiences with theft. It also acknowledges his relationship with his fans in several ways, including its extra length.

> BUNZA V: (*Enters, bows, pauses, smiles sheepishly*) ... (*audience laughter*) Um, thank you. Well, I've shown up again this year. {3} (*laughter*) My name is Katsura Bunza. You can look forward to Katsura Jakki after me. Me, Katsura Jakki, then an intermission. After that I'll tell you one more story, so three stories in all. {1} Thank you in advance for not going home early. {3} (*laughter*)
>
> I hope you've been well. I'm sure you all have many things planned for the New Year. {5} With so much ahead, I hope that everything goes smoothly for you. That would make me very happy. And I hope you enjoy your time here today, too. {2, 3, 5} You often hear the saying, *Ichi go ichi e* 一期一会 (one moment, one encounter). {8} This is about enjoying the same space with others. Not with your family, but those with whom you don't usually spend time. {3, 8} I can't say for sure that you'll enjoy this particular space with me, but I hope that's the case. {3, 6} (*laughter*)
>
> I think you've probably already noticed, but, as usual, we have the "Beauty Corps" sitting here in the front row. {2, 3, 4, 6} (*laughter*) Thank you for always supporting me. {3, 4} It's my goal to eventually have them rushing the stage with LED light sticks. {3, 6} (*laughter*)
>
> It might be a bit impertinent of me to say so, but it's hard to find a nice balance of men and women these days. {5} The word *yose* refers the slots in a show, but also the people who gather, or drop in, to watch shows. It's interesting to observe the many ways that people drop in.[16] {4, 5} I recently performed at a show called the "Parents-and-Kids *Yose*". Of course, I thought it was a show for

The makura *of rakugo, tradition and modernity* 157

young mothers attending with their small children, but at the back was an older woman sitting with a man. {4, 5} Hey, I thought, this is supposed to be a parents and kids show! But it turned out that they actually *were* mother and son. {6} (*laughter*) It was wrong of me to be so narrow-minded. {3}

As for presentation, in *rakugo* one *rakugoka* performs all characters. There aren't multiple actors who exchange lines, after all. {7} We go:
Hello?
Oh, hi, come on in!
Thanks, sorry I've been out of touch.
What are you talking about? It's me who's been out of touch! Please, come in.
No thanks, I'll head home.
Oh, come now, don't be like that ... {6}
One time when I was doing this, a kid in the audience looked at me and said, "Weirdo". {3, 6} (*laughter*) Well, she hit the nail on the head ... {6} (*laughter*) After all, we *rakugoka* do all the talking ourselves. We're *always* alone. {4, 7} And it's hard no matter how you look at it. ... It really is! {3, 6} (*laughter*)

Now, I wonder what I should do for my first story. {4} I'd ask for your ideas, {3} but the truth is I've already decided what I'm going to do. {6} (*laughter*) I thought about it earlier. To start out, I'm going to tell you a story about burglars. {9} I guess I shouldn't say that with a big smile on my face though. {6} (*laughter*) That's right, a story about thieves. Thieves today are different than those long ago. Today, thieves are dangerous and make others feel bad, and this is unacceptable. But thieves in *rakugo* are happy-go-lucky. {7, 9}

I've had quite a few run-ins with thieves. Maybe you have as well. It can be rough out there, especially in Osaka. People are busy and easily irritated. There's a lot of people who leave their bikes in front of train stations, right? {5, 9} I used to live in the Nishinari-ku area of Osaka. My late master, Katsura Bunshi V, lived there. Yes, Bunshi V was my master. I lived with him for fifteen years. {4} And in that period of fifteen years, I had four and a half bikes stolen. {6} (*laughter*) Half because on one occasion somebody just stole the wheel. {6} (*laughter*) Quite a nuisance, really. One time they took just the seat, too. And I had paid to park my bike at the station! I went to work and came back—and my seat was gone. {6} (*laughter*) I was so tired that I initially thought, "Oh, I must have come without my seat this morning". {3, 6} (*laughter*) But who would do that? {6} (*laughter*) "Oh my!", I thought, but there was nothing I could do but walk it home. {6} (*laughter*) That was rough. And that wheel ... You know, if they had taken both wheels I'd have to give up, but with one wheel ... {6} (*laughter*) you can still roll the thing. {6} (*laughter*) So I lifted it up and rolled it home on one wheel. I was exhausted after that one. {3, 6, 9}

I used to live in an apartment building called Rōzen Okamura. It wasn't the best place. The landlord's name was Okamura. It was a four-floor building. Typically, apartment buildings have front entrances with automatic locks and you press the code and room number—*pi-pi-pi*—the door slides open—*uiiin*—then closes. {5} Proper apartments have security systems in place, but this wasn't one of those. The door would open for *anybody* walking by. There was a shelf for shoes at the entrance and I had to walk up the stairs to my room on the fourth floor. {4, 5} Now what kind of apartment is that? {6} (*laughter*) I used to wonder about all this as I lived there.

One day I went downstairs to take out the trash but my shoes were missing from the shoe shelf. {3, 4, 9} Then I wondered again, "Maybe I forgot my shoes the other day", but, nope, somebody had taken them. "Oh no!", I thought. I figured I should go to the police to report the incident. The police are quite used to writing accident and incident reports, after all. {5, 9} When I rang, they said, "Look son, you can't call us every time you lose your shoes". {6} (*laughter*) As if I was talking about something taken from a fruit stand! {6} (*laughter*) "But I've had my bikes stolen too!", I pleaded. He was busy, but I insisted, so he came and asked what had happened. "I've had four and a half bikes stolen", I said. {6} (*laughter*) "Let's forget about the half, okay?" he grumbled. He took off his shoes and came up to my room. He made a report of everything that had been stolen up to that point. {5, 9} When he finished, he went back downstairs, and ... his shoes had disappeared too! {6} (*laughter*) No joke! (*laughter*) Boy, was he was angry. {6} (*laughter*) "I'm going to get that son of a bitch!", he bellowed. He never did though. (*laughter*) Yeah, so all that happened to me. {4} A lot of people have experiences like these though. Some areas are worse than others. {5, 9}

I imagine you've heard of the famous robber Ishikawa Goemon. {5, 8, 9} He appears in *kabuki* and other plays. None of us—including the actors who perform the role—have ever actually met somebody like Goemon though. This is why the theatre is great. They wear beautiful costumes and the actors are so handsome. They put on their makeup and strike beautiful poses, so it's only natural to think, "That's cool, I want to be like Ishikawa Goemon". But the robbers that appear in *rakugo*, as I was telling you earlier, aren't so dashing. They're anything but sophisticated. {7, 8, 9} Instead of Ishikawa Goemons, you have Ishikawa Yoemons. {6} (*laughter*) Or, Ishikawa Niemon-han. {6, 7, 9} (*laughter*)[17]

There's a funny *kobanashi* that I hope you like. It goes something like this ... Oh no, I've forgotten it ... (*laughter*) Um ... okay. It's a *kobanashi* with a character called Ishikawa Nashiemon. Of course, Nashiemon is just an average man like all the others. {7}

Hey, Nashiemon!

Huh?

What is your real name?
Chōjūrō. (laughter)
What's that? Your stage name is Nashiemon, but your real name is Chōjūrō? That's pretty stylish too. How long have you been acting?
Since the Twentieth Century. {6, 8} (laughter)[18]
That's it. Oh boy, I'm glad I could finally remember that one. {3, 6} (laughter)
And speaking of characters, this is where our *rakugo* story begins ... {9} (Uhuhu01)

In *Imodawara*, the story that follows, the thieves' plan is for one of them to hide in a potato sack that they will leave overnight at a merchant's house-shop. The thief inside the sack is to come out after everybody in the house falls asleep at night, then unlock the front door to let in his accomplices. Schemes like this rarely go as planned in *rakugo* and *Imodawara* is no exception.

Analysing Bunza V's *makura*, one can readily tick off the boxes of standard *makura* elements: audience greeting, breaking ice and building rapport, establishment of authenticity, jokes and *kobanashi*, insight about the art, and more. All of this serves to put the audience in a good mood, bring them into the fold, and most importantly, prime them for what is to come. Bunza V allows himself to laugh with the audience and even makes friendly jibes. When performing in a formal *yose*—or for a TV or radio audience—*rakugoka* do not usually take such liberties. But in this intimate setting with his perennial supporters, Bunza V has a better understanding of what his audience wants and how far he can push the limits. By the end of his *makura*, his audience is hooked: there is no other place they would rather be.

Shōfukutei Tama

Tama (see Figure 7.4) began his apprenticeship with Shōfukutei Fukushō in 1998. Tama has earned a reputation for being a gifted and well-rounded performer who has received prizes for his work on stage and he has an enthusiastic fanbase in Osaka and other cities, namely Tokyo (Yamada 2010: 82). Tama presented the following *makura* for a Tokyo audience in 2016. His *hondai* was *Funa Benkei* (*Benkei on the Boat*), a *koten* story about a man who lies to his overbearing and easily irritated wife about where he is going with a friend, and the consequences are comically great (Shores 2021: 104–106, 129–131). Tama's *makura* is based on a personal account of receiving poor service from his internet and phone provider when he moved from one area of Osaka to another. It is quite a long *makura*, a bit like the Western "shaggy-dog" story in which long-windedness itself is funny. He leads the audience up the garden path so that they think they should sympathise with him over his dilemma, only to find that he is poking fun at himself. In this way, the *makura* nicely ties into the theme of the henpecked husband, and bombastic tantrums.

160 *M.W. Shores*

Figure 7.4 Shōfukutei Tama performing *rakugo* on stage.

Source: Photograph copyright Shōfukutei Tama 笑福亭たま, reproduced with kind permission.

TAMA: (*Enters and bows*) *Ee* … Next, I'd like to talk to you a bit about relocation. {1, 5, 6} (*audience laughter*) When moving house, calling to have the internet arranged can be such a pain. The landline too, you know, I've got to have one for dealings with my agency. {4} They've got those optic-fiber lines that let you use phone and internet, right? So, I was moving from Chūō-ku to Fukushima-ku, in Osaka. I had to get the line changed, and I supposed this would also mean getting a new phone number. I believe it's the same for Tokyo—one's phone number usually changes depending on the *ku* 区 (precinct) that one's living in. Osaka numbers start with 06 and, what comes after that changes depending on where you live, but I seemed to think that my phone number might not change because it's linked to my computer.

So, I called my internet provider XXX {6} (*laughter*) and asked, "Is my number going to change?"[19] If it wasn't, I told them, I'll use the number as is. If it was, I'd just as soon pay a disconnection fee, enter a contract

The makura *of* rakugo, *tradition and modernity* 161

with a new company, and get things taken care of more quickly. I'd be better to get my phone and internet settled, so I was fine with cancelling even if it cost more. The line I had, there were certain hours that I couldn't use it, but fine by me if I could just keep the same number. So, I called them up and told them, "I'm happy to stay with you if that's the case".

They told me, "No, your number won't change" and I said, "Oh, okay then". Then they said, "It'll be about a month before we can get everything installed", but it was fine with me to not have a phone or internet during that period if I got to keep the same number. "Yep, okay, I'll keep the number", I said, and they told me that they'd call me in about two weeks to give me the installation date... Hey, you're all following me up to this point, right? {2, 3, 6} (*laughter*) I'd have internet in a month. They'd call me in two weeks to set things up.

So, I got the call and they said, "Okay, we'll be coming in two weeks on this date and you'll have your *new number*." {6} (*laughter*) I was like, is this guy screwing with me? {6} (*laughter*) What the hell have I been sitting around for two weeks for! {6} (*laughter*) I asked him what this was all about and said, "You guys told me that my number wouldn't change!" I was moving but, since I thought my phone number would be staying the same, I went out and bought a bunch of those summer postcards that come with lottery tickets. "I've already printed out my greetings on the backside!" I complained. (*laughter*) I had them ready to send to *hanashika* associates, to my seniors, letting them know that they could use my same number from August, too. {4} "I've got all these postcards ready to go! Now what am I supposed to do?" I protested. "How are you going to make this right?" Then he says, "I'll have you speak with my manager" (*laughter*), and next I get the manager.

The call had been recorded. The manager told me, "Our operator informed you that if the *local exchange prefix* didn't change, neither would your number ..." {6} (*laughter*) Are you following me here? {2, 3, 6} (*laughter*) This is jargon that one hardly ever hears ... The Osaka area code is 06 and what follows that, is the local exchange prefix. The same thing's true for the numbers that follow 03 in Tokyo. If I see the characters for the word, I can tell what it means, but just hearing it ... I thought we were just talking about the area code. The guy then played it back for me ... {6} (*laughter*)

TAMA: *So, my number won't change if the area code doesn't change, right?*

OPERATOR: *That's correct.*

Huh? I piped up, "Well, this isn't my fault then, right?"

Fukushima is in Osaka, so the 06 won't change. I get that much. So I push the manager, "What I'm trying to get at is whether the numbers *after* 06 are going to change ... What's the deal here? I'm asking you if the numbers *after* 06 are going to change or not. You told me that if the local exchange prefix doesn't change, it doesn't change, but this explains nothing! {6} (*laughter*) That's not my question! It's like, I know that H20 is water, but you think I'm asking whether it's H2O!" {6} (*laughter*) "I'm not sure that's the most fitting metaphor for this case" ... {6} (*laughter*) Why's this guy got to correct me on this! {6} (*laughter*)

Then he says, "Well, there hasn't really been a mistake. There wasn't a mistake, but perhaps the explanation wasn't quite adequate." {6} (*laughter*) "Who are you, Masuzoe or something?[20] {6} (*laughter*) What is this!" (*laughter*). "Well, it's a bit difficult to give a precise answer if we don't speak with the installation manager. I think that's the reason we weren't able to give you a suitable answer. We'll have to speak with the installation manager. It would have been *besuto* ベスト (best) if they had spoken to you in the first place." (*laughter*) "What do you mean by '*besuto*'? '*Besuto*'? (*laughter*) This is what comes after *bettaa* ベッター (better), is it not? {6} (*laughter*) Your degrees of comparison are off! {6} (*laughter*) You're talking *guddo* グッド (good), *bettaa*, *besuto* (*laughter*) when you should be talking along the lines of *baddo* バッド (bad), *waasu* ワース (worse), *waasuto* ワースト (worst)! {6} (*laughter*) You should be using *waasuto* or *waasu*, don't you think?" {6} (*laughter*) That one seemed to stump him (*laughter*), so I just figured the guy didn't know anything about comparisons. {6} (*laughter*) But I dug in, "If I draw a line between *guddo* and *baddo* and tell you to choose one of those words, which is it! ... (*laughter*) Got me? I'm talking about the *guddo* of *guddo*, *bettaa*, *besuto* and the *baddo* of *baddo*, *waasu*, *waasuto*! (*laughter*) Well, which is it?" ... {6} (*laughter*) "It's *baddo*." {6} (*laughter*) "Well, there you go. See, you were *baddo*, you bonehead!" {6} (*laughter*)

It took me a month to go through all that and all I wanted in the end was my time back. {6} (*laughter*) I had to wait longer to use my computer because they were slow explaining everything to me. But it turns out that time loss isn't viewed as actual damage. I spoke with a lawyer and was told that only financial loss can be viewed as damage in this case. So, I thought that I should at least get back the money that I spent on those 300 summer postcards. {6} (*laughter*) I didn't really care about the money, but I wasn't happy. I called and asked, "Are you going to reimburse me for the summer postcards I printed that phone number on?" "We're sorry, but we don't think we'll be able to accommodate your request at this time." {6} (*laughter*) "What? So, you're not going to make this right?" "Yes, I'm afraid this is our position at present, but, if you're unhappy, I can have you speak with my manager again." {6} (*laughter*) What! It seemed like they were trying to send a kid to bed crying. {6} (*laughter*) Come on! As far as I see it, if I come to the table having put so much thought into this, shouldn't they have to think about it a bit, too? {6} (*laughter*) It's like, what the hell, you know?

So then I tell him, "Okay fine, I'm just going to cancel my contract and I don't care if I've got to pay for it. If I'm locked into the damn contract and there's a rule that says I've got to pay off the term of the contract, fine, I'll do it. I won't ask you to forgive any fees, but you'll at least pay me back for those postcards, won't you? What does the law have to say about that? Now, if you've got a logical explanation as to why you won't be able to do that, I'll hear you out and, if you can't, I'll accept it. Whatever the case, I want you to give me a clear explanation." ... "Well, I'd have to talk to my manager ..." {6} (*laughter*) "Look, I'm sorry, but you're taking my call and can't answer my questions, right? And just a minute ago, you said we couldn't get a precise answer unless we talk to the installation manager, right? But if you give me to yet another person, wouldn't that be the same as me talking to someone like you—who isn't authorized to give me the correct answer (*laughter*)—and that operator that I spoke to on day one? Isn't that the case? ... Which is it—*guddo* or *baddo*!" {6} (*laughter*)

In the end, I got them to pay for the postcards. {6} (*laughter*) Oh, but boy was it a trying exchange, and quite irritating. (*laughter*) Being summer, I thought one of my veins was going to burst. {6, 9} (*laughter*) Okay, now I'll tell you the story *Funa Benkei* (*Benkei on the Boat*). {9} It's a Kamigata *rakugo* story set in summer—when the hot weather is at its peak. {7, 8, 9}

(Shōfukutei 2016)

One can only guess how much of Tama's *makura* might be factual, but this is part of the fun of *makura*. Bringing the audiences into performers' lives as they do, it does not matter that they might be fiction because fiction too becomes part of the *rakugoka* persona. A similar device was exploited by those Japanese writers who wrote what are known as *watakushi shōsetsu* 私小説 (I-novels, also read as *shi-shōsetsu*), defined by Tomi Suzuki as "an autobiographical narrative in which the author is thought to recount faithfully the details of his or her personal life in a thin guise of fiction" (Suzuki 1996: 1). There is a special attraction for an audience in such a dream world blend of fiction and personal reality. In the *makura*, Tama starts by bowing according to convention but gives no self-introduction or other formal greeting. He essentially jumps right into a protracted *kobanashi* about his trouble with his provider. This is acceptable, however, because he has told a story earlier in the evening and has already gotten a feel for the audience and built rapport. This is evident from their readiness to laugh right away. The lengthy *kobanashi* showing his frustration turning into irritation then rage—and his inability to keep his emotions in check—is apt material to precede *Funa Benkei*, the star of which is Omatsu, arguably Kamigata *rakugo*'s fieriest and most forceful woman character. The points in Tama's *kobanashi* at which he grows angry and speaks faster and faster (particularly the "good-better-best" bit) certainly recall Omatsu's own rapid-fire outbursts.[21] Of course, the *makura* serves to build further rapport with the audience and also establishes Tama's artistic authenticity; it highlights topical material, sparks laughter throughout, and superbly sets up the *hondai*. Since Tama appears to be unable to retain his composure when angry, the jokes he tells are on him: this is consistent with the purpose of bringing the audience into the life of the *rakugoka*.

Those who have heard Tama perform know that he is a meticulous master of words—and *rakugoka* are generally known for being doyens of civility and etiquette (at least in public)—but the fact that he so easily spins out of control serves to render him humbler and more likeable. Nevertheless, this *makura* also serves to establish Tama's authenticity as a professional. He has made the crowd laugh, but also implied that he is an important *rakugoka*, and one who adheres to the rules of hierarchy. Thus, although he is younger than many of his listeners, his right to sit before them and hold the floor is justified. His presumed insider status, and the fact that he has managed to hit it off with the audience mean that he can now allow his audience to enter the virtual fold. This *makura* is successful in every way: it has primed the audience to listen to *rakugo* and specifically the dynamic *Funa Benkei*. Like his illustrious predecessors down the ages, Tama holds his audience in the palm of his hand.

It is noticeable that both Tama and Bunza V (discussed above) employ humour very differently at certain points. Both present themselves as victims of sorts, garnering sympathy from and endearing themselves to their audiences. Yet Bunza V warmly jibes *at* the audience while Tama focuses on (and lambasts) the internet provider that he feels wronged by. There are several reasons for this difference, though it is possible that the choices made would change on a different day with a different audience. One explanation is the performer's persona, although this too can differ with the day or the *hondai*. Considering the present cases, while Bunza V and Tama are both performing at showcase recitals, the former is evidently more at ease and takes more liberties with his audience. This has to do with the informal nature of the show and the fact that most people in the audience are likely to be repeat attenders. Tama's display of exasperation and hot-headedness is tenser, but this fits well with the story he is about to tell. Also, importantly, he is performing in a different region (Tokyo), where people speak a different dialect and hold different expectations than do Osakans, who are more welcoming of humour and *rakugo* (Inoue 2007). Tama thus has to work harder (or appear to be doing so) and be more respectful to gain audience acceptance. As he puts it, all *rakugoka* have to adapt their material differently depending on whether they are playing at "home" or "away".[22]

Conclusion: the weight of a "pillow"

Most *rakugo* stories come with embedded warm-up segments called *makura*. They are typically personalised but do not have to be wholly original, and can be eliminated altogether if needed. As we have seen, *makura* help set the right tone and allow *rakugoka* to accomplish more with the *hondai*. Functioning as "frames" (Masuyama 1997: 13), they allow artists to cast new light—or to re-frame—old material, that is the *hondai*. This is important in the twenty-first century, when audiences are increasingly unfamiliar with the customs, social mores, and values of previous centuries. This was not the case, say during *rakugo*'s golden era around the turn of the twentieth century, because those audiences were not far removed from the world of *rakugo*. In fact, "[i]n the old days, it was often determined which *makura* would go with which story and seniors scolded juniors for 'bad manners' if they carelessly did something different" (Yamamoto 2001: 17). With the many rapid changes that took place in the course of the twentieth century, however, it became helpful (and even necessary) to have amusing professionals liaise between periods and fuse different worlds. As we have also seen, *makura* allow one to "draw on personal experiences or current events to present the materials in the best way as possible to meet the challenging demands of the audience for a novel approach to a familiar story" (Masuyama 1997: 13). *Makura* help *rakugoka* to put individual stamps on the art, keeping it fresh and appealing. This is especially important at a time when there are countless other entertainment options, many available at the tap of a finger and so many with the appealing quality of novelty.

To paraphrase Sawada Kazuya, some *makura* (or *makura* themes) are still meant to go with particular *rakugo* stories; for example, if the *hondai* is about drinking *sake*, it calls for a *makura* about drinking. But *how* a *rakugoka* chooses to present this is important. Should they present a portrait of drunkenness from the current era or from the past? Should one present multiple characters and dialogue in a *kobanashi*? How will this resonate with the audience? Considering that audiences change with every show and over time, *makura* must obviously remain malleable and flexible, able to evolve. Most of all, they need to resonate with the audience (Sawada 1989: 35). If a *makura* fails to capture or to make sense to an audience, it will be harder for them to find interest in the *hondai* that follows. So, in many regards, the weight of *makura* is great. Hayashiya Somemaru IV 四代目林家染丸 (b. 1949) said that if a *rakugoka* is unable to capture the audience and make them want to come to more shows, the blame lies with the *rakugoka*: "It's our job to *sell rakugo*. Say you have a great product, but whether that product sells or not depends on your pitch" (Shores 2021: 137). *Makura* is, in effect, the prime time and way to make this pitch and, ideally, to sink and engage the proverbial hook.

As the discussion and examples given here have shown, *makura* are used to introduce oneself, feel out the audience, break ice and build rapport, establish artistic authenticity, present topical material, tell jokes and *kobanashi*, teach about *rakugo* and elucidate difficult subject matter, transport the audience, and to make a smooth transition into the *hondai*. As a warm-up segment, *makura* allow *rakugoka* to identify things they may have in common with their audience (even if it is just suffering from the summer heat), set the right tone, and prime the audience for laughter. *Rakugoka* know before they take the stage that the audience has paid for tickets and will be waiting in their seats, but they are trained not to take this captive audience for granted. There have, after all, been times in the past when *rakugo* came dangerously close to disappearing. So, to get ahead both professionally and financially, *rakugoka* must ensure that everyone in the audience becomes a repeat customer. Hence the importance of *makura*: they are *rakugo* preludes that allow a more personal and meaningful exchange with the audience, and vice-versa. Thus, they allow the audience to feel a sense of control and ownership of the art, no matter how traditional, and to share the present time with the person on stage and with fellow audience members. *Makura* illustrate that the traditional art of *rakugo* is fresh and alive and that there is more to it than just *hondai* and *ochi*. While *rakugoka* can be expected to tell great stories, audiences always feel comfier with a good *makura*. As light-hearted, humorous, and accommodative prologues, they help update and make *rakugo* much more enjoyable for today's critical audiences.

Notes

1 From the author's email correspondence with *rakugoka* Katsura Ayame III, July 2021.
2 An earlier version of this study appeared in *Asian Theatre Journal*, 38 (2), Fall 2021.
3 Email correspondence with Katsura Ayame III, July 2021.
4 Email correspondence with Shōfukutei Tama in June and July 2021, and Zoom video conference, 3 July 2021.
5 This is a pun. In Japanese, *kamigata* 髪型 means hairstyle and it is also the name of a region, Kamigata 上方 (i.e., Kansai, or western Japan).
6 Translation here and throughout by the author. Given the length of quotations used in this study, English translations only are presented without Japanese text. I have sourced the *makura* examples quoted from the internet or other digital media. Fans regularly upload *rakugo* stories to YouTube and other video-sharing sites without *rakugoka* permission. Most *rakugoka* I have spoken with are not happy about this but do not pursue the matter since the pirated recordings do not appear to be a source of profit.
7 In previous generations, *yose* stages were designed to include *tokonoma* 床の間 (alcoves), which featured aesthetically pleasing items, such as hanging scrolls, flower arrangements, fine pottery, and decorative clocks.
8 Anpanman アンパンマン, created by Yanase Takashi (1919–2013), is a peppy cartoon superhero whose head is made of doughy *anpan* あんパン (pastry filled with sweet azuki paste).
9 "Family" here refers to *ichimon* 一門 or artistic schools. *Ichimon* function like families in the tribal sense, but members are typically not biologically related.
10 In previous generations, it was a given that apprenticing pupils would live in their masters' homes and essentially work as servants as they received training. Today, the practice of *sumi komi* 住み込み (living in) is rarely practiced, mainly because it is inconvenient. One common alternative is for the master to rent a small apartment for her/his pupil nearby. The servant aspect of training is still intact.
11 Email correspondence with Katsura Ayame III, July 2021.
12 *Chiri-tote-chin* (Twing-a-Twang) and *Atagoyama* are well-known *rakugo* titles.
13 In Japan, *matsutake* are usually harvested between September and October.

14 Janet Goodridge believes that "A sense of timing is present in all skilled performance – in contexts as far apart as an operating theatre or a game", adding that "(t)iming in the use of pauses may be particularly expressive" (Goodridge 1999: 45, 46).
15 Email correspondence with Katsura Ayame III, July 2021.
16 Bunza appeared to be bringing up this topic because people continued entering the venue throughout his *makura*—he was buying time and allowing the audience to get settled in.
17 The *go* in Goemon 五右衛門 means five, while the *yo* in Yoemon 四右衛門 means four. Neimon-han 二右衛門半 is a play on "two and a half" (this nicely ties into the joke about four and a half bikes). In other words, thieves in the *rakugo* world are a far cry from strong, brave, handsome *kabuki* thieves, celebrated as heroes of popular culture because they were Robin Hood-like characters.
18 *Nashi* 梨 is the Japanese word for pear. *Chōjūrō* 長十郎 and *nijjiseiki* 二十世紀 (Twentieth Century) are Japanese pear varieties (*Pyrus pyrifolia*).
19 The provider's name has been bleeped out on the CD version. This speaks to the idea that *makura* are private, intended only for those attending the live performance, and that they might invite legal trouble in some contexts.
20 Masuzoe Yōichi (b. 1948) was mayor of Tokyo from 2014 to 2016, when he resigned over the controversy sparked by his misuse of public funds.
21 This rapid-fire speech is referred to as *tateben* 立て弁, a narrative technique in which one speaks so quickly that the sound of one's speech (namely, the staccato therein) can be likened to the sound of *tateita ni mizu* 立て板に水 (water streaming down a washboard) (see Shores 2021: 105).
22 Zoom video conference with Shōfukutei Tama, 3 July 2021.

References

Andō Tsuruo 安藤鶴夫. 1966. *Watashi no yose* わたしの寄席 (*My* yose). Tokyo: Sekkasha.
Boxer, Diana. 2011. *The Lost art of the good schmooze: Building rapport and diffusing conflict in everyday and public talk*. Santa Barbara, CA: Praeger.
Brau, Lorie. 2008. *Rakugo: Performing comedy and cultural heritage in contemporary Tokyo*. Lanham, MD: Lexington Books.
Bushnell, Cade. 2017. She who laughs first: Audience laughter and interactional competence at a *rakugo* performance for foreign students. In T. Greer, M. Ishida and Y. Tateyama, eds., *Interactional competence in Japanese as an additional language*. 81–114. Honolulu, HI: National Foreign Language Resource Center.
Goodridge, Janet. 1999. *Rhythm and timing of movement in performance: Drama, dance and ceremony*. London: Kingsley.
Inoue, Hiroshi. 2007. Osaka's culture of laughter. In Jessica Milner Davis, ed., *Understanding humor in Japan*. 27–35. Detroit, MI: Wayne State University Press.
Kamens, Edward. 1997. *Utamakura, allusion, and intertextuality in traditional Japanese poetry*. New Haven, CT: Yale University Press.
Katsura Beichō 桂米朝. 2004. *Katsura Beichō shūsei* 桂米朝集成 (*Katsura Beichō compilation*), vol. 1. Toyoda Yoshinori and Toda Manabu, eds. Tokyo: Iwanami Shoten.
Katsura Bunshi 桂文枝. 1996. *Ankerasō yawa* あんけら荘夜話 (*Evening tales of an idiot*). Tokyo: Seiabō.
Katsura Shikō 桂枝光 and Doi Jurō 土肥寿朗. 2007. *Chiri-tote-chin no ajiwaikata: Katsura Shikō no rakugo annai 1* ちりとてちんの味わい方 桂枝光の落語案内1 (*How to taste Chiri-tote-chin: Katsura Shikō's Guide to* rakugo 1). Sapporo: Jurōsha.

Katsura Shikō 桂枝光 and Doi Jurō 土肥寿朗. 2008. *Atagoyama no noborikata: Katsura Shikō no rakugo annai 2* 愛宕山の登り方 桂枝光の落語案内2 (*How to climb Mt. Atago: Katsura Shikō's guide to* rakugo 2). Sapporo: Jurōsha.

Kyono, Chiho. 2017. Japanese politeness situated in thanking a benefactor: Examining the use of four types of Japanese benefactive auxiliary verbs. *East Asian Pragmatics*, 2 (1): 25–57.

Masuyama, Eichi Erick. 1997. Towards an understanding of *rakugo* as a communicative event: A performance analysis of traditional professional storytelling in Japan. Unpublished PhD dissertation, University of Oregon.

Miyamoto Kanako 宮本加奈子. 2004. *Rakugoka no makura ni okeru danwa tenkai no shakaigengogakuteki kenkyū: Shinshō to Shinchō oyako o chūshin ni* 落語家の枕における談話展開の社会言語学的研究 志ん生と志ん朝親子を中心に (*A sociolinguistic study of discourse flow in the* makura *of rakugo: Shinshō and Shinchō, father and son*). *Tamamo*, 40: 29–35.

Noma Seiji 沢田一矢. 1933. *Hyōban rakugo zenshū* 評判落語全集 (*Popular* rakugo *anthology*), vol. 1, preface. n.p. Tokyo: Dai Nippon Yūbenkai Kōdansha.

Nomura Masaaki 野村雅昭. 1994. *Rakugo no gengogaku* 落語の言語学 (*Rakugo linguistics*). Tokyo: Heibonsha.

Oda, Shōkichi. 2006. Laughter and the traditional Japanese smile. In Jessica Milner Davis, ed., *Understanding humor in Japan*. 13–26. Detroit, MI: Wayne State University Press.

Okamoto, Shigeko. 2016. Variability and multiplicity in the meanings of stereotypical gendered speech in Japanese. *East Asian Pragmatics*, 1 (1): 5–37.

Ōno Susumu 大野晋, Satake Akihiro 佐竹昭広, Maeda Kingorō 前田金五郎, eds. 2002. *Makura* (entry no. 5). In *Iwanami kogo jiten hoteiban* 岩波古語辞典 補訂版 (*Iwanami's classical language dictionary, expanded*). 13th ed. 1216–1217. Tokyo: Iwanami Shoten.

Sawada Kazuya. 1989. *Makura wa rakugo o sukueru ka* まくらは落語をすくえるか (*Can* makura *save* rakugo?). Tokyo: Chikuma Shobō.

Shores, M.W. 2021. *The comic storytelling tradition of western Japan: Satire and social mobility in Kamigata rakugo*. Cambridge: Cambridge University Press.

Suzuki, Tomi. 1996. *Narrating the self: Fictions of Japanese modernity*. Palo Alto, CA: Stanford University Press.

Takekuro, Makiko. 2006. Conversational jokes in Japanese and English. In Jessica Milner Davis, ed., *Understanding humor in Japan*. 85–98. Detroit, MI: Wayne State University Press.

Ui Mushū 宇井無愁. 1965. *Kamigata hanashi kō* 上方落語考 (*A Study of Kamigata* rakugo). Tokyo: Seiabō.

Yamada Riyoko やまだりよこ. 2010. *Kamigata rakugoka meikan* 上方落語家名鑑 (*Kamigata storyteller directory*). 2nd ed. Osaka: Shuppan Bunkasha.

Yamamoto Susumu 山本進, ed. 2001. *Rakugo handobukku* 落語ハンドブック (Rakugo *handbook*). Rev. ed. Tokyo: Sanseidō.

Digital Media

Edward White. *Rakugo Katsura Ayame Chiri-tote-chin onna baajon de* 落語 桂あやめ ちりとてちん 女バージョンで (*Rakugo* Katsura Ayame Twing-a-twang women's version). At: https://youtu.be/LD9e4YL4VeY (accessed 15 February 2022).

Sandaime Hayashiya Kikumaru kōshiki channeru 三代目林家菊丸公式チャンネル (Sandaime Hayashiya). Vol. 20 *Kōsuke mochi* 「幸助餅」(Vol. 20 Kosuke's *Mochi*). At: https://youtu.be/XLde-X8q4Vo (accessed 15 February 2022).

Nihon no wagei 日本の話芸. Katsura Zakoba *'Nedoko'* 桂ざこば「寝床」(Katsura Zakoba 'Bed'). At: https://youtu.be/GnoWw8MzAwk (accessed 15 February 2022).

Shōfukutei, T. 2016. *Funa Benkei* 船弁慶 (Benkei on the Boat). On *Shōfukutei Tama 1* 笑福亭たま 1 [CD]. Tokyo: Wazaogi.

Terebi bangumi テレビ番組. *Katsura Fukudanji 'Nezumi ana'* 桂福團治「ねずみ穴」(Katsura Fukudanji 'Mousehole'). At: https://youtu.be/hGxuGDIe_Iw (accessed 15 February 2022).

Uhuhu01. *Katsura Bunza no Hōjuji Yose isseki 'Imodawara'* (H29-*nen* 1-*gatsu* 14-*ka*) 桂文三の宝珠寺寄席第 1 席「芋俵」(H29 年 1 月 14 日) (Katsura Bunza's first story at Hōjuji *Yose* 'Sack of Potatoes' [14 January 2015]). At: https://youtu.be/iVbtflyxp1U (accessed 15 February 2022).

8 To joke or not to joke?
Politeness, power and the impact of tradition in Korean workplace humour

HeeSun Kim and Barbara Plester

Introduction

Humour in Korean organisations

This chapter investigates humour within Korean workplaces, with a particular focus on Confucian-based relationships and politeness in communication. Humour is a phenomenon that exists across most cultures (Berger 1987), but how it is used is influenced by the cultural context (Alden et al. 1993). This means that humour use varies in different cultures and its impact is highly contextual. Humour is ambiguous and complex, which may lead to positive or negative outcomes in terms of interpersonal relationships (Cooper 2008), emotions (Kim and Plester 2019), and work performance (Isen et al. 1987).

While humour is generally perceived as a positive form of interaction (La Fave et al. 1976), understanding humour and its uses can be more complicated in Confucian-based cultures. Therefore, our inquiry explores humour in Korean organisations with embedded Confucian cultural values of hierarchy, harmony, and respect, and we focus upon the emphasis on politeness in workplace communication. Language used in Korean workplaces is based on status differences and the use of work and societal titles and honorifics assists in signalling relational hierarchy (McBrian 1978). Language (honorifics) and organisational relationships lie at the centre of this study of how organisational humour and language use are influenced by Confucian values. It offers new perspectives into organisational humour based on culture and politeness and outlines the implications and pragmatic considerations for organisational relationships in Korean workplaces.

Humour, Confucianism and work

Humour is a contextual phenomenon that exists in most cultures (Berger 1987). Generally, humour is considered to create happiness (La Fave et al. 1976) and a sense of commonality (Alden et al. 1993), and thus as a generally positive experience (Ruch 2008) among people. However, the underlying

DOI: 10.4324/9781003176374-8

cultural values of its interacting group and of the wider society may lead to different uses and interpretations of humour. While it is difficult to provide a universal definition of humour (McGhee 1979), it is a multifaceted term which includes both social and psychological processes. Humour may be described as a complex and contextual social interaction which incorporates amusement, laughter, and also unpleasant or unexpected outcomes (Plester 2016); the term also includes the mental process, creation, and emotional responses of and towards funny or laughable gestures and words (Martin and Ford 2018). For example, laughter in Japanese contexts may indicate (negative) interactional problems rather than an enjoyable experience (Tanaka 2018).

Humour may help to describe individual differences (Ruch et al. 2018), to enhance workplace communication (Holmes 2000), and to increase creativity and innovation (Isen et al. 1987). Thus, in an attempt to acquire the beneficial outcomes of humour, organisations often overlook the potentially negative side of humour (Morreall 1983). Humour may be misinterpreted, which can create disruption and conflict (Plester 2016), and it may even exclude some people within the workplace (Plester and Sayers 2007).

Both organisational culture (Plester 2016) and the society in which an organisation is based (Milner Davis 2016) may influence humour significantly. Thus, different cultural assumptions can easily create ambiguity and misunderstanding between communicators in exchanging humour. This is an important aspect of its use, especially in globalised workplace contexts where people from different cultures interact and work together. Cultures that are influenced by Confucian philosophy may approach the idea of humour differently from those in Western contexts (Yue et al. 2016). In Confucian contexts, humour may be perceived as damaging to the authority of individuals of higher organisational status and thus is sometimes considered an inappropriate form of workplace interaction. Individuals in such contexts may use humour based on their cultural backgrounds and associated normative orientation, thus influencing the management of *chemyon* 체면 or face (Kim 2018). Therefore, we argue that workplace humour must be investigated in relation to the associated culture and context.

Confucianism is a philosophy incorporating respect and ethics that has influenced the cultures within diverse East Asian countries such as Korea, China, Japan and Vietnam (Duncan 2002). Everyday practices and the language of Korean people are strongly influenced by such Confucian values which structure societal norms and the ideals of individuals (Choi 2010; Deuchler 1992). Confucianism endorses the value of harmony and interdependency, whereby members within a society should consider hierarchical relationships as a means to maintain respect and collective development (Yao 2000). Authoritarian rule guides the relational role expected between individuals (Rowley and Bae 2003), such that superiors guide and protect subordinates, and subordinates obey and respect superiors (Yao 2000) in order to accomplish group goals and maintain harmony (Hofstede 1984).

Communication processes and language are also influenced by Confucian values which guide relationships within workplaces (Rowley and Bae 2003). Workers in subordinate positions are expected to respond to superiors with silence to show obedience, and are thus restricted in terms of communication (Lim 1999). Respectful behaviour and extensive use of honorifics are expected, based on the relational social and organisational positions (Hwang 1991; McBrian 1978), and thus the ambiguity of humour interactions can create complex dilemmas for both subordinates and managers in Korean workplaces.

Confucian indirectness and humour

Age is an important part of understanding interpersonal relationships within Confucian societies (Yao 2000). Hierarchical status is crafted through a patriarchal or family-like relationship structure, and individuals are expected to behave according to this relational status (Deuchler 1992). This means Korean workplace relationships intersect with Confucian societal roles to guide behaviour and relational interactions. Identifying the relational hierarchy is important to maintain harmonious organisational life in Korean workplaces and hierarchical roles also influence communicative norms (Shim et al. 2008). Since relational status determines the appropriate titles and language to be used between individuals, appropriate language for superiors and subordinates is significantly different. For example, while the title "Mr" or "Miss" (*ssi* 씨 in Korean) may be an adequate way of addressing superiors within Western contexts, in Korea, this is considered rather informal and inappropriate. Instead, more formal titles such as "madam" or "sir" (*nim* 님 in Korean) are more commonly accepted and thus most appropriate to be used towards organisational superiors.

As language must be formally and cautiously structured at work, the use of humour may also need to be carefully considered in organisational communication. While humour still occurs in Confucian-based contexts including Korea (Jung 2014; Kim and Lee 2009), hierarchical dynamics in humour interactions have not been fully investigated (Jung 2014). Furthermore, Cooper (2008) suggests that humour influences the quality of interpersonal relationships between people regardless of their hierarchical differences. Western organisational research (Holmes 2000, 2006; Holmes and Marra 2002; Plester and Orams 2008) has emphasised the reduction of hierarchical levels that occurs when humour is shared at work. However, using workplace humour that reduces hierarchical differences may well be perceived as a challenge in Confucian-based hierarchical structure and could upset the collective identity, behavioural norms and harmony expected in Korean workplaces.

Tanaka (2018) argues that interactional work is facilitated by laughter and that this may be more widely shared across cultural-linguistic contexts that have previously been assumed. The indirectness of humour creates ambiguity which is a feature of humour (Wood 1981). Elements of the "unsaid" or unspoken meaning conveyed by humour further heighten such ambiguity (Dolitsky 1983). It seems however that the indirectness of humour can help to maintain some forms of politeness (Brown and Levinson 1978) and this study links aspects of humour to the politeness and indirectness important in Confucian cultural interactions. While literature suggests that honorifics in Korean language are a form of politeness, and indirectness is somewhat related to being polite (House and Kasper 2011; Upadhyay 2003), further investigation is needed to clarify the link between linguistic indirectness and politeness in Korean workplaces and we would argue that humour should be part of such an investigation—explored from a cultural and contextual perspective. Accordingly, in our pragmatic approach in this chapter, we will demonstrate how the workplace context contributes to the meaning and interpretation of interactional humour. The study analyses linguistic humour and workplace relationships underpinned by Confucian culture in South Korean organisations and its research question asks: "What is the relationship between humour, politeness, and Confucian culture in Korean workplace contexts?"

Methodology

This study adopts an ethnographic approach to investigate humour in Korean workplaces. Humour is a contextual phenomenon that may be interpreted differently and subjectively by communicating individuals (Holmes 2006). Therefore, in order to understand the diverse interpretations of humour, politeness, and Confucian cultural values within Korean workplaces, a multi-voiced interpretivist approach (Alvesson 2010; Cunliffe et al. 2014) is used to investigate the phenomenon. Participant observations, semi-structured interviews and document collection were used to collect data and provide rich descriptions and stories (Bryman and Bell 2015).

Three different Korean companies were selected in an attempt to extend the learning about the phenomenon of interest (Stake 2013). These companies have been assigned the pseudonyms, Wisepath, Mintrack and Truscene. Each company reflects different organisational characteristics, culture, size and industry and the data is drawn from manufacturing, online gaming and Information Technology (IT) industries. The research was undertaken over a period of three months, during which the researcher was fully immersed for observation in each company and its operations for one full month.

Observations focused on markers of organisational culture such as documentary records (e.g. organisational policies), physical manifestations (e.g. symbols and company logo), and the language used between organisational members. The researcher engaged in some organisational activities across working and non-working hours, and undertook work tasks including translating documents, serving in company event booths, and hands-on factory work. In order to understand the subjective experiences and implications for employees, both formal and informal (impromptu) interviews were conducted. Korean language was used in conducting all interviews, as this was the most comfortable language for the participants (Welch and Piekkari 2006). Interviews were later translated into English by the researcher. Across the 3 companies, 46 semi-structured interviews were conducted, and participation was voluntary.

The data collected were analysed using thematic analysis, to understand patterns and themes within the data that provided flexibility and were deemed appropriate for the exploratory nature of this project (Braun and Clarke 2006). The NVivo 12 Plus programme was used to assist the organisation of data during the analysis process. Analysis was conducted in multiple stages, from initial data collection to categorisation and review of combined data. The issue of reflexivity was also considered during the data collection period by using a reflective diary. Notes on the data collected, along with personal reflections on this process, were made by the researcher in order to offer a personalised and reflexive account of significant experiences.

Four broad themes were developed from the collected data. These are: (1) Confucianism and Korean Society; (2) Hierarchy and Managers; (3) Face Saving; and (4) Honorifics. The first theme, Confucianism and Korean Society, addresses the (negative) cultural perceptions towards humour within wider Korean society. The Hierarchy and Managers theme concerns how the use of humour is influenced by the relational hierarchy of communicators, especially those in superior managerial positions. The third theme, Face Saving, encompasses humour used as a method to save or damage face between individuals; and lastly, Honorifics discusses the role of honorifics within humour and different interpretations in terms of politeness and respect.

Confucianism and Korean society

The role of Confucianism within Korean society emerges as an important part of constructing communication and relationships between individuals, even in these organisational contexts. Across all three companies, most participants discussed the influence of Confucianism from the wider Korean society on how humour is shared with other organisational members. Some typical comments (all names are pseudonyms) are:

> It doesn't fit with Korean culture. A workplace needs to be formal. Mixing (humour) with work makes you look arrogant, so it doesn't suit workplace settings.
>
> *Agate, 30, male, Truscene*

> Under the Korean culture, we want discipline. So that's why we are strict on these things ...
>
> *Obsidian, 59, male, Wisepath*

Both these interviewees emphasise the incompatibility between "Korean culture" and humour. While it is unclear what specific aspect of Korean culture is referred to by the participants, the importance of formality and discipline is clearly seen as an important part of it that may be damaged through the use of humour, even resulting in a negative impression ("makes you look arrogant"). Humour is described as a phenomenon that "doesn't suit workplace settings" and it is to be controlled ("we are strict on these things"). Similarly, another participant recounted her observations of a work colleague being punished for the use of humour within the workplace:

> One of my colleagues, he was seriously criticised by the manager for joking around [...] maybe he was over-doing it. But he was so beaten down about it that he never jokes anymore. The same applies to me, so I try not to use humour. I don't even think about the very idea of using humour in the workplace.
>
> *Aquamarine, 20, female, Truscene*

This participant here recalls observing that her colleague (presumably also positioned lower in the organisational hierarchy as the word "colleague" is only used for organisational members in similar hierarchical positions) was once "*seriously criticised*" by their seniors for using humour within the place, and now "never jokes anymore". This implies that humour actions are not approved of by senior members within Truscene and are considered inappropriate, at least for those in lower hierarchical positions ("the same applies to me"). Such disapproval towards the use of workplace humour is attributed by another interviewee to the influence of Confucianism:

> Although I'm not one of those old people emphasising politeness, Korea is still a Confucian-based country. So when you interact with people, you need to have that minimum line [of being polite], but some people don't keep to that line and thinking that they are all funny and good.
>
> *Iolite, 36, male, Mintrack*

> Old people like us have been educated based on Confucianism. Traditionally, our ancestors, father, and mother ... they taught us that joking and laughing makes us look frivolous. Too much of it will make us look vulgar. So these ideas definitely make us different to the younger generation now.
>
> *Obsidian, 59, male, Wisepath*

Confucianism is openly discussed as an important part of guiding behaviour between Korean organisational members ("Korea is still a Confucian-based country"). Iolite suggests that Confucian values should shape how individuals interact and notes that excessive humour has the potential to violate such Confucian values ("some people don't keep to that line and thinking that

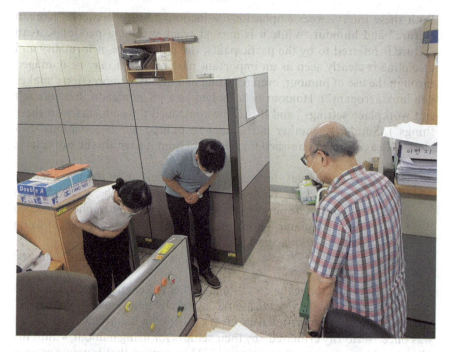

Figure 8.1 Two relatively junior employees working in a semi-open plan office greet their superior as he arrives in their space. He acknowledges but does not respond.

Source: Photography by HeeSun Kim, July 2021; reproduced with kind permission.

they are all funny and good"), and he emphasises politeness ("you need to have that minimum line [of being polite]"). Normal office behaviour in the Korean workplace still insists on many aspects of formality in interpersonal relations, for example, the use of honorifics (as will be discussed below) and behaviours such as the formal bow of greetings given by those in lower hierarchical positions to any older, more senior, or longer tenured employee (for an illustration, see Figure 8.1). Furthermore, Obsidian suggests that under traditional Confucian values, one's own face may be damaged ("look frivolous", "look vulgar") simply by using humour within the workplace; thus, humour is evidently perceived as a negative and risky form of interaction by these workers.

Hierarchy and managers

Another important idea raised by the data involves the influence of hierarchy and how managers and their humour reflect the power differences that exist between organisational members. This is not a simple matter. Within the companies studied, managers' humour was perceived as a positive technique helping to develop organisational relationships. For example, one of the interview participants in a subordinate position described his perception of his own supervisor's use of humour:

> I talk to my manager often, even when he is away on a business trip. He talks in a funny way, and makes me feel quite close [to him]. Of course, not all of his jokes are funny, but he's good. For me, that makes him feel like a brother, or an uncle.
>
> *Apatite, 24, male, Truscene*

While Apatite acknowledges here that his manager's jokes are not always truly funny, he describes his humour as "good". A humorous interaction with a manager seems to help reduce psychological distance with the manager and creates a feeling of closeness ("makes me feel quite close", "feel like a brother, or an uncle"). This implies that, from a subordinate's perspective, a superior's use of humour can be considered as a positive process that helps to develop interpersonal relationships, and thus that it confers some benefits for manager/subordinate relations. Similarly, but from a different point of view, another interview participant in a senior managerial position explained how humour helps managers perform their role as superiors within the workplace:

> As a senior organisational member, I can jokingly tell people off, because I don't want them to cry. I also use jokes to give advice about dating, marriage, and other things, not so serious, but I've lived longer and I care. I think I'm the most caring person in this company [laughs].
>
> *Alexandrite, 42, male, Truscene*

Alexandrite explains that humour may be utilised by managers to perform their role as a manager ("tell people off"), and also by himself as an elderly person ("give advice about dating, marriage, and other things, not so serious, but I've lived longer"). Such use of humour is considered as a signal of "care". This implies that humour initiated by those in superior positions may be perceived as a mode of performing their hierarchical role of "superiors" having an implied duty of care and protection (Yao 2000) towards subordinates.

However, such positive perceptions about humour seemed to be limited to those in superior roles. One of the interview participants occupying a junior organisational position suggested that engaging in humour may be dependent on organisational hierarchy:

> While our company seems really friendly, the whole top-down hierarchy is really important here. Once I got told off by a passing-by manager for joking around with someone in the company kitchen. He asked who has the longer tenure, and only when I told him that we were only a month apart [in organisational tenure] did he back off. It was strange.
>
> *Carnelian, 24, female, Truscene*

This participant explained that hierarchy determines who can initiate humour within the workplace. Her experience of being "told off" by a manager for joking, but later being permitted to use humour with members having similar organisational tenure implies that humour initiated by individuals in relationally lower hierarchical positions is perceived as inappropriate. This is because, at least within the studied Korean workplaces, tenure is an important part of identifying hierarchy between organisational members, because promotion is primarily based on how long someone has been working for the company. Long tenure thus confers seniority upon managers. However, Carnelian also suggested that the manager's behaviour is "strange", implying that those lower in the hierarchy may not agree that those with seniority can use humour how and when they choose.

Responses to humour can also be influenced by organisational hierarchy. The following observational example illustrates how the CEO's humour is accepted by subordinates despite being uncomfortable to them:

> CEO buys a cup of coffee for himself and Citrine at a cafe, and starts to walk back to the office. CEO takes a sip of coffee, and looks at Citrine with a serious expression.
> CEO: Citrine, I think I talked to you about this before, but you really do need to get married before you get too old. I'm really concerned about you.
> CITRINE: [Laughs] Don't worry, I'll get married when I'm ready.
> CEO: You've been saying that for years now. Really, you need to get married. I'm concerned as a senior person. Do you want me to introduce you to someone decent?
> CITRINE: No thank you [laughs]. Let's go and work. Work is important.
> CEO: Women these days, you should really be conscious [laughs].
> CITRINE: [whispers] He's always like this.
> *17 April, Mintrack observation notes*

This observed exchange shows how a subordinate responds positively with laughter towards a superior's inappropriate and intrusive joking remarks about her marriage. Humour is used by the CEO in an attempt to perform his role as a senior (in age) and to demonstrate that he feels a responsibility to look out for his subordinates and their personal lives ("I'm concerned as a senior person"). Citrine does not show resistance but simply accepts the guidance and laughs at the joke. While Citrine's response seems polite, she later admits (via a whisper) that the CEO's joke is not appreciated. Her whispered comment that "he's always like this" implies that the CEO frequently uses humour to discuss the personal lives (such as marriage) of subordinates, and that Citrine is enduring such humour, rather than enjoying it, because of the hierarchical differences between her and the CEO.

Evidently, hierarchical difference between the CEO and Citrine differentiates how each individual interacts and responds to humour, such that individuals in subordinate positions may be relatively restricted in their actions during humorous interactions. In all the workplaces studied, the power embedded in hierarchical position influenced humour interactions, suggesting that humour may in fact be a form of display of power in these organisational relationships, despite its being framed as a duty of care.

Face saving

Not surprisingly, face also emerged as an important issue in discussing the use of humour in these three Korean workplaces. Humour can work to help save face, and saving face at work is certainly important to these participants. The following observation example illustrates how a senior manager used humour to save his face:

> The CEO criticises Jasper's work, in the middle of the company courtyard and leaves. Jasper looks around to check that the CEO has left the courtyard, he looks around again and makes eye contact with other organisational members that were standing around. Jasper spots one young male worker standing approximately two metres away and suddenly starts a conversation in a joking tone of voice.
> JASPER: Hey you, what happened to your surgery? Is your ass-hole okay now? How was your treatment for hemorrhoids?
> Viridine turns around and smiles.
> JASPER: You eat too much, that's your problem. Ladies at the company kitchen always say that you eat too much. That's why your asshole is in such a bad shape [laughs]. Let me have a look at your asshole some time, just to see if it's all right for you to work properly.
> VIRIDINE: [Laughs] Why are you doing this to me?
> Viridine bows and runs away towards the factory.
> JASPER: [Laugh] Oh, I'm such a kind and concerned person. The perfect manager.
>
> *11 June, Wisepath observation notes*

This example illustrates the multidimensional impact of humour in terms of face. First, Jasper initiates a seemingly tendentious joke (a joke which transgresses a social taboo, see Freud 1960) aimed at Viridine (talking about Viridine's intimate body part) which may be an attempt to shift attention from Jasper himself having been shamed (criticised) by the CEO and thus to save Jasper's face. However, he achieves this by damaging the face of a subordinate (Viridine). Joking about Viridine being treated for haemorrhoids is clearly a personal health issue and it is likely that he would want this to remain private. However, by exposing Viridine's health problem through a joke, Jasper temporarily victimises Viridine, suggesting that he may be perceived as compromised in his work capability as well as embarrassing him about his personal problem. This may well protect Jasper's face, however, as he asserts his relational superiority to Viridine, acting as a powerful superior with the ability to embarrass and expose his subordinate.

Interview participants like the following explained that protecting face is an important issue within their workplace, and thus humour may be one of the methods to maintain their face in different situations:

> It kind of emphasises our value on how you are viewed to others.
> *Turquoise, 35, male, Truscene*

Another observation note also indicated that humour may be used to protect face by subordinates. In one of the participating companies (Truscene), humour shared between two organisational members at a similar hierarchical level suggested that subordinates may use humour to protect their own face when interacting with workers of similar (but not equal) organisational hierarchy and age. In this example, Amethyst, Lapis, and Aquamarine engage in humour during their lunchtime. Lapis is not a manager, but is oldest in age among the three women workers in this observation example. All three individuals are at staff level but differ in age and tenure. Amethyst is positioned hierarchically lower than Lapis but slightly higher (in tenure) than Aquamarine.

> Amethyst and Aquamarine run around the office corridor, laughing. Lapis enters the corridor, watches Amethyst and Aquamarine, and shouts at them with a big smile.
> LAPIS: Hey Amethyst, you are sweating like crazy, look at your armpits, oh my god your armpits!
> Aquamarine turns towards Amethyst and pokes her finger at Amethyst's arms
> AQUAMARINE: Oh my god, it is really wet [laughs].
> Amethyst grabs a water dispenser (spray) and starts to spray water on Aquamarine's armpits.
> AMETHYST: [laughs] You know how much I love wet armpits! Let's wet armpits!
> LAPIS: She's obsessed with armpits, she's a pervert, stay away from me, keep your hands where I can see them.
> *14 April, Truscene observation notes*

In this example, Amethyst attempts to protect her face by using humour (spraying water on other people's armpits) to relieve a shameful situation. When Lapis teases Amethyst about sweating, having obviously wet armpits seems to create shame and embarrassment for her. By wetting someone else (Aquamarine)'s armpits, Amethyst jokingly places Aquamarine in a similar position to herself and avoids being the only person with wet armpits. This sequence of actions implies that humour may also be used by individuals in subordinate positions to protect their face, although the humour may not be directed at the superior who has caused the loss of face, at least not in this example.

Honorifics

Honorifics in Korean language are used to construct politeness between communicators by using specific honorifics and titles, depending on the relational hierarchy, between individuals. However, honorifics used in humour interactions can imply messages other than a display of respect and politeness, especially when used by those with superior status. For example, one of the interview participants explained how honorifics and language should be carefully structured even in humour:

> I'm a funny person. I like to joke around. So sometimes I call people names, but obviously maintain some politeness, like calling people by their right titles and using some honorifics, like "*hyung*" 형 [direct translation, "older brother", from younger males] rather than their names. In Korea, calling an older person by their name only is really not a good idea.
>
> *Diamond, 30, male, Mintrack*

This participant implies that, even if he "likes to joke around", politeness needs to be maintained through honorifics and appropriate titles, and that violating such relational structures even in humour is "not a good idea". This suggests that honorifics do indeed play an important role in maintaining hierarchical relationships within the studied workplaces. However, honorifics used in a superior's joke may be a more complex matter, and they may not necessarily signal politeness. One observation example illustrates how a middle manager's use of honorifics in a humorous manner provides a number of different interpretations. This example involves several organisational members interacting during a company workshop, which includes playing games, drinking alcohol and socialising at a holiday house.

EMERALD: Ingredients for the barbeque are almost ready. Hey, isn't it a bit unfair that only the female members are working to prepare for dinner?
IOLITE: Hello, don't forget about me, I'm not a girl, but I work here.
EMERALD: I know, you are an exception.
DIAMOND: Yes, yes, yes ma'am [*ne, ne, ne* 네, 네, 네]. I get your point err.

23 May, Mintrack observation notes

In this observation, Diamond is older and also higher in the organisational hierarchy than Emerald. Nevertheless, he says "*ne, ne, ne* 네, 네, 네", which in Korean is a form of honorific that translates into a very polite, "yes, yes,

yes". Diamond's use of honorifics to respond to Emerald suggests that he is actually unhappy with the fact that Emerald, a subordinate, is wanting another member, a man, to work in the kitchen. It serves as a form of sarcasm to show his discontent, and calling Emerald "*ma'am*" but also making a growling sound, "*err*", shows that Diamond does not at all intend to show respect and politeness towards Emerald by using such honorifics.

Complexity of this kind when using honorifics in humour in relation to different hierarchical standards (of age and organisational position) is also suggested by one of the interview participants:

> Of course, I use honorifics to the CEO and other managers. They are high people [in the organisational hierarchy] in Wisepath [...] but yes, they are much younger than me in age, but they sometimes use different titles and partial-honorifics to me when they joke at social drinking functions. It's good, it's fun, and I know they do it for my sake.
>
> *Coral, 64, female, Wisepath*

Coral is one of the oldest (in age) workers in Wisepath, but nevertheless, she explains that she uses honorifics to the CEO and other managers, due to the organisational hierarchy ("they are high people"). However, she also mentions that the managers use of (partial) honorifics and "different titles". This suggests that managers' use of honorifics in humour ("when they joke at social drinking functions") may be an attempt to regulate the potential problems in showing politeness ("they do it for my sake"), when there are conflicting standards to establish a hierarchy between workers.

Discussion and conclusions

Humour is of course a contextual phenomenon that can be influenced by cultural context as well as by the communicating individuals (Alden et al. 1993). This study investigated the role of Confucian cultural values in using humour within Korean workplaces and its data suggests that the underlying societal values may well influence perceptions and attitudes towards humour usage within the workplace, where Confucian values of formality and hierarchy (Rowley and Bae 2003; Yao 2000) construct humour interactions in a different manner to those in Western contexts (Yue et al. 2016). This finding correlates with existing studies showing that humour in general may not be appreciated in Confucian-based contexts, although they too have shown that humour still occurs within Korean workplaces (Jung 2014; Kim and Lee 2009).

The present study contributes to the extant but limited research into organisational humour in Eastern businesses which are known to be influenced by Confucian values of hierarchy and respect and which emphasise politeness between organisational members. We have argued here that, while humour is generally considered as a positive communication medium that creates enjoyment and develops workplace relationships, such positive experiences may be mostly limited to those with relationally superior status. Most humour observed in the workplaces studied here was initiated by those in relationally superior positions. This superiority is determined by age, organisational position, and by tenure, and a combination of these three factors influences how humour may be used. Superiors are able to use humour more comfortably, while subordinates restrain themselves from initiating humour, since it may be perceived as both inappropriate and impolite, given that obedience is preferred for those in subordinate positions (Lim 1999). This insight extends Smith and Powell's (1988) study, illustrating how hierarchical differences between workers may influence humour interactions. Our observations lead us to argue that humour may serve as a medium for superiors to perform their role as a senior within the Confucian relationship structure (Yao 2000) and that, therefore, humour from a superior, even if not fully enjoyed by all the participants, was mostly accepted by subordinates as a signal of care.

Our observations also suggest that language—and especially humorous language—may need to be constructed and interpreted carefully in non-Western workplaces such as those of Korea. Lower-level employees are highly constrained by politeness norms and therefore both in response to and creation of humour must consider whether the humour interaction meets their societal norms of polite behaviour. Kadar and Spencer-Oatey's (2016) study of politeness evaluations suggests that people who value high "power distance" may evaluate behaviour that challenges others as impolite and they argue that hierarchical relations do in fact affect perceptions of politeness and appropriateness. Building on this notion, many of our younger participants also emphasised the cultural value of politeness but further identified that using humour may itself be perceived as an impolite behaviour in their workplace—making humour somewhat risky for them. Our conclusion is that in the Korean workplaces studied, instigating humour at work is considered a challenging behaviour if and when a subordinate instigates jokes with their (superior) managers; and that upwards joking contravenes politeness norms and is seen as impolite, thus inappropriate. However, when a manager initiates humour in a downwards direction, subordinates are expected to respond positively through smiles or laughter, and thus signal appreciation towards the manager, regardless of their actual evaluation of the humour used.

Participants within these workplaces also used humour to save or protect face within the workplace. These positive uses of humour revealed that the act of laughter and using humour helped individuals to divert attention away from shameful situations, often by involving other individuals in the humour interaction. We saw humour used to disguise mistakes, to offset embarrassment and to redirect a joke's target. The concept of shame appeared relevant to that of face, with participants experiencing shame and embarrassment even in response to minor mistakes. Protecting face through humour is strongly linked to the hierarchical dynamics and relationships that we encountered, as when senior managers sought to take back their superior position and even used humour to denigrate and belittle subordinates in order to firmly re-establish dominance and their superior position. The effectiveness of this technique supports our contention that subordinates within our studied Korean workplaces are tightly bound by politeness rules that constrain their own humour usage, especially towards their managers. This strongly contrasts with much Western research arguing that humour may help subordinates contest and challenge both their managers and organisational decisions (e.g. Holmes and Marra 2002; Plester and Orams 2016).

Honorifics are unquestionably important in Korean culture and those used in everyday work conversations, including humour interactions, are linked to linguistic politeness in Korean as well as in Japanese society (Brown et al. 2014; Shibamoto-Smith 2011). Zajdman (1995) suggests that distance between individuals may be promoted through jokes. The observation above (23 May, Mintrack) in which we saw a senior manager sarcastically use honorifics in his joke to emphasise his hierarchy with a subordinate elaborates this theme. In this case, the sarcastic honorifics did not signal politeness, but instead promoted distance. Although framed in humour, the honorifics signified that the subordinate should recognise her inappropriate behaviour that violated their hierarchical relationships. Therefore, honorifics may not always serve as polite behaviour, but can in fact be used as face-threatening in targeted humour that attempts to reassert workplace relationships.

This focus of this study of humour within Korean organisations has been on the role of the Confucian values of hierarchy, respect and politeness. The findings reinforce and extend the authors' original theorisation (Kim and Plester 2019) of the role of Confucian norms in humour use in Korean workplaces. In particular, they show that humour used by senior managers may differ significantly to how subordinates can use and respond to humour, and how that may impact on the communicators' hierarchical relationships and face. As well as societal values like Confucianism, different language norms such as the use of honorifics construct significant complexities in understanding humour as it occurs in Korean workplace contexts. However, interpreting the hidden messages in that humour may also help to construct different expectations about language relationships and roles within Korean organisations.

References

Alden, D. L., W. D. Hoyer and C. Lee. 1993. Identifying global and culture-specific dimensions of humor in advertising: A multinational analysis. *Journal of Marketing*, 57 (2): 64–75. https://doi.org/10.2307/1252027

Alvesson, M. 2010. *Interpreting interviews*. London: Sage.

Berger, Arthur A. 1987. Humor an introduction. *The American Behavioral Scientist,* 30 (3): 6–15.

Braun, V. and V. Clarke. 2006. Using thematic analysis in psychology. *Qualitative Research in Psychology,* 3 (2): 77–101.

Brown, P. and S. C. Levinson. 1978. Universals in language usage: Politeness phenomena. In E. N. Goody, ed., *Questions and politeness: Strategies in social interaction.* 56–311. Cambridge: Cambridge University Press.

Brown, L. B. Winter, K. Idemaru and S. Grawunder. 2014. Phonetics and politeness: Perceiving Korean honorific and non-honorific speech through phonetic cues. *Journal of Pragmatics,* 66: 45–60.

Bryman, A. and E. Bell. 2015. *Business research methods.* Oxford: Oxford University Press.

Choi, Y. 2010. The History of Confucianism in Korea. In W. Chang, ed., *Confucianism in context: Classic philosophy and contemporary issues, East Asia and beyond.* Albany, NY: SUNY Press.

Cooper, C. 2008. Elucidating the bonds of workplace humor: A Relational process model. *Human Relations,* 61: 1087–1115. https://doi.org/10.1177/0018726708094861

Cunliffe, A., J. Helin and J. T. Luhman. 2014. Mikhail Bakhtin. In J. Helin, T. Hernes, D. Hjorth and R. Holt, eds., *The Oxford handbook of process philosophy and organization studies.* 333–347. Oxford: Oxford University Press.

Deuchler, M. 1992. *The Confucian transformation of Korea: A study of society and ideology.* Boston, MA: Harvard University Asia Center.

Dolitsky, M. 1983. Humor and the unsaid. *Journal of Pragmatics,* 7 (1): 39–48.

Duncan, J. B. 2002. Uses of Confucianism in modern Korea. In B. A. Elman, J. B. Duncan and H. Ooms, eds., *Rethinking Confucianism. Past and present in China, Japan, Korea, and Vietnam.* 431–462. Los Angeles, CA: UCLA Asian Pacific Monograph Series.

Freud, Sigmund. 1960. *Jokes and their relation to the unconscious.* Trans. J. Strachey. London: Routledge and Kegan Paul.

Hofstede, Geert. 1984. *Culture's consequences: International differences in work-related values.* Newbury Park, CA: Sage.

Holmes, Janet. 2000. Politeness, power, and provocation: How humour functions in the workplace. *Discourse Studies,* 2 (2): 159–185.

Holmes, Janet. 2006. Sharing a laugh: Pragmatic aspects of humor and gender in the workplace. *Journal of Pragmatics, Special Issue: Gender and Humor,* 38: 26–50.

Holmes, Janet and Meredith Marra. 2002. Having a laugh at work: How humour contributes to workplace culture. *Journal of Pragmatics,* 34 (12): 1683–1710.

House, J. and G. Kasper. 2011. Politeness markers in English and German. In F. Coulmas, ed., *Conversational routine.* 157–186. The Hague: Mouton.

Hwang, S. J. J. 1991. Terms of address in Korean and American cultures. *Intercultural Communication Studies,* 1 (2): 117–136.

Isen, A. M., K. A. Daubman and G. P. Nowicki. 1987. Positive affect facilitates creative problem solving. *Journal of Personality and Social Psychology,* 52: 1122–1131. https://doi.org/10.1037/0022-3514.52.6.1122

Jung, S. H. 2014. Impact of supervisor's humor on civil servants' innovative work behavior. *Journal of the Korea Contents Association,* 14: 733–743. https://doi.org/10.5392/JKCA.2014.14.12.733

Kadar, Daniel Z. and H. Spencer-Oatey. 2016. The bases of (im)politeness evaluations: Culture, the moral order and the East-West debate. *Journal of East Asian Pragmatics*, 1 (1): 73–106.

Kim, K. H. 2018. Enhancing solidarity through dispreferred format: The nuntey-clause in Korean conversation as a normative basis for leveraging action. *Journal of East-Asian Pragmatics*, 3 (1): 27–57.

Kim, H. S. and Barbara A. Plester. 2019. Harmony and distress: Humor, culture, and psychological well-being in South Korean organizations. *Frontiers in Psychology*, 9: 2643.

Kim, T. Y. and D. R. Lee. 2009. A Sense of humor and performance at work: The Mediating effects of self-efficacy. SSRN Scholarly Paper ID 2638762. Rochester, NY: Social Science Research Network. https://papers.ssrn.com/abstract=2638762

La Fave, L., J. Haddad and W. A. Maesen. 1976. Superiority, enhanced self-esteem and perceived incongruity humour theory. In A. J. Chapman and H. C. Foot, eds., *Humour and laughter: Theory, research, and applications*. London: John Wiley and Sons.

Lim Taesup 임태섭. 1999. *Hankukin-ui communication gach'ikwan: Chont'ong-gwa byonhwa* 한국인의 커뮤니케이션 가치관: 전통과 변화 (*Communication beliefs and values in Korea: Tradition and change*). Communication hak yeongu 커뮤니케이션 학연구 (*Journal of the Communication Association of Korea*), 7: 52–66.

Martin, Rod A. and Thomas E. Ford. 2018. *The psychology of humor. An integrative approach*. 2nd ed. London: Academic Press.

McBrian, C. D. 1978. Language and social stratification: The case of a Confucian society. *Anthropological Linguistics*, 20: 320–326.

McGhee, Paul E. 1979. *Humor, its origin and development*. San Francisco, CA: W. H. Freeman.

Milner Davis, Jessica. 2016. Satire and its constraints: Case studies from Australia, Japan, and the People's Republic of China. *HUMOR: International Journal of Humor Research*, 29 (2): 197–221.

Morreall, John. 1983. *Taking laughter seriously*. Albany, NY: SUNY Press.

Plester, Barbara A. 2016. *The complexity of workplace humour: Laughter, jokers, and the dark side of humour*. London: Springer.

Plester, Barbara A. and M. Orams. 2008. Send in the clowns: The role of the joker in three New Zealand IT companies. *HUMOR: International Journal of Humor Research*, 21: 253–281.

Plester, Barbara A. and J. Sayers, 2007. "Taking the piss": Functions of banter in the IT industry. *HUMOR: International Journal of Humor Research*, 20 (2): 157–187.

Rowley, C. and J. Bae. 2003. Culture and management in South Korea. In M. Warner, ed., *Culture and management in Asia*. London: Routledge Curzon.

Ruch, Willibald. 2008. Psychology of humor. In Victor Raskin, ed., *The primer of humor research*. 17–100. New York: Mouton de Gruyter.

Ruch, Willibald, L. Wagner and Sonja Heintz. 2018. Humor, the PEN model of personality, and subjective well-being: Support for differential relationships with eight comic styles. *Rivista Italiana di Studi sull'Umorismo*, 1 (1): 31–44.

Shibamoto-Smith, J. S. 2011. Honorifics, "politeness", and power in Japanese political debate. *Journal of Pragmatics*, 43 (15): 3707–3719.

Shim, T. Y., M. S. Kim and J. N. Martin. 2008. *Changing Korea: Understanding culture and communication*. New York: Peter Lang.

Smith, C. M. and L. Powell. 1988. The use of disparaging humor by group leaders. *Southern Speech Communication Journal*, 53 (3): 279–292.

Stake, R. E. 2013. *Multiple case study analysis*. New York: The Guilford Press.

Tanaka, H. 2018. Solo or shared laughter in coparticipant criticism in Japanese conversation. *Journal of East Asian Pragmatics*, 3 (1): 125–149.

Upadhyay, S. R. 2003. Nepali requestive acts: Linguistic indirectness and politeness re-considered. *Journal of Pragmatics*, 35: 1651–1677.

Welch, C. and R. Piekkari. 2006. Crossing language boundaries: Qualitative interviewing in international business. *Management International Review*, 46 (4): 417–437.

Wood, A. 1981. Telling it like it is: Teaching Judaism through story and humour. *British Journal of Religious Education*, 3 (4): 151–156.

Yao, X. 2000. *An introduction to Confucianism*. Cambridge: Cambridge University Press.

Yue, X-D., F. Jiang, S. Lu and N. Hiranandani. 2016. To be or not to be humorous? Cross cultural perspectives on humor. *Frontiers in Psychology*, 7. At: https://doi.org/10.3389/fpsyg.2016.01495 (accessed 15 July 2021).

Zajdman, A. 1995. Humorous face-threatening acts: Humor as strategy. *Journal of Pragmatics*, 23 (3): 325–339.

9 Chinese conversational humour over time

Contemporary practice and tradition in Taiwanese cultures

Wei-Lin Melody Chang and Michael Haugh

Introduction

Humour was traditionally known as *huaji* 滑稽 in China, but in recent times, it is usually referred to as *youmo* 幽默. The academic study of humour in China is often traced back to the work of Lin Yutang 林語堂 in the 1920–1930s to promote *youmo*, a transliteration of English word *humour*, the coining of which is indicative of a novel concept (Milner Davis 2013). Despite the fact that debate continues about the relationship between the (traditional) notion of *huaji* and the (contemporary) notion of *youmo* (Liao 2003), the study of humour in Chinese languages arguably offers us a window into an immensely rich and long-standing tradition reaching back more than 3,000 years (Chey 2011; Liao 2001; Santangelo 2012a; Yue 2010). Yet despite this long and venerable history, Chinese conversational humour has only recently gained serious scholarly attention.

Conversational humour arises in interactions between two or more participants.[1] Conversational humour is thus inherently dialogic in nature, that is, it arises through dialogue, and can be contrasted with forms of humour that arise primarily in the context of (extended) monologues or texts produced by one person (often a writer). Conversational humour is sometimes broadly equated with humour that arises in everyday conversations between family and friends. However, while face-to-face interactions between family and friends are clearly ubiquitous—and for some scholars, the most basic, primordial site of sociality (Schegloff 2006)—conversational humour is not limited to interactions in everyday settings. In fact, it can be observed across a wide range of different settings and modes of communication. These include not only everyday conversations but also interactions in workplaces, service encounters and other institutional settings, in digitally mediated interactions via social media platforms and messenger apps, as well as in broadcast settings, including interactions amongst participants in television variety and reality shows, dialogues amongst characters in films and television shows, and, of course, dialogues amongst characters in literary works such as novels and plays.

DOI: 10.4324/9781003176374-9

Yet despite the occurrence of conversational humour in a wide range of discourse types, studies of it have been largely grounded in the here and now, and there has been little consideration of the sociohistorical roots of those contemporary practices. In linguistic research on humour, this reflects a preference for examining cross-cultural variation in conversational humour through a synchronic lens. However, one consequence of this tendency is that there has been little consideration of diachronic dimensions of conversational humour, that is, how contemporary practices have been shaped by practices in the past and how they have changed over time. While the focus on synchronic (i.e. contemporary) variation in conversational humour has proven fruitful, if we situate the study of conversational humour within the broader field of humour studies it becomes abundantly clear that this approach alone will simply not do. From a broader interdisciplinary vantage point, it is clear that contemporary humour practices cannot emerge from nowhere. They are shaped by intersecting societal, cultural and political forces over time.

This chapter proposes that studies of conversational humour in contemporary discourse contexts can be enriched by examining traditional conversational humour practices through a diachronic lens. In this way, the study of conversational humour can be more appropriately situated with respect to time. The study of conversational humour in Chinese is arguably particularly well suited to such investigations, given that it can be traced across literary works that form part of a historical record going back more than 3,000 years (some studied elsewhere in this volume). Given the sheer scale of that historical record, our aims here are rather more modest, in that we limit our discussion to contemporary and traditional conversational humour practices in Taiwan, which forms part of the broader Chinese cultural milieu.

In the following section, we briefly review studies of conversational humour in Chinese languages more broadly, as well as more specifically in the Taiwanese context. In order to explore how we might situate the study of Chinese conversational humour in time, we go on to examine potential cross-generational variation found in recordings of everyday interactions amongst Taiwanese in which conversational humour has arisen. While both younger and older Taiwanese participants engage in mild or gentle teasing, there is a tendency for younger Taiwanese to engage in more biting or harsher forms of teasing, while in contrast, older Taiwanese tend to engage in various forms of wordplay. We suggest that this illustrates how the study of conversational humour can be situated with respect to apparent-time (Labov 1966), and to the possible tendency for different conversational humour practices to be used by different generations of Taiwanese. Our study then briefly outlines how this variation in contemporary conversational humour practice amongst Taiwanese people is mirrored in the occurrence of those different humour practices within literary works published over time in Taiwan. While instances of conversational humour in some more recent novels and short stories do involve examples of biting or harsh forms of teasing, in examples of those published prior to the 1980s, conversational humour tends to arise through various forms of wordplay. We propose that this illustrates how the study of conversational humour can be situated with respect to real-time, and how different types of conversational humour can be tied to sociohistorical points in time, as well as to traditional humour practices in the broader Chinese cultural milieu. We conclude that situating the study of conversational humour in time in this way grounds it more firmly in the broader field of humour studies.

Studies of conversational humour in Chinese

While early studies of conversational humour tended to focus on English (Norrick 1993; Tannen 1984), the past decade has seen an increasing number of studies of conversational humour in other linguistic and cultural settings (Mullan and Béal 2018; Haugh 2017; Sinkeviciute and Dynel 2017). Reflecting this, conversational humour in Chinese is also receiving increasing attention, with many of those studies focusing on various forms of teasing and jocular abuse (Chang and Haugh 2020). Conversational humour can, as noted, arise spontaneously in everyday or institutional conversational interactions, or it can be crafted in dialogues that feature on film and TV or in literary works. It thus occurs in both spoken and written forms, with instances of conversational humour that arise in digitally mediated contexts constituting an interesting blend of spoken and written modes of interaction. Chinese conversational humour has been studied in all of these different discourse contexts, as summarised in Table 9.1 which lists a number of representative studies.

It is clear from the overview of studies to date in Table 9.1 that, while conversational humour is prototypically associated with humour that arises in everyday face-to-face interactions amongst friends and family, a relatively large number of studies of conversational humour in Chinese have examined it in other discourse contexts as well. Television variety and reality shows stand out in particular as an increasingly popular discourse context in which Chinese conversational humour is examined. It is also evident that, for the most part, conversational humour in Chinese has been studied in genres where it is what Tsakona characterises as an "optional but expected feature of the genre" (2017: 495); these include conversational interactions in everyday settings, digitally mediated, and broadcast settings, as well as dialogues in literary works. Whether Li Chuntao's (2020) case study listed in Table 9.1 of an extended bout of teasing in a university workplace telephone call is considered an exception to this overall tendency depends on whether one treats conversational humour in a workplace context as an optional but expected feature of the genre, or optional but unexpected.[2]

Despite the studies of Chinese conversational humour in this wide range of different discourse contexts, few have tackled the issue of whether there

Table 9.1 Overview of studies of conversational humour in Chinese

Discourse context	Representative studies (see references for full detail)
Everyday conversational interaction	Chang and Haugh (2020); Chen, L. (2017); Li, X. (2020)
Institutional conversational interaction	Li, C. (2020)
Digitally mediated conversational interaction	Jin and Chen (2020); Qiu et al. (2021); Su (2009); Zhao (2020)
Broadcast conversational interaction: Television variety and reality shows	Bi and Marsden (2020); Cao (this volume); Chang and Haugh (2021); Chang et al. (2021); Chen, L. (2016a, 2016b, 2017); Gong and Ran (2020); Yang and Ren (2020)
Broadcast conversational interaction: Film and television sitcoms	Cao (2019); Su and Huang (2002); Xu (2014)
Literary works: novels, plays and traditional literature	Chen, X. (2019)

might be any significant variation in the broader Chinese cultural sphere across regions and jurisdictions. Those scholars who have focused more specifically on particular regions or societies have argued, perhaps not surprisingly, that such variation is almost inevitable, given the different sociohistorical trajectories of different regions which include not only Mainland China, but other territories, such as Hong Kong, Taiwan and Singapore, as well as a significant Chinese diaspora spread across countries around the world. Chen (2017: 12), for instance, suggests that the study of conversational humour in Taiwanese society is important in this respect, as it involves consideration of multiple cultural influences, not only traditional Chinese humour practices but also modern Mainland Chinese humour, Hong Kong humour and Japanese humour. However, only a limited number of studies have in fact examined conversational humour in the specific cultural context of Taiwanese society, and there have been no explicitly comparative studies, which make it difficult to interrogate such a claim. We nevertheless hold that it could potentially be fruitful to examine conversational humour in Chinese in different sociohistorical contexts.

Early studies of verbal humour in Taiwan focused on ancient Chinese jokes or *huaji* (Chen, G. 1985; Su 2009), and perceptions of humour by Taiwanese people (Liao 2001, 2003). Subsequent studies have focused on conversational humour in everyday conversational interactions in Taiwan (Chang and Haugh 2020; Chen, L. 2017), in digitally mediated contexts (Su 2009), in television variety shows (Chang et al. 2021; Chen, L. (2016a, 2016b, 2017), and in television sitcoms (Su and Huang 2002). The most comprehensive study of conversational humour in Taiwan to date is that undertaken by Li-Chi Lee Chen (2017), who examined humour in both everyday and broadcast discourse settings. His analysis of conversational humour in recordings of everyday conversations between friends identified a range of different discourse strategies used to generate amusement amongst recipients, including quotations, rhetorical questions, theatrical performances, back-handed remarks, and joint fantasising (which he terms a fictional episode). He also identified a range of different types of conversational humour in the popular Taiwanese television variety show, *Kangxi Lai Le* 康熙來了 (*Kangxi coming*),[3] including personal narratives, wordplay, sarcasm, innuendo, other-deprecating humour (cf. teasing), self-deprecating humour, self-bragging humour, and *wúlítóu* 無厘頭 (nonsense).[4] He argues that while some of these conversational humour practices can be traced to classical Chinese forms of humour (e.g. wordplay), others can be attributed to the influence of humour practices popularised in Hong Kong (e.g. *wúlítóu*) or Japan (e.g. self-deprecating humour).[5] While Chen argues that "modern Taiwanese humour has developed its own characteristics", given it also "overlaps with [mainland] Chinese humour and is greatly influenced by it" (2017: 16), it remains unclear whether the impact of these broader cultural influences on Chinese conversational humour practices is really limited to the Taiwanese cultural context. It seems doubtful.

However, our interest, in this chapter at least, is not on attempting to prove (or disprove) these kinds of putative differences across the broader Chinese cultural sphere, but on a rather intriguing observation that Chen makes in passing in his study, namely, that some commentators have "publicly criticised [*Kangxi Lai Le*] for its rudeness" and claimed that its popularity is "indicative of the deterioration of social values in Taiwan" (2017: 205). This kind of commentary echoes traditional (and neo-Confucian) views on Chinese humour in China in which it is equated with "improperness and immaturity" (Yue 2010: 142). It is also reflected in the findings about contestation of the limits of teasing and when it "goes too far" that apply to both broadcast (Chang et al. 2021) and everyday (Chang and Haugh 2020) settings in Taiwan, in which generational differences in attitudes to humour are explicitly invoked.

In the following sections, we explore the possibility that such attitudes may reflect broader changes over time in conversational humour practices in contemporary Taiwanese society.

Conversational humour in everyday Taiwanese interactions

It has been repeatedly observed that the production or perception of humour can vary across gender, social classes and age; but there are very few studies that have examined the last (Attardo 2020: 309), with the notable exception of recent work by Padilla Cruz (2019) on differences in conversational humour amongst younger and older customers in service encounters in Spain. In the sociolinguistic scholarly tradition, variation in production and perception of humour across age groups can be viewed not only as a form of synchronic variation but also as indicating apparent-time change (Labov 1966). On the latter view, age-related variation is potentially indicative of (ongoing) linguistic change in the society in question.

In an ongoing study of cross-generational differences in conversational humour amongst Taiwanese, Chang (2018) noted that although both younger Taiwanese (in their early 20s) and older Taiwanese (in the late 50s and early 60s) can be observed to engage in light or mild forms of teasing (i.e. *cháoxiào* 嘲笑 or *cháofèng* 嘲諷), younger Taiwanese also have a tendency to engage in more biting or harsh forms of teasing (i.e. *tiáokǎn* 調侃 and *kāiwánxiào* 開玩笑) (Chang and Haugh 2020).[6] Notably, the former, more ridiculing or disparaging forms of teasing are eschewed by older Taiwanese in everyday conversational interactions. Older Taiwanese instead tend to engage more frequently in traditional wordplay, drawing on the long-standing tradition of punning in classical Chinese humour (Chey 2011; see also Leggieri, this volume).

Biting forms of teasing can be observed, for instance, in the following excerpt from a recording of a real-life conversation between two young female friends, Chen and Lin, who are talking about their recent shopping trip.[7]

Example 1 Multilingual Spoken Corpus (MSC) of Taiwanese Mandarin: 'Shopping'

1.	Lin:	阿,還蠻想逛街的,雖然昨天才花了,大失血,呵呵呵
2.	Chen:	哈哈哈,可以不要,不要再亂買了嗎?
3.	Lin:	我也想啊!
4.	Chen:	真是的
5.	Lin:	對不起我爸 呵呵呵
6.	Chen:	對阿,真覺得是那個耶,敗家女
7.	Lin:	屁啦,你們還不是一樣 呵呵呵
8.	Chen:	唉唷,我最近都沒有買東西耶,省錢
9.	Lin:	後火車站怎麼說?
10.	Chen:	後火車站誰買的比較多?
11.	Lin:	哈哈哈
12.	Chen:	想到這個就很厲害
13.	Lin:	我也是逼不得已的
14.	Chen:	你應該要看醫生吧?
15.	Lin:	哈哈
16.	Chen:	幫你介紹精神病院
17.	Lin:	要不然我們下次去士林,士林感覺,便宜,然後
18.	Chen:	我覺得我要在你們身邊,你們才不會亂買,我昨天才離開你們半小時,你們就買了快一萬,呵呵呵
19.	Lin:	呵呵呵,那下次去士林夜市好了
1.	Lin:	Ah, I really want to go shopping although I just spent A lot yesterday he he he
2.	Chen:	Ha ha ha, can you not buy any unnecessary things again?
3.	Lin:	I want to do so

(Continued)

4.	Chen:	Oh
5.	Lin:	I feel sorry for my father he he he
6.	Chen:	Yeah, I really think that you are a shopaholic
7.	Lin:	Nonsense, you guys are the same he he he
8.	Chen:	I haven't shopped at all recently. I'm saving money
9.	Lin:	How do you explain the shopping in the Hou Train station?
10.	Chen:	Who did the most shopping in the Hou Train Station?
11.	Lin:	Ha ha ha
12.	Chen:	When I think of this, I think you are amazing
13.	Lin:	I'm compelled to do it
14.	Chen:	You should see a doctor, huh?
15.	Lin:	Ha ha
16.	Chen:	I can help introduce you to a psychiatric hospital
17.	Lin:	Otherwise we can go to Shilin next time, things are cheaper There and—
18.	Chen:	I think I need to be there with you guys, so you won't buy Unnecessary stuff. Yesterday I was only away for just thirty Minutes and you guys almost spent $NT 10,000 dollars on Shopping, ha ha ha
19.	Lin:	He he he, then let's go to Shilin night market next time

Over the course of a number of turns, Chen teases Lin that when she goes shopping, she always buys more things than she needs. This mild teasing becomes more biting when Chen teases her by saying that she can introduce her to a psychiatric hospital to help treat her "addiction" to shopping (line 16). Throughout the course of Chen's lengthy series of teases, which become increasingly aggressive, Lin not only responds with laughter, but extends this conversational humour episode through her own self-deprecatory humour (e.g. lines 5 and 13) and counter-teases (e.g. line 9, see Haugh and Chang 2015: 403–405) that are directed back at Chen. This extended series of teases, which Attardo (2019: 190) refers to as a form of "sustained humour", is thus actively contributed to by both participants.[8] It is clear that neither of the young women is offended by the apparent criticism and they both appear from the recording to enjoy the banter.

An even harsher instance of teasing can be observed in another example in which two young male friends, Wang and Guo, are talking about something Wang says he overhead another friend, Huang, saying to a mutual female friend.[9]

Example 2 NCCU Corpus of Spoken Chinese (Mandarin): m011

1.	Wang:	他那個時候我在路上就, 于書婷, 是誰把你打成這個樣子
2.	Guo:	哈哈哈 快告訴我, 然後
		((section omitted))
3.	Wang:	也是蠻可愛啊, 就是很像浮, 浮屍

4.	Guo:	[哈哈]
5.	Wang:	[就是]泡在水裡面泡久了然後腫腫的那樣
6.	Guo:	浮屍, 哈哈哈, 我剛以為你要講那種福, 大大福神那種福師, 福師
7.	Wang:	不是啦
8.	Guo:	結果是那個, 浮屍
9.	Wang:	剛剛那些話都是黃跟我講的
10.	Guo:	哈哈哈
11.	Wang:	我覺得他真的很過分, 黃
12.	Guo:	哈哈哈
13.	Wang:	說人家是浮屍
14.	Guo:	哈哈哈, 真的是他講的嗎
15.	Wang:	對啊, 真是要不得
16.	Guo:	哈哈哈
17.	Wang:	哈哈哈
18.	Guo:	我覺得是你講的
19.	Wang:	好啦, 沒有啊, 好朋友才會開這種玩笑
1.	Wang:	I was on the street—and he asked her, "Yushuting, who beat you up like this?"
2.	Guo:	Ha ha ha quickly tell me—then ((section omitted))
3.	Wang:	It is also pretty cute, but it's like a floating, floating corpse
4.	Guo:	Ha ha
5.	Wang:	It's like soaking in the water for a long time
6.	Guo:	Floating corpse, ha ha ha, I thought you were going to say the big Lucky God[10]
7.	Wang:	No
8.	Guo:	And it turns out that you meant floating corpse
9.	Wang:	It was said by Huang
10.	Guo:	Ha ha ha
11.	Wang:	I think Huang went too far
12.	Guo:	Ha ha ha
13.	Wang:	Describing her as a floating corpse
14.	Guo:	Ha ha ha, was it really said by him?
15.	Wang:	Yes, it went too far
16.	Guo:	Ha ha ha
17.	Wang:	Ha ha ha
18.	Guo:	I think it was said by you
19.	Wang:	Okay, no, I think only good friends would joke like this

In this dialogue, Wang tells Guo that he overheard Huang "teasing" a mutual female friend that her face looked swollen as if someone had beaten her up (line 1). After a brief digression (data not shown), Wang goes on to report that Huang even compared her to a "floating corpse" (line 3), seemingly an insulting remark. Guo responds with laughter (lines 4, 6), while Wang goes on to claim that Huang "went too far" with his tease (lines 9, 11, 13). Nevertheless, they both end up laughing about it (lines 16–17), and Guo then turns the tease against Wang by saying that perhaps he is only pretending it was Huang who said it when it was really him (line 18), thereby indicating he does not regard it as a serious infraction. And while Wang criticises his friend, Huang, for the harsh tease (lines 11, 15), he nevertheless laughs at it (line 17), and labels it (line 19) as a just a "joke" (*kāiwánxiào* 開玩笑) amongst friends (see Chang and Haugh 2020: 22).

Instances of this kind of biting or harsh teasing were not found, however, in everyday conversations amongst the older generation of Taiwanese participants in various corpora. Instead, they frequently engaged in wordplay (a form of conversational humour that was also more infrequent amongst the younger Taiwanese). One instance is the following example, a dialogue between two Taiwanese meeting each other for the first time. Wu (a younger male) is asking Zhu (an older female) whether she has a job:[11]

Example 3 Mandarin Conversational Dialogue Corpus (MCDC): 09-02

1.	Wu:	那妳有在上班嗎?
2.	Zhu:	我啊? 我是**櫻櫻美代子**哈哈哈
3.	Wu:	哈哈哈
4.	Zhu:	哈哈哈
5.	Zhu:	其實我本來應該- 我本來在船務公司上班, 那我也工作了十三年
1.	Wu:	Do you work?
2.	Zhu:	Me? I am *yingying meidaizi* ha ha ha
3.	Wu:	Ha ha ha
4.	Zhu:	Ha ha ha
5.	Zhu:	Actually I originally—I worked in a shipping company. I worked for 13 years

Zhu first jokingly responds that she doesn't do anything (characters in bold in line 2), before going on to respond seriously that she started out working for a shipping company (line 5). Notably, Zhu's joke-first response (see Schegloff 1987) involves an instance of wordplay. The expression *yīng yīng měidàizi* 櫻櫻美代子 is a pun on the Taiwanese Hokkien expression *îng îng bô tāi-sì* (literally, idle, nothing), which means to be free without anything to do; but it is also a pun on a Japanese proper name, *Sakura Miyoko* 桜美代子, as pronounced in Mandarin Chinese. Significantly, then, while this wordplay exploits homophones in a manner typical of traditional Chinese humour (Chey 2011), it also invokes three different languages. This kind of cross-linguistic punning is characteristic of a lot of wordplay amongst older Taiwanese who regularly speak both Mandarin Chinese and Taiwanese Hokkien, but are also aware of Japanese influences on Taiwan in the first half of the twentieth century.

In the next conversation between two older Taiwanese male participants, we can also observe instances of wordplay as well as gentle teasing. In the course of this interaction, Chen asks Liu, who owns a car-varnish workshop, to help Chen who has made some art craft-works that need varnishing (names altered, but actual persons and locale shown in

Chinese conversational humour over time 197

Figure 9.1 Photograph by Wei-Lin Melody Chang, 14 June 2010, during recording session in work locale, Yilan, Taiwan.

Source: Reproduced with kind permission of the subject.

Figures 9.1–9.3). The participants spoke primarily in Taiwanese Hokkien, with only a small amount of code-switching into Mandarin Chinese (as indicated in Note 12), so pinyin only is given with the English translation; but Chinese characters are provided for keywords which are bolded and discussed below.[12]

Figure 9.2 Photograph by Wei-Lin Melody Chang, 14 June 2010, during recording session in work locale, Yilan, Taiwan.

Source: Reproduced with kind permission of the subject.

Figure 9.3 Photograph by Wei-Lin Melody Chang, 14 June 2010, during recording session in work locale, Yilan, Taiwan.

Source: Reproduced with kind permission of the subjects.

Example 4 Taiwanese Business Interaction Corpus: 100614_10

1.	Chen:	Lí kin-á-jit ho guá tú-tiòh hāi-a
2.	Liu:	Án-na hāi-a
3.	Chen:	Ū kuí-a tè lí ài kā guá khò khò tsit-ē
4.	Liu:	Tú-tiòh lí wu siánn-mih pāi tāi-tsì ooh?
		%Ni kan, ta dou buyong goutong, hou,
		ta ziranerran ta jiu zhemelihai duibudui?%
5.	Chen:	[ha ha ha]
6.	Liu:	[ha ha ha] lán kham- ài %goutong%? Lí kóng-e- Lí he m̄ sī
		%goutong% (.) he kiò %*jiaodai*%
7.	Chen:	ha ha ha
8.	Liu:	Tiòh bo? eh %*jiaodai*% gah %goutong% tsha tsin-tsē leh
9.	Chen:	ha ha ha %*jiaodai*% si he %tapu%
		((smiles with hand gesture)) (.) %*jiaodai*%
10.	Liu:	Kau-tài lah kau-tài tō sī li- %ta hui ***jiaodai*** hen duo yichan
		gei XXX, na jiao jiaodai, na gen nage jiaodai bang qilai bu
		yiyang
1.	Chen:	It's bad luck [that] you bump into me today
		[see Figure 9.1 for illustration of the apparently straight-
		faced greeting accompanying this line]
2.	Liu:	Why is it bad?
3.	Chen:	There are quite a few, you need to help me brush coating
4.	Liu:	What bad things could happen when I bump into you?
		((turning to the researcher))
		See, he doesn't need to communicate
		he can [give instructions] so naturally and he is so good
		at it

	[see Figure 9.2 for accompanying gesture and expression]
5. Chen:	[Ha ha ha]
6. Liu:	[Ha ha ha] do we need to communicate? What you said—it's not about communication. That was a telling
7. Chen:	Ha ha ha
8. Liu:	Isn't that right? Communication and telling are very distinctive
9. Chen:	Ha ha ha *jiaodai* means tape ((smiles with hand gesture)) (.) *jiaodai*. [see Figure 9.3 for illustration of hand gesture]
10. Liu:	It's telling, telling means—he will transfer his inheritance to XXX, that means telling, that is different from the tape.

Despite the apparently solemn and serious way in which Chen greets Liu in line 1 (and see Figure 9.1), stating that he needs help with work, this exchange is full of gentle teasing. We can observe several instances where Chen is teased by Liu, starting with Liu's hand gesture and words of protest in line 4, illustrated in Figure 9.2. This continues with Liu's laughter lines 6 and 8, to which Chen also responds with laughter. Of particular interest, however, is the explicitly jocular wordplay by Chen in line 9. In response to Liu's tease that Chen is not asking but telling Liu to help with the varnishing (lines 6, 8), Chen laughs and then deflects the teasing through a pun on one of the keywords used, the homophone *jiaodai* (line 6, 8, 9 and 10). When pronounced in Mandarin Chinese, *jiaodai* can mean either "telling 交代 (i.e. instructing)" or "packing tape 膠帶". Notably, Chen marks the latter interpretation as the more salient with a hand gesture (noted in line 9 and illustrated in Figure 9.3), although that interpretation does not of course fit this context. Liu responds to this with a po-face receipt of the tease (Drew 1987), saying in line 10 that Chen meant "telling" in Taiwanese, since "telling" and "packing tape" are pronounced differently in Taiwanese. Liu then goes on to tease Chen that he will instruct someone to pass his inheritance on to his son after he passes away, before repeating his clarification that he knows Chen meant "telling" not "packing tape" (line 10). Chen's clarifications, however, are not serious here and they actually further the joking frame of their interaction.

This section has examined four instances of conversational humour in everyday settings that illustrate the tendency for younger Taiwanese to engage in biting and harsh forms of teasing, and the tendency for older Taiwanese to engage in jocular wordplay. The occurrence of wordplay harks back to long-established and traditional forms of Chinese humour (Chey 2011; Yue 2010), while harsh or ridiculing teasing was traditionally disparaged as an improper form of humour (Santangelo 2012a, 2012b). The question this raises is, whether this observed difference can be regarded not only as evidence of age-based variation in conversational humour practices in Taiwanese, but also as reflecting broader changes in Taiwanese society. To put it another way, are we dealing here with variation that reflects different life stages of those participants, or an apparent-time change that reflects a long-lasting change in linguistic practice? It is difficult to distinguish between these two alternative explanations, or even to be sure about the possibility that both explanations hold good in some respects, as we do not have ready access to recordings of everyday conversations in Taiwan made earlier than the turn of this century. We do not know, therefore, whether older Taiwanese of the present generation might have engaged in harsher forms of teasing when they were younger, and have subsequently shifted to more traditional forms of conversational humour in Chinese, or, alternatively, whether they have always been inclined to engage in jocular forms of wordplay rather than aggressive humour, even when they were younger. In the following section, we move on to consider whether examining instances of conversational humour in literary works published in Taiwan might be able to help distinguish between these alternative ways of situating conversational humour in time.

Conversational humour in Taiwanese literature

Conversational humour in Chinese has been studied primarily from a synchronic perspective in contemporary settings. However, there is no reason—in principle at least—why we might not attempt to study real-time changes in Chinese conversational humour practices from a diachronic perspective. Studies of conversational humour have traditionally favoured analysing instances of humour in recordings of spontaneous conversations interactions. However, as Bednarek (2017) notes, conversational humour in dialogues in television shows are increasingly treated as an important focus of research in their own right. Our view is that we can go further than this, since dialogues in novels and other literary works also constitute an important site of investigation for scholars wishing to study how conversational humour has been shaped by traditional practices, and whether there are significant differences with the ways in which such humour arose in different eras. As Santangelo (2012b) briefly notes in his account of the role of *xiaò* 笑 (smile or laugh) in Chinese humour, we can even find instances of conversational humour in one of the most important literary works in traditional China, *Honglou meng* 紅樓夢 (*The Dream of the Red Chamber*), written by Cao Xueqin 曹雪芹 and Gao E 高鶚 in the middle of the eighteenth century. For example, considering one passage of dialogue in the novel, Santangelo describes how "the participants use light scorn to share humour among each other" (2012b: 33).[13]

One obvious advantage of examining conversational humour in dialogues in literary works is that, unlike television shows, the literary record reaches much further back into time. Another advantage is that the writer provides us—both readers and analysts—with access to the private mental worlds of characters, including their emotions, motivations and state of mind (Santangelo 2012a). Such insights are not readily available in recordings of spoken conversational interactions. Systematic study of conversational humour in literary works thus offers potentially rich insights into contemporary practices. There are questions, of course, about *whose* conversational humour practices are being represented in literary works. The further back one reaches into the historical literary record, the more likely it is that one is tapping into representations of the elite of the day (Chey 2011). However, such caveats aside, valuable insights into both traditional and contemporary practice can emerge from such sources. The role of conversational humour in dialogues in literary works remains a rich, relatively under-utilised vein of research that awaits in-depth exploration.

In this section, we consider some examples of conversational humour identified in dialogues from Taiwanese literary novels and short stories in order to briefly outline this possible line of research. The first example is the following excerpt from the novel, *Da Yiyuan Xiao Yisheng* 大醫院小醫生 (*Big Hospital, Little Doctors,* hereafter *DYXY*), by Hou Weng-Yong 侯文詠, published in 1992. The narrator of this passage from the chapter titled *Mang Yu Mang* 忙與盲 ('Busy and blind') is an intern at a hospital in Taiwan. A patient has just passed away, despite emergency first aid measures being applied. The senior house officer was preparing to announce the patient's death without notifying the senior consultant (a professor). When the senior consultant arrived on the scene, he started shouting furiously at the chief resident:[14]

Example 5 *DYXY* **(1992): Chapter 'Busy and blind', p. 39**

"病人家屬都還沒到,就宣布死亡, 這又怎麼說" 教授又問
　"出血實在太快,我們來不及" 總醫師吞吞吐吐說
　"出血太快?死老百姓, 這像是醫生說的話嗎?" 唰的一聲, 那本病歷被教授丟的好遠
　"那你為什麼不會去走廊大喊救命呢?虧你人長得那麼高, 神經線太長, 傳導比別人久,反應也比別人慢"
　我聽了差點沒笑出來,有人瞪了我一眼, 我連忙低下頭, 乖乖的去把病歷撿回來.

"The death of the patient was declared before his family arrived, how do you explain this?", the professor asked.

"The bleeding happened too fast to be dealt with", the chief resident said.

"The bleeding was too fast? You ignoramus! Is that what a doctor is supposed to say?". The [patient's] medical record was thrown a long way away by the professor.

"Then how come you didn't go [out] into the corridor and shout for help? What a pity you've grown so tall that [your] nerves are too long.

You take longer to transmit messages [to your brain] and you take longer to react than others."

I nearly burst into laughter after hearing that. Someone gave me a look. I lowered my gaze immediately and went to get the case booklet back.

This excerpt describes the professor of medicine, who is higher in status than the chief resident doctor,[15] seemingly abusing the latter for his mistakes. He insults the chief resident doctor about his height, implying that the messages take longer to get to his brain due to his height, thus accounting for his apparent dim-wittedness. However, the subsequent comment (to the reader) by the first-person narrator—the intern, who is in turn lower in status than the chief resident doctor—that the insult nearly caused him to laugh out loud, makes it clear that it is perceived (at least by him) as an instance of jocular abuse (Chen, X. 2019). This jocular abuse by the professor sanctions the chief resident doctor for his shortcomings. But, at the same time, the intern also takes a vicarious pleasure in witnessing the humiliation of the chief resident doctor, who had frequently scolded him in previous encounters. Since the intern suppresses his laughter, his satisfaction with the insult is not obvious to his seniors.

The next example, from the short story, *Wo Ai Mali* 我愛瑪琍 (*I Love Mali*, hereafter *WAM*),[16] by Huang Chun-Ming 黃春明, first published in 1977, is about jocular insults and name-calling of a very different kind. The novel's narrator describes the main character reacting to the way in which his colleagues and boss at work make jokes about his English name. Terms discussed are given in the text in bold.

Example 6 *WAM* (1979): Chapter 1, p. 3

不知道從哪一天開始的，**大衛**這個洋名字,被一些朋友移花接木，改叫他為**大胃**.

這一點可以從幾個朋友留給他的紙條，冒頭稱他為**大衛**即可證明.

那些慣用正宗洋文叫他的朋友,也都叫他**大胃**了. 好在**大衛**與**大胃**的聲音，在中文完全一樣.

這種名字的轉化', 曾經令他感到若有所失似的, 哪知道不多久竟然連他的洋老闆衛門先生,

也用中文發音叫喚他**大胃**了.這一下, 他想一想, 大樂起來,這豈不等於塞翁失馬?

剛開始那一陣子, 他逢人就笑著說:

"真他媽的,我的洋老闆也叫我**大胃**咧! 真他媽的." 說時眼睛瞇成一條線.

他心想洋老闆跟他的關係, 以不同往日,而是更往深一層發展了.

I don't know when it started. His foreign name "**David**" was changed by some friends and they called him "**Big Stomach**". This can be proved by the note that several friends left him saying he had a **big stomach**.

Those friends who used to speak to him in authentic foreign language also called him **Big Stomach**. Fortunately, the pronunciation of

Dawei [David] and *da wei* **[big stomach]** are exactly the same in Chinese. This kind of name change once did make him feel as if he was missing something, but who was to know that] even his foreign boss Edmund also started calling him **Dawei**, in Chinese language. Now he thinks about it, he stands up. Isn't this a blessing in disguise? From then on, he tells people with a smile:

"Damn it, my foreign boss also calls me **Big Stomach** too. Damn it." When speaking about this, his eyes narrow. He thinks to himself that the relationship between the foreign boss and him is different from the past and has deepened further.

In this excerpt, we can observe an instance of jocular wordplay through a pun on the homophone *dàwèi*. While the English name David transliterates as *Dàwèi* 大衛 in Mandarin Chinese, it can also be heard as *dàwèi* 大胃, meaning "big stomach". Through this wordplay or comic naming,[17] the character's colleagues are teasing him about his (plump) figure. However, rather than being insulted, he takes it as a sign of increasing intimacy between himself and his work colleagues and the narrative voice tells us that he regards this as the silver lining of good fortune. His mock complaints about the boss calling him "big stomach" are evidently not too serious, as he makes them with a smile and takes it as a sign he is accepted by all, including his boss, and so can feel much happier than before. Even a brief instance such as this of the conversational humour that regularly occurs between characters in a fictional narrative can provide evidence of their private mental world and state of mind. It also points to the humour practices that characterise their fictional world and which often mirror the social reality of that time.

Given their important role in traditional Chinese humour, it is not surprising that many instances of jocular wordplay can also be observed in earlier Taiwanese novels, such as *Lu Bing Hua* 魯冰花 (*Lupinus*, hereafter *LBH*) by Zhong Zhao-Zheng 鍾肇政, which was published in 1962.[18] This is a novel about a young boy, A-Ming, who comes from a poor family but has a great imagination and is artistically very talented although his work is not discovered until after he dies of a liver condition at the age of ten. The title of the novel is the Latin name of the lupin flower, *lupinus*, symbolising the way in which the main character is like the lupin flower which quietly blooms but remains unnoticed. In one scene, A-Sheng, the younger brother of the main character, A-Ming, has just finished a bottle of milk—a treat that is in scarce supply in their poor household (key terms discussed given in bold):

Example 7 *LBH* **(1962): Chapter 3, p. 54**

正在這貧窮的一家人浸沉在稀有的歡樂當中時, 躲在屋內一角的魔鬼又發出獰笑了這時,媽媽詫異地望著小弟阿生問:
"咦,我好像聽到你肚子咕嚕咕嚕了好幾下"

"嗯,肚子裡有雷公呢!" 阿生答
阿明笑著說他初喝牛奶時的經驗. 他說還記得那時放的響屁一點兒也不臭
又逗得一家人大笑了一陣.

When the poor family was absorbed in this rare joy, the devil that was hiding in the corner of the room gave a malevolent sneer. Then, mum looked at my younger brother in surprise and asked,
"Eh? I seem to hear your belly gurgling"
"Mm, there is a **God of Thunder** in my belly!", A-Sheng replied.
A-Ming smiled when he told of his experience when he first drank milk. He said he still remembers that the fart he made was not smelly at all. Again, this made everyone in the family laugh out loud.

This excerpt contains an instance of wordplay, specifically, the use of hyperbole. It is introduced by the narrative voice telling us that there is a supernatural presence already in the house, a devil hiding in the corner.[19] The little boy's reference to the God of Thunder 雷公 is an exaggerated term for the sound of his belly gurgling after he finished drinking the milk (evidently an unaccustomed part of his diet). According to Taiwanese folk beliefs, the God of Thunder is indeed responsible for thunderclaps. However, the way in which this hyperbolic description elicits from a smile from A-Ming indicates that this hyperbolic statement is not being taken seriously. Instead, it helps alleviate embarrassment on the part of little A-Sheng (Santangelo 2012b) and elicits a follow-up story about his elder brother about his own similar experience when he first drank milk, which makes the whole family laugh.

In this section, we have analysed examples of conversational humour found in literary dialogues. We discussed examples of biting or harsh teasing (*DYXY* 1992) and jocular wordplay (*WAM* 1979; *LBH* 1962) identified in Taiwanese novels and short stories. It is interesting to note that in the previous section, we suggested that the former conversational practice is seemingly favoured by younger Taiwanese, while the latter is favoured by older Taiwanese. This suggests the possibility that the apparent-time change we noted in our analysis of cross-generational variation in everyday conversational interactions may be mirrored in real-time differences in the Taiwanese literary record. We hasten to add that this possibility requires much more rigorous exploration in a larger corpus of literary works.

Conclusion

Studies of conversational humour typically focus on expounding cross-cultural differences of the present time. In this chapter, however, we have suggested that any cultural observations need to be situated within their sociohistorical context, including the role of traditional humour practices. Selecting some examples, we have explored ways in which Chinese conversational humour can be situated in time through two different types of discourse context: everyday conversational interactions and dialogues in literary works.

In examining conversational humour in everyday settings, we began with the established observation that, while younger Taiwanese tend to favour biting or harsh forms of teasing, older Taiwanese appear to favour jocular wordplay (Chang 2018). The examples analysed certainly support such cross-generational variation in conversational humour practices in Taiwan. However, we noted that these observations raise further questions about whether these differences simply reflect synchronic variation in contemporary conversational humour practices, or whether they are evidence of broader diachronic changes in humour practices in Taiwanese society.

In order to explore those questions, we examined some instances of conversational humour found in Taiwanese literary works, specifically, novels and short stories. We noted in our analysis two intriguing parallels: the first, between the conversational humour practices seemingly favoured by older Taiwanese in contemporary recordings of everyday conversational interaction with those occurring in some novels and short stories published in the 1960s–1970s; and the second, between those favoured today by younger Taiwanese with that featuring in a more recent literary work published from the 1990s onwards. It appears that a shift away from traditional forms of wordplay to harsh or biting forms of teasing can be evidenced not only from an apparent-time change perspective (in recordings of everyday conversations interactions amongst Taiwanese of different generations), but perhaps also in a real-time change perspective (in dialogues in Taiwanese literary works across five decades). Thus, observing apparent-time changes (that is, across different generations) may offer us some evidence of broader social change (Labov 1966). However, we have also proposed that a systematic examination of conversational humour practices in dialogues in literary works would be necessary to allow us a window into observing real-time changes in conversational humour practices.

Whether our observations and this approach will hold up in more systematic empirical study remains to be seen. Either way, however, the main point we have been making here remains: situating the study of Chinese conversational humour in time ought to draw on both kinds of time change perspective, apparent and real-time. In studying conversational humour, we need to situate it not only in its cultural context but also in time. Culture is, of course, always a product of its sociohistorical context and the nature of conversational humour in contemporary Taiwanese society is a case in point. While conversational humour practices in Taiwan are clearly rooted in the broader Chinese cultural milieu, some scholars have also argued that Taiwanese conversational humour has been shaped and influenced by forms of conversational humour observed in Hong Kong and Japan, for instance (Chen, L. 2017; Liao 2001). Such claims are difficult to interrogate without systematically examining that broader Chinese cultural milieu and a tradition that can be traced in literary works forming part of a historical record going back more than 3,000 years. Studying conversational humour in a range of different discourse contexts that includes dialogues in literary works not only offers us a potentially fruitful pathway forward in addressing such questions, but is also likely to afford greater cross-fertilisation from different disciplinary perspectives in humour studies. Perhaps it goes without saying that humour is a complex phenomenon requiring concerted interdisciplinary efforts for a full understanding. A volume such as the present is testimony to that. And it is our contention that studies of conversational humour, as well as humour more generally, might benefit from more systematic engagement with the different concepts of time and voice utilised in different disciplinary domains of humour research.

Notes

1 Conversational humour is "an umbrella term for various verbal chunks created spontaneously or repeated verbatim for the sake of amusing the recipient" (Dynel 2009: 1286). Other related terms include "verbal humour" (Attardo 1994) and "conversational joking" (Norrick 1993). While each of these terms draws attention to particular dimensions of humour in interaction (Norrick and Chiaro 2009), this chapter uses the term conversational humour since it is the term most frequently invoked in cross-linguistic or cross-cultural studies of humour (Béal and Mullan 2013; Mullan and Béal 2018; Sinkeviciute and Dynel 2017).
2 Our view is that while in some types of institutional interaction (e.g. service encounters or discussions between colleagues as in Kim and Plester, this volume), conversational humour appears to be an optional but expected feature of the genre, in other types of institutional interaction, it appears to an optional but unexpected feature of the genre (e.g. medical consultations) (cf. Tsakona 2017: 496). Where this line falls, with respect to different types of institutional interaction, is likely to prove an important locus of cross-cultural difference, but further consideration of this point lies outside of the scope of this chapter.
3 *Kangxi Lai Le* 康熙來了 (*Kangxi coming*), was a Taiwanese variety talk show hosted by the celebrities Mr Kangyong Tsai and Ms Xidi Hsu, broadcast from 2004 to 2016 (underlining indicates the combined names giving the title of the show). One of the most popular talk shows in Taiwan, it was also successful in many other Mandarin-speaking countries. Its popularity is often attributed to the hosts' signature style of comic teasing and banter.
4 We reserve the use of tones as indicated here for (Mandarin) Chinese terms that are less commonly used in the academic literature (e.g. *wúlítóu*) or are directly quoted from data extracts.
5 In relation to the latter, Liao's (2001) wry observation that, while Taiwanese scholars have lauded self-deprecatory forms of humour, they rarely practise it, is somewhat germane. It is only in more recent times, according to Chen (2017), and following the increased popularity of Japanese *manzai* or stand-up comedy in Taiwan, that self-deprecatory humour can be more readily observed amongst Taiwanese people.
6 Examples discussed in this chapter are taken from a dataset of over 50 instances of conversational humour identified by the authors through close examination of transcripts/recordings of conversations in a number of extant

corpora of Taiwanese spoken interaction, including the Multilingual Spoken Corpus (MSC) of Taiwanese Mandarin (22 conversations between friends), the NCCU Corpus of Spoken Chinese (Mandarin, Hakka, and Southern Min) (49 conversations between family and friends), and the Mandarin Conversational Dialogue Corpus (MCDC) (thirty conversations between strangers), as well over ten hours of recordings of business interactions in Taiwan collected by the first author between 2010 and 2019 (Taiwanese Business Interaction Corpus).

7 From the MSC, copyright 2006, Tokyo University of Foreign Studies (available on request at: http://www.coelang.tufs.ac.jp/multilingual_corpus/zt/index.html?contents_xml=gaisetsu&menulang=en s). In this and following examples, a transcript of the recording in Chinese is followed by a translation of the dialogue into English by the authors. For reasons of space and readability, pinyin has been omitted and transcriptions simplified. For a more detailed interactional analysis of Chinese conversational humour see, for example, Chang and Haugh (2021).

8 See Haugh and Chang (2015: 404–405) for a more detailed analysis of this teasing sequence.

9 From the NCCU, described in Chui and Lai (2008). The corpus is available at: spokentaiwanmandarin.nccu.edu.tw/corpus-data.html (last accessed 1 July 2021).

10 One of the Japanese Seven Lucky Gods, whose ample figure and fat face represent good fortune.

11 From the MCDC, described in Tseng (2008). Access to the corpus is available on request from the Academia Sinica at: https://www.sinica.edu.tw/en. The key term discussed here is reproduced in bold.

12 From the dataset of ten hours of recordings of business interactions in Taiwan described in Chang (2016). The data is transcribed here using the romanisation system outlined in the *Taiwan Minnanyu Changyongci Cidian* 臺灣閩南語常用詞辭典 (*Dictionary of everyday expressions in Taiwanese Hokkien*) produced by the Taiwanese Ministry of Education (MOE 2011). Code-switching to and from Mandarin Chinese is indicated through the % symbol; descriptions of non-verbal behaviour with double-brackets (( )); overlapping talk with square brackets [ ], and brief micro-pauses with (.).

13 For further discussion of humour in classical Chinese novels, see Leggieri, this volume.

14 From W.-Y. Hou 侯文詠, *Da Yiyuan Xiao Yisheng* 大醫院小醫生 (Taipei: Crown Publishing, 1992).

15 Since in Taiwan, translations into English generally follow American practice, we use the American term chief resident doctor here.

16 *I Love* Mali (*Wo Ai Mali* 我愛瑪琍) first appeared in the *China Times* (*Zhongguo Shibao* 中國時報) in 1977 as part of a short column series. It was republished as a novel in 1979 by Vista Publishing (Yuanjing Chubanshe 遠景出版社, Taipei). The main character in the story works in an international company in Taiwan and is depicted as a person who worships Western culture but despises his own cultural heritage. This extract is taken from the 1979 Vista Publishing edition.

17 For more on comic naming and its role in traditional humour in Chinese languages, see M. Chan, this volume.

18 Lupinus (*Lu Bing Hua* 魯冰花) first appeared in the *United Daily News* (*Lian He Bao* 聯合報) in 1960 as part of a short column series. It was republished as a novel in 1962 by Ming Zhi Publishing (Ming Zhi Chubanshe 明志出版社, Taipei). The extract is taken from this edition.

19 The reference to a devil hiding in the corner in this passage indicates that misfortunate or bad luck is stalking the family and primes the reader to the likelihood that something bad is going to happen to the family again. This ominous hint serves to darken the humour that follows, as is indicated by the reference to the devil's malevolent sneer, an unpleasant form of humour.

References

Attardo, S. 1994. *Linguistic theories of humour.* Berlin: Mouton de Gruyter.
Attardo, S. 2019. Humour and mirth. Emotions, embodied cognition and sustained humour. In J. L. Mackenzie and L. Alba-Juez, eds., *Emotion in discourse.* 189–211. Amsterdam: John Benjamins.
Attardo, S. 2020. *The linguistics of humour.* Oxford: Oxford University Press.
Béal, C. and K. Mullan. 2013. Issues in conversational humour from a cross-cultural perspective: Comparing French and Australian corpora. In C. Béal, K. Mullan and B. Peeters, eds., *Cross-culturally speaking, speaking cross-culturally.* 107–140. Newcastle-upon-Tyne, UK: Cambridge Scholars Press.
Bednarek, M. 2017. The role of dialogue in fiction. In M. Locher and A. Jucker, eds., *Pragmatics of fiction.* 129–59. Berlin: Mouton de Gruyter.
Bi, X. and E. Marsden. 2020. Managing interpersonal relationships: Teasing as a method of professional identity construction. *Journal of Pragmatics*, 165: 18–30.
Cao, Y. 2019. Humour and (im)politeness in Chinese sitcom discourse: A case study of Ipartment. Unpublished PhD thesis, Western Sydney University.
Cao, Y. This volume. *We are real friends*: Constructing Chinese female friendship via teasing in a Chinese reality TV show. In J. Milner Davis, ed., *Humour in Asian cultures: Tradition and context.* Singapore and London: Routledge.
Chang, W. M. 2016. *Face and face practices in Chinese interaction: A study in interactional pragmatics.* London: Equinox.
Chang, W. M. 2018. Cross-generational study of conversational humour amongst Taiwanese speakers of Mandarin Chinese. Paper presented at the 11th International Conference on Im/Politeness, University of Valencia, 4–6 July 2018.
Chang, W. M. and M. Haugh. 2020. The metapragmatics of "teasing" in Taiwanese Chinese conversational humour. *European Journal of Humor Research*, 8: 7–30.
Chang, W. M. and M. Haugh. 2021. Teasing and claims to non-serious intent in Chinese talk shows. *East Asian Pragmatics*, 6: 135–159.
Chang, W. M., M. Haugh and H. Y. Su. 2021. Taking it too far. The role of ideological discourses in contesting the limits of teasing and offence. *Pragmatics*, 31: 382–405.
Chen, G. 1985. *Study of Ancient Chinese Jokes.* Unpublished Master's Thesis, National Taiwan Normal University.
Chen, L. L. 2016a. A socio-pragmatic analysis of *wúlítóu* 'nonsense' in Taiwanese verbal interactions. *Lodz Papers in Pragmatics*, 12: 53–76.
Chen, L. L. 2016b. Laughter, smiling and their pragmatic/interpersonal functions: An interactional linguistic account. *Concentric—Studies in Linguistics*, 42: 135–168.
Chen, L. L. 2017. *Taiwanese and Polish humour. A sociopragmatic analysis.* Newcastle upon Tyne, UK: Cambridge Scholars Press.
Chen, X. 2019. "You're a nuisance!": "Patch-up" jocular abuse in Chinese fiction. *Journal of Pragmatics*, 139: 52–63.

Chey, J. 2011. *Youmo* and the Chinese sense of humour. In J. Chey and J. Milner Davis, eds., *Humour in Chinese life and letters. Classical and traditional approaches*. 1–29. Hong Kong: Hong Kong University Press.

Chui, K and H. Lai. 2008. The NCCU corpus of spoken Chinese: Mandarin, Hakka, and Southern Min. *Taiwan Journal of Linguistics*, 6: 119–144.

Drew, P. 1987. Po-faced receipts of teases. *Linguistics*, 25: 219–253.

Dynel, Marta. 2009. Beyond a joke: Types of conversational humour. *Language and Linguistics Compass*, 3: 1284–1299.

Gong, L. and Y. Ran. 2020. Discursive constraints of teasing: Constructing professionality via teasing in Chinese entertainment interviews. *Chinese Journal of Applied Linguistics*, 43: 64–82.

Haugh, M. 2017. Teasing. In S. Attardo, ed., *Routledge handbook of language and humour*. 204–218. New York: Routledge.

Haugh, M. and W. M. Chang. 2015. Understanding im/politeness across cultures: an interactional approach to raising sociopragmatic awareness. *IRAL: International Review of Applied Linguistics*, 53: 389–414.

Jin, Y. and X. Chen. 2020. "*Mouren*" ("somebody") can be you-know-who: a case study of mock referential vagueness in Chinese Weibo posts. *Journal of Pragmatics*, 164: 1–15.

Labov, W. 1966. *The Social stratification of English in New York City*. Washington, DC: Centre for Applied Linguistics.

Li, C. 2020. Teasing as a practice of managing delicate issues in institutional talk: A case study of request in Mandarin Chinese. *East Asian Pragmatics*, 5: 323–344.

Li, X. 2020. Interpersonal touch in conversational joking. *Research on Language and Social Interaction*, 53: 357–379.

Liao, C. C. 2001. *Taiwanese perceptions of humor: A sociolinguistic perspective*. Taipei: Crane.

Liao, C. C. 2003. Humour versus *huaji*. *Journal of Languages and Linguistics*, 2: 25–52.

Milner Davis, J. 2013. Humour and its cultural context. Introduction and overview. In J. Milner Davis and J. Chey, eds., *Humour in Chinese life and culture*. 1–21. Hong Kong: Hong Kong University Press.

MOE [Taiwanese Ministry of Education]. 2011. *Taiwan Minnanyu Changyongci Cidian* 臺灣閩南語常用詞辭典 (*Dictionary of everyday expressions in Taiwanese Hokkien*). *Zhonghuamingguo Jiaoyubu* 中華民國 教育部 (Ministry of Education), Taipei. At: https://twblg.dict.edu.tw/holodict_new/ (accessed 15 July 2021).

Mullan, K. and C. Béal. 2018. Conversational humour: Forms, functions and practices across cultures. *Intercultural Pragmatics*, 15: 451–456.

Norrick, Neal. 1993. *Conversational joking: Humour in everyday talk*. Bloomington, IN: Indiana University Press.

Norrick, Neal and Delia Chiaro, eds. 2009. *Humour in interaction*. Amsterdam: John Benjamins.

Padilla Cruz, M. 2019. Verbal humour and age in cafes and bars in Seville, Spain. In J. C. Félix-Brasdefer and M. E. Placencia, eds., *Pragmatic variation in service encounter interactions across the Spanish-speaking world*. 169–188. New York: Routledge.

Qiu, J., X. Chen and M. Haugh. 2021. Jocular flattery in Chinese multi-party instant messaging interactions. *Journal of Pragmatics*, 178: 225–241.

Santangelo, Paulo. 2012a. Talking of smile and laughter. In Paulo Santangelo, ed., *Laughing in Chinese*. 5–28. Roma: Aracne.

Santangelo, Paulo. 2012b. Functions of laugh and smile in their Chinese premodern representation: A preliminary survey. In Paolo Santangelo, ed., *Laughing in Chinese*. 29–203. Roma: Aracne.

Schegloff, E. A. 1987. Some sources of misunderstanding in talk-in-interaction. *Linguistics*, 25: 201–218.

Schegloff, E. A. 2006. Interaction: The infrastructure for social institutions, the natural ecological niche for language, and the arena in which culture is enacted. In N. J. Enfield and S. Levinson, eds., *Roots of human sociality: Culture, cognition and interaction*. 70–96. Oxford: Berg.

Sinkeviciute, Valeria and Marta Dynel. 2017. Approaching conversational humour culturally: A survey of the emerging area of investigation. *Language and Communication*, 55: 1–9.

Su, H. Y. 2009. Reconstructing Taiwanese and Taiwan *guoyu* on the Taiwan-based internet. *Journal of Asian Pacific Communication*, 19: 313–335.

Su, L. I. and S. P. Huang. 2002. Harmonious face threatening acts and politeness: A special consideration. *Working Papers in Linguistics (National Taiwan University)*, 5: 175–202.

Tannen, D. 1984. *Conversational style*. Norwood, NJ: Ablex.

Tsakona, Villy. 2017. Genres of humour. In S. Attardo, ed., *Routledge handbook of language and humour*. 489–503. New York: Routledge.

Tseng, S. C. 2004. Processing spoken Mandarin corpora. *Traitement automatique des langues. Special Issue: Spoken Corpus Processing*, 45: 89–108.

Tseng, S. C. 2008. Spoken corpora and analysis of natural speech. *Taiwan Journal of Linguistics*, 6: 1–26.

Xu, Z. 2014. Contextual dimensions in interactional humour: How humour is practiced in selected American and Chinese situation comedies. *Journal of Pragmatics*, 60: 24–35.

Yang, N. and W. Ren. 2020. Jocular mockery in the context of a localised playful frame: Unpacking humour in a Chinese reality TV show. *Journal of Pragmatics*, 162: 32–44.

Yue, X-D. 2010. Exploration of Chinese humour: Historical review, empirical findings, and critical reflections. *HUMOR: International Journal of Humor Research*, 23: 403–420.

Zhao, L. 2020. Mock impoliteness and co-construction of *hudui* rituals in Chinese online interaction. *Chinese Journal of Applied Linguistics*, 43: 45–63.

10 *We Are Real Friends*

Women constructing friendship via teasing in a Chinese reality TV show

Ying Cao

Introduction

Recent studies indicate the growing importance of aggressive but creative use of language in enhancing the humorous effects of television programmes (Culpeper 2005). Some research has focussed on the distinctive characteristics of teasing in Reality Television (RTV) discourse, a format found in many countries in which ordinary people rather than actors are continuously filmed and which is designed to be entertaining rather than informative. Teasing is a distinct linguistic practice that combines (mock) impoliteness and humour and it facilitates humorous and entertaining effects in RTV discourse better than traditional forms of humour such as canned jokes. It also enables new applications of traditional forms like anecdotes and witticisms (Lorenzo-Dus et al. 2013). Reality television, as "a new way of factual TV programming" (Kilborn 2003: 83), offers the viewers the experience of watching celebrities being integrated into ordinary activities, often with "humorous interplay" (Kilborn 2003: 80); and also the opportunity to engage in critical viewing of the attitudes and daily behaviours of well-known people (Hill 2004: 37). Accordingly, RTV shows provide an important site for both participants and TV viewers to establish an affective link through sharing and introspection about their attitudes towards social roles and interpersonal relations. And humour seems to be prominent in this process.

Investigations into the interpersonal functions of humour have emphasised the crucial role of teasing in rapport management in intracultural settings (Beck et al. 2007; Coates 2007; Pichler 2006), and also more generally in intercultural settings (Haugh and Pillet-Shore 2018; Haugh and Weinglass 2018). It appears that teasing facilitates friendship building on various levels: many central friendship activities such as displaying the sharing of common ground, indicating closeness and intimacy, implicitly delivering criticism, reinforcing bonding and so on, can all be discursively performed via teasing (Jones et al. 2005). Yet while teasing has been recognised as a particularly effective means of "doing friendship" in friends' talk (Coates 2007; Eder 1993; Hay 2000; Holmes and Marra 2002), it also delivers an impact at multiple relational levels, creating intimacy, but also carrying aggressive undertones which serve to reconstruct asymmetrical power relationships and which actually harm the target to some extent (Kotthoff 1996).

Being inherently aggressive, teasing is usually considered central to the construction of masculine identities and hierarchies where it seems to be a way of establishing male intimacy and excluding women (Frosh et al. 2002). Research on teasing has mostly focused on interactions among male participants, women's reactions to teasing in mixed-gender talk and their deployment of teasing to assert status in male-dominated discourse, often in the workplace. Few studies look at the link between teasing and friendship-building in women's talk (Pichler 2006). This is particularly surprising since a number of researchers have suggested that the primary goal of talk between women friends is the construction and maintenance of close social relationships (Coates 1997). Teasing, as a type of linguistic practice, requires a collaborative effort: it is not just ancillary to friendship building but is fundamentally grounded in the notion of intimacy (Coates 2007).

The joint nature of teasing has been extensively explored in interactional pragmatics, showing that speakers must be able to gauge when their face-threatening remarks are less likely to be interpreted as having serious implications and more likely to be taken as playful (Kotthoff 1996; Jones et al. 2005; Coates 2007; Haugh and Bousfield 2012; Haugh 2017). To avoid interpretive ambiguity, interlocutors jointly construct a play-frame to show that they have similar attitudes and beliefs about the objects of the jocular acts they perform. It has been argued that Chinese speakers tend to rely on social and cultural knowledge of "face" when constructing a play-frame during interactions (Chen 2013) and culturally imbued characteristics of that framing certainly impact on understanding the jocular tone of teasing in Chinese (Yang and Ren 2020). While this is an important observation, unfortunately, both these studies only mention it in passing.

In response to these research gaps, this study aim to analyse the ways in which teasing is used to construct and maintain friendship in Chinese women's daily interactions, as mirrored in RTV. It demonstrates a diversity of teasing styles and considers the important interactional goal of friendship building, and how the teasing practices of RTV discourse impact on audience perceptions of friendship and gender roles.

Teasing and friendship in women's talk

The conceptualisation of teasing differs somewhat depending on the research paradigm, but it is generally agreed that teasing involves the juxtaposition of an (ostensibly) serious stance and a non-serious stance that is shared by both the teaser and the target of the teasing (Haugh 2017). Teasing involves a speaker figuratively cutting down a target and is accompanied by contextualisation cues signalling that the belittlement is to be taken as playful (Keltner et al. 2001). These clues are both linguistic (e.g. formulaic expressions, incongruities, exaggerations and overt untruthfulness) and paralinguistic (e.g. exaggerated tone of voice, rolling of the eyes, and/or winks, see Haugh 2014; Lampert and Ervin-Tripp 2006). Nevertheless, interpretations of teasing vary depending on how the respective proportions of playfulness and provocation embedded in the tease are construed by the recipients. Factors impacting the recipient's interpretation of teasing include lacking competence in discerning underlying meanings, a negative disposition towards the teaser or teasing *per se*, and even mood of the recipient at that moment (Bollmer et al. 2003; Keltner et al. 2001; Kowalski 2004).

As noted above, teasing is a pervasive strategy in humour with great potential for relationship management and social control in interpersonal interaction. It embodies an interesting mix of "bonding", "nipping" and "biting". Biting refers to teasing that contains overtly aggressive and challenging remarks primarily aimed at putting down the target. Bonding indicates teasing that performs affiliative functions such as highlighting common ground and displaying intimacy rather than challenging or provoking interlocutors (Boxer and Corte-Conde 1997). Nipping indicates teasing of an ambiguous nature: it is normally positioned in between bonding and biting, combining elements of both (Schnurr 2009). While teasing is usually designed to achieve all three effects, its perception by recipients or onlookers may not always be consistent with the speaker's precise goal. A bonding tease may still be perceived as biting and perceptions of teasing vary with gender (Hay 1994). When teasing involves topics such as sex, gender stereotypes and negative evaluations of appearance and body shape, it is more likely to elicit negative responses such as rejection, rebuttal, and correction if it is directed at female targets (Hay 1994; Jones et al. 2005; Lampert and Ervin-Tripp 2006).

Not surprisingly, women's production and interpretation of teasing have been a key focus in humour and gender studies. Generally, females are socialised to have different teasing practices and expectations than males but, significantly, they can strategically deploy teasing to foster new gender roles and relations (Beck et al. 2007). Eder (1993) found teasing was adopted by American adolescent girls to playfully distance themselves from traditional gender roles and simultaneously adhere to societal norms of beauty while socialising each other to feminine norms.

Straehle (1993) and Kotthoff (1996) connect their analyses of teasing among close friends to relationship management. Their finding that adult friends often tease those with whom they enjoy a close relationship or have affection for likely reflects the fact that at the start of a relationship, even moderate teasing can sabotage friendship among women (Kotthoff 1996). Teasing is thus a bonding ritual showing affection and increasing intimacy among close friends. It can be practised because teaser and target tacitly agree that the demands of preserving face should be suspended in the interests of "getting a laugh", and because their relationship is so close and well-established that it cannot be endangered even by seemingly rude utterances (Kotthoff 1996). Friendship clearly attenuates the predicted feelings of negativity associated with teasing and enhances recognition of the humour in teasing situations (Jones et al. 2005). The friendship-building function of teasing is premised on the closeness and mutual understanding that exists between friends and it relies on the teaser's understanding of the target's potential for experiencing genuine pain and a desire to avoid touching upon that. Despite this, it cannot be assumed that teasing will invariably promote bonding between friends.

Much remains to be confirmed in the study of differences in teasing practices and/or different interpretations of teasing across languages and cultures (Haugh 2017). Given the likelihood of culturally imbued characteristics of teasing, and the long traditions governing the use of humour in Chinese cultures noted by many scholars including some in this book, it is important to explore whether there exist particular, perhaps ritualised, forms of teasing characteristic of Chinese cultures and their possibly gender-inscribed nature in women's talk. This study also tests the extent to which systematic approaches grounded in one particular language, namely, English, can accommodate the analysis of teasing in Chinese contexts.

RTV discourse and humour

The reality television show is generally viewed as a type of factual media product. It involves a set of genres based on the conventions of what has been called "the assertive stance to reality" (Blitvich and Lorenzo-Dus 2013). The central premise of the convention is viewers' acceptance of an evident connection between the TV show and reality. The production team deploys a wide range of specific filmic techniques, including location shooting, camera settings and the use of natural lighting and so on, in order to induce viewers to accept scenes they watch on screen as reflections of real situations. However, this assertive real stance does not imply that the identities constructed by actors on screen are always real, nor that viewers should always treat RTV as factual reality. Rather, it guides the RTV production team to work in a way that produces factual outputs seeming to give viewers direct access to some aspects of reality and to a range of apparently real personal and social identities. As Sinkeviciute (2017) has noted, the identities displayed by the people who participate in RTV are in fact distinctly influenced by other fictional TV genres, such as TV series and films, where characters' identities are largely contrived and prefabricated.

While academic interest in RTV has continued to grow in past decades, most published work is rooted in fields such as media, cultural or aesthetic studies. Only a few studies (e.g. Culpeper et al. 2003; Culpeper 2005; Blitvich et al. 2013; Lorenzo-Dus 2006; Thornborrow and Morris 2004; Tolson 2006) have investigated the "language" of RTV discourse with respect to its interactional dynamics. Blitvich and Lorenzo-Dus (2013) suggested the value of a micro-level analysis for enriching studies of language and identity construction in different social and cultural backgrounds. Since focussing on the perceptions of viewers at the macro-level can fail to see the whole picture of RTV discourse (Sinkeviciute 2019), a more language-based approach will be better for understanding underlying functions and deepening insights into how language in RTV discourse impacts people's ways of communication in real-life.

In fact, RTV discourse provides an ideal source for investigating interactional issues such as playfulness and aggression, with studies by Culpeper (2005) and Sinkeviciute (2019) explaining how aggressive expressions are closely related to the success of RTV and examining the multi-layered functions of verbal aggression in RTV discourse. Linguistic aggression is not only deployed as a means of pandering to TV viewers' desire for entertainment value—termed by Culpeper and Holmes (2013) "confrontainment", where humour derives from characters' conflicts—but it also serves as a potent linguistic device for the construction and maintenance of participants' personal and social identities (Blitvich and Lorenzo-Dus 2013). Exploring the semantic features, functions and responses of jocular mockery as a specific form of teasing in Australian and British RTV discourse, Sinkeviciute (2019) found that the use of and response to jocular mockery in these programmes reflects an essential cultural ethos that is widespread in mainstream English-speaking societies, such as the proscription against "taking oneself too seriously".

Analysing teasing in RTV discourse can throw light on the interdependence between aggression and humour in TV genres generally. Specifically, it may provide insights into the multi-faceted aspects of aggressive forms of humour (Blitvich 2009, 2010), as well as into how TV viewers extract amusement from verbal aggression. Conflict has become a staple of RTV and may well be part of the viewers' expectations about interaction within this genre of discourse, and hence not seen as genuine impoliteness. If so, the common use of aggressive expressions in RTV discourse would simply be verisimilitudinous, although it is in sharp contrast—certainly in Chinese societies—to daily societal usage. As Dynel (2013) has observed, the pleasure derived by TV viewers may lie precisely in that contrast. RTV also creates entertainment through its likeness to what audiences recognise as real, providing a feeling that audiences cannot fully experience from scripted fictional discourse. Language that is unscripted (therefore not predictable), unstandardised (not conforming to normative styles of talk) and possibly personal (because not contrived in advance) enhances that sense of the real and makes for exciting TV shows, as Culpeper and Holmes note (2013).

Unsurprisingly, because this TV genre originated in English-speaking countries, most existing research exploring language in RTV discourse is based on English examples and contexts. However, when RTV shows were transported to China, their language and viewers' perceptions might well have embraced new features. Accordingly, before attempting to decode the cultural dimensions of teasing now found in Chinese RTV discourse, the characteristics of Chinese RTV discourse in general need to be addressed. This helps identify the underlying social norms that Chinese audiences abide by in their own lives and that will likely apply when they evaluate participants' humour practices in RTV discourse.

Chinese reality TV shows and *We Are Real Friends*

Reality TV shows were introduced to China in the 1990s and have experienced rapid development in recent decades. In 2004, the great success of *Chaoji Nüsheng* 超级女声 (*Super Girl*), a song contest for female contestants, heralded the first peak in Chinese RTV shows (Yin et al. 2005). It was generally described at the time as the unofficial Mainland Chinese version of the global TV franchise *Pop Idol* and became one of the most popular entertainment shows in China. Following its success, other analogous song contests were subsequently aired, such as *Chaoji Nansheng* 超级男声 (*Super Boy*). The final episode of *Super Girl's* 2005 season peaked at 280 million viewers, dwarfing the 12-million-viewer figure for the finals of *Pop Idol* (Huang 2010). While receiving praise as blazing the trail of cultural democracy, this show was condemned by China Central Television as vulgar and manipulative, and China's State Administration of Radio, Film and Television (SARFT) suspended future production at the end of 2011, citing its hidden moral issues (Huang 2010).

The content of Chinese RTV is required to reflect and strictly abide by traditional Chinese morality (Yang 2015). In addition, rules require that RTV shows should be localised so as to conform to traditional Chinese ethics, and scenes which deviate from traditional Chinese values, such as those containing sex, treachery, deception, disloyalty, and any that invade personal privacy, are banned (Huang 2010). Due to increasing criticisms about the spread of superficiality and the lack of any educational value in RTV shows, SARFT brought forward a series of censorship policies regarding their content and broadcasting times. These motivated RTV producers to transfer their main battlefield from TV to video-sharing platforms. In addition to enjoying the advantage of comparatively loose censorship, online RTV shows are enabled in this way to directly attract the attention of their main target of young audiences who spend most of their time online rather than watching TV.

With the development in the past decade of the major video-sharing platforms, such as IQIYI[1] and Tencent, the RTV show embraced a second wave of fast development with a more versatile form and content. In addition to shows in the forms of a contest, RTV shows based on observations of how celebrities deal with chaotic situations have grasped the audience attention. In these, TV viewers observe celebrities' reactions towards scenarios that are laid out by the production team such as travelling in a foreign place with a tight budget and running a business from scratch. In these shows, cameras are set to fully capture the real-world whereabouts of celebrities so that viewers can observe the celebrities' "real" reactions when facing difficulties and embarrassing moments.

The popularity of this type of show can be ascribed to satisfying the audience's curiosity about the celebrities' daily lives. They arouse sympathy from viewers that celebrities with fame and fortune are also bothered by trivial problems concerning marriage, friendships and careers. In addition to these intriguing scenarios, another key reason for the popularity of such observatory shows is that they incorporate positive content and embrace values (e.g. optimism, righteousness, selflessness and resilience) that conform to traditional Chinese values (Huang 2010).

Among the popular online observatory RTV shows, *We Are Real Friends* (*Wo Men Shi Zhenzheng De Pengyou* 我们是真正的朋友) can be regarded as one of the most representative and outstanding because it is the first Chinese RTV show to concentrate on friendships between women (Chi 2019). This show was released on 9 May 2019, directed by Li Rui 李睿, production by and screening on Tencent Video. It illustrates how four women get along with each other during a trip to Myanmar. These are the actress Barbie Hsu 徐熙媛, singer-songwriter Mavis Fan 范晓萱, and hostesses Elephant Dee 徐熙娣 and Aya Liu 柳翰雅, all of whom have been close friends for over 20 years. The show demonstrates unscripted real-life situations requiring them to arrange their own travel and share their daily routines, for example, travelling to Myanmar to take part in the festival known as "Water Splashing Day" (shown in Figure 10.1; for a more natural portrayal of the four, see Figure 10.2). The producer of the show, Li Xiao 李笑, has said that she was touched by the family-like relationships the four have and she hoped that audiences will learn how to cherish their own long-standing friends after watching the show (Chi 2019). The aim of the show is thus consistent with the core value set down for Chinese RTV shows, that is, apart from amusing viewers, to influence them positively.

Four factors contribute to the distinction and success achieved by *We Are Real Friends*. Firstly, the show is based on female friendship and directly targeted at female viewers who are the main consumers of RTV shows in China (Chi 2019). In addition, the woman director, Li Xiao, knows how to present stories from a female perspective. Secondly, the show deliberately enhances the feeling of reality for its viewers. Instead of choosing the most popular female celebrities so as to attract as many viewers as possible, the production team selected these four women to participate in a friendship-centred show precisely because they are real friends. Thus, when observing how they manage their relationships, viewers are more likely to recognise what they are viewing as real and thus to resonate with the situations and personalities.

Thirdly, the show's aim conforms to the traditional Chinese cultural view of humour and reflects the ethos still widely held by Chinese people today. Traditionally, humour has been seen as a philosophical concept that "reveals a mellow and detached disposition and conveys a certain philosophy of life" (Qian 2011: 203). Despite widespread contemporary use of the neologism

218 Ying Cao

Figure 10.1 Still from Episode 1 (3:41) of *Wo Men Shi Zhenzheng De Pengyou* 我们是真正的朋友 (*We Are Real Friends*), 2019, director Li Rui 李睿, produced and distributed by Tencent Video, showing the four friends entering into the spirit of Myanmar's Water Splashing Day Festival.

Source: From the video version at: https://v.qq.com/x/cover/ud645xiddndklds.html (accessed 8 July 2021).

Figure 10.2 Still from Episode 3 (13:18) of *Wo Men Shi Zhenzheng De Pengyou* 我们是真正的朋友 (*We Are Real Friends*), 2019, director Li Rui 李睿, produced and distributed by Tencent Video, showing the four friends posing as a group for a magazine shoot.

Source: From the video version at: https://v.qq.com/x/cover/khzinb5uhj60fe8.html (accessed 5 August 2021).

youmo 幽默, Wang (2001) has argued that the true Chinese equivalent to the Western term, humour, is *yaxue* 雅谑, comprising *ya* 雅 (elegant) and *xue* 谑 (joke). Both terms encompass a spirit of cheerful happiness and Wang explains that while *ya* represents the basic aspects of people's life, including food, clothing and death, *xue* implies happiness deriving from people's spiritual power even when they can hardly make a living. Thus, in Chinese, as in its original English meaning (Wickberg 1998), humour refers to a sympathetic and reasonable acceptance of life. The bright side of humour that is harmless and benign is central to the traditional philosophical account of humour in Chinese (Chen 2013). Instead of plotting confrontational scenes that afford the viewers a chance to laugh at the inadequacies and embarrassment of participants, the production team of this show focussed on presenting the ordinary daily interaction among the four women and their heartfelt thoughts about life and friendship without contrived conflicts such as are ordinarily found in Western reality TV shows. Interactions are mostly light-hearted, despite occurrences of verbal aggression. These are evidently taken as jocular, and no genuine harm is perceived as occurring. Verbal conflicts involve the women disparaging each other's appearance and body shape, among other things. However, the aggression contained in these verbal exchanges is largely rooted in the paradigm of mock impoliteness, where impoliteness remains at the superficial level.[2] In this way, viewers safely enjoy a moderate amusement that is delivered through the participants' jocularly teasing each other. The show places more emphasis on encouraging its viewers to value and nurture their own friendships than on eliciting laughter from them and harnessing the humour of jocular abuse to these didactic purposes is consistent with traditional concepts of humour in Chinese cultures (Xu 2014).

Finally, an important contribution to the success of the show is that the four women offer viewers a more complex and versatile interpretation of Chinese femininity than is usually available. While successful and dominant in their own professional fields, these four also associate themselves with traditional gender roles, such as the caring sister, the nurturing mother and the considerate wife. Conventionally, females are portrayed in Chinese TV discourse as either powerful iron lady or submissive housewife (Lu 1997), so that the multi-faceted identities of these four display greatly increase the available variety of cultural representations of femininity. They act to reshape stereotypical gender roles, breaking the stigmatised opposition between masculinity (powerful, tough and career-driven) and femininity (caring, submissive, relationship-driven) that is likely ingrained in viewers' expectations.

Data collection and methods of analysis

Data was collected from all ten episodes of *We Are Real Friends*, consisting of approximately 7,500 minutes of video material. A total of 1,378 conversational turns were transcribed to provide the main corpus for this study which was filtered and analysed. First, teasing turns were identified using Haugh's salient design features of jocular mockery which propose to identify a set of both paralinguistic (e.g. laughter, facial expressions and prosodic cues) and linguistic clues (e.g. exaggeration, untruthfulness and incongruities) indicate a speaker's humorous intent (Haugh 2014: 79). Based on these clues, 770 turns of teasing were identified.

Teasing turns were then grouped into units of conversational teasing in order to explore how teasing is constructed and extended in conversations. The boundary of each unit was determined primarily by conversational topic and the pragmatic orientation of each teasing sequence. Thus, if the speaker's utterances were either semantically or pragmatically coherent with previous utterances, those conversational sequences were grouped as one unit. If any linguistic clue explicitly or implicitly indicated a topic transition or the halt of a playful frame, that marked the end of the unit of conversational teasing. These criteria identified ninety-one units of conversational teasing. Data transcription added in brackets contextual information such as the situational context, laughter, and the targets of teasing, to help readers understand the interaction (Zajdman 1991).

The units were then coded as being either a collaborative style of teasing or a non-collaborative style of teasing, a dichotomy developed by Holmes (2006: 114–116). Style here indicates the variety of ways in which participants link their humorous contributions to the contributions of others, resulting in very different effects in terms of the overall style of interaction (Holmes and Marra 2002: 1688). Here, a collaborative style of teasing is defined as a collaborative way of constructing and extending teasing sequences. Participants' contributions aim to reverberate with or reinforce points made by previous speakers and the pragmatic orientation of the teasing sequences is therefore supportive of previous speakers' propositions. A non-collaborative style of teasing indicates cases where the participants extend the teasing sequences in an uncooperative manner by inserting amusing but contestive comments into the exchange to refute each other's points and to rebuke the previous speaker. Cases discussed here may not be completely consistent with the non-collaborative style of humour defined by Holmes (2006: 116). This stresses that the non-collaborative nature of humour is reflected at both the syntactic and stylistic levels, in other words, speakers' humorous sequences are constructed independently with no syntactically integrated structures or only a loose semantic link with previous utterances. However, the non-collaborative style of teasing found in the present data confines its non-collaborative nature to the pragmatic and semantic levels. Thus, if the semantic meanings and the pragmatic force of participants' teasing sentences are negative and contestive, it is treated as a case of non-collaborative style of teasing, despite the fact that these sequences may still be coherent and consistent in terms of stylistic or syntactic features (an illustration in lines 303–304 in Example 2, where the two lines are similar in syntactic structure).

Finally, I explored the strategies adopted by these four women as they construct teasing either collaboratively or non-collaboratively. Previous studies such as Coates (1997) show that women achieve a collaborative style of talk through co-construction of the playful frame (e.g. joint joking), repetition and playing along with the conversational topics and overlapping turns), while challenging, disruptive interruptions and outwitting each other characterise a non-collaborative style of talk (Schnurr 2009). Both studies demonstrated that women's talk conventionally features a more collaborative style and that the strategies used to reinforce their collaboration are also apparent in their humorous exchanges.

Doing friendship through teasing within a play frame

Collaborative style of teasing

Teasing sequences in the collaborative style of teasing are tightly composed so as to create cohesion and a high syntactical integration. Obviously, participants' co-construction of a teasing sequence is indicative of their solidarity and closeness, since participants who collaborate in humorous talk "necessarily display how finely tuned they are to each other" (Davies 2003: 1362). Co-constructed utterances are a more normal feature of all-female talk than of all-male talk and, given that mutual knowledge and closeness are central to women's talk, a collaborative style promotes their togetherness (Coates 2007). Interestingly, however, this study differed significantly from Coates' findings, with the occurrence of the collaborative style of teasing among these four women slightly less than that of the non-collaborative style.

The following example illustrates how these four women jointly build collaborative teasing aided by strategies that include playing along with the conversational theme and joint fantasy. Lines 169–174 below illustrate some of the cohesive devices used, including co-construction of utterances and discourse strategies such as repetition and question used to achieve collaborative humour.[3]

Example 1

Context: Aya always tells others that they should massage their purlicue (that is, the skin between the thumb and forefinger, see Figure 10.3) when they are not feeling well, such as suffering from nausea, headache and so on. Travelling together on the coach, Barbie tells Dee, Aya and Mavis that she is feeling a little under the weather.

164.	Barbie:	*wo jintian yiqilai jiu laduzi.* 我今天一起来就拉肚子。
		I've had the runs ever since I woke up this morning.
165.	Aya:	*dengxia yaobuyao bang ni an xia hukou?* 等下要不要帮你按下虎口。
		Do you need a purlicue massage later on?

(Continued)

166.	Barbie:	\<Smiling face\>
167.	Dee:	*suoyi buguan zenmeyang, doushi an hukou shibushi?* 所以不管怎么样，都是按虎口是不是？ **So just massaging the purlicue can cure us, no matter what's making us feel unwell?**
168.	Aya:	*jiushi tingshuo hukou …* 就是听说虎口 … **I just heard that the purlicue …**
169.	Dee:	***na ruguo jiaochou ye shi an hukou ma*** (laughter)? 那如果脚臭也是按虎口吗 \<laughter\>? **So do I need to have a purlicue massage if I have athlete's foot** \<laughter\>?
170.	Mavis:	\<Laughter\>
171.	Aya:	***ruguo ni toufa fencha, fazhi buhao ye keyi an hukou*** \<laughter\>. 如果你头发分叉，发质不好也可以按虎口 \<laughter\>。 **If your hair develops split ends or you have damaged hair, you could also massage your purlicue** \<laughter\>.
172.	Dee:	\<Laughter\> ***bitou fenci, kebukeyi an hukou, an hukou kebukeyi bian shuang yanpi?*** \<Laughter\> 鼻头粉刺，可不可以按虎口，按虎口可不可以变双眼皮 \<laughter\>? \<Laughter\> **Will purlicue massage cure the acne on my nose? Will I develop double eye-lids if I have a purlicue massage?** \<laughter\>
173.	Mavis:	***ni dang zhebian shi ge duogongneng jian shibushi*** \<laughter\>? 你当这边是个多功能键是不是 \<laughter\>? **You treat your purlicue as a multi-functional button** \<laughter\>?
174.	Dee:	*yinwei wulun shenme shiqing fasheng, Aya dou shuo, wo bang ni an xia hukou* \<laughter\>. 因为无论什么事情发生，阿雅都说，我帮你按下虎口 \<laughter\>。 **This is because no matter what happens, Aya is always saying, I'll help you to massage your purlicue** \<laughter\>.
175.	Aya:	*dan youmeiyou bangzhu ni ziji shuo.* 但有没有帮助你自己说。 **To be honest, does it work for you?**
176.	Dee:	Sometimes *you.* Sometimes 有。 **Sometimes, yes.**
177.	Aya:	\<Laughter\>

When Aya suggests that a purlicue massage for Barbie will alleviate her food poisoning symptoms, Dee initiates the teasing sequence that begins in line 167 by saying, "So just massaging the purlicue can cure us, no matter what's making us feel unwell?", in a slightly ironic and questioning tone to imply that Aya is excessively fond of this form of massage. Without noticing the underlying sarcastic meaning, Aya explains quite seriously the benefits of a purlicue massage to Dee in line 168 and Dee then extends the teasing sequence in a more explicit yet still humorous manner by saying, "So do

We Are Real Friends 223

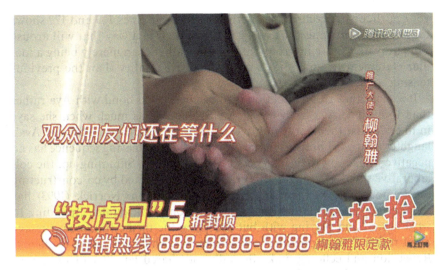

Figure 10.3 Aya giving a purlicue massage. Still from Episode 3 (3: 03) of *Wo Men Shi Zhenzheng De Pengyou* 我们是真正的朋友 (*We Are Real Friends*), 2019, director Li Rui 李睿, production and distributed by Tencent Video. The superscript added by the production team transforms the screenshot into a parodic TV commercial. It reads (down and across): "What are you waiting for, dear audience? Purlicue massage ambassador: Aya Liu. 50% discount on purlicue massage. Call: 888-8888-8888. Aya limited edition, buy now!".

Source: From the video version at: https://v.qq.com/x/cover/khzinb5uhj60fe8.html (accessed 8 July 2021).

I need a purlicue massage if I have athlete's foot?" Several linguistic and suprasegmental features mark the humorous frame of this exchange, such as the unrealistic content of the tease (that this massage will cure athlete's foot is obviously a fantastic exaggeration), Dee's rising tone of voice (Drew 1987) and then outright laughter. Laughter in line 170 by Mavis, the other participant, is additional recognition and appreciation of Dee's humorous intent.

Interestingly, Aya recognises Dee's intentional teasing and co-constructs and extends her teasing sequence with another teasing exaggeration: "If your hair develops split ends or you have damaged hair, you could also massage your purlicue". This is despite the fact that the target of the teasing is herself and what the others see as her abnormal behaviour. Her behaviour indicates that the close and solid friendship between the speakers is not undermined by such ritualised playful insults. In line 172, Dee extends the teasing sequence by asking about even more far-fetched cures and her laughter at the beginning of the teasing implies an extension of the play frame to cover what she says. Then Mavis joins in the teasing by asking if purlicue massage is being treated as a "multi-function button" or cure-all. In what follows, Dee concludes the teasing in line 174 by spelling out the problem in a way that echoes her first tease at line 167: "No matter what happens, Aya is always saying, I'll help you massage your purlicue". A comparison with her teasing in lines 169 and 172 shows that this final instance of teasing is formulated in a way that will arouse sympathy and share in-group knowledge, rather than merely being a jocular statement. It embodies a more affiliative quality than the previous teasing sequences.

It is clear that Dee's intention is to use teasing to bond with Aya rather than to exclude Aya from the group. She admits as much when she says in line 176 that this therapy only works for her sometimes. This and Aya's laughter in line 177 both reinforce the point that this teasing sequence has no negative impact on their interpersonal relationship. Summing up, the collaborative style of teasing in this example is constructed by co-constructing the humour and by thematic and verbal repetition. Norrick (1993) has shown that humour co-construction relies on participants responding to what is said and playing with but accepting the theme (purlicue massage here), rather than responding to what is meant, which might lead to offence. Repetition and echoing make the talk and shared laughter of these four women textually cohesive and allow the teasing sequence to be extended without giving or taking offence.

Non-collaborative style of teasing

The relatively loosely semantically connected teasing contributions from the speakers designated as a non-collaborative style of teasing are often built up in a disruptive manner so as to stake out the claims being made by the speaker. This kind of teasing sequence is premised on the notion of "ritual abuse" (see Sinkeviciute and Dynel 2017), where insulting and challenging messages are produced and received within a playful frame and so in certain communicative contexts serve to build solidarity.

Reciprocation is also an important feature of non-collaborative teasing. Participants try to outdo one another by "recycling" part of the original teasing and by reconstructing the original teasing sequence to reciprocate with what Eder (1990: 67–68) has called an "even more clever, outrageous, or elaborate reply". Thus, non-collaborative teasing constitutes a more competitive style of teasing that includes ritual teasing sequences by both speaker and targets. In spite of how aggressive these teasing sequences can be, both speaker and targets tacitly seem to understand that the aggression remains superficial. While these practices are likely not as common among people with a certain social distance between them, they are frequently observed among close friends (Eder 1990).

In this study, the four women, Aya, Barbie, Dee and Mavis, often use the strategies of competing, challenging, distorting, and dominating the conversational flow to extend a teasing sequence in a non-collaborative manner, even when the topics are quite personal and insulting, as Example 2 illustrates.

Example 2

Context: Dee is complaining to Aya about why Barbie looks better than herself on camera, and Barbie intervenes to reply that she has been more beautiful than Dee ever since they were born and Dee responds.

287. Dee:	\<laughter\> *ni jingran shuo de chu, zheme mei renxing de hua* \<laughing voice\> *cong chusheng dao xianzai, jiu bi wo piaoliang.* \<laughter\> **suanle, xinghao haiyou Aya zai wo shenbian, gei wo liliang.** \<laughter\> 你竟然说得出,这么没人性的话 \<laughing voice\> 从出生到现在,就比我漂亮。\<laughter\> 算了,**幸好还有阿雅在我身边,给我力量**。 \<laughter\> How dare you be so mean to me as to say \<laughing voice\> you've been much more beautiful than me ever since we were born. \<laughter\> Never mind, **at least I have Aya to keep me company, and that gives me comfort**.
288. Aya:	*WEI!* 喂! HEY!
289. Dee:	\<laughter\>
290. Aya:	*wo ZHENDE meiyou juede ziji bu piaoliang.* 我真的没有觉得自己不漂亮。 I TRULY don't think I'm not pretty.
291. Dee:	*haola, ni you ziji de weidao* \<smiling voice\>. 好啦,你有自己的味道 \<smiling voice\>。 **Fine, you have your own style** \<smiling voice\>.
292. Barbie:	*meigeren douyou ziji de weidao a.* 每个人都有自己的味道啊。 Everyone is beautiful in their own style.
293. Dee:	*wo ye zhibuguo shi kai yige wanxiao, ni gamma zheme jijiao* \<exaggerated facial expression\>? 我也只不过是开一个玩笑,你干嘛这么计较 \<exaggerated facial expression\>? **I was just joking. Why you being so serious** \<exaggerated facial expression\>?
294. Aya:	\<laughter\> \<laughter\>
295. Barbie:	*ke ni zhege wanxiao kaile ershiji nian ei.* 可你这个玩笑开了二十几年诶。 **But you've kept on using this joke for over twenty years.**
296. Barbie, Dee, Aya:	\< shared laughter\>
297. Barbie:	*waibiao zhishi pinang, you shenme zhongyao de.* 外表只是皮囊,有什么重要的。 It doesn't matter what you look like on the outside.
298. Dee:	*ZUIHAO SHI, na ni gamma meng jianfei* \<laughter\>. 最好是,那你干嘛猛减肥 \<laughter\>。

(Continued)

		YEAH, RIGHT! You are not on a crash diet <laughter>.
299.	Barbie:	*jianfei shi weile JIANKANG HE GONGZUO.* 减肥是为了健康和工作。 Keeping fit is for HEALTH AND WORK.
300.	Dee:	<laughter> FANGPI. <Laughter> 放屁。 <laughter> BULLSHIT.
301.	Barbie:	*ni kan wo feidudu de chulai gongzuo, bushi geng mei ren yao wo le ma?* 你看我肥嘟嘟得出来工作,不是更没人要我了吗? If I was chubby, I will get far less jobs than now, right?
302.	Dee:	*ni kan adaier duo zixin.* 你看阿黛尔多自信。 Look at Adele,[4] she is charming and confident.
303.	Barbie:	*yinwei ta hen hui CHANGGE a.* 因为她很会唱歌啊。 Because she is a great SINGER.
304.	Dee:	***ni ye keyi zuo ge hen hui yanxi de pangzi a*** <laughter>. 你也可以做个很会演戏的胖子啊 <laughter>。 **You can also be a great but chubby actress** <laughter>.
305.	Barbie:	***NI YOU BING A!*** 你有病啊 <laughing voice>! **WHAT'S THE PROBLEM WITH YOU** <laughing voice>!
306.	Dee:	***wo zhege bing a, dou de le sishiyi nian le*** <laughter> ***haobuliao le.*** 我这个病啊,都得了四十一年了 <laughter> 好不了了。 **Yeah, I've had this problem for forty-one years** <laughter> **and I will never ever do well.**

It is clear that Barbie, Aya, and Dee are competing for the floor and vying with each other to produce witty one-liners and pejorative remarks. Typically, women do not like negative comments on their body shape and looks. Notwithstanding the seemingly aggressive nature of these contestive teasing sequences, in fact, they invariably prompt rapport and serve to create a higher level of intimacy between those present. The teasing exists entirely within a mutually accepted play-frame. In line 287, Dee responds to Barbie's comments with a jocularly challenging tease, asking how she dares to say that she is more beautiful than Dee. Although this conveys a face-threatening message to Barbie, Dee's non-serious intentions are made clear by her own laughter. She then diverts the target of her teasing to Aya by saying, "At least I have Aya …". This teasing implies that Aya is also less beautiful than Barbie, which is comforting because she is not alone. Attacked in this way, Aya wishes to defend herself and registers her objection with the exclamation "Hey!" in a rising and assertive tone. Seeing Aya's apparently serious reaction, Dee responds with laughter to reframe her previous remark in a playful tone. However, Aya ignores Dee's revocation of serious intent and responds with an emphatic and serious justification of her position, asserting with a double negative that she does think of herself as pretty: "I TRULY don't think I'm not pretty". To mitigate the tension, Dee demonstrates her agreement with Aya by saying, "Fine, you have your own style", and then Barbie also joins in to comfort Aya in line 292.

Evidently, Dee feels some embarrassment, as she re-initiates the teasing frame by saying, "I was just joking ...", but accompanies this with an exaggerated facial expression. She is implying that Aya seemingly overreacted to her previous teasing. Aya then responds with laughter, indicating that she is not genuinely offended by Dee's teasing. After that, Barbie extends Dee's teasing frame further by accepting the ridiculous premise that the two women have differed in beauty since birth and accusing Barbie of using the same joke for over twenty years. This reduction of the argument to absurdity produces mutually shared laughter, implying that the ultimate communicative effect of all the teasing sequences from lines 287 to 296 is positive, not negative.

Interestingly, the pragmatic orientation of the whole teasing sequence above cannot strictly be categorised as non-collaborative, since it is all co-constructed around a consistent topic or theme, that of beauty. The instances of teasing from lines 297–306, however, are marked by a non-collaborative style. When Barbie expresses her opinion in a serious manner in line 297, Dee starts another ironic teasing by saying emphatically, "Yeah, right ...". This implies that Barbie does indeed have rigid control over her looks and body shape while suggesting that others should not pay such excessive attention to their appearance. In line 299, Barbie replies in a serious tone and with a rising pitch to defend herself. Dee continues teasing Barbie by saying, "bullshit", very emphatically. Dee's swearing implies two levels of meanings. At the superficial level, she is expressing her disbelief about Barbie's words, and at the underlying level, she is reproving Barbie for being so unauthentic while on camera (line 300). Looking at lines 301 to 304, it is clear that Dee keeps on refuting Barbie's claims, so that these conversational sequences are obviously non-collaborative in style with each of the participant vying with each other. When Dee jocularly teases Barbie by pointing out that despite being chubby she could be still a great actress, Barbie replies with the jocular question, "What's the problem with you?", an insult spoken in a laughing voice. In what follows, Dee concludes the teasing sequence with self-denigrating humour acknowledging her reputation for having a sharp tongue (line 306). Although the content of this teasing is mostly semantically contestive, its playful frame is reaffirmed by both Dee and Barbie's laughter.

Ritualised playful teasing is an important way to demonstrate closeness, intimacy and mutual-understanding among friends, since they know there is no serious intention underlying these ostensible aggressive remarks. Participants can constantly reclaim and confirm the playful nature of the teasing during such interactions (Pichler 2006), as happens here. For example, when Dee's teasing seemingly provokes Aya in line 288, Barbie joins the teasing sequence to divert the teasing to target Dee. This helps counteract the negative impact of Dee's teasing. In the same way, when teasing seems to impact the target too negatively after several turns of constantly negative messages (as from lines 297 to 306), the speaker can reclaim her playful intent by directing the teasing to herself as the target and defusing the tension. Evidently, in this example of friends' talk, friendship is indexed via non-collaborative teasing by confirming that the teasing is produced and accepted as playful by all participants throughout the whole interaction.

Interaction of collaborative and non-collaborative styles of teasing

It is sometimes difficult to sustain a clear boundary between the different styles of teasing since the discourse style of teasing is not always developed in a consistent manner in any one context. The data contains a number of examples demonstrating an interaction between collaborative and non-collaborative styles of teasing in the same unit of conversational humour. Speakers adopt the two styles alternately to achieve different communicative goals; however, the central aim of building friendship is actually completed dynamically through this interaction between the two styles.

Interaction typically happens when the four women are engaged in a serious talk, even in disputes or complaints about each other, and when they wish to disguise serious (normally negative) views about each other in a socially acceptable manner. In this vein, teasing is mostly constructed in a non-collaborative manner at the beginning, and then shifts to collaborative. This may suggest that, although the contestive content embedded in the non-collaborative teasing style is mostly tacitly interpreted as playful and non-serious among close friends, it nonetheless has the power to inflict genuine hurt on the target of the teasing. This would explain why, when a speaker observes from the target's initial reactions that the teasing might result in an adverse effect, they shift the teasing sequences from non-collaborative to collaborative to avoid the negative information being taken seriously by the target and to allow an opportunity for retaliation.

The interaction of the two styles of teasing is usually jointly completed by both speaker and target with the speaker initiating the transfer and the target accepting it. Speakers and targets co-construct this mixture of styles in order to achieve different communicative purposes at different stages of serious talk. At the beginning of a serious talk (e.g. a dispute or a complaint), the participants wish to deliver their dissatisfaction and vent their negative emotions through the non-collaborative style of teasing; however, their central aim is to trump others by their ideas and arguments rather than to disassociate themselves from the group. Therefore, at the second stage, they turn to the opposite style of talk, hoping to appease the quarrel, mitigate the tension, and reconcile the group.

As might be expected, there is also the case when the discourse style of teasing is constructed firstly in a collaborative manner and then diverted into a non-collaborative style. Unfortunately, the range of examples in the present study only contains a shift of styles from non-collaborative to collaborative and no vice versa cases. But these certainly deserve further exploration in future studies.

Example 3 below illustrates the interaction of different styles of teasing which start in a non-collaborative manner with contestive contributions from both parties and then end up with a markedly collaborative style through overlapping turns from both speakers and hearers.

Example 3

Context: Aya has invited Barbie and Dee to come rowing along the river after dinner, but Barbie and Dee did not show great interest. Although they finally agreed with Aya's plan and joined the boat-trip, Aya felt somewhat unhappy about their nonchalant and uncaring looks.

147. Aya:	*suoyi xushi jiemei, nimen zhende shi bujiefengqing.* 所以徐氏姐妹,你们真的是不解风情
	So, Xu sisters, both of you are indeed unromantic.
148. Dee:	*weishenme ba wo ye suan jinqu?* 为什么把我也算进去?
	Why did you include me?
149. Aya:	*yinwei wo zhuan guoqu* <laughter> *ni hai xiaozhe gen wo shuo,* SUOYI AYA NI MANYI LE BA <laughter>? 因为我转过去 <laughter> 你还笑着跟我说,所以阿雅你满意了吧 <laughter>?
	This is because, when I turned my back <laughter>, you were smiling and saying to me, SO, AYA, ARE YOU SATISFIED NOW <laughter>?
150. Dee:	<laughter> *suoyi qishi wo shi, wo de manyi ba, shuo de shi,* **okay, we are all here on the boat!** *zhe you shenme hao shengqi de ya!* <Laughter> 所以其实我是,我的满意吧,说的是, **okay, we are all here on the boat!** 这有什么好生气的呀 <laughter>!
	So, I meant, when I was saying, are you satisfied, **I meant, okay, we are all here on the boat! There is nothing that should piss you off.**
151. Aya:	<laughter> NI! <laughter> 你!
	<laughter> YOU!
152. Dee:	*xinyan hao xiao,* ZHEME XIAO. 心眼好小,这么小!
	You are such a petty person, SO PETTY!
153. Aya:	<laugh> *danshi wo you mei zenyang a,* **shui yao ni xianzai ba zhege dongxi you liao qilai** <laugh>. <laugh> 但是我又没怎样啊, **谁要你现在把这个东西又聊起来** <laugh>.
	<laugh> But I didn't say anything then, **it's you who started up this topic again** <laugh>.
154. Dee:	*meiyou, wo zhishi xiang rang dajia zhidao, women si jiemei hen zhidao, dajia [de ... dian].* 没有,我只是想让大家知道,我们四姐妹很知道,大家[的点]

(Continued)

	No, I just wanted to let you know, four sisters really do know [each other's concerns].
155. Aya:	\<Smiling face\> [*de dian*] *zai na*. \<Smiling face\> [的点] 在哪。
	\<Smiling face\> What [each other's concerns] are.

Aya and Dee are arguing while Barbie is just listening. The argument is obviously constructed non-collaboratively, where each contribution is inserted to reprove others and defend oneself. When Aya complains in line 147 about Dee and Barbie's aloof attitude towards Aya's romantic outing on the river, Dee replies in a rising pitch defending herself by saying, "Why did you include me?". This implies that she should not be blamed for being unromantic since she actually accepted Aya's proposal and joined in the boat-trip, even though she might look reluctant. Aya then rebuts Dee by repeating and stressing Dee's own words when they arrived on the boat, "So, Aya, are you satisfied now?" (line 149). We can infer that although Aya recognised that Dee uttered these words with a smiling face, she still perceived the underlying negative connotation that Dee is not genuinely enjoying Aya's sightseeing arrangements. Dee continues to defend herself by clarifying her intended meaning, that since they are all on the boat, there is no reason to be annoyed (line 150). Dee intensifies her voice and switches her words alternately from Chinese to English and her exaggerated words imply that Aya is too sensitive and has over-interpreted her words. Feeling insulted but not knowing quite how to defend herself, Aya replies by exclaiming the single word, "YOU" (line 151), to express her frustration. Having trumped Aya, Dee maintains her superior position by denigrating her as "such a petty person, so petty" with a stress on "so petty" (line 152). Aya defends herself by clarifying that Dee herself re-initiated this topic and that Aya is not taking it personally (line 153). She thus passes the buck back to Dee, the initiator of this childish quarrel.

Beneath the aggressive and competitive surface meaning of these conversational turns (lines 147–152) are highly salient nonverbal cues indicating non-serious intent by both Aya and Dee. When their argument seems to escalate (lines 149–151), they both accompany their words with laughter, especially Aya, who both starts and ends her aggressive words with laughter (line 149 and 153). By attending to these nonverbal cues and accompanying facial expressions and gestures, we can infer that despite the disagreement, both women wish the other not to be genuinely offended and have no desire for any negative impact on their friendship.

The following two turns (lines 154–155) are evidently collaborative contributions. Dee concedes a point, explaining herself by saying, "We four sisters truly know all our concerns …", and Aya overlaps Dee's words *wǒmén de diǎn* 我们的点 (each other's concerns) to complete her sentence with *zài nǎli* 在哪里 (what [each other's concerns] are). While these overlapping turns are not teasing, they form the response to Aya's previous tease about Dee's behaviour (line 153) and are therefore the concluding part of the teasing sequences. These were initiated non-collaboratively (lines 147–153) with each contribution having a semantically negative orientation and a loose cohesive link for all the talk and then concluded with collaborative turns (lines 154–155) which are neatly syntactically integrated. The interaction between the two styles of teasing implies that while this example is not explicitly inscribed with agreement, it features much invoked evaluative meaning that is linked to inclusiveness, mutual understanding and thereby negotiates affiliation among the group.

Aspects of teasing and identity

Besides friendship building, other interesting characteristics of the teasing and identities displayed by these friends can be noted. Firstly, laughter and laughing voice emerge as the most efficient devices to affirm the teasing's jocular tone. In all the examples, laughter occurs frequently in the turns of both speaker and target. This reinforces the affiliative nature of laughing together (Coates 2007) and allows participants to signal their involvement in what is being said and their continued collaborative presence, demonstrating "togetherness" with interlocutors (Norrick 1993).

Secondly, while some normal characteristics of teasing in women's talk are found in the teasing between these four Chinese women, it also possesses its own features. The topics of teasing are mostly the same in both: appearance and body shape which are heatedly discussed by these four, as Examples 1 and 2 demonstrate. The differences that emerge are the preference in style of teasing and in ways of delivering aggression.

More non-collaborative instances of teasing are deployed than the opposite, which diverges from Coates' (1997, 2007) findings that women normally speak collaboratively. Although the difference may not be very great, it is present in example after example, indicating that these four actually enjoy displaying subversive aspects of talk that transgress normative gender behaviour. In addition, the way in which they convey aggression in teasing is characteristically implicit and covert, not overt. Dee's teasing, for example, rather than overtly disparaging her target's appearance or body shape, degrades the target implicitly so that negative meanings can hardly be inferred without full knowledge of the context. In Example 2, line 287, Dee teases, "At least I have Aya to keep me company, and that gives me comfort", and in line 290, "Fine, you have your own style": in neither of these statements is aggression obvious. Line 287 even delivers a positive meaning if we view the surface meaning alone. The disparaging force that is contained in these teasing sequences can only be fully grasped with the aid of contextualisation cues such as Dee's stressed tone of voice and her arrogant facial expression; and, most directly, in the responses of the target, Aya, who says with some emphasis, "I TRULY don't think I'm not pretty". Dynel (2008) notes that a speaker needs to be certain about sharing common ground with a target (and other interlocutors) for teasing with aggressive potential to be used with complete rapport. Mutually shared ground facilitates the intended humorous interpretation and reception by the hearer. The examples presented show that the successful "rapport teasing" among these Chinese women denotes the hearers' full knowledge of shared common ground and their complete understanding of the speaker's intentions. Since teasing competitively and aggressively lies at the heart of customary joking relationships among intimate friends, any failure by the hearer to decode aggressive messages would here as elsewhere negate the intention to promote intimacy through teasing.

Lastly, in these examples, teasing serves to convey multi-faceted aspects of the women's identities in a way that reproduces but also reshapes traditional femininity in Chinese society. While these four portray themselves as caring, supportive and considerate—all characteristics typically associated with femininity in Chinese as in many other cultures—they also speak in a way that distances themselves from gender stereotypes. Among the four, Dee is probably the most distinctive. As can be seen in Example 1, line 176 ("Sometimes") and Example 3, line 150 ("okay, we are all here on the boat"), she even mixes English expressions with Mandarin. By doing so, she intentionally portrays herself as a well-educated, international celebrity who speaks fluent English. In addition, her incongruously boastful way of speaking imbues her personality with a vibe of humour. She is also the dominant teaser who initiates most of the teasing sequences in the group's interactions.

Dee's identity as humorous and intelligent subverts viewers' expectations of traditional femininity. Even in today's Mainland China, humorous and highly educated females are frowned on, as indicated by the classical proverb *"nüzi wu cai bian shi de* 女子无才便是德 (too much learning does not become a virtuous woman)". Although this proverb is constantly criticised for its gender-biased view, a significant number of people in contemporary China, especially in rural areas (Sun 2004) still uphold the stereotypical view that erudite women are not attractive and are unlikely to get married. In addition, Dee's use of swearwords (e.g. "BULLSHIT" in both Mandarin and English in Example 2) reinforces her willingness to deploy subversive and stereotypically masculine traits. Her ability to combine elements of a relatively feminine style of interaction with more masculine ones assists her in presenting an unconventional yet intriguing female image in Chinese RTV discourse.

Conclusions

This study of teasing in the micro context in Chinese RTV discourse confirms that a collaborative style of teasing serves to: display intimacy (Norrick 1993); share in-group knowledge; express gentle criticism (Pichler 2006); create positive identity, mitigate tension and build friendship

(Dynel 2008). What is unique is the finding that a non-collaborative style of teasing exists that conveys face-threatening forcefulness (e.g. pointed criticism and dismissal of assertions) but both by itself and in interaction with collaborative teasing discursively reinforces friendship among these Chinese women.

Using representative examples, analysis of the frequent occurrence of teasing between the four reveals an expectation that teasing will itself constitute a crucial strategy in reinforcing their friendship. It also suggests that teasing is important in Chinese RTV discourse as an effective way of displaying celebrities' positive identities as authentic, humorous and down-to-earth. These women play out being themselves on TV for a popular audience and their creative deployment of teasing sequences implies two levels of meaning, both subverting audience expectations about gender roles. First, it diverts Normal expectations of how women reinforce friendship in Chinese discourse and expectations of how celebrities will speak and behave in TV genres are both subverted. In normal life, it is expected that female relationships are built through sharing sympathy, compliments and understanding (Zhang 1995), rather than by teasing and disparaging each other. In addition, celebrities are expected to speak and behave in a morally and socially appropriate manner rather than displaying their genuine flawed selves—especially in Chinese TV discourse, where censorship strictly evaluates the role-modelling effect of celebrities' behaviour.

In this TV show, female friendship is built not only by teasing but also by appropriate deployment of the teasing sequence, especially when non-collaborative teasing is used. The four women aptly deploy contextualisation cues such as laughter and exaggerated facial expressions to signal their non-serious intention and make timely use of remedial strategies such as shifting between the two styles of teasing and providing explanations. This successfully saves/maintains their friendship despite their practice of non-collaborative teasing. This is a unique feature of their friendship-building strategies and its repeated performance across the whole season of *We Are Real Friends*, means it is expected by women members of the audience. Given normal modelling effects, the ways these celebrities do their friendship will likely influence audiences' own practices in teasing with competence and consideration.

Besides type and style of teasing, indexicality at the discourse and ideological level seems unique to this kind of friendship building. Topics invoked through teasing index a range of micro and macro social meanings. Some, like appearance, beauty and body shape, follow the norms of stereotypical femininity, but these women also appreciate and often discuss each other's professional success and achievements (as Example 2 revealed). This allows them to construct themselves in opposition to mainstream femininities, to signal their membership of a community of independent and smart women, and to index authenticity. The four authenticate themselves by constructing their identities as friendship-centred and fun but also as independent and career-valuing, signalling alignment with more modern interpretations of femininity in Chinese society.

Considering the complicated relationships between teasing, gender and friendship, humour seems important at both the micro contextual level of the immediate co-textual environment and at the macro-institutional level of the norms and goals of Chinese society. Future studies might with benefit focus on how teasing arises in female discourse in contemporary Chinese societies and how role-modelling teasing helps modern women construct themselves and female friendships in specific environments.

Appendix

Table 10.1 Transcription conventions

She's out.	Period shows falling tone in preceding element
Oh yeah?	Question mark shows rising tone in preceding element
damn	Bold characters indicate emphatic stress
(0.2)	Brackets enclose the time length (second as a unit) of the speaker's noticeable pause between words
but	Underline indicates an incomplete or cut-off sentence
[at all]	Aligned brackets enclose simultaneous speech by two or more participants
<laughter>	Angle brackets indicate non-verbal clues

Notes

1 Chinese online TV shows are mostly found on four Chinese video-sharing platforms, namely, IQIYI, Tencent Video, Youku and Mango TV. IQIYI is reportedly top, closely followed by Tencent Video, according to 2019 view-ratings (data available at: https://zhuanlan.zhihu.com/p/139717425, accessed 17 February 2021).
2 For a detailed discussion of this linguistic construct, see Haugh and Bousfield 2012.
3 For transcription conventions, see Table 10.1 in the Appendix. Key phrases discussed are bolded.
4 Adele Laurie Blue Adkins (b. 1988) is a famous English singer and songwriter. She was a little plump until she lost about one hundred pounds at the end of 2019 with a healthy diet and workout regime (at: https://www.womenshealthmag.com/weight-loss/a30443070/adele-weight-loss-diet/, accessed 3 July 2021).

References

Beck, S., S. E. Clabaugh, R. A. Clark, M. C. Kosovski, R. Daar, V. Hefner et al. 2007. Teasing among college men and women. *Communication Studies*, 58 (2): 157–172.

Blitvich, Pilar Garcés-Conejos. 2009. Impoliteness and identity in the American news media: The "Culture Wars". *Journal of Politeness Research Language Behaviour Culture*, 5 (2): 273–303. https://doi.org/10.1515/JPLR.2009.014

Blitvich, Pilar Garcés-Conejos. 2010. A genre approach to the study of impoliteness. *International Review of Pragmatics*, 2: 46–94.

Blitvich, Pilar Garcés-Conejos and Nuria Lorenzo-Dus. 2013. Reality television: A discourse-analytical perspective. In N. Lorenzo-Dus and P. G.-C. Blitvich, eds. *Real talk: Reality television and discourse analysis in action*. 9–23. New York: Palgrave Macmillan.

Blitvich, Pilar Garcés-Conejos, Patricia Bou-Franch and Nuria Lorenzo-Dus. 2013. Identity and impoliteness: The expert in the talent show "Idol". *Journal of Politeness Research*, 9 (1): 97–121. https://doi.org/10.1515/pr-2013-0005

Bollmer, J. M., M. J. Harris, R. Milich and J. C. Georgesen. 2003. Taking offense: Effects of personality and teasing history on behavioral and emotional reactions to teasing. *Journal of Personality*, 71: 557–603.

Boxer, D. and F. Corte-Conde. 1997. From bonding to biting: Conversational joking and identity display. *Journal of Pragmatics*, 27 (3): 275–294. doi:10.1016/s0378-2166(96)00031-8

Chen, Guo-Hai. 2013. Chinese concepts of humour and the role of humour in teaching. In J. M. Davis and J. Chey, eds., *Humour in Chinese life and culture*. 193–214. Hong Kong: Hong Kong University Press.

Chi Tongtong 迟彤彤. 2019. *Duihua Women Shi Zhenzheng De Pengyou: Cong zhenrenxiu dao zhenqingxiu de juli* 对话《我们是真正的朋友》: 从真人秀到真情秀的距离 (Talking with *We Are Real Friends*: The distance from reality show to real sentiments show). *Dianshi zhinan* 电视指南 (*TV Guide China*—Special report): 16–19.

Coates, J. 1997. Women's friendships, women's talk. In R. Wodak, ed., *Gender and discourse*. 245–262. London: Sage Publications.

Coates, J. 2007. Talk in a play frame: More on laughter and intimacy. *Journal of Pragmatics*, 39 (1): 29–49. doi:10.1016/j.pragma.2006.05.003

Culpeper, Jonathan. 2005. Impoliteness and entertainment in the television quiz show, *The Weakest Link*. *Journal of Politeness Research*, 1 (1): 35–72.

Culpeper, Jonathan, Derek Bousfield and Anne Wichmann. 2003. Impoliteness revisited: With special reference to dynamic and prosodic aspects. *Journal of Pragmatics*, 35: 1545–1579.

Culpeper, Jonathan and Oliver Holmes. 2013. (Im) politeness and exploitative TV in Britain and North America: *The X Factor* and *American Idol*. In N. Lorenzo-Dus and P. G.-C. Blitvich, eds., *Real talk: Reality television and discourse analysis in action*. 169–198. London: Palgrave Macmillan.

Davies, C. E. 2003. How English-learners joke with native speakers: an interactional sociolinguistic perspective on humor as collaborative discourse across cultures. *Journal of Pragmatics*, 35: 1361–1385.

Drew, Paul. 1987. Po-faced receipts of teases. *Linguistics*, 25: 219–253.

Dynel, Marta. 2008. No aggression, only teasing: The pragmatics of teasing and banter. *Lodz Papers in Pragmatics*, 4 (2): 241–261. doi:10.2478/v10016-008-0001-7.

Dynel, Marta. 2013. Impoliteness as disaffiliative humour in film talk. In M. Dynel, ed., *Developments in linguistic humour theory*. 105–144. Amsterdam and Philadelphia: John Benjamins.

Eder, D. 1990. Serious and playful disputes: Variation in conflict talk among female adolescents. In Allen D. Grimshaw, ed., *Conflict talk*. 67–84. Cambridge, UK: Cambridge University Press.

Eder, D. 1993. Go get ya a French: Romantic and sexual teasing among adolescent girls. In D. Tannen, ed., *Gender and conversational interaction*. 17–31. Oxford: Oxford University Press.

Frosh, S., A. Phoenix and R. Pattman. 2002. *Young masculinities*. London: Palgrave.

Haugh, Michael. 2014. Jocular mockery as interactional practice in everyday Anglo-Australian conversation. *Australian Journal of Linguistics*, 34 (1): 76–99. doi:10.1080/07268602.2014.875456

Haugh, Michael. 2017. Teasing. In Salvatore Attardo, ed., *Handbook of language and humour*. 204–218. London: Routledge.

Haugh, Michael and D. Bousfield. 2012. Mock impoliteness, jocular mockery and jocular abuse in Australian and British English. *Journal of Pragmatics*, 44 (9): 1099–1114.

Haugh, Michael and D. Pillet-Shore. 2018. Getting to know you: Teasing as an invitation to intimacy in initial interactions. *Discourse Studies*, 20 (2): 246–269.

Haugh, Michael and Lara Weinglass. 2018. Divided by a common language? Jocular quips and (non-)affiliative responses in initial interactions amongst American and Australian speakers of English. *Intercultural Pragmatics*, 15 (4): 533–562.

Hay, J. 1994. Jocular abuse patterns in mixed-group interaction. *Wellington Working Papers in Linguistics*, 7 (1): 26–55. doi:10.1177/104649647600700102

Hay, J. 2000. Functions of humour in the conversations of men and women. *Journal of Pragmatics*, 32 (6): 709–742. doi:10.1016/s0378-2166(99)00069-7

Hill, A. 2004. Watching *Big Brother UK*. In E. Mathijs and J. Jones, eds., *Big Brother International: Formats, critics and publics*. 25–39. London and New York: Wallflower Press.

Holmes, Janet. 2006. *Gendered talk at work*. London: Blackwell Publishing.

Holmes, Janet and Meredith Marra. 2002. Over the edge: Subversive humor between colleagues and friends. *HUMOR: International Journal of Humor Research*, 15 (1): 65–87. doi:10.1515/humr.2002.006

Huang Shenghui 黄生晖. 2010. *Dianshi zhenrenxiu yanjiu zongshu* 电视真人秀研究综述 (An overview of reality television shows). *Xinwen Daxue* 新闻大学 (*Journalism Research*), 3: 151–154.

Jones, D. C., J. B. Newman and S. Bautista. 2005. A three-factor model of teasing: The influence of friendship, gender, and topic on expected emotional reactions to teasing during early adolescence. *Social Development*, 14 (3): 421–439.

Keltner, D., L. Capps, A. M. Kring, R. C. Young and E. A. Heerey. 2001. Just teasing: A conceptual analysis and empirical review. *Psychology Bulletin*, 127: 229–248.

Kilborn, R. 2003. *Staging the real: Factual TV programming in the age of "Big Brother"*. Manchester, UK and New York: Manchester University Press.

Kotthoff, Helga. 1996. Impoliteness and conversational joking: On relational politics. *Folia Linguistica*, 3 (4): 299–326.

Kowalski, R. M. 2004. Proneness to, perceptions of, and responses to teasing: The influence of both intrapersonal and interpersonal factors. *European Journal of Personality*, 18: 331–349.

Lampert, M. D. and S. M. Ervin-Tripp. 2006. Risky laughter: Teasing and self-directed joking among male and female friends. *Journal of Pragmatics*, 38 (1): 51–72. doi:10.1016/j.pragma.2005.06.004

Lorenzo-Dus, Nuria. 2006. Buying and selling: mediating persuasion in British property shows. *Media, Culture and Society*, 28 (5): 739–761.

Lorenzo-Dus, Nuria, P. Bou-Franch and P. G.-C. Blitvich. 2013. Impoliteness in US/UK talent shows: A diachronic study of the evolution of a genre. In N. Lorenzo-Dus and P. G.-C. Blitvich, eds., *Real talk: Reality television and discourse analysis in action*. 199–217. New York: Palgrave Macmillan.

Lu Ye 陆晔. 1997. *Zhongguo dianshi chuanbo zhong nüxing xingxiang de yanjiu* 中国电视传播中女性形象的研究 (Research on female images in media). *Xinwen daxue* 新闻大学 (*Journalism Research*), 10: 32–40.

Norrick, Neal R. 1993. *Conversational joking: Humor in everyday talk*. Bloomington IN: Indiana University Press.

Pichler, P. 2006. Multifunctional teasing as a resource for identity construction in the talk of British Bangladeshi girls. *Journal of Sociolinguistics*, 10 (2): 225–249. doi:10.1111/j.1360-6441.2006.00326

Qian Suoqiao. 2011. Discovering humour in modern China: The launching of *Analects Fortnightly Journal* and the "Year of Humour" (1933). In J. Milner Davis and J. Chey, eds., *Humour in Chinese life and letters*. 191–218. Hong Kong: Hong Kong University Press.

Schnurr, Stephanie. 2009. Constructing leader identities through teasing. *Journal of Pragmatics*, 41 (6): 1125–1138. doi:10.1016/j.pragma.2008.10.002

Sinkeviciute, Valeria. 2017. Variability in group identity construction: A case study of the Australian and British Big Brother houses. *Discourse, Context and Media*, 20: 70–82.

Sinkeviciute, Valeria. 2019. *Conversational humour and (im)politeness: A pragmatic analysis of social interaction*. Amsterdam and Philadelphia: John Benjamins.

Sinkeviciute, Valeria and Marta Dynel. 2017. Approaching conversational humour culturally: A survey of emerging area of investigation. *Journal of Language and Communication*, 55: 1–9.

Straehle, C. A. 1993. "Samuel?" "Yes, dear?": Teasing and conversational rapport. In D. Tannen, ed., *Framing in discourse*. 210–230. Oxford: Oxford University Press.

Sun Yan 孙燕. 2004. *Nüxing xingxiang de wenhua chanshi* 女性形象的文化阐释 (A study of female image from the perspective of culture). *Zhongzhou xuekan* 中州学刊 (*Academic Journal of Zhongzhou*), 5: 79–81.

Thornborrow, Joanna and Deborah Morris. 2004. Gossip as strategy: The management of talk about others on reality TV show "Big Brother". *Journal of Sociolinguistics*, 8 (2): 246–71.

Tolson, Andrew. 2006. *Media talk: Spoken discourse on TV and radio*. Edinburgh: Edinburgh University Press.

Wang Dingtian 王定天. 2001. *Lun zhongguo youmo de lilun xingtai* 论中国幽默的理论形态 (A study on theoretical form of humour in Chinese). *Xinan shifan daxue xuebao* 西南师范大学学报 (*Journal of Southwest China Normal University*), 27 (2): 101–107.

Wickberg, Daniel. 1998. *The senses of humor: Self and laughter in modern America*. Ithaca, NY: Cornell University Press.

Xu, Weihe. 2014. Confucianism., In S. Attardo, ed., *Encyclopedia of humor studies*. Vol. 1: 173–174. Thousand Oaks, CA: Sage Publishing.

Yang, H. 2015. A review of Chinese sitcoms in past twenty years. *Media in Contemporary China*, 2: 89–94.

Yang, N. and W. Ren. 2020. Jocular mockery in the context of a localised playful frame: Unpacking humour in a Chinese reality TV show. *Journal of Pragmatics*, 162: 32–44.

Yin Hong 尹鸿, Lu Hong 陆虹, Ran Ruxue 冉儒学. 2005. *Dianshi zhenrenxiu de jiemu yuansu fenxi* 电视真人秀的节目元素分析 (Elements of TV reality shows). *Xiandai chuanbo* 现代传播 (*Modern Media*), 5: 47–52.

Zajdman, Anton. 1991. Contextualization of canned jokes in discourse. *HUMOR: International Journal of Humor Research*, 4 (1): 23–40. doi:10.1515/humr.1991.4.1.23

Zhang Ailing 张爱玲. 1995. *Lun nüxing yuyan de tedian ji qi wenhua neihan* 论女性语言的特点及其文化内涵 (A study of the characteristics of women's language from a cultural perspective).*Waiguoyu* 外国语 (*Foreign Languages*), 1: 73–77.

11 My Unfair Lady
Gender, *sajiao* and humour in a Hong Kong TV series

Marjorie K. M. Chan

Introduction

Television Broadcasts Limited (TVB) in Hong Kong produces a number of Cantonese-language television series each year. That was no less true in 2017. Debuting that May to much anticipation, was a 28-episode TV series entitled, *Budong Sajiao de Nüren* 不懂撒嬌的女人, with the tantalising English title, *My Unfair Lady*, cheekily playing off the title of the beloved 1964 American film, *My Fair Lady*, starring Audrey Hepburn and Rex Harrison in the title roles. That association, plus the adding of "un" to "fair" for an impish homonymic pun, guaranteed that fun and mischief was afoot.[1] The Chinese title of the TV series literally translates as "Women who don't know how to *sajiao*", where *sajiao* has been variously translated as "to act cute, to be cutesy, to be flirtatious". It is a communication style that is primarily performed by females, particularly those whose image "embodies cute, baby-like, childish, and sweet elements" and whose demeanour reflects innocence, cuteness, dependence, and submissiveness (Yueh 2017: 48). The TV series title further implies that *sajiao* is a skill that is acquired, in combination with other desirable attributes, such as youth, feminine bodies, and physical attractiveness (Chan and Lin 2019). Among the women in this TV series, those from Taiwan especially, and also those from Mainland China (*dalu* 大陸), are presented as more skilful *sajiao* performers than the local Hong Kong ladies.

The TV series' title also harks back to a recent Mandarin-language film directed by Pang Ho-cheung, namely, his 2014 romantic comedy, *Women Who Flirt* (*Sajiao Nüren Zui Hao Ming* 撒嬌女人最好命, literally, Women who *sajiao* have the best fate). This is a title taken from a 2005 book written by Lover Man (Luo Fuman 羅夫曼, although a more apt parsing of this author's pseudonym, overriding the monosyllabic surname, would be Luofu Man, Lover Man). Here, the English-translated title is, *Everyone Loves a Tender Woman*. The book became so wildly popular that Lover Man (LOVERMAN) wrote a collection of follow-up volumes, providing instructions to women on how to acquire the skills of *sajiao* with the express aim of attracting men in order to enjoy a happy and fulfilling married life.[2]

DOI: 10.4324/9781003176374-11

In the case of our TV series, which offers a broad, social context that spans personal and professional settings, only some of the females know how to perform *sajiao* (*hui sajiao* 會撒嬌, or in Cantonese,³ *sik1 de2* 識嗲),⁴ while others do not.

With this playful linking to other media for both the Chinese and English titles of this Hong Kong TV series, the stage is set for anticipating humour amidst the interplay of gender, romance, and the central role of *sajiao* in this TV series directed by Kwan Shu Ming 關樹明. The 28 episode, 21-hour long series was scripted by Chu Kang Kei 朱鏡祺 and his wife, Lau Siu Kwan 劉小群, both of whom started their screenwriting career at TVB in 1988. The current study begins by examining the fundamental issue of name-use for the six main characters in the series. This includes proper names used in isolation or in conjunction with prefixal forms and kinship terms, as well as nicknames that may be used as terms of address, and/or as terms of reference. The study then examines three short scenes that highlight different aspects of humour intersecting with various gender-driven issues such as envy, admiration, scorn, or jealousy. It concludes with a short discussion of some real-world, recalcitrant societal issues that are tackled in this series, thus pointing to more serious topics that appear amidst an otherwise fairly light-hearted comedy of social interactions among friends, lovers, relatives, and co-workers, all of whom may be peers, subordinates, or superiors in the context of their TV narrative.

What's in a name?

We may never fully know what was intended by Confucius in *The Analects* in his remarks on *zheng ming* 正名, conventionally translated into English as "rectification of names", or issues brought up later in the fourth century BCE by another famous Chinese philosopher, Xunzi 荀子, regarding the relationship between the word and that which it names (see Wang 1989). With respect to specific naming practices for people, personal names, titles, kinship terms, as well as terms of address and terms of reference, these have all played an important part in both religious and secular activities in China's long history, dating back at least to the Zhou Dynasty if not back to the Shang Dynasty.⁵ An interesting case is the universal taboo in the imperial realm on the use of the emperor's *ming* 名 (personal name), as well as that of his heir apparent, the *taizi* 太子. As Cohen (2000: 472) observes, the prohibition on writing the Chinese characters of the emperor and his heir's *ming* even extended to place names. The solution adopted is illustrated in Cohen's example drawn from the Tang Dynasty (618–907 CE) and quoted below (Cohen 2000: 472–473). Hanyu Pinyin is used here in lieu of Cohen's use of the older Wade-Giles romanisation system.

> In order to resolve this problem, it was customary to substitute other characters for the forbidden ones. These substitutions might be done

on the bases of phonetic, semantic, or graphic similarities. For example, the second emperor of the Tang Dynasty was named Li Shimin 李世民 (r. 626–649). Therefore, the characters of his *ming*, Shimin, were tabooed from the time of his ascension to the throne in 626 until the end of the Tang Dynasty, i.e., all writings between 626 and 907 should not contain the characters *shi* and *min*. In order to observe the taboo it was common practice to write the character *shi* 時 ('season; time') in place of *shi* 世 ('generation'), and the character *ren* 人 ('person') in place of *min* 民 ('people').

Within a given dynasty, the naming taboo problem is easily solved by the selection of rare characters for the *ming* of later heirs to the imperial throne.

While imperial taboos are avoided by the use of near-synonyms and (near-)homophones, other circumventions involving naming taboos are also practised at the familial and lineage levels of the common people. (For example, in a traditional Chinese family, one would not find a son bearing the same name as the father, as in the case of Joseph Robinette Biden Jr., the 46th President of the United States of America.) Aside from naming taboos, the ubiquity of homophones in the Chinese language also lends itself to other uses, particularly when (near-)homophony may have auspicious or inauspicious connotations, as is well documented by Sung (1979). The technique permeates the lives of the common people, forming an integral part of traditional Chinese culture that affects all stages of a person's life, from birth to marriage and childbirth, and ultimately death.

Homophony in wordplay and witticism involving names also finds a place in the people's popular literature, such as Cao Xueqin's classic novel, *Dream of the red chamber* (*Hongloumeng* 紅樓夢), where the opening poetic line contains *jia* 假 (false, fake or fictitious) and *zhen* 真 (true, genuine, or real), which are coupled with Cao's choice of Jia 賈 for the surname of the main family, juxtaposing that with another family's surname, Zhen 甄. Scholars of Redology[6] (*Hongxue* 紅學, Red + -ology)—that is, the academic study of the *Dream of the red chamber* (*Hongloumeng* 紅樓夢)—have devoted many delightful hours to analysing and interpreting this opening couplet and the author's deliberate pairing of *zhen* (甄 and 真) and *jia* (賈 and 假) in the novel.

Our Hong Kong TV series lacks the weight of imperial taboos and the witticisms of classic novels. Nonetheless, it offers some very witty wordplay in the selection of names and nicknames for quite a few of the characters. Wordplay using proper names as well as nicknames and adopted English language personal names is widespread in Hong Kong culture, and this is a hallmark of the humour in this TV series. In Chinese culture, names are not arbitrarily and haphazardly chosen just because something sounds good or someone is popular at the time, nor do they plummet in popularity, as the case may be.[7] The care in naming selection also applies to at least some of the names in this TV series, including even the choice of surnames. We will focus mainly on the names given to the six main characters who appear in the TV series. In the process, we also highlight some interesting observations on a few other names.

Molly

The main female protagonist is Molly Ling, whose Chinese name in Cantonese is *Ling4 Man5* 凌敏 (cold, ice + quick, nimble). She is indeed ice-cold and brusque. She is addressed as "Mall *ze1* Mall 姐", where the kinship term, *ze1* (older sister), is added to a given name, a common practice that in Hong Kong, may be placed after a Chinese given name or an English one. The corresponding name in the English subtitle is "Sis Mall". Molly is sometimes simply addressed by others as "Molly", her English name, as well as by her Cantonese given name (e.g. by her father) with the vocative prefix *Aa3-* 阿 added to give *Aa3-Man5* 阿敏. Later in the series, after she gets married to Gordon Man (*Man4 Nim6 Sam1* 文念深), her ex-boyfriend from years ago, her co-workers sometimes address her as "*Man4 Taai3* 文太, Mrs Man", which, in Mandarin, would be "*Wen Taitai,* 文太太, Mrs Wen".

Molly, born in 1975, is aged 42 at the start of the series in Episode 1. Cast in the role of Molly is veteran Hong Kong actress, Jessica Hsuan 宣萱, born in 1970, and thus, in fact, in her 40's. At the start of the story, Molly Ling is the General Manager (GM) of the Leasing Department of Sirius Bright Asset Management Co. Ltd. (傲星資產管理有限公司), which oversees twelve shopping malls in Hong Kong. One can readily see that "Sis Mall" is a term of address that cleverly plays off the pun of her name, "Moll(y)", and "Mall". She later becomes the GM of a new unit that is the merger of her original Leasing Department and that of the Promotions Department, and is then forced to share the management of this combined department with her ex-boyfriend, Gordon Man. He has been hired by the big boss of the company, Mr Yau (*Jau4 Zeon3 Git6* 游俊傑, swim + hero/person of outstanding talent), to re-shape Molly's department.

Ice-cold, curt, and super-professional in her conduct, Molly Ling is a survivor who has climbed the corporate ladder, and is a no-nonsense, fast-talking, tough-as-nails executive. She is also a control freak who attends to details and demands flawless perfection. She barks and snaps at her subordinates, and expects absolute obedience, including total compliance by not disrupting their meetings in wasting time going to the washroom. They can go before or after the meeting, but not during it. A hint to her managerial style can be seen in the sequence of text messages given in Table 11.1, which provides the senders' names and their mixed, Cantonese and English texts. The context is that one morning at 6:57 a.m., because of an early morning flight that day, Molly asks Cherry, her younger cousin and subordinate, to contact their team to meet 3 minutes earlier than their usual time of 7:00 a.m., for a meeting during which they normally combine jogging with updating on the business of the day. Except for Tet-yan Lui (*Leoi4 Tit3 Yan4* 雷鐵仁, thunder + iron + benevolence), the other co-workers all use English

Table 11.1 Group text messages

Cherry:	Mall 姐今日早機. 緊急呼喚.
	要早 3 分鐘見人開會!
	Sis Mall has an early flight, meet 3 minutes early.
Annie:	Arrived. Warming up,
	come within 30 sec.
Elaine:	Sorry, 去咗廁所,
	1 分鐘到
	Sorry, in the toilet. Give me 1 minute.
鐵仁:	廁所都唔去,
	衝緊嚟!
	Skipping toilet, be right there.

names in their text messaging app. The English provided below is from the DVD's subtitles.

Not only do Molly's team members snap to attention; even her dog, a French bulldog that she named Mooney (*Soeng4 Mun5* 常滿, eternal + contented), obeys her instantly. In the above scenario of early morning jog-cum-meeting, with Mooney in tow, Molly crisply commands her dog to poop, ordering her in English, "Go potty!", Mooney poops on the spot, earning words of astonished praise and admiration from a passer-by, "Wow! It's so obedient! It poops as soon as it's told!" (*Waa3, gaau3 dak1 gam3 teng1 waa6 ge2! Jat1 giu3 zau6 o1!* 嘩! 教得咁聽話嘅! 一叫就屙!). Molly replies emphatically, in mixed English and Cantonese, "Training! Rigid training". (*Training! Jim4 gaak3 ge3 training.* Training! 嚴格既 training.) Rigid training, indeed! And that also applies to her equally well-trained team.

The example in Table 11.1 gives a very vivid portrayal of the domineering protagonist. Jilted some fifteen years earlier by her boyfriend, Gordon Man, when he left Hong Kong for the Mainland and all the swooning, *sajiao*-savvy females, Molly has determined to marry her life to her career. As the old saying goes, "Hell hath no fury like a woman scorned" and this is our Molly as she navigates the corporate world. She admonishes her younger cousin, Cherry, who works closely and loyally under her. Molly's mindset and her harsh tone can be gleaned immediately in Episode 1, in her dialogue with Cherry, which is quoted in Table 11.2 in vernacular Cantonese, and using the English subtitles from the DVD. In this exchange, Cherry has just told Molly that she had followed a Shanghai girl back to Shanghai, someone who seems to have become her boyfriend Hanson's new Mainland girlfriend, that is, a *xiaosan* 小三 (literally, little three, which is Taiwan Mandarin slang for "mistress").

The depiction of Molly that emerges is of a severe woman who is the exact opposite of a sweet, cuddly, demure, male-dependent *sajiao* performer seeking a mate. The humour deriving from Molly's character comes precisely from this stark, exaggerated contrast between a woman who shuns *sajiao* and any hint of feminine charm (*nüren wei* 女人味), and those who practise such charms naturally and (almost) unconsciously.

Table 11.2 Molly warns Cherry about men

M:	賤男人,上親大陸就去 掘。見上海妹追上海妹,見台灣妹追台灣妹。全用下邊諗嘢,要嚟做乜嘢?女人冇男人使死。 Creeps! All men are busy chasing skirts in China, whether they're from Shanghai or Taiwan. They all think with the organ below the belt. Who needs them?
C:	我 32 歲啦。 But I'm 32.
M:	我四字頭添啦。冇拍拖, 冇結婚, 有乜問題? 男人會呃你, 份工唔會。好似我咁, 嫁咗俾公司, 咁重有尊嚴, 咪重好? And I am in my 40's. So what if I'm single and not dating anyone? Men lie to you, but not your job. Like me, you should marry the office. You will live in dignity. Isn't that better?

Amazingly, despite the severity of Molly's countenance and her harsh managerial style, there is one young man in her managerial team who is infatuated with her. This is Tet-yan, whose composite name is shown above (*Leoi4 Tit3 Yan4* 雷鐵仁, thunder + iron + benevolence). He is the only male on the team and the only one lacking an English name. Consequently, there is no plethora of names and nicknames for him as for others. Despite his surname meaning "thunder", Tet-yan is actually a very mild-mannered young man. His given name, Tet-yan, is homophonous with *Tit3 Jan4* 鐵人 (iron man). But ironically, just as he is no personification of thunder, he is also definitely not a man of steel either. Throughout an entire meeting, he ignores his natural urges to go to the washroom in order to obey Molly's dictum on attendance and ends up being rushed to the hospital for a kidney stone operation. Still, he returns later and gets back to work. He makes up for lack of steeliness with determined grit.

After Molly follows Gordon in leaving the company and together with him starts a match-making company in Hong Kong and several strategic cities in China (they briefly return later to the original company), Tet-yan meets up with Molly over lunch. During their conversation (Episode 19), Tet-yan professes his interest in joining their new company; in the process, he also declares his love interest in her. Molly is, of course, astonished and reminds him that she was born a zodiac cycle (i.e. twelve years) or so earlier than him.[8] Undaunted, he declares his strong preference for someone older, for example, than his fellow co-worker, Elaine (who is already older than him), whom he finds not mature enough. He has no feelings for her, he says in mixed Cantonese and English: *m4 gau3 mature, mou2 feel*, 唔够 mature, 冇 feel (not mature enough, no feel). Instead, he prefers someone who is older and wiser, and has seen a lot of life. Tet-yan tells Molly further that he gains confidence and learns a lot from her each time he talks to her. Moreover, he does not think that Molly looks her age. Why, when he showed his friends a photo taken of him with her last year, guess what? "They thought the two of us looked nice together, they said you are pretty and at most two years older than me!" (*Keoi5 dei6 waa6 ngo5 gan1 nei5 hou2 can3, waa6 nei5 hou2 leng3, zung6 waa6 nei5 zeoi3 do1 daai6 ngo5 loeng5 seoi3* 佢哋話我跟你好親, 話你好靚, 重話你最多大我兩歲。). Molly responds by abruptly thanking him for the lunch and leaving. Here, counter to the homophony of his name, Tet-yan is more of a puppy dog than an iron man, or man of steel.

Cherry

The second female protagonist is Cherry, who, as noted above, is Molly's younger cousin, and works on Molly's team as an assistant manager. Cherry has stayed in Hong Kong to work with Molly even though her family has migrated to Canada. At the start of the series, Cherry's boyfriend is Hanson. Not only do they work in the same company, but they have been together for four years, although they are sometimes apart when the company sends him to the Mainland. At age 32, Cherry Ling (*Ling4 Jyu5 Kan4* 凌禹勤) worries about her biological clock, and hopes to get married before she turns 35. The actress who plays Cherry is Natalie Tong 唐詩詠, born in 1981 and so 36 at the time of the series' production—hence, cast very age-appropriately. As in the case of Molly being addressed as Mall *ze1* (Mall 姐), Cherry is also sometimes addressed with her English name plus a suffix, -*ze1* 姐 (older sister), thus: Cherry *ze1* (Cherry 姐). A very diligent worker, Cherry has also earned the nickname, *Kan4 lik6 mui1* 勤力妹 (Hardworking girl), with *kan4 lik6* 勤力 (hardworking) cleverly incorporating the second morpheme from her given Chinese name.

Unlike Molly, Cherry does see herself as someone who can *sajiao*. However, her *sajiao* performance is very superficial and is strictly work-related, being limited to such tasks as sweet-talking mall tenants in order to smooth out problems, as in one scenario in Episode 1. Indeed, she is the designated *sajiao* performer in Molly's Leasing team. She adopts a sweeter, gentler tone of voice, adds a reduplicated form and sentence-final particles to her speech, bats her eyelashes, touches her hair, and acts a bit flirtatious in speaking to the mall tenants. These are all men who, just a few minutes earlier, were angry and frustrated because a huge crowd of women had swarmed through the place looking for bargains at the big annual lingerie sale being held in the next shop. Even though Cherry asserts that Hongkongers know how to *sajiao* and that she herself can do it, her superficial *sajiao* capability does not impress her three friends. One of them, Debbie, dismisses it with the observation that Hong Kong girls only *sajiao* on the guy's payday, while Mainlanders will do it for free any time. So, she concludes, if you are a guy, which girl would *you* choose?!

When the four friends spot Hanson's new girlfriend in the mall (having already determined earlier with whom she had conversed on her phone), they see that she not only knows how to *sajiao*, but that she also has additional endowments that Cherry lacks. Unlike Cherry and other Hong Kong girls who wear small A cup bras—according to the knowledgeable Debbie, who works as a sales clerk in a lingerie shop in the mall—this girl has big boobs. They are even the size of the Big Ben clock (*Daai6 Ban6 Zung1* 大笨鐘), London's famous clock, the largest in the world when it was built in 1859. After making this observation, Cherry's friends gleefully refer to Hanson's new girlfriend as "Big Ben Boobs" (*Daai6 Ban6 Hung1* 大笨胸), which rhymes nicely in Chinese—both Cantonese and Mandarin—with Big Ben Clock (*hung1*/*xiōng* 胸 and *zung1*/*zhōng* 鐘). As a family-oriented program, the humour in this television series should not and does not get much more risqué than this.

There is in fact an additional layer of humour here regarding "Big Ben". Another, more frequently used transliteration in Chinese for the Big Ben Clock is *Da Ben Zhong* 大本鐘. Here, *Daben* 大本 means "basis, essence", clearly a dignified and appropriate choice of morpheme for the stately clock, in contrast to the *daben* 大笨 above, which means "big and stupid". In Mandarin Chinese, both 本 and 笨 are *ben*, differing only prosodically, as is shown with tone diacritics: *běn* (Tone 3) versus *bèn* (Tone 4). That is not the case in Cantonese, where the two graphs differ both tonally and segmentally: *bun2* 本 (basis, origin) versus *ban6* 笨 (stupid, dumb, clumsy). The choice of *ban6* [pɐn] 笨 (stupid), with vowel [ɐ] in Cantonese, is closer in vowel quality to the English vowel, [ɛ] in "Ben", than is the vowel [u] in *bun2* 本, and thus piles multiple layers of humorous meaning onto the Cantonese dialogue in the choice of *daai6 ban6 hung1* 大笨胸 for Big Ben Boobs, literally, big dumb boobs. (Hereafter, her nickname is shortened to "Big Boobs". Her actual name in the TV series is Li Yanfang 李燕芳.)

In the meantime, despite touting her own prowess at *sajiao*, Cherry is not at all successful in using that style of persuasion when she is sent to Taiwan on a short business trip. In fact, she is a flop next to such natural *sajiao* performers as Wen Chunchun 溫純純 (warm + pure, innocent + pure, innocent), the younger cousin of Saving, who has become Cherry's new boyfriend after she dumped Hanson. Chunchun, who is secretly in love with her cousin Saving, becomes a new competitor to Cherry. As is reflected in her name, Chunchun is the epitome of the warm, sweet, cuddly, and innocent *sajiao* girl who can melt not only any man's heart, but even that of a female Taiwan shopkeeper, getting some free stuff before heading to Hong Kong in hopes of celebrating her birthday with Saving. The audience must ask itself, who can resist a soft-spoken, pretty, lithesome damsel with such a sweet-looking face, pouty lips, and puppy-dog eyes?! The emotions that she displays are very genuine and heart-warming. Poor Cherry.

Gordon

While the story centres around the two female protagonists, the source of Molly's single-minded devotion to her career is Gordon, who left her some fifteen years earlier in order to escape from her controlling personality and work on the Mainland. There, he has been very successful, both in his career and in his wide choices of beautiful women while managing to maintain his bachelorhood. Gordon Man (*Man4 Nim6 Sam1* 文念深, culture + think + deep) is variously called "Gordon", "Gordon *go1*" (Gordon 哥), where the kinship term, *go1* (older brother), is added to his English given name, and also "*Man4 Saang1* 文生 (Mr Man)", which, in Mandarin, would be "*Wen Xiansheng* 文先生 (Mr Wen)".

Given his capability and sophistication, the selection of Gordon's surname as *Wen* 文 (which is fairly rare, and is not among today's top hundred most common Chinese surnames, cf. *2021 Nian Baijiaxing Paihang*) is quite deliberate and goes beyond its associated meaning of "culture". It is also significant that his surname, pronounced *Man4* [mɐn] in Cantonese, is romanised as "Man" and pronounced as in the English word, "man" [mæn], when pronounced together with "Gordon": Gordon Man [gɔrdən mæn], thus making Gordon very much a "cultured man". A suave and handsomely debonair visionary who is re-entering the company as a co-manager, Gordon brings many fresh and exciting business ideas. In the midst of re-kindling an old flame with Molly, his life gets more complicated when he also becomes the love interest of a new staff member who has been hired by Molly, a managerial trainee from the Mainland named Tin Mat (*Tin4 Mat4* 田蜜, field + honey).

In the series, Gordon is also unflatteringly referred to as "*Zin6* Gor 賤 *Gor*", where *zin6* can be translated as "cheap, shameless, despicable", that is, the depiction of someone of low morals. Played by veteran actor Frankie Lam 林文龍, who was born in 1967 and was forty-nine at the completion of the series production, Gordon was the Pacific Marketing Director of Soul & Soul, Asia, before he resigned, accepting a manager position created by Mr Yau, the big boss of Sirius Bright Asset Management Co. Ltd., after the formation of the Leasing and Promotions Department. This is a merger of two separate departments, one headed by Molly and the other by Cherry's boyfriend, Hanson. In creating the new department with a change in structure and with the potential aim of eventually removing Molly, Mr Yau assigns Gordon and Molly as co-managers of the new unit. In addition, Hanson is fired at some point but then later re-hired by Molly as part of her team, against Cherry's wishes. As one can imagine, this scenario allows for ample fireworks between the different members of the staff.

Tin Mat

Tin Mat (*Tin4 Mat6* 田蜜, field + honey)—played by Samantha Ko 高海寧, a former Miss Hong Kong contestant who was born in 1987 in Nanjing, China—is Molly's new MT (Management Trainee) from Shanghai. A two-time divorcée, she is a femme fatale and the top villain in this story. Gordon, on first seeing her in the office (in Episode 4) and recognising her from a former meeting in China, calls her *Suzhou guniang* 蘇州姑娘 (Suzhou damsel), which reminds us of Suzhou's renown for its beautiful women, be they in the inner chambers of wealthy homes or in the pleasure quarters of painted boats. Tin Mat is the only staff member who occasionally switches from Cantonese to Mandarin during working hours in the office, an occasional reminder to viewers that she is an outsider.

Tin Mat knows how to cultivate trust, first from Molly and then from Mr Yam Siu Tung (*Jam6 Siu6 Tung1* 任兆通, appoint + omen + connect), the CEO who works directly under big boss, Mr Yau. Tin Mat rises quickly from being Molly's MT (in Episode 4) to personal assistant to the CEO (in Episode 10). In this latter position, Molly actually needs to speak to her to make an appointment if she wishes to talk to Mr Yam. This new status is a promotion of six grades, all in one leap. It is no wonder that her co-workers, formerly working directly under Mr Yam and now ostensibly demoted, do not like her. In Episode 14, Tin Mat is raised further to manager status.

Unlike the sweet innocence of Chunchun's *sajiao* style, Tin Mat's style involves a more subtle, feminine allure, more appropriate to a career professional in a working environment. Strategically directing her thoughtful and kindly attentiveness, she seeks out opportunities to assist her male superiors and, in the process, gains their trust and increases their reliance on her. The CEO, Mr Yam, as is clear from the outline above, repays her attentiveness with opportunities for rapid advancement, a strategy that she herself is pursuing, in the hope of replacing Molly in her managerial position. In the case of Gordon, Tin Mat cultivates his concern, empathy, and compassion outside the office. She also uses her sensual appeal to try to seduce him, to lure him into a deeper, personal relationship. But when she sees Gordon re-establishing a connection with Molly, she turns on him in revenge and seizes an opportunity to falsely accuse him of sexual harassment. Nonetheless, Tin Mat still seeks to get close to her object of desire: after Gordon and Molly are married, she magnanimously tells Molly that she is ready and willing to share Gordon with her!

By Episode 13, Tin Mat has earned the nickname of "*Saat3 Po3 Long4* 撒破郎" or, in Mandarin, *sapolang* (to scatter + break + young man), abbreviated as "SPL" in the series' English subtitles. The first morpheme is a ready reminder of the first morpheme in *sajiao* 撒嬌 (to scatter + tender, delicate), which forms an important part of the title of this series. Its Hong Kong women are neither *sajiao* performers nor invincible, male destroyers. Significantly, there is yet an extra layer of wordplay in the Cantonese nickname, "*Saat3 Po3 Long4* 撒破郎". *Saat3* 撒 in Cantonese is homophonous with the word for "to kill", *saat3* 殺 (but not quite homophonous is the Mandarin [Putonghua] *sha*). Thus, the homophonous nickname is even more lethal in Cantonese: "*Saat3 Po3 Long4* 殺破郎 (Male slayer)"!

Another nickname for Tin Mat is suggested by Hanson in Episode 16, based on further wordplay with her name. Since Tin Mat is from the Mainland, the pronunciation of her surname in Mandarin Chinese is worth noting, since *tian* (*tin4* 田, field) is homophonous with *tian* (*tim4* 甜, sweet), The two graphs are not homophonous in Cantonese, although they are quite close phonetically, differing only in the nasal coda: *tin4* versus *tim4*. Thus, in

Mandarin at least, Tin Mat's name, "*Tian Mi* 田蜜 (field honey)", is homophonous with *tianmi* 甜蜜 (sweet honey). Given her meteoric rise to become Mr Yam's personal assistant, plus her ambition in eyeing Molly's vacated position as general manager, Tin Mat very much earns the black humour arising from her nickname that is used behind her back: "*Duk6 Mat6* (*dumi* 毒蜜, poison honey)". To grasp the critical meaning of this humour, it is important to know that Tin Mat's local Hong Kong co-workers need to deal with Mainland visitors and others who only speak Mandarin Chinese. Hence, all her co-workers are able to recognise the perfect homophony in Mandarin Chinese of *tianmi* (田蜜/甜蜜), and the extension to wordplay and word-substitution that yields *Duk6 Mat6* (*dumi* 毒蜜, poison honey).[9]

Older Hong Kong TV series only use Cantonese, mixed with some English. In this series, however, some Mandarin Chinese utterances and dialogues are incorporated, along with code-mixing with English. In fact, this series even uses additional dialects and other languages. For example, in Episode 10, Molly's father, a former seaman who has travelled to numerous countries over the decades, speaks in French with a Frenchman he meets in the mall and helps the young man who has lost his passport. Episode 21 has Saving and Hanson's mother both engaging in a lively phone conversation using the more rural Weitou 圍頭 (walled village) dialect of Cantonese, while Hanson himself stands by, excluded and bewildered, even though it is *his* mother on the other end of the phone chatting with Saving. (See below for some comments on Weitou dialect.) In Episode 23, Chunchun uses some Taiwanese (Southern Min dialect) when speaking with Saving; and in Episode 24, assistant manager Annie practices Shanghainese in the hope of promotion to oversee operations in Shanghai. Using additional dialects and languages in this way contributes to the playfulness and light-hearted liveliness of the television series, and extends its entertainment value, a strategy that Hong Kong films have used at least since the end of the Second World War if not earlier.

Hanson

Hanson Ho (*Ho4 Zi3 Ciu1* 何志超), whose mother calls him *Aa3-Ciu1* 阿超, is "Hanson *go1* Hanson 哥" to his co-workers. His four-year relationship with Cherry has included purchasing a flat together, which they are still paying for at the start of the story. As noted earlier, he is Molly's counterpart in the company, serving as manager of the Promotions Department. However, when Mr Yau merges their two departments, conflict arises, and he and Molly are in competition. For various reasons, Hanson quits but is later re-hired by Molly in her subsequent competition with Gordon, with whom she is co-managing the newly merged department.

Hanson also has a nickname, "*Zin3* Han 賤 Han (Cheap Han)", a name he deserves much more than Gordon does his rather disparaging one, and it is one that he proudly owns and touts almost as a personal trademark. He even gets called the Cantonese slang word for "dirty old man" (*haam4 sap1 lou2* 鹹濕佬, salty + wet + guy). Hanson's shameless behaviour includes seeing nothing wrong with men having both girlfriends and Mainland mistresses (*xiao san* 小三) when they are sent there for business. This, of course, infuriates his girlfriend, Cherry. To hide his activities, he pretends that his smartphone is free from any hanky-panky and lets Cherry scour through his phone records. This is fine except that sneakily, he actually has two phones and only shows Cherry his "clean" one while hiding the other. Cherry soon enough finds out the truth, of course, and breaks up with him. He immediately brings his new girlfriend, "Big Boobs" (Li Yanfang 李燕芳), to live in the apartment that he shares with Cherry. Adding insult to injury, the two of them take over the large bedroom, relegating Cherry to the small one. As can be imagined, there is a great deal of situational comedy in these scenes.

Hanson's Mandarin is very strongly accented and he has confusion with some words, giving rise to much unintentional humour on his part. One example is when he says *pang* 胖 (fat) when he should have said *bang* 棒 (excellent). *Pang* 胖 is not quite how Big Boobs would like to be described. Adding another layer of multilingual humour is the series' witty translation of *bang* 棒 and *pang* 胖 as "fit" and "fat". Not learning from his first error, Hanson repeats this mispronunciation elsewhere as well. Interestingly, in this bilingual wordplay, the Chinese words, *bang* 棒 and *pang* 胖, form a rhyming pair, while the corresponding English pair, "fit" and "fat", differ only in their vowel, a case that we will treat as one of "mock apophony". Genuine apophony involves grammatically induced vowel alternations, and is a more general term than "ablaut" in English and other Germanic languages (an example is *sing, sang, sung*). This carefully crafted bilingual set of rhyming pair and near-rhyming pair, both with amusingly contradictory meanings, offers further instances of the creative humorous wordplay that characterises this series.

Hanson is played in the series by Chris Lai 黎諾懿 (a stage name, his real name being 黎日升), who was born in 1980. Over the course of the series, his character becomes a better and more responsible person, who ultimately succeeds to the position of new CEO of the company, replacing Mr Yam, who turns out to be a scoundrel. In the last episode, set two years later than the first, Hanson has become Chunchun's boyfriend. As a term of endearment, she sweetly calls him "Han Han": this is a reduplication process that is one of the prominent features of the *sajiao* speech style, playing to his preferences. Chunchun, Saving's younger cousin from Taiwan, is the best example in the series of a naturally sweet, *sajiao* performer. She is also the only character whose given name itself consists of a reduplication with, as noted above, a highly appropriate meaning: Chunchun 純純 (pure, innocent).

Saving

Saving is the nickname given to *Cing4 Jat6 Fai1* 程日暉, a nickname earned by his frugality and efforts to save money. He had his own small production company before joining Molly's company as a managerial trainee (MT), but is soon fired by Molly when he gets into a fight with Hanson, even though it was Hanson's fault. The series carefully evens the score by showing Hanson then getting into trouble with his own mother, who beats him up. Despite his frugality, Saving helps Cherry by buying out Hanson's share of the flat and thus kicks out Hanson and his Big Boobs girlfriend. As one can imagine, two single people of the opposite sex sharing a common living space can lead to some additional, light-hearted, sit-com-type humour. Saving and Cherry eventually fall in love with each other.

During Chunchun's visit in Episode 21, Cherry contributes one more nickname to add to the list of Saving's nicknames, one that involves a homonymic pun. While Cherry prepares bedding for Chunchun to sleep in Saving's bedroom, Chunchun asks where her cousin will sleep. Conversing in Mandarin, since Chunchun is from Taiwan and is not familiar with Cantonese, Cherry replies that he can sleep "outside", by which she means the living room. She then tells Chunchun that the expression in Cantonese for him occupying the living room is that he is the "living room guard". To emphasise this Cantonese term, she switches to Cantonese and pronounces it as [tʰɛŋ tsœŋ] (*tingzhang* 廳長, living room + head). Without any hint of mischief, Cherry then teaches Chunchun how to pronounce the word in Cantonese and encourages her to call Saving by that title. Chunchun repeats the phrase slowly in Cantonese. However, in China, *tingzhang* 廳長 is a lofty, official post, that of the head of a provincial governmental department: it is therefore a highly ironic title for poor Saving, who is merely the lowly keeper of their tiny living room!

Saving is played by actor and singer Vincent Wong (王浩信, original name 王昊), who is a tall (six-foot-one), lanky, good-looking fellow. Relevantly, he was born in Xinjiang in 1983 and moved with his father (ethnic Chinese) and mother (Uighur) to Hong Kong in his youth.[10] With his multilingual background, he is well suited to the character of Saving, who converses with his cousin Chunchun in Mandarin, and with his Hong Kong friends and co-workers in Cantonese. In addition, Vincent Wong makes use of his proficiency in the rural, Weitou 圍頭 dialect of Cantonese, a dialect spoken natively by one of Hong Kong's most famous actors, Chow Yun-fat, who was born on Lamma Island in the New Territories. Vincent Wong's use of the Weitou dialect invokes for Hongkongers his first starring role, playing a Weitou village chief in the previous year's TV series, *Over Run Over* (*EU* 超時任務, Emergency Unit overtime assignment). Both role and use of the Weitou dialect are then uncanny reminders for Hongkongers of a young, fast-talking Chow Yun-fat in a similar 1992 role as a Weitou village chief, although in that case, in a lively, bidialectal (Standard Cantonese, and Weitou dialect) comedy film, *Now You See Love, Now You Don't* (*Ngo5 oi3 nau2 man4 caai4* 我愛扭紋柴, literally, I love naughty child). Wong shows off his linguistic prowess in an amusing scene in Episode 21 during which he fires away in a rapid-paced exchange with Hanson's mother over the phone. The conversation takes place right in the middle of a job-seeking interview for Saving and Cherry with Hanson Ho. To impress Hanson, who is very

My Unfair Lady 251

Figure 11.1 A still from *Budong Sajiao de Nüren* 不懂撒嬌的女人 (*My Unfair Lady*), director Kwan Shu Ming 關樹明, production by Television Broadcasts Limited (TVB), Hong Kong, distributed by U Media Global and TVBI, 2017. The still, from disc 4, episode 21, shows Hanson and Saving, interviewer and interviewee in identical tan-colour two-piece suits, with Saving chatting with Hanson's mother while Hanson tries to listen in on the conversation. L-R: Cherry (seated), Hanson and Saving.

Source: From DVD box-set of *Budong Sajiao de Nuren* 不懂撒嬌的女 (*My Unfair Lady*), 2017, owned by Marjorie Chan.

knowledgeable about haute couture, Saving shows up for his interview wearing an expensive, tan-coloured two-piece suit that just happens to be identical to the one Hanson is wearing that day. Smack in the middle of Hanson's tough interview, his mother calls him on his smartphone and, much to his bewilderment, asks to speak to Saving. Hanson reluctantly hands his phone over to his interviewee but moves very close to him. As shown in Figure 11.1, Hanson tries intently to listen to his mother's end of the conversation, which is inaudible to the audience.

What is actually heard is Saving blithely and cheerfully engaging Hanson's mother in conversation, calling her by the familiar title of "Auntie" (*baak3 mou5* 伯母), asking her if she has eaten, and then reminding her to take her medication: three white pills three times a day, and two yellow pills twice a day. Clearly, he knows her very well, and the audience can infer that he joined Cherry in taking her to see her doctor during Hanson's absence. Then Mrs Ho asks about her son. We are only privy to Saving's end of the conversation in which he re-assures Mrs Ho that Hanson has not (or not since?) done anything horrible at work. Evidently, Mrs Ho then confides to Saving that Hanson was really naughty when he was a kid, because Saving utters some words of sympathy and comfort about this. All this while, Hanson helplessly has been listening in. Apparently, he had not heard his mother speak in the Weitou dialect before and is confused, hearing Saving's conversation with her, to learn that she can speak it. After Saving hands the phone back to Hanson, his incredulous reaction tells us that his mother is urging him to learn from Saving and to hire both him and Cherry! At this point, Saving hands Hanson a pen and he duly signs the two contracts. In hiring Saving, thanks to a well-timed phone call from a prescient and wise mother, Hanson gains a friend who offers him constructive advice that ultimately helps him get past his "Cheap Han" image and earn the position of CEO. This takes him well beyond his initial ambition of heading the Leasing and Promotions Department and allows him to beat both Tin Mat and Annie, Molly's very capable assistant manager.

By dumping Hanson and choosing Saving as a boyfriend, it turns out that Cherry has exchanged one set of problems for another as she encounters a new series of obstacles to her set goal of getting married before turning thirty-five. The problem is that Saving suffers from gamophobia, the fear of marriage commitment. As an indication of the cliffhanger nature of the ending of the series, *The Straits Times* (2017) indicated that "the finale for My Unfair Lady drew the largest audience for a TVB drama in Hong Kong this year, with 1.9 million viewers watching the last scene in which fan favourites, will-they-won't-they couple Saving and Cherry, meet on a flight of steps".[11] The article adds, "the finale broadcast on Sunday averaged 27.3 points, and the last scene between Saving (Vincent Wong) and Cherry (Natalie Tong) drew a high of 29.3 points, said *Sing Tao Daily*".

This study has focused on the six main characters of this relatively lengthy television series, examining the relationship between their characters and personalities and their names and nicknames, particularly in relation to wordplay and also to some gender-related topics that arise in their interactions. While there are many more characters who could also be examined, space dictates a limit.

Three scenes

Moving from wordplay to other realms of humour, three scenes have been selected to allow an analysis of humour in action, combining comedy of character with comic plot. These all focus on Molly and Cherry. The first, Scene 1 below from Episode 1, is about a chauffeur who serves as improvised boyfriend. Scene 2, also from Episode 1, concerns the cracking of a Facebook password; while Scene 3, from Episode 14, offers a glimpse into a bathroom bathing scene.

The transcriptions provided for the scenes are given verbatim rather than in standard (Mandarin) Chinese. Hence, the words are transcribed in whichever language they were spoken in, be it in English, Cantonese, or Mandarin Chinese, including code-mixing within an individual utterance.

My Unfair Lady 253

The English translation largely follows the English subtitles in the series but has some authorial tweaking for intelligibility. This also allows for the translation for each scene not to be constrained by the fact that subtitles need to fit the allotted space on the television screen. Turn-taking by each speaker is indicated by their name-code and a number to assist in referencing.

Scene 1. The improvised boyfriend

This scene, involving a fast-paced, one-and-a-half minute dialogue, opens with Molly (M) and Hanson (H) in Shanghai on a short business trip, and soon to meet up with the CEO, Mr Yam. Driving them is a local chauffeur, Xiao Huang[12] (XH, 小黃, *Siu2 Wong4*, in Cantonese). Just before getting out of the car, Hanson, in the back seat, suddenly spots Gordon (G), in a formal dinner suit and bowtie, exiting a fancy hotel, accompanied by a beautiful young lady, Tyra (T), in full wedding ensemble. The two get ready to step into the waiting bridal car and the scene plays out as follows in Table 11.3.

There are at least three sources of humour in this Scene 1. One is that Molly initially takes the bridal ensemble at face value—which is the reason that she co-opts Xiao Huang to play her boyfriend—only to realise, on seeing and recognizing Tyra, that this is simply a commercial event. We are amused by Molly's antics that were born of pride but we also understand her motivation and can empathise with her not wanting to be humiliated. This empathy is deepened when it turns out that her play-acting, her charade, is for naught.

A second source of humour is Xiao Huang's behaviour, which is visually comic. Not knowing Cantonese and, hence, being unable to follow the conversation between Molly and Gordon, Xiao Huang behaves like a little kid, dragged off somewhere by his mother who is busy chatting with her adult friends, while his eyes wander around and alight on whatever catches his attention and strikes his fancy. Not a man of sophistication like Gordon, Xiao Huang stares unblinkingly at Tyra, an action that is made all the more hilarious by the camera's close-up of his wide-eyed stare which is unabashedly fixed on Tyra's well-endowed bosom. As the audience is well aware, all the while he is supposed to be acting the part of Molly's boyfriend and should be attentive to her, not gawking at another woman's bosom.

The third source of humour, the final surprising blow, comes from the discovery of how it is that Gordon knows Xiao Huang's name. The assumption, common to both Molly and the audience, is that Xiao Huang is an unknown entity, a stranger to Gordon. However, Gordon sets up a different scenario by using Xiao Huang's name (*Siu4 Wong4*, in Cantonese) when he speaks to Molly. To resolve matters, Molly seeks an answer from Xiao Huang, who sheepishly explains that he has not only driven for Gordon's company but that he has driven Gordon personally a number of times. At this point, the scene resembles the theatre of the absurd, full of crossed wires as the different characters talk across each other. That is compounded by Molly switching from

Table 11.3 Gordon to Molly: "Your boyfriend?"

H (1):	(sees and recognises Gordon)
	Gordon Man 喎。
	("Man" is pronounced as in the English word [mæn])
	Hey, it's Gordon Man.
M (1):	(about to get out of the car but then turns to Xiao Huang and snaps at him in Mandarin)
	脫手套，下車。
	Take off your gloves. Get out!
	(They exit the car with Molly's arm around Xiao Huang's, giving the impression that he is her boyfriend)
G (1):	(in Mandarin to Tyra, as she is about to step into the bridal car)
	小心
	Be careful.
G (2):	(Molly clears her throat; Gordon sees her and walks over)
	Molly?
M (2):	(as if surprised to see Gordon, replies brightly)
	Hi
G (3):	(in Cantonese to Molly)
	好耐冇見喎。
	Long time no see.
H (2):	(eyes on Tyra, gravitates towards her)
	Hi
T (1):	Hello
M (3):	(recognises Tyra and remarks in Cantonese)
	哦，原來係 Tyra. 電視台女主播。
	Oh, it's Tyra. TV anchor.
T (2):	(in Cantonese, in response to Hanson's words that are muffled in the crosstalk)
	多謝。
	Thanks.
M (4):	(to Gordon in Cantonese)
	搞 event? 梗係 launch 你哋 Soul & Soul 同 Vila L'Amour Crossover 嘅婚紗 line 啦。
	You have an event? It must be the crossover bridal gown line between Soul & Soul and Vila L'Amour.
G (4):	梗係搞 event。就算我真係要結婚我又點會搞埋晒呢啲咁嘅嘢。
	Of course, it's an event. If I were getting married, I wouldn't do any of this.
	(Molly looks intently on hearing this.)
T (3):	(comes over and greets Molly)
	Hi
M (5):	(a bit brusquely in reply)
	Hi
G (5):	(looks at Xiao Huang and asks Molly in Cantonese)
	你男朋友啊？
	Your boyfriend?
M (6):	(replies indirectly in Cantonese)
	有乜問題？
	What's the problem?

(Continued)

Table 11.3 Gordon to Molly: "Your boyfriend?" *(Continued)*

G (6):	(comments quietly and amusedly in Cantonese) 你有冇發覺小黃對眼一直望住邊度啊? Have you noticed where Siu Wong's eyes have been staring straight at? (Xiao Huang's eyes are wide-open, ogling Tyra's well-endowed bosom, partially revealed in her low-cut wedding gown.)
M (7):	(eyes quickly darting between Tyra and Xiao Huang, then glares at Xiao Huang, gives him a hard nudge, and declares abruptly in Cantonese) 趕時間, 我哋走先。 We're in a hurry. We have to go.
H (3):	(goes over to Gordon, smiles, and shakes his hand) Gordon (Hanson then joins Molly and Xiao Huang, as the three stand outside their car watching as Gordon drives away in the bridal car)
H (4):	(turns to Molly in Cantonese) Tyra 明明係 Soul & Soul 大老闆嘅女朋友。Gordon 同大老闆爭女呀哈? Tyra is the girlfriend of Soul & Soul's big boss. Gordon is vying with his boss for the girl?
M (8):	(annoyed, replies gruffly in Cantonese) 佢爭女人關我咩事。爭邊個女人做咩同我講? What does it matter to me if he is vying for a girl? Why are you telling me that?
M (9):	(suddenly turns to Xiao Huang, and asks him in Mandarin) 他怎麼知道你姓黃的? How does he know your surname is Huang?
XH (1):	(laughs, a bit embarrassed) 文先生公司之前請我開過車。我載過文先生好幾趟了。 Mr Man's company once hired me. I have driven Mr Man quite a few times before.
M (10):	(to Xiao Huang in Cantonese, flustered) 你做咩唔同我講啊? Why didn't you tell me?! [Editorial comment: Not that she has given him a chance!]
H (5):	(in Mandarin to Molly) 他不懂廣東話的。 He doesn't understand Cantonese.
M (11):	Shut up!

Mandarin to Cantonese to speak to Xiao Huang, who does not understand Cantonese, and Hanson, in turn, switching from Cantonese to Mandarin in speaking to Molly—for the express purpose of reminding Molly of Xiao Huang's ignorance of Cantonese—when all along both of them are native Cantonese speakers. To top it off, Molly ends all that by switching to English and very curtly telling Hanson to shut up. Given the crosscurrents of gender, seniority and language culture between the characters, and the highly entertaining comic effect of using code-switching, this is a perfect and ironic closure. It illustrates the rich layers of different forms of humour that can be achieved in even such a short scene, only one-and-a-half minutes in length.

Scene 2. Cracking a Facebook password

This scene is the first minute of a two-minute conversation between Cherry (Ch) and her three close friends who all work in the mall, Coco (Co), Debbie (De) and Miki (Mi). They are hanging out together, standing along a safety-glass railing on the second level of the mall, above a large lobby area. The scene begins with a conversation among them concerning Cherry's boyfriend, Hanson, and his new girlfriend from the Mainland, leading them to discuss how Cherry can ascertain what Hanson is up to. Since in a couple of places, it is impossible to determine which of Cherry's friends is speaking, speaker assignment is an educated guess by the present author, but the selection does not impinge on the flow of the conversation.

Humour has many components. Here in Scene 2, there is the basic comic situation in which Cherry's three close friends eagerly, nosily, and noisily try to help her guess Hanson's password to his Facebook account. The aim is to spy on his dallying with the Mainlander with the big boobs. This sets the stage from the start of this scene as an opposition between the playboy and his show-off girlfriend on the one side and the girls' club on the other. There are two unsuccessful attempts—the first using Hanson's birthdate and then, the bust size of his new girlfriend, "36-24-36" (in the scene, viewers can assume that Debbie knows this from having met her earlier that day at her lingerie shop). Figure 11.2 shows the girls clustered eagerly around Cherry as she enters the bust size. But it is the third try that proves to be the lucky charm. Having grabbed the smartphone, Miki inserts the extra-large bra-cup size, E, into the set of paired numbers, speaking as she inputs the text: 36E 24 36 (*saa4 luk6 E, jaa6 sei3, saa4 luk6* 卅六E, 廿四, 卅六). Then, bingo! Success! The password speaks volumes about Hanson's value system. Adding to the humour is the fact that Hong Kong girls' typical cup size (including Cherry's) is only A. As Debbie has told Cherry earlier, "Hong Kong is an A-cup city, and you're the representative". Thus, to the gender wars, the scene adds both culture wars and geographical wars.

These efforts to crack the Facebook password provide the context linking what is already a daring activity of invading someone's privacy to something even more risqué, bosoms and bras. But in humour as in other things, sex sells, right?[14] It certainly preoccupies the girls just as much as Hanson: first, there is Coco's exaggeration in Co (4), a case of hyperbole, in which she exclaims that those boobs are bigger than her head, even bigger than the Big Ben clock![15] Furthermore, citing Cherry's competitor, Big Boobs, as being an E-cup is something of an exaggeration since this not only exceeds the normal range, but even exceeds the well-known D-cup size of Hollywood's two 1950s sex symbols, Jane Russell (Nawab 2021) and Marilyn Monroe (Hiskey 2012). This is then contrasted with sweet Cherry's measly A-cup size. The comparison between Big Boobs and Cherry is thus especially brutal, confirming Hanson's lecherous reputation as a dirty old man,[16] and making the contrast between the two girls an even more devilish case of humorous hyperbole.

My Unfair Lady 257

Figure 11.2 A still from *Budong Sajiao de Nüren* 不懂撒嬌的女人 (*My Unfair Lady*), director Kwan Shu Ming 關樹明, production by Television Broadcasts Limited (TVB), Hong Kong, distributed by U Media Global and TVBI, 2017. This still, from disc 1, episode 1, has a caption showing the almost-but-not-quite-correct password for Hanson's Facebook account. L-R: Coco, Debbie, Cherry and Miki.

Source: From DVD box-set of *Budong Sajiao de Nuren* 不懂撒嬌的女 (*My Unfair Lady*), 2017, owned by Marjorie Chan.

Scene 2 also introduces humour in two cases of witty wordplay via rhyming. One case is limited to Chinese but the other brings in English as well, through the English subtitles. The first occurs in the turn Co (4) in Table 11.4. It ignores the sentence-final particle, *wo3* 喎—as is conventional in Chinese rhyming practices that date back to the Zhou Dynasty *Shijing* 詩經 (*Book of Songs*)—and thus rhymes *zung1* 鐘 (bell, clock) with *hung1* 胸 (chest, breast, bosom), as noted earlier in the discussion of Big Ben and Big Boobs. The pairing is shown in Table 11.5 with literal translations. Pinyin romanisation is used with tone diacritics for Mandarin placed in parentheses.

The second case of wordplay, shown in Table 11.6 with a literal translation, involves rhyming in the turn Mi (2). The rhyming pair of syllables in Cantonese is *coeng4* 長 (long) and *koeng4* 強 (strong). Mandarin pronunciation is given here in Pinyin romanisation within parentheses. The witty rhyming extends even to the English subtitles in the rhyming pair, *longer* and *stronger*, in the deliberately chosen literal translation of *chang* (*coeng4* 長, long), instead of a more appropriate translation of "deep", as the collocate for cleavage which would not rhyme with "strong"! The rhyming in these examples reminds one of what is found in English doggerel poetry, trivial rather than lofty in form, and comedic without being serious in content or message. It is nevertheless amusing and serves to strengthen the overall humorous effect of the scene, denigrating Big Boobs and all she stands for.

Table 11.4 Cracking Hanson's Facebook code

Mi (1):	第二招, 人肉搜尋。
	Second move, the Human Flesh engine.[13]
Ch (1):	唔, 我日日都睇佢 Facebook, 都冇嘢。有嘢我會知嚟嘛。
	(Sighing) I check his Facebook every day, there's nothing. I'll know if there's something wrong.
Co (1):	哎呀! 唔該你啊, 喐吓個腦啦, 好唔好啊! 人哋啊梗係block 晒嚟啦! 你係入呢, 直情入佢個 Facebook 度。Okay?
	Oh, please! Use your brain, would you? He obviously blocked you. If you go in, log into his Facebook account. Okay?
	(Miki nods in agreement)
	有冇密碼?
	Do you have his password?
Ch (2):	梗係冇啦
	Of course not.
Co (2):	撞啦, 係咪仲要教啊?
	Guess, okay? Do I have to tell you everything?
Ch (3):	生日啦, 好唔好?
	His date of birth?
Co (3):	好。試。
	Good. Try it.
Ch (4):	(Cherry inputs "19790923")
	唔係佢生日喎。我生日囉。
	Not his birthdate. How about mine?
De (1):	欸, 嘥氣啦你。欸? 頭先個男人呢咪喺個電話嗰度讚個女人身材正嘅?
	Oh, please! You waste your breath. A while ago a man on the phone praised a woman's figure.
	(She proceeds to announce the numbers one by one) 362436
All:	(Cherry's friends clamour excitedly for her to try those numbers)
	一定係, 試試佢。試試佢。試試佢。
	Must be. Try it. Try it. Try it.
Ch (5):	(Cherry punches in the number sequence but it doesn't work.)
	唔啱啊。
	That's not it.
De (2):	(In the atrium below, Hanson's new girl comes into view, holding some shopping bags. The four friends have a great view of her upper body.)
	條女出嚟啦, 睇吓幾大波。
	Here she comes! Look at how big her boobs are!
Co (4):	(unclear) 你老闆吖, 真係大過我個頭喎。人哋係警鐘胸, 佢大過大笨鐘喎。
	Oh no, your boss! They're really bigger than my head! Others' boobs look like alarm bells, but hers are huge, bigger than the Big Ben!
De (3):	唔係喎。佢條事業線呢真係長咗成吋喎。
	No, look at her cleavage!
	It's longer than a whole inch [not shown in English subtitle but spoken in Cantonese]
Mi (2):	一吋長, 一吋強啊, 吓。試吓先。
	An inch longer, an inch stronger! Let's try this …
	(grabs the phone from Cherry and tries again, calling out the numbers and letters in pairs while the subtitle displays the sequence of entered text)
	36E2436
	(Bingo! Miki has got into Hanson's Facebook account. Everyone is excited.)
De (4):	真係得咗, 都話嘅啦!
	That worked! See? Told you!
	(The conversation continues …)

Table 11.5 Rhyming pun, Example 1

人哋係警鐘胸
Jan4 dei6 hai6 ging2 zung1 **hung1** (*xiōng*)
Others' [boobs] are alarm bells

佢大過大笨鐘
Keoi5 daai2 guo3 daai2 ban6 **zung1** (*zhōng*)
Hers are bigger than Big Ben

Table 11.6 Rhyming pun, Example 2

一吋長
jat1 cyun3 **coeng4** (*yī cùn **cháng***)
one inch *long* / an inch **longer**

一吋強
jat1 cyun3 **koeng4** (*yī cùn **qiáng***)
one inch *strong* / an inch **stronger**

In Table 11.6, the third row first provides the literal word-by-word translation, and then the actual English subtitle with the comparative forms, *longer* and *stronger*.[17] Thus, the English subtitle is displayed as follows: "An inch longer, an inch stronger!"[18]

Scene 2 hides yet one more gem in wordplay within Co (4). Sex sells and so does coarse language, it seems. Coco utters the phrase, *nei5 lou5 baan2* 你老闆 (your boss), which seems out of place, since there are no bosses referred to in this conversation. The English subtitle for this only shows, "Oh no!" Here is added the literal translation, "your boss". Why should "your boss" appear here? The secret being referred to is another phrase that sounds very close to it and is far more titillating: this is the Cantonese vulgar slang, *nei5 lou5 mou2* 你老母 (literally, your mother). This expression is vulgar because it is a euphemism, an abbreviation for *diu2 nei5 lou5 mou2* (written as 屌你老母 or as 閪你老母), where both the shortened phrase and the full one carry the meaning of "f**k your mother". As for Coco, she coyly substitutes for the original slang an innocuous-sounding phrase, *nei5 lou5 baan2* 你老闆 (your boss). The humour, then, depends on recognising the substitution of one of a number of phrases[19] standing for the real, intended phrase, and it is a shared transgressive pleasure for the Cantonese-viewing audience.

Scene 3. "You betrayed me!"

The third and final scene to be analysed is again only one-and-a-half minutes in duration and is shown in Table 11.7. It takes place at Molly's home, the morning after Gordon has spent the night there. It begins with Molly waking up and hearing Gordon's voice coming from the bathroom. He is speaking very slowly and patiently, as if he were coaxing a child, or perhaps

Table 11.7 Molly to Gordon, "You betrayed me!"

G (1):	(from the bathroom) 嗱, 你乖乖哋, 嗱, 咁 massage 係咪好舒服? Be good, okay? Isn't this massage nice? (Molly peels off her blanket) 嗱, 唔好郁啊吓。喂, 喂, 喂, 唔好整..哎呀你睇吓你彈到我都 我濕哂啦。 Don't move! Stop it. See? You got me all wet. (Molly scrambles out of bed) 你乖乖哋, 唔好郁啦, 好唔好啊? 係咪好舒服先。 Stay still, okay? Isn't that comfy? (Molly heads to the bathroom door and listens) 嗱, 如果你唔舒服你話俾我聽喇。 Tell me if you're not comfy. (Molly opens the bathroom door, and whips aside the shower curtain, revealing Gordon seated, helping to bathe a young lady in the bathtub)
M (1):	(exclaims in shock and dismay) 文念深, 你對得我住! Man Nim-sum, you betrayed me!
G (2):	(replies quietly and nonchalantly) 噚晚同你玩吓㗎啫嘛。你當真㗎? I was toying with you last night. You think it was for real?
M (2):	你又呃我。 You lied to me.
G (3):	慣㗎啦, 又唔係第一次。我話過我唔單只會攞哂你啲場, 連 Mall-Plus 都會係我。你唔係咁天真, 真係以為我會同翻你噉哋一齊呀嘛? Should be used to it. It's not the first time. I told you I'll take all your malls. Even Mall+ will be mine. Are you that naive to think we can be together again? (The next moment, the scene changes to show Molly still lying in bed, eyes wide open, staring up at the ceiling. Her eyes dart in the direction of the empty half of the bed.)
G (4):	(from the bathroom) 嗱, 你乖乖哋, 嗱, 咁 massage 係咪好舒服? Be good, okay? Isn't this massage nice? (Molly gets out of bed and stands outside the bathroom door, listening intently.) 嗱, 唔好郁啊吓。喂, 喂, 喂, 唔好整...哎呀你睇吓你彈到我都...我濕哂啦。 Don't move! Stop it ... See? You got me all wet. (Molly opens the door quickly. Gordon is seated facing the bathtub, with the shower curtain half closed, shielding whoever is in the bathtub.) 你乖乖哋, 唔好郁啦, 好唔好? 係咪好舒服先。嗱, 如果你唔舒服你話俾我聽喇。 Be good. Stay still, okay? See? Isn't that comfy? Tell me if you're not comfy.
M (3):	(flings open the shower curtain and starts to bark at Gordon but breaks off in mid-sentence) 文念深, 你 ... Man Nim-sum, you ... Standing on a small, white stool, contentedly covered in soap suds is her dog, Mooney.

a girlfriend? To be begin with, the camera shows Molly's shocking discovery, but then proceeds to re-run the scene from another point of view.

One can easily see that there are two intersecting events in this scene, the one imagined by Molly and the one actually taking place. Gordon's tone of voice coming from inside the bathroom sets up the expectation that he is speaking to some female, coaxing her as one would a lovey-dovey girlfriend or wife. The audience also hears Molly's anguished cry in response, "You betrayed me!" (This cry, given here and used as the title of this scene, replaces the wording actually given in the English subtitle, "How could you?"). Gordon's voice, that was warm, kind and tender just a minute ago speaking to someone else, is replaced by a cold and callous tone of voice in the imagined reaction to Molly's outcry of betrayal.

The first, imagined scene thus sets up an expectation, priming the audience to anticipate witnessing an unfaithful Gordon in the bathroom with some beautiful damsel, and in Molly's own flat and bathtub. The reality, however, is very different and the object of Gordon's gentle massaging efforts, is none other than the innocent Mooney, Molly's beloved dog. Humour is derived from the surprise denouement, which reveals a descending incongruity between Molly's expectations of high drama and the reality that is shown, not in words but in the visual impact of Mooney appearing, happily soaped-up in the bathtub.

In sum, these three short scenes, totalling just four minutes, offer a glimpse into the rich array of the tools and structural types of humour buried in this treasure trove of twenty-one hours of TV programming.

Conclusion

In the 28 episodes of *My Unfair Lady* many gender-related issues are raised that are not only treated with humour but may also pertain to more serious topics, resulting in a complex tapestry of issues that confront and challenge thoughtful viewers. One that has already been mentioned in this study is Cherry's concern about her biological clock, which guides her decision on whether to stay with the gamophobic Saving, or to make another decision about her future. Since Natalie Tong, the actress who plays Cherry, is in the same age range as her character, this topic becomes a more realistic one for viewers to ponder over concerning their favourite star actress, regardless of whether their own reluctant boyfriend might be truly gamophobic or simply nervous about making the legal, long-term commitment to them.

Similarly, for Jessica Hsuan, who plays Molly, both she and her character in the series are in their early forties. All professional women face a dilemma as to what extent they wish to choose a career over marriage and raising a family, or whether they can try to have it all. And as more women in China and Hong Kong take on managerial roles in the professions, this is a current topic of enormous import to the local audience. The series reveals that Molly has had a hysterectomy and is unable to have children. Even though on the evening before Scene 3, Gordon has embraced her tightly in the office and told her that he wants her to control him and that he does not mind her not being able to have children, Scene 3 shows that she still feels very vulnerable and does not have full trust and confidence in Gordon—especially having been deserted once by him before. While the scene is depicted with humour, Molly's fear is palpable, and it lingers in the audience's awareness as an undercurrent to the comedy.

Another serious family and career topic involves Annie, Molly's competent assistant manager, who grapples with the dilemma of whether to raise her young son as a single, divorced mother, or to give up custody to her ex-husband and his new girlfriend, in order to pursue promotion to general manager position. At the same time, having been unsuccessful in her first marriage, she hesitates to respond to her co-worker, Oscar, who is in love with her and genuinely cares for both her and her son.

Other issues raised in the series include Molly's background of having been abandoned by both her parents, and then raised by a cold, unfeeling uncle, as well as her love-hate relationship with her father who tries hard to re-connect with her after having spent decades at sea. It was her father, for example, who told Gordon about her hysterectomy. Molly's father had come across her medical report one day and made tremendous efforts to get help to understand its contents. Also touched upon are issues of age disparity between two partners, as in the case of Tet-yan's infatuation with Molly, who is more than a zodiac cycle over his age, and Molly's father's tender relationship with a Mainlander who is at least half his age or younger still and whom he eventually marries.

As is conventional in a comedy, all's well that ends well. The final scene shows Molly, not only content in her marriage to Gordon but also surrounded by a gaggle of children, suggesting that they have been adopted by the happy pair. Molly is a clear-headed heroine, recognises that she does not know how to *sajiao*, but is unfazed by that, as she has managed to gain happiness without those alluring, feminine skills.

All in all, the twenty-eight episodes add up to a warm, sympathetic depiction of family, lovers, friends and co-workers, a depiction filled with both humour and pathos. But the humour is warm-hearted, rising above all the problems and accepting human foibles. The television series achieves this by making use of a variety of devices to evoke humour, from simple antics and sight gags to use of irony, hyperbole, mock apophony and other wordplay (such as cheekily adding the negative prefix, *-un*, to *My Fair Lady*, playing with rhyming reminiscent of doggerels, etc.). In addition, it exploits the use of code-switching between other dialects and languages, modulation of speech tempo and tone of voice (be it for coaxing, *sajiao* or other purposes), as well as using more cerebral wit in wordplay that involves puns, especially in the realm of naming practices. In themes and depiction of women's roles it is decidedly modern, but its humour is in some ways very traditional, reflecting the history of cultural practice as well as the nature of the rich array of Chinese language available to the modern-day Hongkonger.

The power of homophony in the Chinese language has guided naming taboos since antiquity, and has inspired creative punning in Chinese social, cultural and literary realms up to and during the present era. Among educated Chinese in modern times, perhaps the greatest punster was renowned Chinese linguist, Chao Yuen Ren 趙元任 (1892–1982), who famously composed a narrative poem, perhaps in the 1930s or earlier still (*Pinyin News* 2010), that consists entirely of the syllable, *shi*, when read in Mandarin Chinese. The title of this tongue-in-cheek poem, containing just under 100 characters, is (with tone diacritics included to assist the reader) *Shī shì shí shī shǐ* 施氏食獅史 (Lion-eating poet in the stone den).[20] Chao (1959) is likely also the earliest person to conduct a linguistic inquiry into homophony and homonymy, as part of his analysis of ambiguity in the Chinese language. Although later scholars (e.g. Sung 1979, Li and Costa 2009, Lu and Wang 2013, including references therein) have further studied punning, none focus on linking it with humour. The universality of punning and humorous wordplay is however well-known (Attardo 2018, Attardo et al. 2017, Smith et al. 2020, etc.), and studies on that topic exist for other East Asian languages (e.g. Nishimura 2012, Oh et al. 2021). Clearly, it offers a rich backdrop for further research on punning, humour and the Chinese language, including a new layer of creative punning that juxtaposes multiple dialects and languages.

This study of *My Unfair Lady* has taken the humble pun as its launching ground to focus on the comic depths offered by the names and nicknames of the six major characters in this television series. The pun, with its ability to engage the brain in the linguistic task of simultaneously juggling multiple meanings of words, entertains while it teases and hints at critical truth. In the process of dissecting the rich offerings of the TV series, this study has invited side glances at a few other characters in the interplay of naming, gender, and the performance of *sajiao*, and how all this represents a challenge for the modern working woman in Hong Kong, and perhaps elsewhere. While puns are only one part of the comic mix here on offer, they are by no means the least, and deserve Pollack's (2011: 152) ardent defence: "Ultimately, puns keep our minds alert, engaged and nimble in this quickening world, revealing new connections and fresh interpretations. And that's why, even as we hurtle into a future of uncertain opportunities, puns will always be more than some antics".

Notes

1. I would like to express my appreciation and gratitude to Jessica Milner Davis for her support, encouragement and helpful feedback during the writing process. Thanks also go to my colleagues and graduate students, and especially to Jennifer W. Jay and Jinwei Ye for their valuable input in the transcription of the three scenes, and to Wei William Zhou, Paul Cockrum, and Jocelyn Chey for their helpful feedback on early drafts.

2   Yueh (2017: 44) notes that "[a]s of 2015, Lover Man has published thirty-four books concerning love and relationships, and all of them emphasise women's *sajiao* skills toward men". Including news articles and books by other authors, tips and instructions on *sajiao* have become a veritable cottage industry!
3   Hanyu Pinyin romanisation (without tone diacritics) is used throughout for Mandarin Chinese, and Jyutping romanisation with tones (numbers 1 to 6), developed by the Linguistic Society of Hong Kong, is used for romanisation of Standard Cantonese where Cantonese pronunciation is needed.
4   The Cantonese dialect word corresponding to Mandarin Chinese *sajiao* is *dia* 嗲 (*de2* in Cantonese). Hence, a word-for-word, vernacular Cantonese version of the title for this TV series would be *m4 sik1 de2 ge3 neoi5 jan2* 唔識嗲嘅女人 (women who do not know how to act cute). On *de2* 嗲 per se, the earliest sociolinguistic study is Light's (1982) article, "On being *déing*: How women's language is perceived in Chinese".
5   Adamek's (2012) Leiden University dissertation provides a valuable source on the tabooing of names in China, or *bihui* 避諱, based on written sources going back to the Shang Dynasty oracle bones. A key observation is, "The names of sovereigns, ancestors, officials, teachers, etc. were taboo, meaning that it was prohibited to pronounce or record them. This custom had an enormous impact on Chinese culture and serious consequences for the daily lives of many Chinese, as well as for Chinese historiography". Other sources dealing with the complexity in interpreting naming taboo in early sources include Beck (1987) and Venture (2011).
6   Research interest in one of China's greatest classical novels, *Dream of the Red Chamber*, became so intense and extensive that, by late 19th century, the flurry of academic activities spawned a whole subfield in Chinese literature dedicated to its study, *Hongxue* 紅學, "Redology".
7   Naming has real-life consequences. As an example of the latter case, in the United States, the name "Donald" is apparently no longer *très chic* for naming one's baby, having become linked to Donald Trump, its 45th President: Pennyfarthing (2021) notes that "[a]ccording to the Social Security Administration's latest list of popular baby names, the popularity of 'Donald' saw a big decline in the year 2020. The name fell 55 places, from the 555th most popular name for boys in 2019 to the 610th last year—its lowest-ever ranking on the annual list, which dates back to the 1880s".
8   It is customary in Chinese culture to quote the zodiac sign of one's birth year rather than the calendar year, thus giving an approximate idea of the decade into which one was born.
9   Samantha Ko, who plays Tin Mat, is not normally cast in the role of a villain. Not surprising, then, at the end of this lighthearted television series, Tin Mat does not actually try to destroy Molly and Gordon's marriage. Instead, she reconnects with her first husband, whom she had originally divorced because he was too absorbed in his work to nurture their marriage. As one of the supporting characters, the audience eventually sees that he is a smart, visionary businessman who is reasonable and trustworthy—the very qualities that had attracted Tin Mat to Gordon—and, importantly, one who could be a better partner to Tin Mat the second time around.
10 Two online sources are used for information on Vincent Wong's background, one using his English name, Vincent Wong, and the other his Chinese name 王浩信. (see Wong, Vincent, personal website and Wang Haoxin, personal website)
11 The figure of 1.9 million viewers may seem small but it represents a whopping 25.6% of the Hong Kong population that year (based on the Hong Kong government's population figure of 7,409,800 for the end of 2017, see Year-end Population for 2017). For comparison, Wikipedia gives the following statistics for

the very popular American TV series, *Friends,* which ended its ten-season run in 2004: "The series finale aired on 6 May 2004, and was watched by around 52.5 million American viewers, making it the fifth most-watched series finale in television history, and the most-watched television episode of the 2000s" (Friends 2021). As the US population on 1 July 2004 was 292,801,000 (Statistical Abstracts of the United States: 2004–2005), the viewership for that series finale was only about 18% of the total US population at the time, far short of the 25.6% for *My Unfair Lady.*

12 *Xiao* 小 (young; literally, little) is a commonly used prefix before a surname in Mandarin Chinese for younger people, while older folks have their surnames prefixed by *Lao* 老 (old).

13 人肉搜尋 (Human flesh engine, in the English subtitle) refers to the "Human Flesh Search Engine", a concept similar to "doxing" (or "doxxing") that involves "a group endeavour to reveal someone's identity and personal details online" (Brancart 2018).

14 Hongkongers of post-WWII generations are well aware that sex sells. As avid followers of tabloid news on Hollywood celebrities and sex symbols, they have gleefully and liberally alluded to them in their comedic Cantonese operas and early Cantopop songs, such as "Love you to the bone" (*Oi3 nei5 jap6 gwat1* 愛你入骨), which has even Miss Jane Russell—despite her famous hourglass figure (38-24-36)—sighing in envy at the sexy figure of the Hong Kong damsel who is the young man's love interest (see Chan and Chey 2013).

15 In fact, the English subtitle more modestly claims that the boobs are equivalent to, not bigger than, the size of Big Ben: "Hers are huge like the Big Ben!".

16 Note that in Scene 1 above, Hanson's chief interest is in introducing himself to the glamour girl Tyra, and that he pays no attention to Gordon until departing. This is not a matter of him merely being polite.

17 The English indefinite article, "a(n)", and "one" are both translated as *yī* (*jat1* 一, one) in Chinese.

18 Could the English subtitling team be hinting at a particular male body part?!

19 Hutton and Bolton (2005: 94–95) offer some other partial euphemistic variants, including a semantic substitution, by replacing the disyllabic noun, in *nei5 lou5 mou2* 你老母 (your mother) with a synonym from literary Chinese, *nei5 noeng4* (or *loeng4*) *can1* 你娘親 (your mother). Phonetic substitution is also used, by replacing the disyllabic noun with near homophones, in *nei5 lou5 mei2* 你鹵味 (your roasted meat), and *nei5 lou5 mei2* 你老尾 (your old tail). In other words, Hongkongers can be as creative as they wish in dreaming up a partial euphemistic alternative. In Coco's case, she semi-hides the taboo expression by omitting the offensive verb and by substituting "your mother" with "your boss". (Note: Jyutping romanisation here replaces the Yale romanisation used in this dictionary.)

20 For a recent literary analysis of Chao's poem, see Slider (2012).

References

2021 Nian Baijiaxing Paihang 2021 年百家姓排行 (2021 ranking of the top 100 surnames). 2021. At: https://www.10ce.com/home/baijiaxing.html (accessed 12 June 2021).

Adamek, P. 2012. *A good son is sad if he hears the name of his father: The tabooing of names in China as a way of implementing social values.* Unpublished PhD dissertation, Leiden University.

Attardo, S., ed. 2017. *The Routledge handbook of language and humor.* New York, NY: Routledge.

Attardo, S. 2018. Universals in puns and humorous wordplay. In E. Winter-Froemel and V. Thaler, eds., *Cultures and traditions of wordplay and wordplay research*. 89–109. Berlin: De Gruyter.

Beck, B. J. M. 1987. The First Emperor's taboo character and the three day reign of King Xiaowen: Two moot points raised by the Qin chronicle unearthed in Shuihudi in 1975. *T'oung Pao (2nd Series)*, 73 (1/3): 68–85.

Brancart, B. 2018. After more than a decade, the Human Flesh Search Engine is still raging across Chinese social media: At times unjust, excessive, or even illegal – but the Human Flesh Search still is an inherent part of Weibo. Posted 6 February 2018. At: https://www.whatsonweibo.com/decade-human-flesh-search-engine-still-raging-across-chinese-social-media/ (accessed 15 July 2021).

Chan, M. K. M. and J. Chey. 2013. "Love you to the bone" and other songs: Humour and *rusheng* 入聲 rhymes in early Cantopop. In J. M. Davis and J. Chey, eds., *Humour in Chinese life and culture: Resistance and control in modern times*. 103–130. Hong Kong: Hong Kong University Press.

Chan, M. K. M. and Y. Lin. 2019. Chinese language and gender research. In C. R. Huang, J. S. Zhuo and B. Meisterernst, eds., *The Routledge handbook of Chinese applied linguistics*. 165–181. New York, NY: Routledge.

Chao, Y. R. 1959. Ambiguity in Chinese. In S. Egerod and E. Glahn, eds., *Studia Serica Bernhard Karlgren dedicata*. 1–13. Copenhagen: Ejnar Munksgaard. (Reprinted in Y. R. Chao. 1976. *Aspects of Chinese sociolinguistics: Essays by Yuen Ren Chao*. Selected and introduced by A. S. Dil. 293–308. Stanford CA: Stanford University Press.)

Cohen, A. P. 2000. *Introduction to research in Chinese source materials*. New Haven, CT: Far Eastern Publications.

"Friends". 2021. Wikipedia site, edited 27 June 2021. At: https://en.m.wikipedia.org/wiki/Friends (accessed 28 June 2021).

Hiskey, D. 2012. Marilyn Monroe was not even close to a size 12–16. Posted 17 April 2012. At: https://www.todayifoundout.com/index.php/2012/04/marilyn-monroe-was-not-even-close-to-a-size-12-16/ (accessed 6 July 2021).

Hutton, C. and K. Bolton. 2005, *A Dictionary of Cantonese slang: The language of Hong Kong movies, street gangs and city life*. Honolulu, HI: University of Hawai'i Press.

Li, C. D. S. and V. Costa. 2009. Punning in Hong Kong Chinese media: Forms and functions. *Journal of Chinese Linguistics*, 37 (1): 77–107.

Light, T. 1982. On being *dě*ing: How women's language is perceived in Chinese. *Computational Analysis of Asian and African Languages*, 19: 21–49.

Nawab, N. 2021. Jane Russell measurements, bio, height, weight, shoe, bra size. Last updated 9 February 2021. At: https://www.gistrat.com/jane-russell-measurements/ (accessed 6 July 2021).

Nishimura, Yukiko. 2012. Puns in Japanese computer mediated communication: Observations from misconversion phenomena. Papers from the 2012 AAAI Fall Symposium on Artificial Intelligence of Humor, November 2–4, Arlington VA, USA. *AAAI Technical Paper FS-12-02*: 38–45. At: http://www.aaai.org/ocs/index.php/FSS/FSS12/paper/view/5586 (accessed 30 May 2021).

Oh, S., J. Kim, S. Lee and E. Park. 2021. *Jujeop*: Korean puns for K-pop stars on social media. *Proceedings of the Ninth International Workshop on Natural Language Processing for Social Media, Association for Computational Linguistics*. 170–177. At: https://aclanthology.org/2021.socialnlp-1.15 (accessed 27 June 2021).

Pennyfarthing, A. 2021. The name 'Donald' is plunging in popularity, as is 'Karen.' Is there any wonder why? Posted 11 June 2021. At: https://m.dailykos.com/stories/2021/6/11/2034780/-The-name-Donald-is-plunging-in-popularity-as-is-Karen-is-there-any-wonder-why?detail=emaildkre (accessed 18 June 2021).

Pinyin News. 2010. Roots of the stone lions story. Posted 20 August 2010. At: http://pinyin.info/news/2010/roots-of-the-stone-lions-story/ (accessed 28 June 2021).

Pollack, J. 2011. *The pun also rises: How the humble pun revolutionized language, changed history, and made wordplay more than some antics.* New York, NY: Penguin Random House.

Slider, R. 2012. "Shi and the ten stone lions": Riddle or nonsense? Posted 11 November 2012. At: https://finecha.wordpress.com/2012/11/11/red-slider/ (accessed 28 June 2021).

Smith, R. H., C. E. Hoogland and E. G. Brown. 2020. Once a pun a time: Exploring factors associated with perceptions of humorous punning. *Humor: International Journal of Humor Research*, 33 (1): 7–28.

Statistical Abstracts of the United States. 2004–2005. At: https://www.census.gov/library/publications/2004/compendia/statab/124ed.html (accessed 28 June 2021).

Sung, M. 1979. Chinese language and culture: A study of homonyms, lucky words and taboos. *Journal of Chinese Linguistics*, 7 (1): 15–28.

The Straits Times. 2017. TVB romance *My Unfair Lady*'s open-ended finale draws high ratings and brickbats. Posted 30 May 2017. At: https://www.straitstimes.com/lifestyle/entertainment/tvb-romance-my-unfair-ladys-open-ended-finale-draws-high-ratings-and (accessed 10 June 2021).

Venture, O. 2011. *Caractères interdits et vocabulaire officiel sous les Qin: L'Apport des documents administratifs de Liye. Études Chinoises*, 30: 73–98.

Wang Haoxin 王浩信. Personal website. At: https://zh.wikipedia.org/wiki/%E7%8E%8B%E6%B5%A9%E4%BF%A1#%E7%B0%A1%E6%AD%B7 (accessed 10 June 2021).

Wang, W. S. Y. 1989. Language in China: A chapter in the history of linguistics. *Journal of Chinese Linguistics*, 17 (2): 183–222.

Wong, Vincent. Personal website. At: https://en.wikipedia.org/wiki/Vincent_Wong_(Hong_Kong_actor) (accessed 7 July 2021).

Year-End Population for 2017. The Government of the Hong Kong Special Administrative Region. At: https://www.info.gov.hk/gia/general/201802/13/P2018021300299.htm (accessed 28 June 2021).

Yueh, H. I. 2017. *Identity politics and popular culture in Taiwan: A Sajiao generation.* Lanham, MD: Lexington Books.

Index

Note: References to figures are indicated in *italics* and references to tables in **bold**. References to endnotes consist of the page number followed by the letter 'n' followed by the number of the note, e.g. 206n5.

Adamek, P. 264n5
adaptive/maladaptive humour 5
Addison, Joseph 24
advertising: Australian National Meat and Livestock Board's lamb advertising campaign 2–3; humorous advertising on social media 8
affiliative humour 12, 84, 85, 213, 224, 231
age: and styles of humour 7; *see also* Taiwanese conversational humour (Wei-Lin Melody Chang and Michael Haugh)
aggressive humour: and Reality Television 215; *see also* teasing and female friendship in Chinese reality TV show (Ying Cao)
alliteration, in Balinese *wewangsalan* 76, 77
allo-repetition, in Japanese *angama* humour 109–110, 111
Allport, Gordon 3
ambiguity: in Balinese *cecangkitan* 63, 78, 80–82, 85; in Chinese language 263; and indirectness of humour 172–173; in Mencius' conversations 31; in South Korean workplace humour 172; and teasing 212
American sitcoms 8
ancient Greece: philosophy and humour 36n2; rhetorical tradition 19
Andō Tsuruo (1908–1969) 150
angama ritual and banter on Ishigaki Island, Japan (Makiko Takekuro): chapter overview 8, 9; festival of *sōron* and *angama* (characters, costumes and masks) 88, 92–93, *93*; focus on banter as poetic performance 90, 111, 112; humour as plurimodal poetic performance 90–91, 110, 111, 112–113; Ishigaki Island *89*, 92; Japanese humour studies 88–90; methodology of case study 93–94; performance example (Ishigaki Store band question) 95–99, *95*, 103; performance example (*ushumai's* teeth question) 99–102, 103; performance with children (*ushumai* trying to find boy in audience) 108–110; performance with children (*ushumai's* teeth question) 103–108, *104*; rhythm, importance of 98, 102, 103, 111; role of *boke* (jokester) 111; rules of communication 94–95; use of falsetto tone by ancestors/dead spirits 94; use of local material and regional identity 95, 103, 110, 111–112; use of onomatopoeia 99, 102, 111; use of parallelism 99, 102, 109, 111; use of quick-witted answers 94, 103, 111; use of repetition 99, 102, 109–110, 111; use of standard Japanese 93, 94, 112; use of Yaeyaman languages 94, 112; visual humour 94–95; wordplays 111
apuroochi '("approach" in Japanese *makura* of *rakugo*) 139
Aristotle, *eutrapelia* 8
Arnawa, Nengah *see* Balinese traditional oral humour (Nengah Arnawa)
Ashley Cooper, Anthony, 3rd Earl of Shaftesbury 24–25

Index 269

assonance, in Balinese *wewangsalan* 76, 77
Attardo, Salvatore 49, 59n19, 118, 120, 194, 206n1
Australia, National Meat and Livestock Board's lamb advertising campaign 2–3

Bagus, I Gusti Ngurah 63
balé kedék (Balinese "vehicle for laughter" TV programmes) 64
Balinese culture: *bebanyolan* (Balinese humour) 4, 64; *bondrés* (masked comic performing art) 64; *drama gong* (traditional drama) 63–64, 65, 83; family groupings (*banjar* and *témpékan*) 83; *humor* term 4; I Cupak (traditional comic figure) 84; *mabebanyolan* (funny stories) 64; *magegiakan* (laughing out loud) 64; *magegonjakan* (conversing using humour) 64; *makedékan* (joking) 64; *paribasa* (proverbs) 63, 65; politeness rules and humour 5, 9; punning (wordplay) 5; *satua* (folk tales) 63; *satua banyol* (funny folk tales) 65; *séndratari* (drama with dance) 64, 65, 83; verbal humour, early study of 13n3; *see also* Balinese traditional oral humour (Nengah Arnawa); *wayang kulit* (Balinese shadow puppet theatre)
Balinese language: speech levels and caste/social status 62–63; speech levels (high, general, low) 62
Balinese traditional oral humour (Nengah Arnawa): chapter overview 4, 6, 62; complexity of Indonesian languages 62; features of Balinese language and social status 62–63; humour and Balinese language 63; humour and Balinese literature genres 63; humour and Balinese traditional theatre performances 63–64; humour-related Balinese terms 64; linguistic anthropological approach and sources 64–65; linguistic constructs: *bladbadan* 63, 69–75, **71**, **72**, *72, 73*, **74**, 84; *cecangkitan* or *raos ngémpélin* 63, 78–82, **79**, *79*, 85; *cecimpedan* 63, 65–69, 83–84; *wewangsalan* 63, 75–78, **76**, **77**, **78**, 84–85; social functions of Balinese humour 83–85; *tokoh banyol* (famous contemporary comedians) 83; wordplay (punning) 73–74; *see also* separate Balinese terms
banjar (Balinese family grouping) 83
banter *see angama* ritual and banter on Ishigaki Island, Japan (Makiko Takekuro)
Bauman, R. 90
Beattie, James 36n3
bebanyolan (Balinese humour) 4, 64; *see also* Balinese traditional oral humour (Nengah Arnawa)
Bednarek, M. 200
Beeman, W. O. 90
Bi, X. **191**
bisociation 118
bladbadan (in Balinese humour): affiliative style of humour 85; example from Cenk Blonk *wayang kulit* 70–71, **71**, **72**, *72*, 73–74, *73*; examples from printed collection 74–75, **74**; form of sound play with meaning transposition 63; frame, denotative and associative meanings 69–70, **72**; and incongruity theory of humour 71, 73–74; morphology of term 69; and relief theory of humour 75, 84; speech interaction context 70, 84; and superiority theory of humour 73–74, 84
Blitvich, Pilar Garcés-Conejos 214–215
bodily humours, theory of 3
boke (jokester in Japanese culture) 111
Bolton, K. 265n19
bondrés (Balinese masked comic performing art) 64
Bourdieu, P., "*habitus*" concept 91
Boxer, Diana 144
Brandstadter, Susanne 13n1
Brau, Lorie 150, 151
Briggs, C. 90
British Psychological Society, Welsh Branch, inter-disciplinary conference on humour and laughter (Cardiff, 1978) 1
Budong Sajiao de Nüren see gender, *sajiao* and humour in Hong Kong *My Unfair Lady* TV series (Marjorie K. M. Chan)
bugaku (Japanese court music) 150
bunraku (or *ningyō jōruri*, i.e. Japanese puppet theatre) 137, 151; *gidayūbushi* (musical narrative) 138
Bushnell, Cade 149
business relations, and humour 2–3

Cai Guoliang 46, 49, 59n10
Caizi jiaren (*Brilliant scholar and beautiful maid*) Chinese stories 42
Cantonese Chinese language 51, 238, 248; Weitou (dialect of Cantonese) 248, 250
Cantonese operas (Hong Kong) 265n14
Cantopop songs 265n14
Cao, Ying **191**; *see also* teasing and female friendship in Chinese reality TV show (Ying Cao)
Cao Xueqin (1715?–1763?), *Honglou meng* (*The Dream of the Red Chamber*) 40, 200, 240
The Carnal prayer mat see under Li Yu (1611–1680?)
Carnival celebrations (Europe) 8
cartoons *see* Hasegawa's cartoons (Sachiko Kitazume)
cecangkitan (or *raos ngémpélin* in Balinese humour): affiliative style of humour 85; ambiguity-based puzzle 63, 78, 80–82, 85; example from Cenk Blonk *wayang kulit* 78–80, **79**, 79; examples from printed collection 80–82; morphology of term 78; used to make fun/joke around 78
cecimpedan (in Balinese humour): *cecimpedan* associative 66–69; *cecimpedan* onomatopoeia 65–66; children's riddles 63, 66; and incongruity theory of humour 66, 67, 68, 83; morphology of term 65; and relief theory of humour 69, 83–84
Cenk Blonk *see* I Wayan Nardayana, alias Cenk Blonk (b. 1966)
Chan, Marjorie K. M. *see* gender, *sajiao* and humour in Hong Kong *My Unfair Lady* TV series (Marjorie K. M. Chan)
Chan, Shirley 2, 4, 6, 7, 8, 59n11; *see also* Mencius and humour as rhetorical discourse (Shirley Chan)
Chang, Wei-Lin Melody **191**, 192, 193; *see also* Taiwanese conversational humour (Wei-Lin Melody Chang and Michael Haugh)
chao (derision in Chinese) 37n4
Chao Yuen Ren (1892–1982) 263
cháofěng (light teasing in Chinese, Taiwan) 193
cháoxiào (light teasing in Chinese, Taiwan) 193
Chaplin, Charlie 8

Chen, L. L. 191–192, **191**, 206n5
Chen, X. **191**
Chen Huiqin 43, 59n10
Chey, Jocelyn 13n1, 36n3
children: and Balinese *cecimpedan* 65, 66; and Japanese *angama* ritual 92, 95, 103–110, 111, 112
China: Ming dynasty (1368–1644) 7, 40, 41, 44, 47, 58; Qin dynasty (221–206 BCE) 7, 21; Qing dynasty (1644–1911) 40, 42; Shang dynasty (c.1600 BC–c.1046 BC) 239; Tang dynasty (618–907 CE) 239–240; Warring States period (475–221 BC) 7, 20, 21; Zhou dynasty (c.1046–256 BCE) 21, 239, 257
China (People's Republic of China): Mainland Chinese humour 191; neo-Confucian views on humour 192; traditional view of femininity 232; *see also* teasing and female friendship in Chinese reality TV show (Ying Cao)
Chinese culture: *chao* (derision) 37n4; Chinese humour, scarcity of English-language studies on 2; Chinese humour, studies on 13n1; Chinese humour, use of and adaptive humour style 5; Chinese Theory of the Humours 14n6; *e'gao* (spoofing on internet) 7; *huaji* (laughable) 4, 6, 7, 20, 37n4, 188, 191; *ji* (to ridicule) 37n4; naming taboos 239–240, 263, 264n5; wordplay (punning) 7, 192, 193, 199, 240–241, 262, 263; *xiangsheng* (crosstalk) 7; *xiao* (laughable) 4; *xie* (glib or laughable) 37n4; *xue* (joking) 37n4; *yaxue* (humour) 219; *youmo* (humour) 4, 12, 20, 188, 219; *see also* Chinese literature; Chinese philosophy; Confucianism; Hong Kong culture; Taiwanese culture
Chinese languages: ambiguity in 263; Cantonese Chinese 51, 238, 248; homophony in 240, 263; Mandarin Chinese 11, 51, 196, 197, 199, 203, 248; Taiwanese Hokkien 11, 196, 197; Weitou (dialect of Cantonese) 248, 250; Wu (Suzhounese) dialect 51
Chinese literature: folly-and-consequence stories 52; *huaben* (novella, short story) 40, 42, 43, 58; *Shijing* (*Book of Songs*) 257; *see also Guzhang juechen* (Antonio Leggieri)

Chinese philosophy: Daoism 20, 55; early Chinese texts 29, 37n6; Legalist philosophers 20, 37n8; Mohism 24, 33–34; rhetorical tradition 19; *see also* Confucianism; Mencius and humour as rhetorical discourse (Shirley Chan)
Chow Yun-fat (b. 1955) 250
Chu Kang Kei (active 1988–) 239
Clap your hands and rid yourself of dust (*Guzhang juechen*) *see Guzhang juechen* (Antonio Leggieri)
clowns *see punakawan* (clown figures in Balinese *wayang kulit*)
Coates, J. 221, 231
co-construction (in humour) 221, 224
cognitive studies (on humour) 1
Cohen, A. P. 239–240
coincidence, and humour 58
community: community-based humour in Japanese *angama* 95, 103, 110, 111–112; "humour community" concept 49, 52
Confucianism: Confucian concept of appropriate humour 5, 7, 8, 11, 12, 20; Confucian-based relationships 10, 170; and hierarchy/humour in South Korean workplace 170, 171–172, 174–176, 183, 184; and Mencius 8, 21, 22–24, 25, 28, 34, 38n20; neo-Confucianism 7, 192; and self-cultivation 38n14; and Shōtoku Taishi 10, 131, 133
Confucius (trad. 551–479 BCE): on "rectification of names" (*The Analects*) 239; *see also* Confucianism
context 118, 119, 120–121, 124; context of culture 118, 121; context of situation 118, 121; conventional context 118; *see also* cultural context and humour (Jessica Milner Davis)
conversational humour 188–189; *see also* Taiwanese conversational humour (Wei-Lin Melody Chang and Michael Haugh)
Cooper, C. 172
Coulson, Seana 119
Cui Chengxiu (d. 1627) 43, 46–48
Culpeper, Jonathan 215
cultural context and humour (Jessica Milner Davis): cognitive and affective elements of humour 1; concept of humour and cultural contexts/traditions 2–3; concept of humour in Asian contexts 3–4; continuity and change in humour 6–7; continuity and tradition in humour 7–8, 13; cultural conventions, personal preferences and humour 4–6; interdisciplinary scholarship on humour 1; laughter vs. humour 1, 2; parallels between Asian and Western humour 8; scarcity of English-language studies on Asian humour 2; studies on Japanese, Chinese and Taiwanese humour 13n1; studies on Singaporean and Balinese humour 13n3; summaries of book chapters (humour and cultural evolution) 10–12; summaries of book chapters (humour and cultural tradition) 8–10
culture wars 6

Daoism 20, 55
Davies, C. E. 221
Davis, Jessica Milner *see* Milner Davis, Jessica
Délem (Balinese *punakawan* clown) 70–71, **71**, *72*, *73*, 76, **77**
diplomatic relations, and humour 2
discourse strategies 192, 221
Dittmer, Jason 13n4
Dolar *see* I Wayan Tarma, alias Dolar (1954–2016)
double entendre 52
drama gong (Balinese traditional drama) 63–64, 65, 83
The Dream of the Red Chamber see under Cao Xueqin (1715?–1763?)
Du Fu (712–770) 55–56
Du Plooy-Cilliers, F. 121
dwipura (reduplication of front part of word), in Balinese humour 75, 78
Dynel, Marta 206n1, 215, 231–232

Eder, D. 213, 224
Edo period (Japan, 1600–1868) 150
e'gao (spoofing on internet in China) 7
Elephant Dee *see* Hsu, Dee (Xú Xîdì aka Elephant Dee, b. 1978)
English culture: evolution of 'humour' concept 3, 4; George Meredith's conception of humour 6, 36n3
esprit, vs. *humour* 3
European medieval period: Carnival celebrations 8; farces 8

face, and play-frames 212
face saving 174, 179–181, 183–184

facial expressions: in Japanese *angama* humour 110; and teasing 233
Fan, Mavis (Fàn Xiaoxuân, b. 1977) 217, 221–223, 224
farce: European farce 8; medieval farce 8
Fauconnier, Gilles 119
Feng Menglong (1574–1646), *Sanyan* 42
The Flowers in the Mirror see under Li Ruzhen (c.1763–1830)
folly-and-consequence Chinese stories 52
frames: in Balinese *bladbadan* 69–70, **72**; frame-based theories of humour 118–119; *makura* as 164–165; play-frames 212, 221, 224, 226–227
French culture, *humour* vs. *esprit* 3
friendship *see* teasing and female friendship in Chinese reality TV show (Ying Cao)
fūshi (satire in Japanese) 4

gakaku (Japanese dance) 150
Gao E (c.1738–c.1815) 200
Gaozi (c.420–350 BCE) 27, 34
gender: and teasing 212, 213, 221, 231, 232; *see also* gender, *sajiao* and humour in Hong Kong *My Unfair Lady* TV series (Marjorie K. M. Chan); women
gender, *sajiao* and humour in Hong Kong *My Unfair Lady* TV series (Marjorie K. M. Chan): chapter overview 7, 12; Chinese naming taboo tradition 239–240, 263; Chinese wordplay tradition 240–241, 262, 263; names, nicknames and wordplay in TV series: Cherry 244–245, *251*; Chunchun 245, 246; Gordon 245–246; Hanson 248–249, *251*; Molly 241–244, **242**, **243**; Saving 249–252, *251*; Tet-yan 243–244; Tin Mat 246–248; *sajiao*, concept of 238–239; *sajiao* and Cherry 244, 245; *sajiao* and Chunchun 245, 249; *sajiao* and Molly 242, 262; *sajiao* and Tin Mat 247; scene analysis: "cracking Facebook password" 252, 256–257, *257*, **258–259**; "improvised boyfriend" 252, 253, **254–255**; "You betrayed me!" 252, 259, **260**, 261; series finale and audience statistics 252; type of humour and devices used 262–263; use of different languages and dialects 248, 255, 262–263; women's issues 261–262; wordplay in scenes 257, 259, **259**
General Theory of Verbal Humour 49, 118
geopolitics, and humour 13n4
gestures, in Japanese *angama* humour 102, 110, 111
gidayūbushi (musical narrative of Japanese *bunraku* puppet theatre) 138
Gong, L. **191**
Goodridge, Janet 167n14
Granny Mischief see Ijiwaru Baasan (Hasegawa's comic strip)
Grice, H. Paul: Cooperative Principle 120; Maxims of Conversation 120; theory of implicature 118, 120
Guzhang juechen (Antonio Leggieri): chapter overview 7, 8–9; fiction and humour in late-Imperial China 40, 58; *huaben* genre 40, 42, 43, 58; nature and structure of work 41–42, 58; original plates (1631) *44*, *45*, *57*; plots, events and non-events 42–43; references to past/previous works and intertextuality 54; satirical humour and Wei Zhongxian 43–50, *45*, 52; section 1: *Feng* (Wind) 41, 42, 55–56, 58; section 2: *Hua* (Flowers) 41, 42–43, *44*, 50–51, 58; section 3: *Xue* (Snow) 41, 42, 51–54, 55, 56–57, *57*; section 4: *Yue* (Moon) 41, 42, 43–50, *45*, 58; subversive parody and coincidence 58; subversive parody and register humour 56–57; verbal humour (exaggeration, colourful language, double entendre) 51–52; verbal humour in folly-and-consequence story 52–54; verbal-visual humour 50–51; voice of narrator and literary sabotage 54–56

ha (breach or development in Japanese) 150
"habitus" concept 91
Halliday, M. A. K. 118, 121
Han Feizi (c.280–233 BC) 37n8
Hanan, Patrick 41–42, 45–46, 59n4
hanashika or *rakugoka* (Japanese storytellers) 143; *see also makura* of *rakugo* (M.W. Shores); *rakugo* (Japanese storytelling)

haori (kimono jacket), removal of during *makura* 151–152
Harbsmeier, Christoph 37n6
Hasegawa Machiko (1920–1992): awards received by 122; Tokyo street named after 122; *see also* Hasegawa's cartoons (Sachiko Kitazume); *Ijiwaru Baasan* (Hasegawa's comic strip); *Sazae-san* (Hasegawa's comic strip)
Hasegawa Machiko Art Museum 122
Hasegawa's cartoons (Sachiko Kitazume): chapter overview 7, 9–10; comic strip *Ijiwaru Baasan (Granny Mischief)* 117, 118, 121–122, 128–133; comic strip *Sazae-san* 117, 118, 121, 122–128, 133; context 118, 119, 120–121, 124; context of culture 118, 121; context of situation 118, 121; conventional context 118; criticism of frame-based theories of humour 118–119; implicature 118, 119, 120, 126, 129, 134; implicature, conversational 118, 120; Japanese people's use of humour 117; methodology 118; text 118, 121; Twist theory 118, 119–120, 134; Twist theory and *Ijiwaru Baasan* 129–130, 131, 132, 133; Twist theory and *Sazae-san* 118, 123, 124, 126–128, 133; *see also Ijiwaru Baasan* (Hasegawa's comic strip); *Sazae-san* (Hasegawa's comic strip)
Haugh, Michael **191**, 192, 220; *see also* Taiwanese conversational humour (Wei-Lin Melody Chang and Michael Haugh)
Hayashiya Kikumaru III (b. 1974) 148–149
Hayashiya Somemaru IV (b. 1949) 165
Hayashiya Someta (b. 1975) 143
Hegel, G. W. F., on Socratic Method 32, 33
hierarchy: and Confucianism in South Korean workplace 170, 171–172; and humour in South Korean workplace 182–183, 184; and managers' humour in South Korean workplace 174, 176–179
Hofstede, Geert 5
Holmes, Janet 220
Holmes, Oliver 215
homonymy 82, 85, 238, 263
homophony (in Chinese language) 240, 263

hondai (stories in Japanese *rakugo*) 137, 138–140, 147, 149, 150–151, 159, 164–165, 166
Hong Kong culture: Cantonese operas 265n14; Cantopop songs 265n14; cultural and linguistic distinctiveness 2; wordplay 7; *wúlitóu* ("silly talk/nonsense") 192; *see also* gender, *sajiao* and humour in Hong Kong *My Unfair Lady* TV series (Marjorie K. M. Chan)
honorifics: in Japanese culture 98, 142, 143, 184; in South Korean culture 170, 172, 173, 174, 176, 181–182, 184
honpen ("main part" in *makura* of Japanese *rakugo*) 139–140
Hou Weng-Yong (b. 1962), *Da Yiyuan Xiao Yisheng (Big Hospital, Little Doctors)* 201–202
Hsu, Barbie (Xú Xîyuán, b. 1976) 217, 221–222, 224–228, 229–230
Hsu, Dee (Xú Xîdì aka Elephant Dee, b. 1978) 217, 221–228, 229–231, 232
Hsuan, Jessica (b. 1970) 241, 261
Hu Shiying 42
huaben (Chinese novella, short story) 40, 42, 43, 58; folly-and-consequence stories 52; *see also Guzhang juechen* (Antonio Leggieri)
huaji (laughable in Chinese) 4, 6, 7, 20, 37n4, 188, 191
Huang, S. P. **191**
Huang Chun-Ming (b. 1935), *Wo Ai Mali (I Love Mali)* 202–203
Hui, King of Liang (400–319 BC) 30–31
humor (in Indonesian and Balinese) 4
humour: adaptive vs. maladaptive 5; affiliative 12, 84, 85, 213, 224, 231; aggressive 215; and business/diplomacy/tourism 2–3; and coincidence 58; evolution of concept 3; and geopolitics 13n4; vs. laughter 1, 2; "national sense of humour" notion 6; and philosophy 19; and psychology 1, 3, 5; recurrent themes in Asian and Western humour 7–8; self-deprecating 3, 5, 143, 192, 194, 227; *see also* conversational humour; cultural context and humour (Jessica Milner Davis); humour studies; irony; laughter; sarcasm; satire; teasing; theories of humour; verbal humour; wit
"humour community" concept 49, 52

humour studies: Asian humour, scarcity of English-language studies on 2; Balinese humour 13n3; Chinese conversational humour 189, 190–192, **191**; Chinese humour 13n1; cognitive studies 1; Japanese humour 13n1, 88–90; Singaporean humour 13n3; Taiwanese humour 13n1

humours: bodily humours, theory of 3; Chinese Theory of the Humours 14n6

Hutton, C. 265n19

I Cupak (traditional Balinese comic figure) 84

I Made Mundra, alias Sakuni (aged 62) 83

I Nyoman Subrata, alias Petruk (b. 1949) 83

I Wayan Nardayana, alias Cenk Blonk (b. 1966) *64*, 70–71, **71**, **72**, 73–74, 78–80, **79**, 83

I Wayan Tarma, alias Dolar (1954–2016) 83

Ijiwaru Baasan (Hasegawa's comic strip): character of mischievous old woman (*Granny Mischief*) 117, 128; character's popularity and Japanese morals 118, 131, 132, 133; extracts used in study 121–122, 128; four-frame strip with speech balloons 122; "rewarding-good-and-punishing-evil" 131, 133; strip 1: lost cat 128–130, *129*, 132; strip 2: foot warmer and trap 130–131, *130*, 132–133; strip 3: feeding a stray dog 131–132, *132*, 133; Twist theory of humour 131, 132, 133; Twist theory of humour in Hasegawa's *Ijiwaru Baasan* 129–130; *see also* Hasegawa's cartoons (Sachiko Kitazume)

implicature 118, 119, 120, 126, 129, 134; conversational implicature 118, 120

incongruity theory of humour: in Balinese *bladbadan* 71, 73–74; in Balinese *cecimpedan* 66, 67, 68, 83; in *Guzhang jueehen* 49; in Mencius 19, 31, 35; and philosophers/psychologists 36n3; and Twist theory 119

Indonesia: *humor* term 4; scarcity of English-language studies on humour 2, 13n1

Indonesian languages 62, 80

Indonesian Modern Humor Institute (IHIK) 4

internet: Chinese Reality Television shows 216–217; *e'gao* (spoofing in China) 7; humorous memes 8; *see also* social media; YouTube

intertextuality 54

irony: and humour 2; in Mencius 19, 24, 25–26, 27, 29, 34–35, 36

Ishigaki Island 92; map *89*; *see also angama* ritual and banter on Ishigaki Island, Japan (Makiko Takekuro)

Ishikawa Goemon (1558–1594) 158

Japan: Edo period (1600–1868) 150; Meiji period (1868–1912) 143, 147

Japanese culture: *boke* (jokester) 111; *bugaku* (court music) 150; *bunraku* (or *ningyō jōruri*, i.e. puppet theatre) 137, 138, 151; *fūshi* (satire) 4; *gakaku* (dance) 150; *haori* (kimono jacket) 151–152; honorifics 98, 142, 143, 184; humour, attitude to 117, 146; humour, state-sponsored adoption of Western models of 7; humour studies on Japanese humour 13n1; humour studies on Japanese humour, scarcity of in English 2; *jiuta* music 137–138; *jo, ha, kyū* (prelude, breach, quick) 150; *kabuki* (dance-drama) 137, 148, 151, 158; *koten* (classical performing arts) 10, 137, 148, 152, 153, 156, 159; *koto* music 138; *kyōgen* (comic playlets) 8, 137; Lunar New Year village performances 6; *ma* (interval/timing) 151; *manzai* (stand-up comedy duo) 6, 110, 206n5; *nō* theatre 137, 150; politeness rules and humour 5; satire 75; self-deprecating humour 192; *shi-shōsetsu* (*watakushi shōsetsu*, I-novels) 163; sumō wrestling 148–149; *uitto* (wit) 4; wordplay 5, 7, 111, 146; *yūmoa* (humour) 4; *see also angama* ritual and banter on Ishigaki Island, Japan (Makiko Takekuro); Hasegawa's cartoons (Sachiko Kitazume); Japanese poetry; *makura* of *rakugo* (M.W. Shores); *rakugo* (Japanese storytelling)

Japanese languages: Ryukyuan languages 113n8; standard Japanese 93, 94, 112; Yaeyaman languages 94, 112

Japanese poetry: integration of in *makura* 149–150; *makura kotoba* ("pillow words" in Japanese poetry) 137; *uta makura* (Japanese "poem pillows") 137–138

ji (to ridicule in Chinese) 37n4
Jiang, Tonglin 5
Jin, Y. **191**
jiuta music (Japanese genre) 137–138
jo (prelude or introduction in Japanese) 150
jocular: jocular abuse in Chinese conversational humour 190, 219; jocular abuse in Taiwanese humour 202–203; jocular mockery, design features of 220; jocular mockery in Reality Television 215; jocular wordplay in Taiwanese humour 199, 203, 204; *see also* teasing
Jonson, Ben 8
jōruri see bunraku (or *ningyō jōruri*, i.e. Japanese puppet theatre)

kabuki (Japanese dance-drama) 137, 148, 151, 158
Kadar, Daniel Z. 183
kāiwánxiào (heavy teasing) 193
Kamens, Edward 137–138
Kangxi Lai Le (Taiwanese TV variety show) 192
Kant, Immanuel 36n3
Kardji, I Wayan 63
Kataoka, K. 91
Katsura Ayame III (b. 1964) 136, 139, 145, 152, *153*; analysis of her *makura* 152–155
Katsura Beichō III (1925–2015) 141, 144, 145, 148
Katsura Bunshi V (1930–2005) 145, 152, 155, 157
Katsura Bunza V (b. 1967) 145–146, *155*; analysis of his *makura* 152, 155–159, 164
Katsura Fukudanji IV (b. 1940) 140
Katsura Harudanji III (1930–2016) 151
Katsura Mikisuke III (1902–1961) 149–150
Katsura Shikō (b. 1959) 148
Katsura Zakoba II (b. 1947) 144, 145
Kilborn, R. 211
Kim, HeeSun 206n2; *see also* Korean workplace humour and Confucian politeness (HeeSun Kim and Barbara Plester)
Kitazume, Sachiko *see* Hasegawa's cartoons (Sachiko Kitazume)
Ko, Samantha (b. 1987) 246
kobanashi (short tales/jokes in Japanese *rakugo*) 139, 146–147, 150, 158, 159, 163, 165

Koestler, Arthur 118
Korea *see* Korean workplace humour and Confucian politeness (HeeSun Kim and Barbara Plester); South Korean culture
Korean workplace humour and Confucian politeness (HeeSun Kim and Barbara Plester): chapter overview 7, 10–11; Confucianism, politeness and humour 170, 172–173, 182, 184; Confucianism and hierarchy 171–172; Confucianism and negative perceptions of workplace humour 174–176; face saving 174, 179–181, 183–184; formal bow of greetings 176, *176*; hierarchy and humour 182–183, 184; hierarchy and managers' humour 174, 176–179; honorifics 170, 172, 176; honorifics and politeness 173, 174, 181–182, 184; humour as contextual/complex phenomenon 170–171, 182; humour as source of conflict in organisations 171; methodology (ethnographic approach) 173–174; politeness vs. humour 170, 173, 174, 175, 176, 183, 184; work/social titles and hierarchy 170, 172
koten (Japanese classical performing arts) 10, 137, 148, 152, 153, 156, 159
koto music (Japanese music) 138
Kotthoff, Helga 213–214
Kwan Shu Ming (active 1994–) 239
kyōgen (Japanese comic playlets) 8, 137
Kyono, Chiho 142
kyū (quick or conclusion in Japanese) 150

Lai, Chris (Lai Yatsing, pseud. Lai Lokyi, b. 1980) 249
Lam, Frankie (b. 1967) 246
Lau Siu Kwan (active 1988–) 239
laughter: vs. humour 1, 2; and incongruity 36n3; Plato on 36n2; and teasing 231, 233
Legalist philosophers (China) 20, 37n8
Leggieri, Antonio *see* Guzhang juechen (Antonio Leggieri)
Li, Chuntao 190, **191**
Li, X. **191**
Li Bai (701–762) 55–56
Li Luo 50, 55, 59n10
Li Rui (b. 1989) 217
Li Ruzhen (c.1763–1830), *Jing hua yuan* (*The Flowers in the mirror*) 40

Li Shimin, Emperor (r. 626–649) 240
Li Xiao (b. 1972) 217
Li Yu (1611–1680?): *Rou pu tuan* (*The Carnal prayer mat*) 40; *Wusheng xi* (*Silent operas*), first story 54
Liao, Laura Chao Chih 13n1, 206n5
Lin Yiqing 59n8
Lin Yutang (1895–1976), *Lun youmo* (*On humour*) 3–4, 6, 20, 37n8, 188
Ling Mengchu (1580–1644) 43; *Chuke pai'an jingqi* (*Slapping the table in amazement*) 41
Liu, Aya (Liu Hànya, b. 1978) 217, 221–227, *223*, 229–231
Liu Ling (221–300) 56
Lorenzo-Dus, Nuria 214–215
Louw, M. 121
Lover Man (Luo Fuman's pseud.), *Everyone Loves a Tender Woman* 238
Lunar New Year village performances (Japan) 6

ma (interval/timing in Japanese) 151
mabebanyolan (Balinese funny stories) 64
magegiakan (laughing out loud in Balinese) 64
magegonjakan (conversing using humour in Balinese) 64
makedékan (joking in Balinese) 64
makura see makura elements; *makura* examples; *makura* of *rakugo* (M.W. Shores)
makura elements: 9 elements, list and order of 139–140, **139**; breaking ice, building rapport 143–144; establishing artistic authenticity 145; "feeling out" audiences 142–143; greeting audiences 142; presenting safely topical material 145–146; setting up smooth transitions into *hondai* 150–152; teaching audiences about *rakugo* past and present 147–149; telling *kobanashi* and other jokes 146–147; transporting audiences to different time/place 149–150; *see also apuroochi* ("approach" in Japanese *makura* of *rakugo*); *honpen* ("main part" in Japanese *makura* of *rakugo*); *tsukami* ("catch" in Japanese *makura* of *rakugo*)
makura examples: Hayashiya Kikumaru III on sumō wrestling 148–149; Katsura Ayame III's *makura* analysed 152–155; Katsura Bunza V on living with master Katsura Bunshi V 145; Katsura Bunza V on New Year and enjoying the moment 145–146; Katsura Bunza V's *makura* analysed 152, 155–159, 164; Katsura Fukudanji IV's brief *makura* before *Nezumi ana* tale 140; Katsura Mikisuke III reciting Matsuo Bashō's verse 149–150; Katsura Zakoba II on his own life 144; Shōfukutei Tama's *makura* analysed 152, 159–164
makura kotoba ("pillow words" in Japanese poetry) 137
makura of *rakugo* (M.W. Shores): chapter overview 6, 10; defining *rakugo* 136–137; *makura* (lit. pillows) as warm-up segments 136, 164; *makura* as "frames" 164–165; *makura* in other arts 137–138; *makura* of *rakugo* neglected by scholars 138; *makura* on YouTube 166n6; *makura* removed from YouTube or TV/radio broadcasts 138; nine elements of *makura* 139–140, **139**, 142–152; performers' different approaches 138–139, 140–141; performers' job to "sell *rakugo*" 165–166; three *makura* analysed 152–164; women as *rakugoka* 136, 152–156; *yose* (play-houses) 136, 141, *141*; *see also makura* elements; *makura* examples; *rakugo* (Japanese storytelling)
Malinowski, B. 121
Mandarin Chinese language 11, 51, 196, 197, 199, 203, 248
manzai (stand-up comedy duo in Japan) 6, 110, 206n5
mapping (cognitive process) 119
Marsden, E. **191**
Masuyama, Eichi Erick 164–165
Matsuo Bashō (1644–1694) 149–150
medieval period *see* European medieval period
Meiji period (Japan, 1868–1912) 143, 147
memes, humorous 8
Mencius (Mengzi, 372?–289? BCE) 2, 7, 9, 10, 128; *see also* Mencius and humour as rhetorical discourse (Shirley Chan)
Mencius and humour as rhetorical discourse (Shirley Chan): chapter overview 2, 7, 8; Chinese rhetorical tradition 19; humour, philosophy

and incongruity 19, 31–32, 35; humour, philosophy and persuasion 20, 31–32, 36; humour, *youmo* and other Chinese terms 20; humour and Confucian tradition 25; humour and Confucianists/Legalists vs Daoists 20; Lin Yutang on Mencius' cerebral wit (not humour) 37n8; Mencius and *shi* (gentry scholars) 21, *23*, 24, 25–26, 27, 30, 38n20; Mencius as portrayed in *Myths and Legends of China* 22; Mencius' Confucianism 21, 22–24, 25, 28, 34, 38n20; Mencius' criticism of Gaozi 27, 34; Mencius' criticism of Mohists 24, 33–34; Mencius' criticism of Yang Zhu 24, 33–34; Mencius' rhetorical techniques 24, 35–36; Mencius' technique compared to Socratic Method 32–33; Mencius' use of humour 24–25, 35–36; nature and purpose of *The Works of Mencius* 21–22; story of King Hui of Liang seeking governing advice 30–31, 35; story of King Xuan of Qi seeking advice about expanding his power 29–30; story of King Xuan of Qi seeking advice about reducing mourning period 28; story of King Xuan of Qi seeking governing advice 31–32, 35; story of man of Qi (hypocritical/pedantic *shi*) 25–26, 35; story of man of Song (moral self-cultivation) 26–27, 35; story of tax collector (government corruption) 27–28; story of Wu Lu's query about food/sex and rituals 28–29; using humour to advise the powerful 29–33; using humour to criticise contemporary teachings 33–35; using humour to instruct 25–29; widespread use of expressions/sayings from *Works of Mencius* 34 35, 36

Merdah (Balinese *punakawan* clown) 76, **77**, 78, **79**, *79*

Meredith, George 6, 36n3

Miao Zhuang 50, 55, 59n10

Milner Davis, Jessica 13n1; *see also* cultural context and humour (Jessica Milner Davis)

Ming dynasty (China, 1368–1644) 7, 40, 41, 44, 47, 58

Minsky, Marvin Lee 118–119

Miyamoto Kanako 144

mock impoliteness 211, 219

Mohism 24, 33–34

Molière 8

Morreall, John 36n3

My Fair Lady (American film) 238; *see also* Shaw, George Bernard

My Unfair Lady (TV series) *see* gender, *sajiao* and humour in Hong Kong *My Unfair Lady* TV series (Marjorie K. M. Chan)

names: comic names in Hasegawa's *Sazae-san* comic strip 122; comic naming in Taiwanese humour 202–203; naming taboos in China 239–240, 263, 264n5; *see also* gender, *sajiao* and humour in Hong Kong *My Unfair Lady* TV series (Marjorie K. M. Chan)

National Meat and Livestock Board (Australia), lamb advertising campaign 2–3

Nevo, Ofra 13n3

nicknaming 7; *see also* gender, *sajiao* and humour in Hong Kong *My Unfair Lady* TV series (Marjorie K. M. Chan)

ningyō jōruri see bunraku (or *ningyō jōruri* i.e. Japanese puppet theatre)

nmī (female ancestral spirit) 92, *93*; *see also angama* ritual and banter on Ishigaki Island, Japan (Makiko Takekuro)

nō (Japanese theatre) 137, 150

Noma Seiji (1877–1938) 138

Nomura Masaaki 142

Norrick, Neal R. 206n1, 224

ochi (punchline in Japanese humour) 137, 138, 143, 146, 150, 153, 166

Oda, Shōkichi 146

Okamoto, Shigeko 147

onomatopoeia: *cecimpedan* onomatopoeia 65–66; in Japanese *angama* humour 99, 102, 111

organisational relationships, and humour 170

Ortega, M. Balén Alvarado 70

Padilla Cruz, M. 192

Pang Ho-cheung (b. 1973), *Sajiao Nüren Zui Hao Ming* (*Women Who Flirt*) 238

parallelism, in Japanese *angama* humour 99, 102, 109, 111

paribasa (Balinese proverbs) 63, 65

parody 56–58
People's Republic of China (PRC) see China (People's Republic of China)
performance, and poetics 90–91
Petruk see I Nyoman Subrata, alias Petruk (b. 1949)
philosophy: and humour 19; and incongruity theory of humour 36n3; see also Chinese philosophy
Plaks, Andrew 42
Plato, on laughter 36n2
play-frames 212, 221, 224, 226–227
Plester, Barbara 206n2; see also Korean workplace humour and Confucian politeness (HeeSun Kim and Barbara Plester)
"pluri-modality" concept 90, 91; see also angama ritual and banter on Ishigaki Island, Japan (Makiko Takekuro)
poetics: and performance 90–91; and pluri-modality 91
politeness: in Balinese culture 5, 9; and Confucianism 5, 10; in Japanese culture 5; see also Korean workplace humour and Confucian politeness (HeeSun Kim and Barbara Plester); mock impoliteness
political satire 8
Pollack, J. 263
Powell, L. 183
"power distance" 183; see also hierarchy
pragmatics 88–89, 112, 118, 119, 120, 173; interactional pragmatics 212
PRC (People's Republic of China) see China (People's Republic of China)
psychology: and humour 1, 3, 5; and incongruity theory of humour 36n3
Puja Astawa (b. 1974) 83
punakawan (clown figures in Balinese *wayang kulit*): Cenk Blonk example 64, 70–71, **71**, **72**, 73–74, 78–80, **79**; Délem and Sangut 70–71, **71**, *72*, *73*, 76, **77**; Merdah and Tualén 76, **77**, 78, **79**, *79*
punning see wordplay (punning)
puppet theatre see bunraku (or *ningyō jōruri*, i.e. Japanese puppet theatre); *punakawan* (clown figures in Balinese *wayang kulit*); *wayang kulit* (Balinese shadow puppet theatre)

Qi Yukun 43, 59n10
Qian Suoqiao 217

Qin dynasty (China, 221–206 BCE) 7, 21
Qin Shihuangdi, Emperor (259–210 BCE) 21
Qing dynasty (China, 1644–1911) 40, 42
Qiu, J. **191**
Quentin, Cecil Robert Burnett vii, xviii, xix–xx

rakugo (Japanese storytelling): books about rakugo traditions 147; comic storytelling 6, 136–137; components (*makura, hondai* and *ochi*) 137, 138; Edo/Tokyo tradition 137, 147, 148, 152; Kamigata tradition 137, 140, 147, 148, 152, 163; making a living 137; number and gender of *rakugoka* 136; old tales and new stories 137; reworking of stories and new language 137; social media presence 137; training 137, 144, 145; see also hondai (stories in Japanese *rakugo*); kobanashi (short tales/jokes in Japanese *rakugo*); makura of *rakugo* (M.W. Shores); ochi (punchline in Japanese humour)
rakugoka or *hanashika* (storytellers in Japanese) 143; see also makura of *rakugo* (M.W. Shores); *rakugo* (Japanese storytelling)
Ran, Y. **191**
raos ngémpélin see cecangkitan (or *raos ngémpélin* in Balinese humour)
Raskin, Victor 48, 118, 120
Rea, Christopher 13n1
Reality Television (RTV) 211, 214–215; see also teasing and female friendship in Chinese reality TV show (Ying Cao)
register humour 56
relief theory of humour, and Balinese humour 69, 75, 83–84
Ren, W. **191**
repetition, in Japanese *angama* humour 99, 102, 109–110, 111
rhetoric see Mencius and humour as rhetorical discourse (Shirley Chan)
rhythm, in Japanese *angama* humour 98, 102, 103, 111
"ritual abuse" concept 224
Roman Stoicism 24
Russell, Bertrand 31
Ryukyuan languages 113n8

sajiao ("be flirtatious") see gender, *sajiao* and humour in Hong Kong *My*

Unfair Lady TV series (Marjorie K. M. Chan)
Sakuni *see* I Made Mundra, alias Sakuni (aged 62)
Sangut (Balinese *punakawan* clown) 70–71, **71**, *72*, *73*, 76, **77**
Santangelo, Paulo 13n1, 200
sarcasm 2, 10, 11, 182, 184, 192, 222
satire: in Balinese *wewangsalan* 75; in Chinese culture 3–4, 43; in Chinese novels (late-Imperial period) 40; in Japanese culture 4, 75; in Mencius 19, 24, 25–26, 36; political satire in Korean masked dance-drama 8; *see also Guzhang juechen* (Antonio Leggieri)
satua (Balinese folk tales) 63; *satua banyol'* (funny folk tales) 65
Sawada Kazuya 165
Sazae-san (Hasegawa's comic strip): cheerful but careless housewife 117, 122; common view of human nature as good but flawed 128, 133; English version (*The Wonderful World of Sazae-san*) 118, 122, *123*, *125*, *127*; extracts used in study 122–123; family members and comic sea-related names 122; first published in local and national newspapers 121; four-frame strips with speech balloons 122; longest-running animated television series 117, 121; statues and public places in honour of series 122; strip 1: bus queue 123–124, *123*; strip 2: beauty cream 124–126, *125*; strip 3: Father's Day 126–127, *127*; Twist theory of humour 118, 123, 124, 126–128, 133; *see also* Hasegawa's cartoons (Sachiko Kitazume)
Schopenhauer, Arthur 36n3
Schwartz, Shalom H. 14n9, 14n10
self-deprecation 3, 5, 143, 192, 194, 227
self-repetition, in Japanese *angama* humour 109–110, 111
Semantic Script-based Theory of Humor 118
semiotic signs 91, 112
séndratari (Balinese drama with dance) 64, 65, 83
shadow puppet theatre *see punakawan* (clown figures in Balinese *wayang kulit*); *wayang kulit* (Balinese shadow puppet theatre)
Shaftesbury, Lord *see* Ashley Cooper, Anthony, 3rd Earl of Shaftesbury

Shang dynasty (China, c.1600 BC–c.1046 BC) 239
Shaw, George Bernard: *Pygmalion* 12; *see also My Fair Lady* (American film)
Sherzer, Joel 13n3
shi (Chinese gentry scholars) 21, *23*, 24, 25–26, 27, 30, 38n20
Shijing (*Book of Songs*, China) 257
shi-shōsetsu (*watakushi shōsetsu*, Japanese I-novels) 163
Shōfukutei Fukushō (b. 1949) 139, 159
Shōfukutei Tama (b. 1975) 139, 140, *160*; analysis of his *makura* 152, 159–164
Shores, M.W. *see makura of rakugo* (M.W. Shores)
Shōtoku Taishi, Prince (574–622) 10, 131, 133
Sima Qian (145?–86? BCE) 20, 37n7
Simpen, I Wayan 63, 66, 75, 76, 80
Singapore, study of humour use in 13n3
Sinkeviciute, Valeria 214, 215
Smith, C. M. 183
social media: humour on 8; *rakugoka* active on 137; *see also* internet; YouTube
Socratic Method 32–33
sonority theory 77
sōron (Japanese *Bon* festival) 88, 92, 94, 102; *see also angama* ritual and banter on Ishigaki Island, Japan (Makiko Takekuro)
South Korean culture: honorifics 170, 172, 173, 176, 181–182, 184; political satire in masked dance–drama 8; scarcity of English-language studies on humour 2, 13n1; *see also* Korean workplace humour and Confucian politeness (HeeSun Kim and Barbara Plester)
Spencer-Oatey, H. 183
Staroverov, P. 77
Steinmüller, Hans 13n1
Stoicism 24
storytelling *see rakugo* (Japanese storytelling)
Straehle, C. A. 213
Su, H. Y. **191**
Su, L. I. **191**
Sumarsono 82
sumō wrestling 148–149
Sung, M. 240
superiority theory of humour, and Balinese humour 73–74, 75, 84–85

Suzhounese (Wu) Chinese language 51
Suzuki, Tomi 163
Suzuki Mutsu 143

Taiwanese conversational humour (Wei-Lin Melody Chang and Michael Haugh): chapter overview 7, 11; conversational humour from diachronic perspective 188–189, 200, 204–206; conversational humour in everyday Taiwanese interactions 189, 192–200, 205; conversational humour in Taiwanese literature 189–190, 200–204, 205–206; literary example from Hou Weng-Yong (jocular abuse) 201–202, 204; literary example from Huang Chun-Ming (jocular wordplay and comic naming) 202–203, 204; literary example from Zhong Zhao-Zheng (jocular wordplay) 203–204; studies of conversational humour in Chinese languages 189, 190–191, **191**; studies of conversational humour in Taiwan 191–192; teasing and cross-generational differences 189, 192–193, 199–200, 204, 205; teasing example ("floating corpse" joke) 194–196; teasing example (shopping) 193–194; wordplay and cross-generational differences 190, 193, 199, 204, 205; wordplay example (cross-linguistic punning) 196; wordplay example (with gentle teasing) 196–199, *197*, *198*

Taiwanese culture: cultural and linguistic distinctiveness 2; Taiwanese humour, study on 13n1; TV variety show *Kangxi Lai Le* 192; *see also* Taiwanese conversational humour (Wei-Lin Melody Chang and Michael Haugh)

Taiwanese Hokkien 11, 196, 197
Takekuro, Makiko 146; *see also* angama ritual and banter on Ishigaki Island, Japan (Makiko Takekuro)
Tanaka, H. 172
Tang dynasty (China, 618–907 CE) 239–240
teasing: in Chinese conversational humour 190, 192; Chinese terms for different kinds of 193; *see also* jocular; Taiwanese conversational humour (Wei-Lin Melody Chang and Michael Haugh); teasing and female friendship in Chinese reality TV show (Ying Cao)

teasing and female friendship in Chinese reality TV show (Ying Cao): chapter overview 11–12; data collection and methods of analysis 219–221; Reality Television (RTV) and teasing 211; RTV discourse and aggressive humour 214–216; RTV in China on TV and online platforms 216–217; teasing, aggressive undertones of 212; teasing, collaborative style of 220–224, *223*, 231, 232–233; teasing, non-collaborative style of 220–221, 224–228, 231, 233; teasing, non-collaborative/collaborative styles, interaction of 228–231, 233; teasing and friendship-building 211–212; teasing and friendship-building in women's talk 212–214, 233; teasing and identity 231–232; teasing and mock impoliteness 211, 219; teasing and play-frames 212, 221, 224, 226–227; teasing process and linguistic/paralinguistic clues 212–213; teasing strategy (bonding, nipping, biting) 213; versatile interpretation of Chinese femininity 219, 232, 233–234; *We Are Real Friends* (*Wo Men Shi Zhenzheng De Pengyou*) 217, *218*, 219; *yaxue* vs. *youmo* 219

television comedy *see* gender, *sajiao* and humour in Hong Kong *My Unfair Lady* TV series (Marjorie K. M. Chan); teasing and female friendship in Chinese reality TV show (Ying Cao)

témpékan (Balinese family grouping) 83
Tenma Tenjin Hanjōtei (Osaka *yose*) *141*
text 118, 121; *see also* context
theories of humour: frame-based theories 118–119; General Theory of Verbal Humour 49, 118; relief theory 69, 75, 83–84; Semantic Script-based Theory of Humor 118; superiority theory 73–74, 75, 84–85; *see also* incongruity theory of humour; Twist theory of humour

tiáokǎn (heavy teasing in Chinese, Tiawan) 193
timing (in comedy) 151
Tinggen, I Nengah 63, 66, 77
titles: and hierarchy 170, 172; *see also* honorifics
tokoh banyol (Balinese comedians) 83

tonchi de kaesu (providing quick-witted answer in Japanese *angama* humour) 94
Tong, Natalie (b. 1981) 244, 261
tourism, and humour 2
transgressive language/humour 48, 52, 231, 259
Tsakona, Villy 190
tsukami ("catch" in Japanese *makura* of *rakugo*) 139, 143
Tualén (Balinese *punakawan* clown) 76, **77**, 78, **79**, *79*
Twist theory of humour 118, 119–120, 134; and Hasegawa's *Ijiwaru Baasan* 129–130, 131, 132, 133; and Hasegawa's *Sazae-san* 118, 123, 124, 126–128, 133

Ui Mushū 140
uitto (wit in Japanese) 4
Unofficial history from the forest of literati see under Wu Jingzi (1701–1754)
ushumai (male ancestral spirit) 92, *93*; *see also angama* ritual and banter on Ishigaki Island, Japan (Makiko Takekuro)
uta makura (Japanese "poem pillows") 137–138

verbal humour: concept 206n1; General Theory of Verbal Humour 49, 118; in *Guzhang juechen* 50–54; study of Balinese verbal humour 13n3; *see also* Balinese traditional oral humour (Nengah Arnawa); conversational humour; Semantic Script-based Theory of Humor 118
Verschueren, Jef 121, 124

Wang Dingtian 219
warm-up segments (of *rakugo*) 136, 164, 165
Warring States period (China, 475–221 BC) 7, 20, 21
watakushi shōsetsu (*shi-shōsetsu*, Japanese I-novels) 163
wayang kulit (Balinese shadow puppet theatre) 6, 9, 64, 65; *see also* Balinese traditional oral humour (Nengah Arnawa); *punakawan* (clown figures in Balinese *wayang kulit*)
We Are Real Friends (Chinese online RTV show) *see* teasing and female friendship in Chinese reality TV show (Ying Cao)

Wei Zhongxian (1568–1627) 43–49, *45*, 52
Weitou (dialect of Cantonese) 248, 250
Wells, Marguerite A. 13n1
Werner, E. T. C., *Myths and Legends of China* 22
wewangsalan (in Balinese humour): affiliative style of humour 84; consisting of two rhyming lines 63, 75; morphology of term 75; and relief theory of humour 75, 84; rhyming 75–76, **76**; rhyming and interpretation 76–77, **77**; satirical use to mock or insult 75; sonority 77–78, **78**; and superiority theory of humour 75, 84–85
wit: in Balinese culture 67, 71, 75, 85; in Chinese culture 3, 7, 240; in Chinese reality TV show 211, 226; English wit 4; French *esprit* 3; in *Guzhang juechen* 50; in Hong Kong *My Unfair Lady* 240, 249, 257, 262; in Japanese *angama* humour 99, 111; in Japanese culture 4; in Mencius 24, 28, 33, 35, 36, 37n8
Wo Men Shi Zhenzheng De Pengyou (Chinese online RTV show) *see* teasing and female friendship in Chinese reality TV show (Ying Cao)
women: as *rakugoka* 136, 152–156; *see also* gender; gender, *sajiao* and humour in Hong Kong *My Unfair Lady* TV series (Marjorie K. M. Chan); teasing and female friendship in Chinese reality TV show (Ying Cao)
Wong, Vincent (Wong Ho, pseud. Wong Hoshun, b. 1983) 250
wordplay (punning): in Balinese culture 5, 73–74; in Chinese cultures 7, 192, 193, 199, 240–241, 262, 263; in Japanese culture 5, 7, 111, 146; in Taiwanese humour 190, 193, 196–199, *197*, *198*, 203, 204, 205; *see also* gender, *sajiao* and humour in Hong Kong *My Unfair Lady* TV series (Marjorie K. M. Chan)
workplace humour *see* Korean workplace humour and Confucian politeness (HeeSun Kim and Barbara Plester)
Wu (Suzhounese) Chinese language 51
Wu Jingzi (1701–1754), *Rulin waishi* (*Unofficial history from the forest of literati*) 40, 49–50
wúlitóu ("silly talk/nonsense", Hong Kong) 192

xiangsheng (cross-talk in China) 7
xiao (laughable in Chinese) 4, 200
xie (glib or laughable in Chinese) 37n4
Xu, Weihe **191**
Xuan, King of Qi (d. 312 BC) 28, 29–30, 31–32, 35
xue (joking in Chinese) 37n4
Xunzi (Hsün Tzu, c.310–c.220 BCE) 239

Yaeyaman (*angama*) festival *see* *angama* ritual and banter on Ishigaki Island, Japan (Makiko Takekuro)
Yaeyaman languages 94, 112
Yamamoto Susumu 165
Yang, N. **191**
Yang Zhu (c.440–c.360 BCE) 24, 33–34
yaxue (humour in Chinese) 219
yose (Japanese play-houses) 136, 141, 146, 151, 156, 159; Tenma Tenjin Hanjōtei (Osaka) *141*
youmo (humour in Chinese) 4, 12, 20, 188, 219

Young, Dominic 123, 128
Young, Jules 123, 128
YouTube 6, 64, 70, 138, 166n6
Yue, Xiao Dong (or Xiaodong) 13n1, 192
Yueh, H. I. 238, 264n2
yūmoa (humour in Japanese) 4

Zajdman, Anton 184
Zeami (c.1363–c.1443) 150
Zelizer, Craig 13n4
Zhao, L. **191**
Zhong Zhao–Zheng, *Lu Bing Hua* (*Lupinus*, published 1962) 203–204
Zhou dynasty (China, c.1046–256 BCE) 21, 239, 257
Zhu, Ping 13n1
Zhu Quan (1378–1448) 41
Zhu Xi (1130–1200) 38n20
Zhuang Zhou (c.369–c.286 BC) 37n7